SECOND EDITION

BASIC BOOKKEEPING

★

An Office

Simulation

★

BROOKE C.W. BARKER

ANNE L. CORRIGAL

ELSIE KLIM

Nelson Canada

I(T)P An International Thomson Publishing Company

Toronto • Albany • Bonn • Boston • Cincinnati • Detroit • London • Madrid • Melbourne • Mexico City
New York • Pacific Grove • Paris • San Francisco • Singapore • Tokyo • Washington

I⊤P™
International Thomson Publishing
The trademark ITP is used under licence

Published in 1995 by
Nelson Canada
A Division of Thomson Canada Limited
1120 Birchmount Road
Scarborough, Ontario M1K 5G4

Canadian Cataloguing in Publication Data

Barker, Brooke C.W.
Basic bookkeeping: an office simulation
2nd ed.

ISBN 0-17-604862-6

1. Bookkeeping. 2. Bookkeeping — Problems, exercises, etc.
I. Corrigal, Anne. II. Klim, Elsie.
III. Title

HF5635.B37   1994   657'.2   C94-931477-3

Acquisitions Editor	Peter Jackson
Production Editor	Tracy Bordian
Developmental Editor	Yuval Kashdan
Senior Production Coordinator	Sheryl Emery
Art Director	Liz Nyman
Cover Design	Liz Nyman
Cover Photo	Susan Ashukian
Interior Design	Word & Image Design
Composition Analyst	Frank Zsigo

Printed and bound in Canada

98 97 96 95 (WC) 1 2 3 4

OTABIND

Bound to stay open

The pages in this book open easily and lie flat, a result of the Otabind bookbinding process. Otabind combines advanced adhesive technology and a free-floating cover to achieve books that last longer and are bound to stay open.

Contents

CHAPTER 9   **BANK RECONCILIATION**   **151**

CHAPTER 10   **GOODS AND SERVICES TAX**   **171**

CHAPTER 11   **PARTNERSHIPS**   **187**

CHAPTER 18   **OTHER RECORDING SYSTEMS**   **289**

CHAPTER 19   **COMPUTERS AND ACCOUNTING**   **309**

APPENDIX A   **ANSWERS TO THINK ABOUT IT!**   **321**

GLOSSARY   **328**

CHART OF ACCOUNTS   **KBC DECORATING CO.**   **339**

C H A P T E R

An Introduction to Bookkeeping

CHAPTER OBJECTIVES

After completing this chapter, you will be able to:
- define the three forms of business organization
- define the five categories of accounts: assets, liabilities, owner's equity, revenues, and expenses
- classify accounts according to the five categories

IMPORTANT WORDS AND TERMS IN THIS CHAPTER

Account	Endorsement
Assets	Expenses
Bookkeeper	Liabilities
Bookkeeping	Merchandise
Capital	Net Worth
Cheque	Owner's Equity
Corporation	Partnership
Depositor	Proprietorship
Deposit Slip	Revenue

· · · · · · · · · · ·

The procedure known commonly as **bookkeeping** is the record-keeping phase of accounting that involves compiling the monetery values of daily business activities. In simpler terms, bookkeeping is the process of keeping track of cash spent and cash received, sales and purchases, and other monetary activities in which the business is involved. On a basic level, bookkeeping can be compared with the process of keeping track of financial activities in a personal chequing account—a record of money spent and money received.

DATE 19 –	CHEQUE NO.	CHEQUES ISSUED TO OR DESCRIPTION OF DEPOSIT		CHEQUE AMOUNT		✔	DEPOSIT AMOUNT		deduct cheque add deposit	BALANCE FORWARD 930	00
April 1	64	TO	Hill Realty						CHEQUE − DEPOSIT +		
		FOR	rent	450	00				BALANCE ▶	480	00
4	65	TO	Food Basket						CHEQUE − DEPOSIT +		
		FOR	groceries	50	00				BALANCE ▶	430	00
6	66	TO	Provincial Power						CHEQUE − DEPOSIT +		
		FOR	hydro bill	95	00				BALANCE ▶	335	00
11	67	TO	Food Basket						CHEQUE − DEPOSIT +		
		FOR	groceries	70	00				BALANCE ▶	265	00
15		TO							CHEQUE − DEPOSIT +		
		FOR	paycheque				672	50	BALANCE ▶	937	50
16	68	TO	Gregg's Garage						CHEQUE − DEPOSIT +		
		FOR	tune up	45	00				BALANCE ▶	892	50
19	69	TO	Corner Store						CHEQUE − DEPOSIT +		
		FOR	groceries	20	00				BALANCE ▶	872	50
23	70	TO	Man-Tel						CHEQUE − DEPOSIT +		
		FOR	telephone bill	45	00				BALANCE ▶	827	50
25	71	TO	Top Tailors						CHEQUE − DEPOSIT +		
		FOR	clothing	55	00				BALANCE ▶	772	50
26	72	TO	Food Basket						CHEQUE − DEPOSIT +		
		FOR	groceries	60	00				BALANCE ▶	712	50
30		TO							CHEQUE − DEPOSIT +		
		FOR	paycheque				672	50	BALANCE ▶	1385	00
30	73	TO	Petro-Can						CHEQUE − DEPOSIT +		
		FOR	gas & oil	150	00				BALANCE ▶	1235	00
		TO							CHEQUE − DEPOSIT +		
		FOR							BALANCE ▶		

Figure 1.1   Chequebook Record

A chequebook provides a record of all deposits made and all cheques issued. (See Figure 1.1.) But where did the money come from that was deposited to the account? To whom were the cheques sent? What were those cheques paying for? Most people are careful about recording every activity that affects their bank accounts. But just how important is this information? Perhaps more important than you think, because a record of cashflow helps you plan your spending over the next days, weeks, and months. If, for example, you have only a small amount of money in your bank account, you likely would not be planning a night on the town or the purchase of a shiny new sports car.

Marvin Reese, for instance, has his eye on a new car, but he is not sure whether he can afford it. His bank account shows a balance of only $1,235. Hardly enough for his dream car! From the chequebook record in Figure 1.1, we get a picture of Marvin's spending habits. A simple chart will help us see at a glance where his money comes from and where it goes.

Cash In (deposits)		Cash Out (cheques)	
Paycheques	$ 672.50	Rent	$ 450.00
	672.50	Utilities	140.00
		Food	200.00
		Automobile	195.00
		Miscellaneous	55.00
	$1,345.00		$1,040.00

On the one side, we see the money he deposits (usually his paycheque), and on the other is a list of those living costs paid every month. Simple arithmetic shows us that Marvin would be able to save $1,345 − $1,040 = $305 each month. (However, we have not yet taken into consideration the annual insurance premiums on his car and his apartment, any regular or unforeseen car repairs, and clothing costs.) At this rate, Marvin could be saving for many years before he has enough money to buy a new car.

As an alternative to saving the money he needs for the car, Marvin could borrow the money from the bank. Before he visits the bank, Marvin will make a list of everything he owns, including any investments (such as savings bonds and college funds), and all debts he currently owes, including any other bank loans, student loans, and amounts on credit cards. The bank will use this information to determine Marvin's eligibility for a bank loan.

Things I Own		Debts I Owe	
Cash	$1,235.00	Credit Cards	$ 450.00
Car	1,500.00	Top Tailors	390.00
Furniture	2,000.00	Gregg's Garage	270.00
Savings Bonds	2,500.00		
	$7,235.00		$1,110.00

This kind of detailed personal record-keeping helps to plan not only day-to-day decisions about spending but also long-term goals for major purchases. By looking back over the financial activities of past months and years, we get a picture of spending habits. This is helpful in establishing a budget so that money is spent wisely.

Looking at bookkeeping from a slightly different perspective, Lance Reed is a high-school student with his own part-time business doing yard work for his neighbours—cutting grass in the summer and clearing snow in the winter. For his business Lance will keep track of essentially the same information that Marvin does; that is, where the money comes from and how it is spent.

Cash In (deposits)		Cash Out (cheques)	
Earnings from yard work:			
J. McWhinney	$ 32.00	Gas for mower	$16.00
E. Porth	25.00	Garbage bags	14.50
B. Woodward	27.00	Miscellaneous	5.00
D. Essig	20.00		
	$104.00		$35.50

Also, Lance will prepare a statement listing those things his business owns (called assets) and all debts he owes (called liabilities).

Things Owned (Assets)		Debts Owed (Liabilities)	
Lawnmower	$250.00	Loan from father	$120.00
Other tools	40.00		
	$290.00		$120.00

Based on these figures, we can see that Lance's personal investment in his business is $290 − $120 = $170. This value represents Lance's equity in his business.

After graduating from high school, Lance has decided to operate his business on a full-time basis. To get off on the right foot, he has prepared the two statements that we discussed above and is going to present this information to the bank in order to get a loan so that he can buy a used truck and more equipment (some tools and another lawnmower).

The bank has asked that the information be prepared in a more formal fashion. The statement of assets and liabilities and owner's equity is commonly called a **balance sheet**. (See Figure 1.2.)

The statement that itemizes his business earnings and operating costs isincome statement. (See Figure 1.3.)

Assuming that the loan has been granted to Lance and that he has purchased the additional items he needs, Figure 1.4 illustrates a new balance sheet showing the financial position of his business today.

You can see from the discussion so far that the information recorded by a company and the information recorded by an individual are virtually the same. Company information, however, is generally kept more formally and displayed formally for others who must also interpret it.

THREE FORMS OF BUSINESS ORGANIZATION

Since the focus of this program is to learn how to keep books for business, we must consider the different forms of business organization. All businesses, regardless of size or nature, fall into one of three basic forms of organization: a proprietorship, a partnership, or a corporation.

Lance Reed Balance Sheet June 30, 19—							
ASSETS							
Equipment:							
Lawnmower					2	5	0	00
Tools						4	0	00
					2	9	0	00
LIABILITIES							
Loan					1	2	0	00
OWNER'S EQUITY							
Capital, L. Reed					1	7	0	00
					2	9	0	00

Figure 1.2 Balance Sheet

Lance Reed Income Statement for 3 months ending June 30, 19—						
REVENUE						
Yard Service				1	0	4	00
OPERATING COSTS						
Gas	1	6	00			
Garbage bags	1	4	50			
Miscellaneous		5	00		3	5	50
NET INCOME					6	8	50

Figure 1.3 Income Statement

Lance Reed Balance Sheet July 2, 19—							
ASSETS							
Cash					1	4	0	00
Truck				3	0	0	0	00
Equipment:							
Lawnmowers					5	6	0	00
Tools						9	0	00
				3	7	9	0	00
LIABILITIES							
Loans:							
Father					1	2	0	00
Bank				3	5	0	0	00
OWNER'S EQUITY							
Capital, L. Reed					1	7	0	00
				3	7	9	0	00

Figure 1.4 Balance Sheet

1. **Proprietorship** refers to a business owned by one person, such as a grocery store, a dress shop, or a restaurant. (Lance Reed's business is a proprietorship because he is the sole owner.) The owner acts as the manager, makes all business decisions, and is personally responsible for all the debts incurred by the business, such as bank loans, mortgages, and accounts owing to suppliers.

2. **Partnership** refers to a business owned by two or more persons. These co-owners combine their skills and financial resources (money) in forming what is hoped to be a more successful and profitable business. The partners share the decision-making and are fully responsible for all debts incurred by the business. Common examples of partnerships include law firms, medical clinics, and accounting firms. But this does not mean that only professional groups may form partnerships. Any two or more people who have combined their skills and financial resources to operate a hardware store, a restaurant, or a video store, for example, also have formed a partnership.

3. **Corporation** refers to a separate legal entity operating under a government charter. *Entity*, in a business context, means that the business is separate from the owners (called *shareholders* or *stockholders*). The ownership of a public corporation is divided into shares or stocks that are generally bought by and sold to the public through a stock exchange. The most familiar examples include large national and international companies, such as IBM (International Business Machines Corp.) and Air Canada. Both proprietorships and partnerships can become private corporations by applying for either federal or provincial incorporation. Such an action separates the owners (now known as shareholders) from the business entity and, as a result, protects them against the liabilities incurred by the corporation.

Whether the business is large or small, or whether it is a single proprietorship, a partnership, or a corporation, the basic principles of bookkeeping are exactly the same. A clear, accurate record of its business activities must be maintained and results must be reported in a form that can be verified and interpreted by others.

BANKING

When Lance Reed expanded his yard work business, he went to the bank to get advice on typical banking services that his business would be using. Until now, he had been using his own savings account for depositing his earnings and for paying for gas and supplies. In order to keep his personal financial activities separate from those of his business, the bank suggested opening a *current account*.

A current account is very much like the personal chequing account held by most private citizens, except that a current account usually does not earn interest. Depending on the bank, the service fees charged each month are usually on a per-cheque or per-entry basis. A cheque that has been written on a current account and has cleared the bank is returned to the client at the end of the month with the bank statement as evidence that the cheque was cashed and that the amount was deducted from the account.

At the time the account is opened, the customer is given a supply of cheques and deposit slips. Most businesses will have cheques printed with the company name, address, and logo (the company emblem or symbol). These cheques are pre-numbered in sequence and are encoded with MICR (magnetic ink character recognition) characters across the bottom of each (see Figure 1.5). These special characters allow the bank's computers to read and process the cheques quickly and efficiently. The information represented by those characters includes the cheque number, the transit (branch) number, the bank number, and the customer's account number. After the cheque is cashed, the amount of the cheque will be encoded as well.

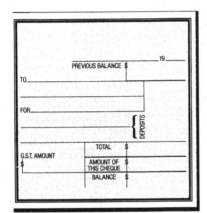

Figure 1.5 Sample Cheque

The bank will require that a signature card be signed by all signing officers (those company personnel authorized to sign cheques on behalf of the company). This card is kept on file by the bank and is used to compare unusual or unfamiliar signatures that may appear on the cheques.

The bookkeeper will keep a close watch on the balance in the chequing account to avoid issuing cheques for amounts greater than the balance (which means the cheques would "bounce") and to avoid balances that are larger than the amount required to meet current needs. Excessive balances mean idle cash, and since a current account earns no interest, any excess funds should be invested to earn additional money for the business. If the company has been maintaining a balance of $10,000 in its account but needs only $2,000 on an on-going basis to meet immediate needs, the extra $8,000 might be put into a short-term investment. Alternatively it might be used to purchase additional equipment that will increase income. Most banks will accept a minimum investment deposit of $5,000 for as few as 30 days.

When Lance receives a cheque from one of his customers, he will deposit it into his company's bank account. Whenever a person cashes or deposits a cheque, he or she signs the back of the cheque when it is presented to the bank teller. This is known as *endorsing* the cheque. A rubber stamp impression is used in the case of an endorsement by a company. Figure 1.6 shows both types of endorsement.

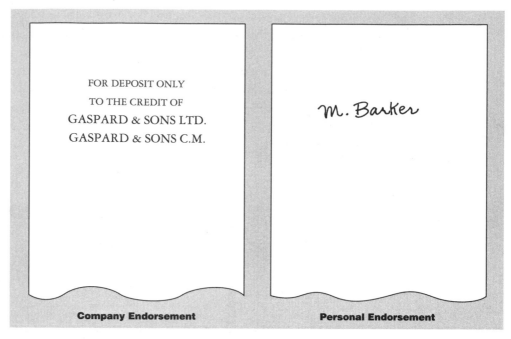

FOR DEPOSIT ONLY
TO THE CREDIT OF
GASPARD & SONS LTD.
GASPARD & SONS C.M.

M. Barker

Company Endorsement   **Personal Endorsement**

Figure 1.6   Cheque Endorsements

A **deposit slip** is a list of all currency, coins, and cheques being deposited into an account. Company deposits are usually prepared in duplicate; the original copy is retained by the bank and the duplicate copy is stamped by the teller and remains part of the deposit book. A sample deposit slip is shown in Figure 1.7.

Each month, the bank will send out a statement to each of its current account customers as a record of that customer's banking transactions. The bank statement, as shown in Figure 1.8, provides the following information:

1. The balance at the beginning of the month.
2. All deposits made to the account during the month.
3. All cheques and other authorized payments processed by the bank during the month and subsequently deducted from the account.
4. The balance at the end of the month.

All cancelled cheques (those that have been cleared by the bank and deducted from the account) listed on the bank statement are returned to the company with the statement each month.

SIMPLE BOOKKEEPING DEFINITIONS

To further understand the concepts of bookkeeping, we will now consider some of the basic terminology that is used. These terms apply whether we are talking about the financial activities of an individual, such as Marvin Reese, or of a business, such as that of Lance Reed.

Assets (sometimes called economic resources) are things of value that are owned by the business, such as cash, land, buildings, furniture, equipment, etc., including inventories of merchandise and supplies, that are expected to benefit the business into future years. Amounts owing to the business from its customers (called *Accounts Receivable*) are also of value to the business and are considered assets as well. Lance Reed's business assets include the lawnmowers, the truck, and any other tools he uses in his yard work. If any of his customers have not yet paid him for the work he has done, these amounts owing are his accounts receivable and are part of his total assets.

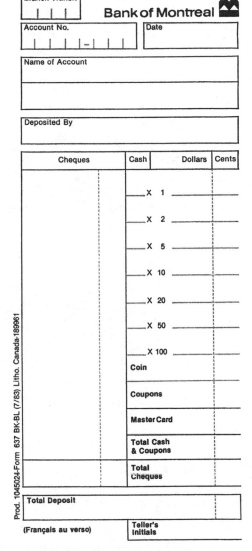

Figure 1.7 Deposit Slip

Liabilities are claims by creditors against the assets of the business. More simply stated, liabilities are the debts owing to others; for example, debts owing to suppliers (called *Accounts Payable*) and debts to a bank or mortgage company (*Bank Loan Payable* and *Mortgage Payable*). If Lance had bought tools from a local hardware store and had agreed to pay the amount owing within 30 days, this debt would be considered an account payable; and the loan from the bank would be shown on his books as Bank Loan Payable.

Owner's Equity is the owner's claim against the business assets. In simpler terms, owner's equity represents the value of assets remaining after all liabilities have been deducted. The owner's equity comes from two sources:

1. Investments by the owner, such as the cash, furniture, equipment, etc., to start the business. (Lance Reed invested a lawnmower and cash when he started his business.)

2. Profits (or losses) earned from operations. The goal of almost every business is to earn a profit. These profits, if retained within the business, increase its worth.

The Royal Canadian Bank
3000 Pembina Highway
Winnipeg, Man. R3G 9C2

Statement of account with:

KBC Decorating Co.
79 Buffalo Place Industrial Park
Winnipeg, Man. R3C 2S4

Account No. 654-789-7
Page 1
Statement date: 30 June 19—
Balance forward from previous
statement: $8,292.96

Cheques	Cheques	Deposits	Date	Balance
950.00		1,309.04	June 1	8,652.00
		541.08	2	9,193.08
1,800.00	140.00	1,057.04		
140.00			3	8,170.12
50.00	86.20	2,898.81	8	10,932.73
506.00 D/M	70.00		9	10,356.73
50.00	275.00	438.38	10	10,470.11
23.00		1,737.53	15	12,184.64
		864.24	17	13,048.88
		2,255.54	25	15,304.42
452.75		775.64	26	15,627.31
578.08 D/M			30	15,049.23

Figure 1.8 Bank Statement

On the balance sheet for Lance Reed's business, his owner's equity value can be seen as **Capital**, the usual name given to the owner's investment. Capital is determined by calculating the difference between the total of all assets and the total of all liabilities ($1,490 − $1,320 = $170).

Revenue is the earnings from the sale of goods or services to customers, and represents an inflow of assets (cash or accounts receivable). In Lance's case, some of his customers will pay immediately for his work on their yards; others might arrange to pay him on a specified future date. Regardless of when he receives the money for his work, Lance will record the revenue as having been earned. As Figure 1.9 shows, businesses can have more than one source of earnings.

Expenses are the costs of operating the business. They include rent, salaries, utilities, telephone, advertising, and delivery costs, to name just a few. If we do not pay the rent on the store, we will not be allowed to stay in business at that

TYPE OF BUSINESS	PRIMARY REVENUES	SECONDARY REVENUES
Department Store	Sales of Merchandise	- sales of services - cafeteria - parking lot - interest on charge accounts
Doctor, Lawyer, Dentist	Professional Fees	
Colleges & Universities	Tuition Fees Grants	- sale of books & supplies - cafeteria - parking lot
Real Estate Broker	Commissions Earned	- interest - real estate rental - rent from student housing

Figure 1.9 Sources of Revenue

location; if we do not pay our utilities, we will not have electricity for the lights or gas for the furnace. These costs are incurred in the process of earning revenue. Lance's expenses are few: gas and oil for the equipment, garbage bags, and any costs associated with getting his equipment to and from the work sites. Each of these expenses is necessary to Lance's ability to provide service to his customers.

Figure 1.10 shows sample account names that are commonly used by a variety of businesses. An account name should indicate its purpose and, when necessary, its classification. For example, office supplies can be either an asset or an expense; therefore, when referring to the expense, the account name is Office Supplies Expense, and when referring to the asset, the account name is Office Supplies Prepaid. (When naming accounts, however, some accountants will take shortcuts by dropping the word "Prepaid," thus referring to the asset simply as Office Supplies.) Similarly, when interest is earned by the business, the account is called Interest Revenue or Interest Earned; but when interest is paid by the business, it is called Interest Expense.

ASSETS VS. EXPENSES

At initial glance, the definitions given for assets and expenses may seem quite similar. To understand the difference between these two categories is to recognize the length of time for which the asset or expense is expected to be carried on the books. The general rule of thumb is that expenses contribute to the business only during the current operating year, whereas assets contribute not only to the current period but also into future operating years.

For example, on November 15, $150 was spent on office supplies, such as stationery, pens, pencils, etc. If these supplies are expected to be consumed (used up) before the end of the current operating year (December 31), this cost may immediately be recognized as an expense. However, if some of these supplies are not expected to be used until the next operating period (after January 1), they are considered assets because the cost is being spread over two or more operating years. In such a case, the supplies are identified using the term *prepaid*, such as Office Supplies Prepaid.

In another example, a one-year insurance policy on a building was purchased on July 1 at a cost of $397. If the operating year ends on December 31, half the cost of the policy will contribute to operations in the current operating year and half will contribute to next year's operations. As a result of affecting two operating years, this cost is recognized as an asset and identified as Insurance Prepaid. On the other hand, if a special two-month insurance policy is purchased on July 1 to cover an unusually large inventory of merchandise in the warehouse, this policy will expire before the end of the current year (December 31); therefore, the cost of this policy will be recognized as an expense (Insurance Expense).

Whether to recognize costs as assets or expenses is often at the discretion of the accountant, and the decision is based on when and how often such costs are incurred.

SAMPLE ACCOUNT NAMES

Assets	Liabilities	Owner's Equity	Revenues	Expenses
Bank (or Cash)	Accounts Payable	Capital	Sales	Merchandise Purchases
Accounts Receivable	Suppliers Payable	Equity	Service Income	Freight Costs
Merchandise Inventory	Bank Loan Payable	Drawings	Interest Earned	Delivery Expense
Supplies Prepaid	Loans Payable	Withdrawals	Interest Income	Advertising Expense
Office Supplies	Mortgage Payable	Retained Earnings	Rent Earned	Maintenance
Store Supplies	Interest Payable	Income Summary	Fees Earned	Business Taxes
Shop Supplies	GST Payable	Profit & Loss	Medical Fees Earned	Property Taxes
Shipping Supplies	GST–ITC		Dental Service Income	Licenses
Warehouse Supplies	PST Payable		Professional Fees	Depreciation Expense
Insurance	Sales Tax Payable		Tuition Revenue	Donations
Land	Salaries Payable		Legal Fees Earned	Office Supplies Expense
Buildings	Wages Payable		Advertising Revenue	Store Supplies Expense
Office & Warehouse	Payroll Payable		Passenger Revenue	Warehouse Supplies Expense
Trucks	CPP Payable		Green Fees Earned	Supplies Expense
Vans & Trucks	UI Payable		Pro Shop Sales	Interest Expense
Delivery Equipment	Pensions Payable		Parking Fees Earned	Bank Charges
Service Equipment	Income Tax Payable			Interest & Bank Charges
Rental Equipment	Union Dues			Interest on Mortgage
Autos				Postage
Vehicles				Salaries (Payroll) Expense
Tools & Equipment				Telephone Expense
Office Furniture				Travel Expense
Office Equipment				Utilities
Furniture & Equipment				
Telephone Equipment				
GST Recoverable				

Figure 1.10 Sample Account Names

A WORD ABOUT MERCHANDISE

Several terms are commonly used to refer to the merchandise that a business handles in its daily operations, whether it is invested by the owner, bought for resale, sold to the public, or counted as inventory. To understand how these terms should be used correctly, study these explanations:

- **Merchandise Sales** (often called *Sales*) refers to the merchandise that has been sold to customers, whether for cash, on credit cards, or on account (to be paid for by a specified date). Merchandise Sales is a revenue account.

- **Merchandise Purchases** (often called *Purchases*) refers to the goods that have been bought by the business for the purpose of resale to the public. Merchandise Purchases is an expense account because the goods are expected to be sold during the current operating year.

- **Merchandise Inventory** (often called *Inventory*) refers to the merchandise that was originally on hand when the business was started. It also refers to the unsold merchandise on hand at the end of the operating year that is expected to be sold in the next operating year. Merchandise Inventory, therefore, is considered an asset account because it is a value contributing to more than one operating period.

The word "merchandise" does not specifically identify whether the goods in question are being bought or sold; therefore, "merchandise" by itself should not be used as an account title. To simplify the references to merchandise, it is recommended that the terms Sales, Purchases, and Inventory be used instead.

▶ PRACTICE EXERCISE 1

Using the definitions explained in this chapter (assets, liabilities, owner's equity, revenues, and expenses), determine the classification of each of the following account names. If necessary, refer to Figure 1.10. To get you started, we've done the first one for you.

	Account Name	Class
1.	*Cash*	*Asset*
2.	Delivery Truck	
3.	Bank Loan Payable	
4.	Telephone Expense	
5.	Salaries & Wages	
6.	Sales of Merchandise	
7.	Office Supplies Prepaid	
8.	Accounts Receivable	
9.	Sales of Service	
10.	Capital	
11.	Tools & Equipment	
12.	Building	
13.	Mortgage Payable	
14.	Rental of Equipment	
15.	Advertising	
16.	Insurance Prepaid	
17.	Utilities	

18. Interest Earned
19. Bank
20. Office Equipment

► **PRACTICE EXERCISE 2**

Classify each of the following account names as an asset, liability, owner's equity, revenue, or expense.

	Account Name	Class
1.	Vans and Trucks	
2.	Accounts Payable	
3.	Sales of Service	
4.	Cash	
5.	Mortgage Payable	
6.	Office Supplies Prepaid	
7.	Capital	
8.	Accounts Receivable	
9.	Bank Loan Payable	
10.	Typewriters & Computers	
11.	Sales of Merchandise	
12.	Shipping Supplies Prepaid	
13.	Office Building & Warehouse	
14.	Interest Expense	
15.	Advertising	
16.	Inventory of Merchandise	
17.	Office Supplies Expense	
18.	Parking Fees Earned	
19.	Salaries and Wages	
20.	Taxes Expense	

► **PRACTICE EXERCISE 3**

Classify each of the following account names as an asset, liability, owner's equity, revenue, or expense.

	Account Name	Class
1.	Land	
2.	Income Tax Payable	
3.	Property Taxes	
4.	Travel Expenses	
5.	Commissions Earned	
6.	Automobiles	
7.	Accounts Receivable	
8.	Service Revenue Earned	
9.	Accounts Payable	
10.	Shop Supplies Prepaid	
11.	Pro Shop Sales	

12. Building
13. Postage
14. Interest on Bank Loan
15. Legal Fees Earned
16. Business Taxes
17. Rent Earned
18. Mortgage Payable
19. Rent Expense
20. Interest Earned

THINK ABOUT IT!

1. The basic principles of bookkeeping remain the same for all types of businesses. True or False?
2. The most common type of bank account used by businesses is a current (chequing) account. True or False?
3. The bank does not charge for the handling of cheques and deposits affecting the business's bank account. True or False?
4. Once cheques have been cleared and cancelled by the bank, the bank keeps them. True or False?
5. A business's bank account earns no interest. True or False?
6. How does a proprietorship differ from a partnership? from a corporation?
7. What is the difference between an asset and an expense?
8. (a) Give an example of an asset (other than cash).
   (b) Give an example of a liability.
9. What is capital?
10. What is a person's usual source of earnings? What is a business's source of revenue?

2

The Accounting Equation

CHAPTER OBJECTIVES

After completing this chapter, you will be able to:
- define debit and credit as used in the process of bookkeeping
- record simple bookkeeping transactions in a general journal

IMPORTANT WORDS AND TERMS IN THIS CHAPTER

Accounting Equation	General Journal
Balance Sheet	Liabilities
Compound Journal Entry	Simple Journal Entry
Credit	Source Documents
Debit	T-Accounts
Double-Entry System	Transactions

············

When someone talks about "balancing" a chequebook or when a company "balances" its books, what are they talking about? Balancing refers to maintaining equality. For example, when you receive your bank statement at the end of the month, you probably check the figures on it with those recorded in your chequebook. If all entries correspond and if both you and the bank agree on the amount of money you have in your account, your chequebook balances. The concept is similar when applied to a company's books.

Perhaps the easiest way to express this important concept is by means of a simple arithmetic equation, called the **accounting equation**:

ASSETS = LIABILITIES + OWNER'S EQUITY (or CAPITAL)

Simply stated, the total of all business assets (things of value) must equal the combined total of all liabilities (debts) and owner's equity (sometimes called net worth). With assets on one side of the equation, we show all those who provided the assets on the other side of the equation. The owner likely invested the initial assets (usually cash), which represent the amount known as Capital. Also, the bank has likely lent money to the business, which would allow the owner to buy other assets, and other companies would have sold items to the business on credit, with the balance to be paid by a specified date. The debts owing to the bank and to other companies are the liabilities.

To illustrate the use of the accounting equation, we will assume that you are planning to go into business for yourself and already have assets to invest in your new business, such as cash, equipment, etc. If these assets are worth $150,000, your equity in the business is $150,000, provided you have no debts (liabilities). Here is how the values would be shown in the accounting equation:

Assets = Liabilities + Owner's Equity
$150,000 =   Ø   + $150,000

If, on the other hand, you still owe $50,000 on the assets you turned over to the business, your net worth in respect of the business is now $150,000 − $50,000 = $100,000.

Assets = Liabilities + Owner's Equity
$150,000 = $50,000   + $100,000

If you decide that you need other furniture and equipment before you open your doors to the public, you might buy another $50,000 worth of assets from a company that has granted credit to you. In this case, your total assets have increased by $50,000 to $200,000; and because you owe the money on these new assets, your liabilities have increased by $50,000 to $100,000.

$$\text{Assets} = \text{Liabilities} + \text{Owner's Equity}$$
$$\$200,000 = \$100,000 + \$100,000$$

As may be seen, although the values change within the accounting equation, the equation always remains in balance.

▶ **PRACTICE EXERCISE 1**

Calculate the value of the missing number on each line of the following chart that will balance the accounting equation.

	ASSETS	=	LIABILITIES	+	CAPITAL
Example:	$25,000	=	$15,000	+	?
	Answer: $25,000 – $15,000 = $10,000				
1.	32,000	=	12,000	+	?
2.	60,000	=	?	+	17,000
3.	?	=	24,000	+	13,000
4.	?	=	600	+	2,040
5.	3,290	=	1,750	+	?
6.	104,750	=	?	+	82,900
7.	93,400	=	13,640	+	?
8.	1,340 + 725	=	?	+	600
9.	?	=	2,120 + 320	+	1,850
10.	? – 1,630	=	11,800	+	35,000
11.	16,240	=	7,290	+	?
12.	12,200	=	?	+	9,000
13.	?	=	17,450	+	13,500
14.	21,350 – ?	=	8,300 + 1,725	+	9,000
15.	7,340 + 8,250	=	6,330 + ?	+	7,500

BALANCE SHEET

The formal representation of the accounting equation is the **balance sheet**. Total assets must always equal the combined total of liabilities and owner's equity. John Brown's business balance sheet is shown in Figure 2.1. One side shows what the business owns (assets), while the other shows who supplied those assets (liabilities and owner's equity). You can easily see that the total of the assets is equal to the combined total of the liabilities and owner's equity.

John Brown Repairs
Balance Sheet
December 31, 19—

ASSETS							LIABILITIES & CAPITAL						
Cash	150	0	0	0	00		Liabilities	50	0	0	0	00
							Capital, J. Brown	100	0	0	0	00
	150	0	0	0	00			150	0	0	0	00

Figure 2.1 Balance Sheet

If John Brown spends $30,000 of the cash to purchase new shop equipment, the asset Cash is decreased by $30,000 and the new asset Equipment is increased by $30,000. Figure 2.2 shows the effect of this transaction on the balance sheet. One asset (Cash) was used to acquire another asset (Equipment); therefore, total assets remain at $150,000, liabilities remain at $50,000, and Capital is still $100,000.

John Brown Repairs
Balance Sheet
December 31, 19—

ASSETS						LIABILITIES & CAPITAL					
Cash	120	0	0	0	00	Liabilities	50	0	0	0	00
Equipment	30	0	0	0	00	Capital, J. Brown	100	0	0	0	00
	150	0	0	0	00		150	0	0	0	00

Figure 2.2 Balance Sheet

If John Brown then decides to pay $10,000 toward his liabilities, the asset Cash is decreased by $10,000 because a cheque has been issued, and the total liabilities would also decrease by $10,000. Notice the effect of this transaction on the balance sheet in Figure 2.3.

John Brown Repairs
Balance Sheet
December 31, 19—

ASSETS						LIABILITIES & CAPITAL					
Cash	110	0	0	0	00	Liabilities	40	0	0	0	00
Equipment	30	0	0	0	00	Capital, J. Brown	100	0	0	0	00
	140	0	0	0	00		140	0	0	0	00

Figure 2.3 Balance Sheet

Regardless of the business activities that occur and how the values are represented in either the accounting equation or the balance sheet, the equation must balance.

DEBITS AND CREDITS

Another equation that is important in the accounting process is:

$$DEBIT = CREDIT$$

Debit (abbreviated Dr.) refers to the left side of the equation, while **credit** (abbreviated Cr.) refers to the right side.

You will notice in Figure 2.3 that assets are on the left side of the balance sheet. They are said, then, to be on the debit side. Liabilities and Capital, on the other hand, are on the right side of the statement; therefore, they are on the credit side.

A *word of caution*: Do not associate any other meanings with the terms debit and credit. Remember, debit is left; credit is right.

BASIC RULES FOR DEBIT AND CREDIT

The word "account" will be used throughout the following discussions. But what is an account? An **account** is a concise record of the increases and decreases affecting a given financial item. If you think of your personal bank account, the chequebook or passbook itemizes the activities (deposits, withdrawals, and cheques) that have affected the balance in your account. The same idea applies to bookkeeping. Each financial item requires its own account; for example, all money received or paid out is recorded in the Bank (or Cash) account; the furniture owned by the company would be recorded in the Furniture account; and the amount paid for each month's telephone bill would be recorded in the Telephone Expense account.

Here are some basic rules for applying debits and credits:

- *An account increases on the side of origin.* "Origin" refers to the side on which the account appears on the balance sheet.

- *An account decreases on the side opposite of origin.* If an account increases on the debit side of the balance sheet, for example, it will decrease on the credit side.

Assets increase on the debit side because assets appear on the left side of the balance sheet (see Figure 2.3); assets decrease, then, on the credit side. If we are recording an entry that results in an increase in total assets, it is recorded as a debit entry. If the entry will result in a decrease in total assets, it will be recorded as a credit entry.

Liabilities and Capital will increase on the credit side because they appear on the right side of the balance sheet; liabilities and Capital decrease, then, on the debit side. If we record an entry that results in an increase in total liabilities or Capital, it is recorded as a credit entry. If the entry will result in a decrease in total liabilities or Capital, it will be recorded as a debit entry.

Figure 2.4 uses simple T-accounts to show the effects of debit and credit entries on assets, liabilities, and owner's equity. They are called T-accounts because they are shaped like the letter T and represent the debit and credit sides of a simple balance sheet. The left side of the T is the debit side and the right side is the credit side.

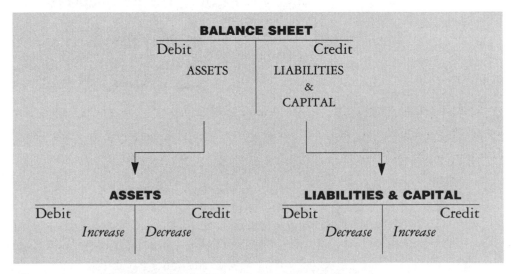

Figure 2.4 How Debit and Credit Affect Assets, Liabilities, and Capital

- *Revenues increase on the credit side and decrease on the debit side.*

Revenue and expense accounts can be thought of as part of owner's equity. Revenue represents the earnings of the business; so as revenues increase, the owner's equity in the business is likely to increase. Since owner's equity increases on the credit side, revenue accounts will increase on the credit side as well. (See Figure 2.5.)

- *Expenses increase on the debit side and decrease on the credit side.*

Expenses are the operating costs that are paid regularly to keep the business alive. Since an increase in expenses reduces the amount of "profit" the business will earn, it is reflected on the debit side as a decrease in the owner's equity in the business. Expenses, therefore, increase on the debit side. (See Figure 2.5.)

It is important to know the definitions of each class of accounts as discussed in Chapter 1, and to understand the effect that these basic rules have on each class.

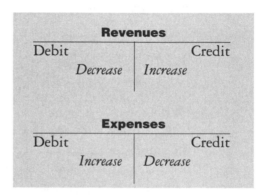

Figure 2.5 How Debit and Credit Affect Revenues and Expenses

PRACTICE EXERCISE 2

For each of the following account names, indicate its classification (asset, liability, equity, revenue, expense) and indicate whether the account increases on the debit or on the credit. Use the definitions of classification from Chapter 1 to help you determine which class is appropriate.

	Account Name	Class	Increases on Dr./Cr.
Example:	*Cash*	*Asset*	*Dr.*
1.	Bank Loan Payable		
2.	Telephone Expense		
3.	Rent Expense		
4.	Furniture		
5.	Service Revenue		
6.	Equipment		
7.	Accounts Receivable		
8.	Accounts Payable		
9.	Utilities		

10. Salaries
11. Sales
12. Rental Revenue
13. Office Supplies Prepaid
14. Capital
15. Bank
16. Plumbing Equipment
17. Green Fees Earned
18. Wrapping Supplies Expense
19. Sales Tax Payable
20. Plumbing Supplies Prepaid

▶ ### PRACTICE EXERCISE 3

On June 10, 19—, you were given $500 by your employer with instructions to pay amounts owing by the business and to collect amounts owing to the business. Set up the T-account for Bank illustrated below and record the receipts and payments for the month. After all entries are recorded, calculate the cash balance on June 30 by subtracting the total of credit entries from the total debit entries. (*Remember*: Bank increases on the debit side and decreases on the credit side.)

To help you get started, copy this T-account and the opening balance onto a sheet of blank paper and record the cash items listed below.

(Debit)	Bank	(Credit)
June 10 500.00		

June	10	Received from B. Moore	$215.25
	12	Paid J.S. Shaw	412.40
	14	Paid F. Salter	54.23
	16	Received from H.D. Trent	114.72
	16	Received from G.L. Roy	94.19
	17	Paid L. Ritchie	421.60
	21	Received from L. Olson	77.23
	23	Received from J. Rielh	313.62
	24	Received from A.B. Hoyle	123.77
	26	Received from Bob King	25.79
	27	Paid S.R. Aikens	111.39
	28	Received from G. Fisher	22.13
	30	Received from B. Smith	140.16

DOUBLE-ENTRY SYSTEM OF BOOKKEEPING

Every bookkeeping transaction affects at least two accounts. One account will be debited and another account will be credited for an equal value. In other words, for every debit entry, there must be an equal credit entry. If, for example, $35 is recorded as a debit entry to an account, a credit entry of $35 must be recorded to another account. This is called the **double-entry system** of bookkeeping, which ensures that every transaction is balanced; therefore, the accounts remain in balance and the balance sheet remains in balance.

When a transaction consists of one debit entry and one credit entry of equal value, this is known as a **simple journal entry**. A **compound journal entry**, on the other hand, will have any number of debit entries and any number of credit entries, provided the total debits equal the total credits. Every bookkeeping entry, whether single or compound, must always balance.

Simple Entry				Compound Entry		
Debit		**Credit**		**Debit**		**Credit**
$35	=	$35	OR	$75	=	$50
						+25

ANALYZING A TRANSACTION

In order to record a transaction correctly, analyze it by considering the following questions:

1. What accounts will be affected by this transaction?

2. What is the classification of each account (asset, liability, owner's equity, revenue, or expense)?

3. Will these accounts increase or decrease as a result of the transaction?

4. Will the accounts be debited or credited?

Example 1

Cash was received for over-the-counter sales, $525.00.

1. *What accounts are affected?* Since money is directly involved in this transaction, the Cash account is affected. (Many businesses prefer to use the name "Cash" for the account representing the inflow and outflow of money; others prefer to use "Bank." Companies with several bank accounts might choose to use the actual name of the bank as the name of the account on the books; for example, "Royal Bank." In general terms, however, *Cash* and *Bank* are interchangeable.) The cash was received as a result of the sale of merchandise; therefore, the other account affected is Sales.

2. *What classification is each account?* Cash is something of value to the business, so it is an asset account. The sale of merchandise (or services) is the business's source of earnings; therefore, Sales is a revenue account.

3. *Will the accounts increase or decrease?* We now have more money in our possession, so the Cash account has increased. And because more merchandise was sold, additional revenue was earned; therefore, the Sales account has increased as well.

4. *Will the accounts be debited or credited?* We have learned that assets increase on the debit side. Since Cash is an asset that is increasing in this transac-

tion, the Cash account will be debited. We also learned that revenue accounts increase on the credit side; so, because Sales is a revenue account that is increasing, the Sales account will be credited in this transaction.

Here is a chart that summarizes how this transaction was analyzed:

Analysis	Rule	Entry
The asset Cash is increased.	Assets increase on the debit side.	Debit: Cash
The revenue Sales is increased.	Revenues increase on the credit side.	Credit: Sales

Example 2

A cheque for $48.95 was issued in payment of this month's telephone bill.

1. *What accounts are affected?* Since money is directly involved in this transaction, one account affected is Cash (or Bank). In bookkeeping, cheques are treated as cash. This cheque was issued in payment of the telephone bill; therefore, the other account affected is Telephone Expense.

2. *What classification is each account?* Cash is something of value to the business, so Cash is an asset. The telephone bill is a cost of operating the business, so Telephone Expense is an expense.

3. *Will the accounts increase or decrease?* Each month's telephone bill represents an additional cost of operating the business; therefore, the Telephone Expense account is increasing. The cheque represents cash going out of the bank account; therefore, the Cash account is decreasing.

4. *Will the accounts be debited or credited?* We have learned that expenses increase on the debit side. Since the telephone cost is an expense that is increasing, the Telephone Expense account will be debited in this transaction. Because the cheque that was issued will decrease the bank balance, the Cash account will be credited to represent the decrease in the asset account.

Analysis	Rule	Entry
The Telephone expense is increased.	Expenses increase on the debit side.	Debit: Telephone Expense
The asset Cash is decreased.	Assets decrease on the credit side.	Credit: Cash

The process described in the preceding examples should be used when analyzing any transaction, whether simple or complex. With a little practice, you will easily determine which accounts will be affected in any transaction.

ANALYZING A TRANSACTION (CARTER'S WINDOW COVERINGS)

The concept of analyzing transactions is perhaps the most important aspect of the bookkeeping process and deserves closer examination. Tom Carter has just started a business that specializes in window coverings, such as venetian and vertical blinds.

June 1   Tom Carter invests $80,000 cash in his new business.

Analysis	Rule	Entry
The asset Bank is increased.	Assets increase on the debit side.	Debit: Bank
Owner's equity is increased.	Owner's equity increases on the credit side.	Credit: Capital, T. Carter

$$\text{Assets} = \text{Liabilities} + \text{Capital}$$
$$\$80,0000 = \emptyset + \$80,000$$

New businesses often begin with the owner's contribution of his or her own money. (Throughout these illustrations, we have chosen to use the name Bank rather than Cash for the cash transactions.)

June 3   Land was purchased as a future building site. A cheque was issued for $25,000.

Analysis	Rule	Entry
The asset Land is increased.	Assets increase on the debit side.	Debit: Land
The asset Bank is decreased.	Assets decrease on the credit side.	Credit: Bank

In this case, one asset was given away in order to acquire another asset. Therefore, the total value of assets remains unchanged.

Assets		=	Liabilities	+	Capital
Cash	Land				
$80,000		=	∅	+	$80,000
−25,000	+$25,000				
$55,000	$25,000	=	∅	+	$80,000
$80,000		=	∅	+	$80,000

June 7   Constructed a small building, $100,000. Paid $30,000 down and arranged for a $70,000, 15-year mortgage.

Analysis	Rule	Entry
The asset Building is increased.	Assets increase on the debit side.	Debit: Building
The asset Bank is decreased.	Assets decrease on the credit side.	Credit: Bank
The liability Mortgage Payable is increased.	Liabilities increase on the credit side.	Credit: Mortgage Payable

The value of the building on the debit side is offset by two values on the credit side: the cash down payment and the mortgage. This is an example of a compound entry.

June 8   Purchased equipment for the store, $5,000, from Strands Office Equipment Co. on terms of net 10 days. (Credit terms are often expressed as net 10 days, indicating that the invoice must be paid within 10 days of the invoice date, in this case, by June 18.)

Analysis	Rule	Entry
The asset Office Equipment is increased.	Assets increase on the debit side.	Debit: Office Equipment
The liability Accounts Payable/Strands Office Equipment Co. is increased.	Liabilities increase on the credit side.	Credit: Accounts Payable/Strands Office Equipment Co.

The Equipment account is used to record such assets as cash registers, typewriters, computers, and fax machines. Some bookkeepers would not include desks, chairs, and filing cabinets in this account because these items cannot really be defined as equipment; they are furniture. For such assets, a Furniture account would be used. Other bookkeepers, however, will combine both equipment and furniture in the same account, called Furniture & Equipment. Whether this asset account is named Equipment or Furniture or Furniture & Equipment, it is recorded as the debit entry to represent the increase in the total of the assets owned by the business.

The credit entry to Strands Office Equipment Co. includes the term "Accounts Payable" to clearly indicate that this company is a creditor, not a customer. If it were a customer, the term "Accounts Receivable" would be used. Experienced bookkeepers often prefer not to use either term because they know from experience which companies they deal with are customers and which are creditors. But as a new bookkeeper, you should be sure to include the terms so that there is no confusion.

June 10   Bought a quantity of merchandise (venetian blinds) for an upcoming sale; paid $8,000 cash.

Analysis	Rule	Entry
The expense Purchases is increased.	Expenses increase on the debit side.	Debit: Purchases
The asset Bank is decreased.	Assets decrease on the credit side.	Credit: Bank

Purchases is the typical account name used when merchandise is bought for the purpose of resale to customers. The word "Merchandise" should *not* be used as the account name because it will lead to confusion later.

June 18   A payment of $5,000 was made to Strands Office Equipment Co. in full payment of the balance owing to them.

Analysis	Rule	Entry
The liability Accounts Payable/Strands Office Equip. Co. is decreased.	Liabilities decrease on the debit side.	Debit: Accounts Payable/Strands Office Equipment Co.
The asset Bank is decreased.	Assets decrease on the credit side.	Credit: Bank

Again, notice that the term "Accounts Payable" is used when identifying the name of the creditor.

June 20   Cash sales of merchandise to date, $5,500. (This is a very common transaction—one that you will see frequently.)

Analysis	Rule	Entry
The asset Bank is increased.	Assets increase on the debit side.	Debit: Bank
The revenue Sales is increased.	Revenues increase on the credit side.	Credit: Sales

June 30   Issued a cheque in payment of the June telephone bill, $145.

Analysis	Rule	Entry
The Telephone expense is increased.	Expenses increase on the debit side.	Debit: Telephone Expense
The asset Bank is decreased.	Assets decrease on the credit side.	Credit: Bank

Although adding "Expense" to the names of expense accounts is not always necessary, it can be helpful to do so. Accounts such as Interest and Rent, which can also be revenue accounts, should be given names that clearly indicate the correct classification: Interest Revenue, Interest Expense, Rent Revenue, Rent Expense.

► ### PRACTICE EXERCISE 4

Set up the following ten T-accounts on a sheet of blank paper: Cash (or Bank); Office Equipment; Furniture & Fixtures; Delivery Equipment; Land; Building; Accounts Payable/Hill Office Furniture Co.; Accounts Payable/Murray Auto Sales; Bank Loan Payable; Capital, W. Stubbs.

Using the process of analyzing transactions discussed in this chapter, record the following transactions directly into the T-accounts. (The first transaction has been done for you, but be sure to include it in your T-accounts.)

19—

Feb   1   William Stubbs invested $75,000 cash in a hardware store.

Dr.	Cash	Cr.	Dr.	Capital	Cr.
75,000.00					75,000.00

2   Borrowed $20,000 from the bank.

3   Bought a building and lot for $80,000. The building is valued at
    $63,000 and the lot at $17,000. Paid by cheque.

4   Bought a cash register for $950 (Office Equipment). Issued a cheque.

5   Bought a desk and chair for the office (Furniture & Fixtures), $1,200,
    from Hill Office Furniture Co. on account.

6   Bought a used delivery truck for $6,100 on account from Murray
    Auto Sales.

7   Made a partial payment on the bank loan, $500.

8   Paid Hill Office Furniture Co. $400 on account.

9   Bought an office calculator from Hill Office Furniture Co. for $250.
    Paid $150 cash and agreed to pay the balance in 10 days.

▶ █ **PRACTICE EXERCISE 5** █

Set up the following T-accounts, allowing the number of lines indicated for each:
Cash (9); Accounts Receivable/John A. Bell (2); Accounts Receivable/A. Carter
(2); Furniture & Equipment (1); Automobiles (1); Accounts Payable/Coldwell
Wholesalers (1); Accounts Payable/McCleod Co. (1); Bank Loan Payable (1);
Capital, John A. Walters (1); Sales (6); Purchases (2); General Expense (1);
Insurance Expense (1); Salary Expense (2); Utilities Expense (1).

Record each transaction directly to the appropriate T-accounts, being sure
that each transaction is balanced.

19—

May   2   John A. Walters has started his business by investing $18,000 in
          cash.

      2   Bought merchandise, issuing a cheque for $985.60 (Purchases)

      3   Bought wrapping supplies and other materials for wrapping parcels,
          $126. Paid by cheque.

      4   Bought a cash register, $625, from McCleod Co., paying $300 down
          and owing the balance in 10 days.

      5   Paid the water bill, $52 (Utilities Expense)

      6   Cash sales, $216.45.

      8   Paid bi-weekly salaries, $625.

      9   Sold merchandise to these customers on account: John A. Bell, $47;
          A. Carter, $59. Payment from these customers is due in 10 days.

     10   Borrowed $5,000 from the bank.

     11   Purchased a second-hand truck from Like-Nu Motors. Paid them by
          cheque, $5,000.

     11   Bought merchandise from Coldwell Wholesalers on terms of net 30
          days, $427.70.

     12   Cash sales, $241.60.

13   Sold merchandise on account to John A. Bell, $45.50, due in 10 days. Today he paid $25 on his previous invoice owing from the 9th.

14   Paid McCleod Co. $325 for the balance owing on the account.

15   Sold merchandise on account to A. Carter, $34.75.

16   Paid for insurance for one month, $35.

22   Paid bi-weekly salaries, $625.

25   Received payment from these customers on account: John A. Bell, $40; A. Carter, $25.

SOURCE DOCUMENTS

All entries recorded in the books must originate from information found on business documents that provide evidence that a financial activity has occurred. These are called **source documents**. Some examples of source documents are:

Activity	Source Document
Purchase of merchandise	Purchase invoice
Sale of merchandise	Sales invoice
Receipt of cash	Receipt duplicate, or cash register total
Payment of cash	Cheque stub
Payroll	Time cards, or payroll chart
Sale of a service	Work order

THE GENERAL JOURNAL

As each transaction is analyzed, it is recorded in an appropriate journal-in this case, the general journal. A **general journal** is the formal record of the financial activities that have affected the business or organization, recorded in chronological order (day by day). This journal (see Figure 2.6) captures all the important information about each activity: the date the transaction occurred, the names of the accounts affected, and the amounts affecting these accounts. The amounts are recorded in the debit column or the credit column, depending on whether the account is being increased or decreased as a result of the activity.

The transactions discussed previously for Carter's Window Coverings are shown in general journal form in Figure 2.6. As you read through the following steps for recording journal entries, compare the explanations with the corresponding entries in Figure 2.6 so that you can see how transactions are recorded properly.

1.   Analyze the transaction as discussed earlier. Determine the account that is to be debited and the account that is to be credited. The general journal requires that the debit side of each transaction be recorded before the credit side is recorded. This is in accordance with the Generally Accepted Accounting Principles that have been defined by the professional accounting organizations.

2.   Write the date of the transaction in the Date column of the journal. The year is written at the top of every page and the month may be abbreviated if necessary. Only the day of the month is recorded for each successive

GENERAL JOURNAL
PAGE ___GJ1___

DATE		ACCOUNTS & DESCRIPTION	F.	DEBIT	CREDIT
19— June	1	Bank		80 0 0 0 00	
		Capital, Tom Carter			80 0 0 0 00
		Investment in business.			
	3	Land		25 0 0 0 00	
		Bank			25 0 0 0 00
		Purchased land for cash.			
	7	Building		100 0 0 0 00	
		Bank			30 0 0 0 00
		Mortgage Payable			70 0 0 0 00
		Bought building, assuming 15-year mortgage.			
	8	Office Equipment		5 0 0 0 00	
		Accts. Pay./Strands Office Equipment Co.			5 0 0 0 00
		Bought equipment, terms net 10 days.			
		Due June 18.			
	10	Purchases		8 0 0 0 00	
		Bank			8 0 0 0 00
		Bought merchandise for cash.			
	18	Accts. Pay./Strands Office Equipment Co.		5 0 0 0 00	
		Bank			5 0 0 0 00
		Paid account in full.			
	20	Bank		5 5 0 0 00	
		Sales			5 5 0 0 00
		Cash sales to date.			
	30	Telephone Expense		1 4 5 00	
		Bank			1 4 5 00
		Paid telephone bill.			

Figure 2.6 General Journal Entries for Carter's Window Coverings

transaction. The month and year are repeated only at the top of a new page or when either the month or the year changes on the existing page. (Revenue Canada requires that all financial records be kept for a period of at least six years, so the year date is essential on all journal pages and other financial documents to distinguish one year's activities from another's.)

3. On the same line as the date, beginning at the date margin in the Accounts & Description column, write the name of the account to be debited and enter the dollar amount in the debit column. The account to be debited must be entered *before* the account to be credited. If the amount has no cents, a dash may be used rather than entering ".00" in the cents column. Generally, both methods are acceptable.

4. On the next line, indent about 2 cm from the date margin and record the account name to be credited, then enter the amount in the credit column. Again, a dash may be used rather than ".00" for representing no cents. The credit entry is always indented to distinguish it visually from the debit entry.

5. On the next line, starting at the date margin again, write a brief explanation of the transaction. All transactions should be explained so that anyone examining the books, even a year from now, will have a full understanding of the activity being recorded. This explanation will often include invoice numbers, due dates, and any other information that helps to fully explain the details of the activity.

6. Leave a blank line after each transaction to make it stand out clearly. If no blank lines are left, the journal entries will be very difficult to read.

7. Do not split a transaction between the bottom of the current page and the top of the next page. If the entire transaction cannot be recorded on the same page, begin at the top of a new page.

8. All pages of the journal are numbered consecutively; for example, GJ1 (general journal page 1), GJ2, GJ3, etc.

9. Dollar signs, decimal points, and commas are not required on amounts recorded in journals. Also, all numbers recorded in money columns should be written the same size—the cents figures are no less significant than the dollar figures. Also, numbers should be written clearly to avoid misreading the amounts.

▶ ### PRACTICE EXERCISE 6

On April 1, 19—, James Mead opened a grocery store. You will be recording the transactions for his business in a general journal as explained in this chapter. Provide suitable explanations for all transactions.

The assets and liabilities invested by Mr. Mead appear on the following chart. Record the investment of these items. Because this transaction will consist of two entries in the debit column and two entries in the credit column, it is a compound entry.

James Mead's Investment					
ASSETS					
Cash	2	5	0	0	0	00
Inventory		1	0	0	0	00
	2	6	0	0	0	00
LIABILITIES & CAPITAL					
Accounts Payable		1	0	0	0	00
Capital, J. Mead	2	5	0	0	0	00
	2	6	0	0	0	00

Continue by recording the following activities in the general journal.

April 2 Bought merchandise from Green Wholesalers Ltd., $353. Issued cheque #1.

2 Paid the store rent for April. Issued cheque #2 for $400.

4 Sold merchandise to A. Hill on 10-day terms, $28.50; sales invoice #1.

7 Bought merchandise from Weston Grocers on 10-day terms, $170.00; purchase invoice is #342.

9 Cash sales for this week, $185.30.

12 Sold merchandise on 30-day terms to James Miller, $18.10, sales invoice #2; Jack Abbot, $23.60, sales invoice #3; and James Wood, $16.00, sales invoice #4. (Prepare this as a compound entry.)

14 Received a cheque from A. Hill for the amount owing on sales invoice #1, $28.50. (Since cheques are treated as cash, you will be debiting Bank [or Cash] for this transaction.)

16 Cash sales for the week, $96.90.

17 Issued cheque #3 to Weston Grocers in full payment of account (see the April 7 entry).

23 Cash sales for the week, $123.80.

30 Issued cheque #4 to City Hydro to pay the electricity bill, $117.60. (Utilities Expense).

30 Cash sales for the week, $134.65.

▶ **PRACTICE EXERCISE 7**

Prepare general journal entries for the following transactions. Each transaction requires a proper explanation.

19—

May 1 James Kennedy has invested $25,000 in a shoe store. The money was deposited into the business account.

2 Rented a building from Greenway Properties for $600 per month, making the payment for May by cheque #1.

3 Bought store fixtures from Consolidated Enterprises, $1,650. Issued cheque #2.

3 Bought wrapping supplies and twine, $85.30. Issued cheque #3. (Wrapping Supplies Prepaid)

4 Bought a company car from Carman Auto Sales, $16,500. Paid $10,000 down (cheque #4) with the balance due in 90 days, purchase invoice #8625.

5 Bought merchandise, $1,825, from Dominion Shoe Co.; purchase invoice #842. This invoice must be paid within 30 days. (Purchases)

6 Cash sales, $420.15.

9 Sold merchandise on account, $97.50, to Tom Watson on sales invoice #1. Payment is due in 20 days.

10 Cash sales, $464.75.

11 Sales on credit: A.W. Trent, $47.95; G.R. Roberts, $63.50; F.W. Grant, $75. Sales invoices #2, #3, and #4 respectively, due in 20 days. (This should be recorded as a compound entry.)

13 Purchased merchandise on account, $1,550, from Standard Footwear Ltd. Terms are net 30 days on purchase invoice #441.

14 Paid salaries by cheque, $500. Cheque #5.

15 Paid Dominion Shoe Co. $1,825 for balance owing on purchase invoice #842. Issued cheque #6.

16 Cash sales, $527.45.

17 Sales on credit: F.W. Grant, $23.50; A.W. Trent, $36.75; G.R. Roberts, $19. Terms are net 20 days on sales invoices #5, #6, and #7 respectively.

18 Received a cheque from F.W. Grant as partial payment on invoice #4, $60.

20 Cash sales, $746.95.

25 Sales on credit: A.W. Trent, $45; G.R. Roberts, $32.95. Terms are net 20 days; sales invoices #8 and #9 were issued.

26 Purchased merchandise, $895, from Dominion Shoe Co. Terms are net 10 days; purchase invoice #930.

28 Paid salaries, $500. Cheque #7.

29 Paid telephone bill, $80. Cheque #8. (Telephone Expense)

29 Received a cheque from Tom Watson on sales invoice #1, $97.50.

▶ ### PRACTICE EXERCISE 8

Robert Waters has started a plumbing business under the name of The Village Plumber. Record the following transactions for the month of June in the general journal.

19—

June 1 Robert Waters invested cash, $10,500, and a truck, $6,500, into the plumbing business.

2 Rented a portion of a building from Heswell Properties and paid rent for June, $700; cheque #101.

2 Purchased tools and plumbing equipment from Sam's Plumbing Supply, $2,200; cheque #102. (Tools & Equipment)

3 Bought supplies for the office from Chang Stationery, $35.90; cheque #103. (Office Supplies Expense)

3   Performed repair work for Country Hardware on account, $267. This is work order #1, payment due in 10 days. (Repair Service Revenue)

5   Purchased an answering machine for the office from Tony's Electronics, $250; cheque #104. (Office Equipment)

7   Installed a new water heater and new pipes for Gerald Wallace; work order #2. Collected $1,020 as full payment for the work performed.

10   Newspaper advertising is to appear in the *Selkirk Journal* on June 15. Purchase invoice #327 for $75 is due in 10 days.

13   Collected the amount owing from Country Hardware, $267.

15   Completed repairs for Harris Drugs, $310, to be collected June 25; work order #3.

19   Received purchase invoice #752 from Acme Service Station for repairs and gasoline for the truck, $283. Payment in 10 days. (Truck Expense)

20   Paid *Selkirk Journal* $75 on account; cheque #105.

21   Completed plumbing repairs for Mrs. Anne Brill, $96 cash. Work order #4.

25   Collected the amount owing from Harris Drugs for repairs completed on June 15, $310.

29   Paid the telephone bill, $123; cheque #106.

29   Paid the amount owing to Acme Service Station, $283; cheque #107.

30   Paid salaries, $820; cheque #108.

▶ **PRACTICE EXERCISE 9**

The following transactions for the Elbran Company occurred during the month of October. Prepare the general journal entries, complete with suitable explanations.

19—

Oct.   1   Ann Brell, the owner, started the business by investing $82,000 cash.

2   Purchased land and a building, making a $40,000 down payment and signing a mortgage at Bank of Montreal for the balance of $60,000. Value of land, $45,000; value of building, $55,000. Cheque #1.

4   Bought a desk and chair for the office from Sears, $1,050. Cheque #2.

6   Bought merchandise from C. Barker & Co., $725. Cheque #3.

6   Purchased a typewriter, $545, and supplies for the office (Office Supplies Prepaid), $65.20; purchase invoice #342 from Kirkfield Equipment Co.; terms net 30 days. (This will require a compound entry.)

8   Bought merchandise from Riverside Company on account, $894; purchase invoice #306, payment due in 10 days.

8   Paid $361 to General Insurance Co. for a one-year fire insurance policy. Cheque #2. (Insurance Prepaid)

10   Sold merchandise on credit to Brad Abbot, $229; terms net 10 days; sales invoice #1.

11   Sold merchandise for cash, $432.

14   Paid $55 to the *Local Gazette* for advertising. Cheque #5.

15   Paid salaries: bookkeeper, $650; sales representative, $700. Cheques #6 and #7. (Separate salary accounts are required for each employee.)

18   Received $229 from Brad Abbot on account for sales invoice #1.

19   Purchased merchandise from C. Barker & Co., $525. Cheque #8.

20   Paid Riverside Company $894 on account. Cheque #9.

23   Sales on credit: Martha Corrigal, $64.50; Tim Dunphy, $46; and Michelle Parent, $32.50. Sales invoices #2, #3, and #4 respectively. Terms net 30 days.

26   Purchased merchandise from Ritchie & Co. on credit, $493. Purchase invoice #498, due in 30 days.

30   Paid the first installment on the mortgage (withdrawn by the bank), $900. Interest of $600 is included in this payment. (A compound entry is required.)

31   Paid salaries: bookkeeper, $650; sales representative, $700. Cheques #10 and #11.

31   Paid the telephone bill, $46.70. Cheque #12

THINK ABOUT IT!

1.   The term debit is abbreviated Dr. True or False?
2.   The term credit is abbreviated Cr. True or False?
3.   Debit means the right side of the account. True or False?
4.   An account increases on the side of origin. True or False?
5.   The accounting equation is Assets + Liabilities = Capital. True or False?
6.   Every bookkeeping transaction must balance. True or False?
7.   Bookkeeping should be done in pencil so that all errors can be corrected easily. True or False?
8.   What is a journal?
9.   (a) Which side of the transaction is recorded first, debit or credit?
      (b) Can a transaction be split between two pages?
      (c) In what order are the pages in a journal numbered?
10.   Why is the year date required on each page?
11.   Is it necessary to explain every transaction?

3

The Ledger

CHAPTER OBJECTIVES

After completing this chapter, you will be able to:

- assign account numbers according to a predetermined chart of accounts

- post transactions from the general journal to a general ledger

- prepare a trial balance from the general ledger

IMPORTANT WORDS AND TERMS IN THIS CHAPTER

Audit Trail
Chart of Accounts
Compensating Errors
General Ledger
Ledger Account
Posting

Posting Marks
Slide Errors
Transposition of
   Figures
Trial Balance

In Chapter 2, we learned that the journal is used for recording business transactions on a daily basis. But the journal is only one phase of the bookkeeping process. If, at the end of the month, we want to know how much money Tom Carter's business has in its Bank account, can we tell just by looking at the journal? Not very easily. The cash transactions are scattered throughout the pages of the journal. In order to get this kind of information, we will need to transfer each transaction from the journal to another set of records called the general ledger.

The **general ledger** is a book or file that holds all ledger accounts in one place. The **ledger accounts** show the increases and decreases (debit and credit entries) of each specific asset, liability, owner's equity, revenue, and expense account. All the Bank (or Cash) transactions, for example, come together in the Bank ledger account, with the final balance representing the amount of money available at that time. Likewise, all Sales transactions will be shown in the Sales account, representing the revenue earned to date from the sale of merchandise or services.

Such ledger accounts are usually printed on loose-leaf sheets or cards and are stored in a binder or in filing trays. Computerized accounting systems store this information in a similar fashion on computer disks. (Computerized accounting will be discussed in Chapter 19.)

In a small business, such as Tom Carter's, a single ledger file or book will accommodate all the ledger accounts that the business is likely to require; however, organizing and using a set of ledger accounts can be enhanced by dividing it into three sections:

1. general ledger;

2. accounts receivable ledger (sometimes called the customers' ledger); and

3. accounts payable ledger (sometimes called the creditors' ledger).

In a large business, it is probably more practical to use several ledger files in order to keep the number of accounts from becoming too numerous in any single file and to provide an opportunity to divide the work involved in maintaining the ledger accounts. This subdivision of labour allows more than one employee to work on the ledger accounts at the same time. For example, a business with a large number of customers might find it more practical to divide the work of maintaining the accounts receivable ledger among two or more employees. One employee could be in charge of customers whose names start with A to L, and another could be in charge of customers whose names start with M to Z. A business with a large number of creditors (suppliers) could divide the accounts payable ledger among two or more employees in a similar fashion.

The accuracy of the ledger file is extremely important because:

• The ledger file is the basis for the preparation of financial statements.

• The ledger files provide management with useful information for decision-making purposes during the accounting period, such as how much cash is available in the bank account, how much is owing to the business by its customers, and how much is owing by the business to its creditors.

THE LEDGER ACCOUNT

Each ledger sheet or card is headed with all the pertinent information that identifies the account, such as the account name, the account number, and the sheet (page) number. (See Figure 3.1.) Each account starts with Sheet 1; then as that page is filled, a second page is started (numbered Sheet 2), and so on.

ACCOUNT	A/R Devon Lauryl Company													ACCT. NO.	137	
TERMS	n/30					CREDIT LIMIT	$3000							SHEET NO.	4	

DATE		MEMO	DISC. DATE	F.	✓	DEBIT	✓	CREDIT	✓	DR. CR.	BALANCE
19— Oct.	1	Bal. Fwd.								Dr.	3 0 0 00
	7	inv. #387		SJ7		2 5 0 00					5 5 0 00
	13	paid on a/c		CR5				3 0 0 00			2 5 0 00
	26	inv. #419		SJ8		8 0 0 00					1 0 5 0 00

Figure 3.1 Customer's Ledger Account

The Date column records the date that was entered in the journal. A year date is entered at the top of each ledger page and whenever a new year begins.

The Memo (or Explanation) column contains any particulars important to a transaction. Although memos are not always necessary in general ledger accounts, they can be particularly helpful in the customers' and creditors' accounts. Such memos help to provide a complete picture of the transactions and are helpful when looking for unusual transactions or for possible errors.

Folios, sometimes called posting references, provide a cross-reference for the transactions that are transferred from the journal to the ledger accounts. In the journal, the Folio column shows the number of the account to which the entry was transferred, while in the ledger account, the Folio column shows the journal page number from which the entry was transferred. These posting references, in the journal and in the ledger account, provide evidence that the transfer of each journal entry to its respective ledger account has been completed.

The Debit column shows the amounts transferred from the Debit column in the journal. If the entry was recorded in the Debit column in the journal, it must appear in the Debit column in the ledger account if the books are to remain in balance.

The Credit column is for amounts transferred from the credit column in the journal. If the entry was recorded in the credit column in the journal, it must appear in the credit column in the ledger account if the books are to remain in balance.

The Balance column shows a running dollar balance for that account. Some bookkeepers prefer to wait until all entries for the month have been posted to the account before computing the balance; however, we recommend that the balance be computed after each transaction has been entered.

Accounts Receivable (customer) ledger accounts and accounts payable (creditor) ledger accounts will also show the customers' and creditors' addresses and the credit limit allowed.

A **chart of accounts** is a list of ledger account titles and the account numbers assigned to them. The number of accounts and the names of those accounts will depend on the size of the business and the nature of its operations. The accounts are arranged and numbered in a standard order according to the classifications defined in Chapter 1, such as:

Assets	100–199
Liabilities	200–299
Owner's Equity	300–399
Revenues	400–499
Expenses	500–599

The range of numbers assigned to each category will depend on the number of ledger accounts that must be accommodated. Some businesses, for example, may have so many different operating expenses that the range 500 to 599 shown above might have to be increased to, for example, 500 to 699; or a wider range might be required for assets, such as 100 to 299. Also, account numbers that are four digits long, or five, rather than only three as shown here, might better accommodate the specific needs of the business. The chart, then, is flexible and can be altered easily to meet the business's changing needs, such as when the transition is made from a manual accounting system to a computerized system. The following chart illustrates how flexible the structure of a chart of accounts can be and how different companies might set up their charts of accounts:

	Northern Steelworks Ltd.	Western Workwear Co.	Eastern Auto Repairs
Assets	1001–1199	100–299	1–19
Liabilities	2001–2999	300–499	20–29
Owner's Equity	3001–3999	500–599	30–39
Revenues	4001–5999	600–699	40–49
Expenses	6001–8999	700–999	50–75

▶ **PRACTICE EXERCISE 1**

Using the standard chart of accounts explained above, assign an appropriate three-digit account number to each of these general ledger accounts. Be sure not to use any number more than once.

Drafting Supplies Prepaid	Capital, Arthur Fraser
Donations	Cash (or Bank)
Land	Accounts Payable
Sales	Building
Telephone Expense	Rent Expense

Accounts Receivable	Purchases
Interest Expense	Mortgage Payable
Salaries	Interest Revenue
Service Equipment	Insurance Prepaid
Rental Revenue	Sales Tax Payable
Office Furniture & Equipment	Delivery Expense
Bank Loan Payable	Advertising Expense

POSTING

The process of **posting** involves copying the information that is recorded in the journal into the individual ledger accounts. Every debit and credit entry in the journal is posted to its respective ledger account in the order in which it appears in the journal, including the date of the entry, the amount of the transaction, and any other details deemed important to note.

To demonstrate how posting is accomplished, the first two general journal entries for Carter's Window Coverings (discussed in Chapter 2) will be illustrated and explained. As you read through the following steps, refer to Figure 3.2, which illustrates the posting of Tom Carter's transactions from the journal to the ledger accounts.

1. Locate the ledger sheet for the first account named in the first general journal entry. In this case, the account is Bank.

2. Enter the date of the transaction in the Date column of the ledger account. The month and year are recorded only for the first entry in each account. Do not repeat them for subsequent entries in the same account, except when the account transactions are continued on the next page or when the month or year changes.

3. Write a suitable explanation in the Memo column, if one is required. This might include an invoice number, a cheque number, or a special notation related to the transaction.

4. Enter the amount ($80,000) that appears in the debit column of the journal into the Debit column of the ledger account. Care must be taken to ensure that all amounts are copied accurately.

5. Calculate the balance of the account and enter it into the Balance column. Since this is the first entry in the Bank account, the balance will be the same amount ($80,000). Later, when the next entry is posted to the Bank account (the credit side of the June 3 entry), it will be deducted from this balance to arrive at a new balance ($80,000 − $25,000 = $55,000). Be sure to write all numbers legibly.

6. Mark the status (debit or credit) of this balance in the column located between the Credit column and Balance column, marked DR./CR. You will write either Dr. or Cr. depending on the current status of the newly calculated balance. Here's an easy way to determine the status of any balance in any account: add up all the entries in the Debit column and add up all the entries in the Credit column. Whichever is the larger total determines the status of the balance. In the illustration of the Bank account in Figure 3.2, there was a debit entry recorded on June 1 but no

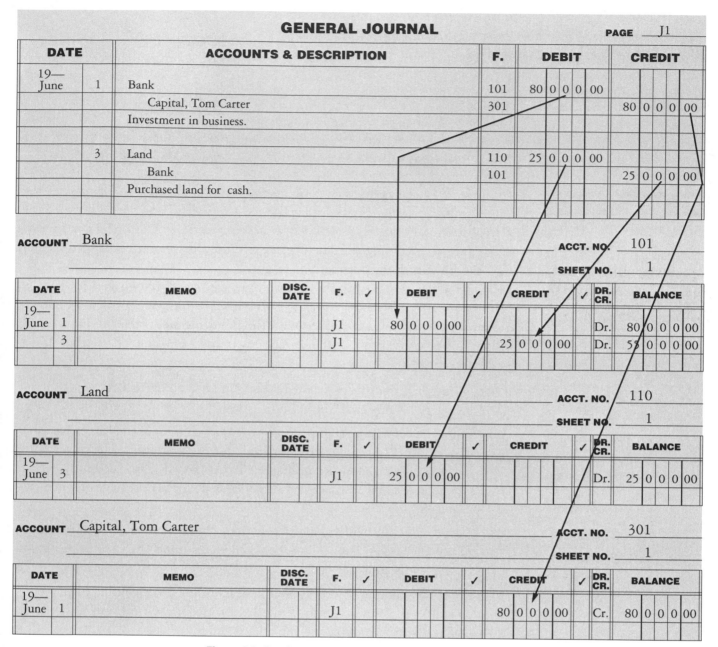

Figure 3.2 Posting to Ledger Accounts

credit entries; therefore, the $80,000 balance on that date is a debit balance. Later, when the June 3 entry is posted, the Debit column will have a total of $80,000 while the Credit column will have a total of $25,000. Since the Debit column is still larger than the Credit column, the new balance of $55,000 is a debit balance.

7. Two posting references (often called posting marks or folios) are required for every amount posted: (a) In the Folio or posting reference column of the ledger account, write J1 (or GJ1) to indicate that the transaction was transferred from page 1 of the general journal. (b) In the Folio column in the general journal, write the ledger account number (101 in this case) to indicate that the transaction was posted to that specific ledger account. These posting marks serve two important purposes: (i) they show that the transfer of the entry is complete; and (ii) they assist in locating an entry

that may be questionable or requires a correction. Posting references provide an **audit trail**, the means of following a transaction from the source document to the journal and to the various ledger accounts affected by the transaction, or from the ledger account back to the journal entry and to the source document.

8.   Repeat the posting process for the credit (Capital) part of the transaction in the journal. To avoid omissions and errors, it is advisable to post the debit and credit entries line by line down the journal page. In the Carter's Window Coverings journal, we would post to Bank first, then to Capital, then to Land, and then to Bank again. Balances in the ledger should be computed after each entry has been posted. This provides a running balance of each account.

THE TRIAL BALANCE

After all entries in the journal have been posted to the ledger accounts, a trial balance is prepared. A **trial balance** is a list of all accounts in the ledger book or file and their balances. If no errors are made in posting from the journal, the total of the debit balances should equal the total of the credit balances.

The trial balance for Carter's Window Coverings ledger is shown in Figure 3.3. This statement begins with a three-line heading identifying who, what, and when. This heading shows *who* the trial balance was prepared for, *what* the name of the statement is, and *when* the trial balance was prepared (usually the last day of the month).

Carter's Window Covering
Trial Balance
June 30, 19—

	Account	Debit	Credit
101	Bank	17 3 5 5 00	
112	Office Equipment	5 0 0 0 00	
121	Land	25 0 0 0 00	
122	Building	50 0 0 0 00	
213	Mortgage Payable		20 0 0 0 00
301	Capital, T. Carter		80 0 0 0 00
401	Sales		5 5 0 0 00
501	Purchases	8 0 0 0 00	
506	Telephone Expense	1 4 5 00	
		105 5 0 0 00	105 5 0 0 00

Figure 3.3 Trial Balance (Carter's Window Coverings)

All accounts are listed in the same order as they appear in the ledger, that is, in numerical order, with the current balance of each placed appropriately in the debit or credit column. A total is then calculated for each column. To complete the statement, a single line is drawn above the totals and a double line is drawn below the totals.

But what is the purpose of preparing a trial balance? The trial balance proves that:

(i)   equal debits and credits have been recorded for all transactions; and

(ii)   the balance of each account has been computed correctly.

If the totals of the trial balance do not equal, it is likely that one or more of the following errors were made:

1. Entering a debit amount into the Credit column in a ledger account, or vice versa.

2. Listing a debit balance in the Credit column of the trial balance, or vice versa.

3. Making errors in computing account balances.

4. Copying figures incorrectly from a ledger account to the trial balance or from the journal to a ledger account.

5. Adding the debit and credit columns of the trial balance incorrectly.

A trial balance is a proof that the ledger accounts are still in balance after posting is completed; that is, that debits still equal credits. But there are certain kinds of errors that the trial balance will not disclose:

1. Posting to the wrong ledger account.

2. Omitting an entire transaction during posting.

3. Compensating errors (an error on the debit side that offsets an error of equal value on the credit side).

LOCATING ERRORS IN A TRIAL BALANCE

Every bookkeeper (whether new or experienced) is occasionally faced with a trial balance that does not balance. The process of locating the error (or errors) is not as difficult as it may initially appear.

Here are a few simple steps that will help to locate just about any error that you are likely to encounter:

1. Double-check the addition of the trial balance. The error may just be an amount keyed incorrectly into the calculator.

2. Compare the amounts on the trial balance with those in the ledger accounts. Copying errors are quite common.

3. Calculate the difference between the debit and credit totals on the trial balance to determine the amount out of balance. This difference may reveal that one of the accounts was omitted by mistake or that a journal entry has not yet been posted.

4. Divide the difference by 2 and look for that amount. This amount may have been placed on the wrong side of the trial balance, or it may have been posted to the wrong side of an account. For example, if the difference is $72, divide by 2 to get $36; then look for a possible incorrect balance or entry of $36.

5. Divide the difference by 9. If the difference is divisible by 9, the error is usually a transposition of figures, such as $96 entered as $69, or $572 entered as $527. Errors of this kind could also be the result of a "slide," such as $2,157.00 entered as $21.57.

6. Check the calculation of the balance in each ledger account.

7. If the above steps do not reveal the error, a thorough check of all postings from the journal to the ledger accounts should be made. Check each entry carefully to ensure that it has been posted accurately.

The procedure described above for locating errors in a trial balance is the regular bookkeeping cycle in reverse: checking the trial balance, tracing the figures back to the ledger accounts, then tracing them back to the journals and, if necessary, going back to the source documents. All errors must be located and corrected before the next month's transactions are recorded and posted.

CORRECTING WRITING ERRORS

Once errors are found, they must be corrected properly by observing a few common-sense procedures. As discussed earlier, all financial records must be kept for a minimum period of six years. Anyone looking back through the books of previous years must be able to read every word and every figure clearly.

Erasures, white-out, and writing over figures are not permitted in accounting records. All accounting work should be done with blue or black pen, *not in pencil*. When writing errors are detected, they should be corrected by neatly crossing out the incorrect figures or words with a single line (without obliterating the original characters) and writing the correct information neatly above. Figure 3.4 shows how best to correct writing errors.

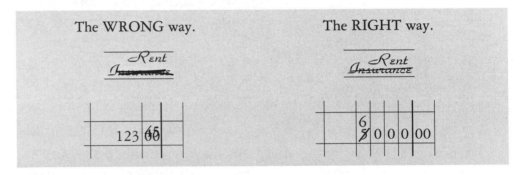

Figure 3.4 How to Correct Writing Errors

This correction method is suitable if a simple writing error occurs in the journal or the ledger accounts *before* the trial balance has been prepared. But if an error is discovered after the month is closed (that is, after the trial balance has been completed), a more practical solution is to record a correcting journal entry with a detailed explanation of its purpose. This correcting entry will be posted to the ledger accounts, in effect reversing or nullifying the original incorrect entry. (Correcting journal entries will be discussed in detail in Chapter 13.)

▶ PRACTICE EXERCISE 2

The following activities are to be recorded in the books of H. Brown Real Estate Services.

(a) Select blank ledger sheets from your supplies and open the following accounts using the account numbers indicated. All ledger accounts will be marked Sheet 1, except Bank, which will require two ledger sheets, marked Sheet 1 and Sheet 2 respectively.

Bank, 101; Office Furniture & Equipment, 102; A/R Benson, Michael, 110; A/P Kran's Typewriter Co., 201; Capital, Henry Brown, 301; Commission Revenue, 401; Rent Expense, 501; Office Salaries, 502; Office Supplies Expense, 503; Telephone Expense, 504.

(b) Record the following transactions in a general journal. The account to be used for revenues earned from the sale of real estate is Commission Revenue.

19—

Mar. 12   Henry Brown has invested $18,000 cash in his real estate business.

1   Paid rent for the month of March to Masc Group, $350. Issued Cheque #1.

2   Bought office furniture, $2,575 from City Furniture Co. Cheque #2.

3   Purchased a computer on credit from Kran's Typewriter Co., $995. Payment is due in 30 days. Purchase invoice #322.

8   Closed a sale on a house for Tom Dunphy and received a commission cheque for $2,250. The contract number of this sale is #0001.

10   Bought office supplies from Wilson's Stationery Co., $33. Cheque #3.

15   Closed a sale on a farm property for Michael Benson, earning a commission of $3,000, which has not yet been received. Sales contract #0002.

18   Closed a sale on a city lot for Marcel Parent, contract #0003. Received a commission cheque of $1,125.

30   Received a cheque from Michael Benson for $2,000 on account.

30   Paid Kran's Typewriter Co. the balance owing. Cheque #4.

31   Paid the telephone bill, $83.90. Cheque #5.

31   Paid office salaries for the month, $1,200.00. Cheque #6.

(c) Post the entries to the ledger accounts as explained and illustrated in this chapter. Be sure that all entries in the journal and all entries in the ledger accounts have appropriate posting references.

(d) Prepare a trial balance like the one in Figure 3.3, including a suitable three-line heading.

▶ **PRACTICE EXERCISE 3**

(a) Jack Herta, the owner of Red River Moving & Storage, started his business on February 1, 19—. Before recording his business activities in the journal, open the following ledger accounts, using the account numbers indicated. All ledger accounts will be marked Sheet 1. (Bank will require two ledger sheets.)

Bank, 101; A/R Smith, Edward, 105; Swain, Jack, 106; Moving Van, 112; Office Equipment, 113; A/P Peckoff Equipment Co., 201; Bank Loan Payable, 220; Capital, J. Herta, 301; Moving Service Revenue, 401;

Storage Fees Revenue, 402; Interest Revenue, 405; Gasoline Expense, 501; Maintenance Expense, 502; Rent Expense, 503; Utilities, 504.

(b) Here is a statement of the assets and liabilities that Jack has invested in the business:

Statement of Assets, Liabilities, and Owner's Equity **February 1, 19—**					
ASSETS					
Cash	20	0	0	0	00
Moving Van	40	0	0	0	00
	60	0	0	0	00
LIABILITIES & OWNER'S EQUITY					
Bank Loan	15	0	0	0	00
Capital, J. Herta	45	0	0	0	00
	60	0	0	0	00

Prepare the general journal entry for the above investment and record the following transactions for the month of February. Each transaction requires a suitable explanation.

19—

Feb. 2 Purchased office equipment from Peckoff Equipment Co. on 30-day credit terms, $1,390. Purchase invoice #2071.

3 Edward Smith has stored his furniture for one month. Storage fees are $180. Received a $50 deposit and the balance will be paid in 20 days. Sales invoice #1.

3 Paid National Agency for February rent, $2,000. Cheque #1.

5 Received $2,380 from William Butler for moving services.

10 Charged Jack Swain $1,975 for moving services, to be paid on March 2. Sales invoice #2.

15 Paid Shell Canada for gasoline for moving vans, $400; cheque #2.

23 Received a cheque from Edward Smith to cover the balance of his account.

25 Received $3,250 from Philip Webster for moving services provided today.

26 Issued cheque #3 for $150. to Fred's Garage for maintenance work on the van.

28 The bank deposited $200 in our account for interest earned on a short-term investment.

28 Issued cheque #4 for the light and heating bill, $150.

(c)   Post the journal entries to the ledger accounts as illustrated in this chapter.

(d)   Prepare a trial balance, complete with an appropriate three-line heading.

► ## PRACTICE EXERCISE 4

(a)   Select blank ledger sheets from your supplies and open the following accounts using the account numbers indicated. All ledger accounts will require only one sheet, marked Sheet 1, except Bank, which will require two ledger sheets.

Bank, 101; A/R Hartley, S., 110; A/R Judy's Dress Shoppe, 111; A/R Nash, Ellen, 112; A/R Rennie's Auto Sales, 113; Cleaning Equipment, 120; Store Fixtures, 130; Delivery Equipment, 140; A/P Brown's Equipment Suppliers, 201; A/P Bruce Auto Sales, 202; A/P Daily Press, 203; Bank Loan Payable, 220; Capital, John Grady, 301; Service Revenue, 401; Advertising Expense, 501; Cleaning Supplies Expense, 502; Rent Expense, 503; Salaries Expense, 504; Telephone Expense, 505; Utilities, 506.

(b)   Journalize the following transactions, complete with appropriate explanations, for Rainbow Rug & Furniture Cleaners.

19—

Oct.   1   John Grady started his business by investing the following assets and liabilities: Bank, $18,000; Cleaning Equipment, $8,000; Store Fixtures, $3,000; and Bank Loan, $5,000. (Hint: Determine the Capital value needed to balance this transaction.)

2   Issued cheque #1 to Deutsch Holdings for $325 to pay the October rent.

2   Purchased a truck for $16,900 from Bruce Auto Sales; paid $6900. down; terms net 90 days. Purchase invoice #773; cheque #2.

4   Purchased additional cleaning equipment, $3,000, and supplies, $800, from Brown's Equipment Suppliers. Payment is due in 10 days. Purchase invoice #663.

5   Received $175 from Tony Laicini for cleaning services rendered.

7   Sent a bill to S. Hartley for services provided; terms net 10 days; sales invoice #01; $225.

9   Placed a newspaper advertisement in the *Daily Press*, to be paid in 10 days; $85. Purchase invoice #113.

11   Billed Rennie's Auto Sales $425.00 for cleaning floor rugs in their showroom; 10-day credit terms; sales invoice #02.

12   Received $195 cash from Sally Ritchie for cleaning rugs and furniture.

14   Issued cheque #3 for $3,800 to pay the balance owing to Brown's Equipment Suppliers.

17   Received from S. Hartley on sales invoice #01, $225.

19   Issued cheque #3 on account to the *Daily Press*, $85.

21 Received $425 from Rennie's Auto Sales on sales invoice #02.

22 Sent a bill to Judy's Dress Shoppe for cleaning services rendered on 30-day terms, $345; sales invoice #03.

23 Sold services for cash to Rozmin Jamal, $165.

25 Paid telephone bill, $27, with cheque #5.

26 Services rendered on credit to Ellen Nash, $145; terms net 10 days; sales invoice #04.

30 Services provided to John Carter for cash, $130.

30 Paid utilities, $65. Cheque #6.

31 Paid monthly salaries to two employees, $1,050 each. Cheques #7 and #8.

(c) Post the general journal entries to their respective ledger accounts.

(d) Prepare a trial balance in proper form.

▶ **PRACTICE EXERCISE 5**

James Martin, the owner of the Family Shoe Store, has employed you as his bookkeeper.

(a) Set up ledger accounts in the order stated below. The Bank account will require three ledger sheets; all others will require only one each. Assign an appropriate account number to each using the account classification guide shown in the Chart of Accounts section of this chapter.

Bank; A/R Crawford, W.A.; A/R Dickson, R.G.; A/R Fuller, W.F.; Office Supplies Prepaid; Delivery Equipment; Store Fixtures; A/P Canada Auto Sales; A/P Dominion Shoe Co.; A/P Royal Stationery; Capital, J. Martin; Sales; Purchases; General Expense; Rent Expense; Salary Expense.

(b) Record the following transactions in the general journal. All payments are to be made by cheque, beginning with cheque #1. Record the cheque number issued in the explanation portion of the entry.

19—

May 1 Mr. Martin invested $35,000 cash into his business and deposited the money in the bank.

2 A rental agreement was signed today with Pelletier Properties for the use of a store for $600 per month. (No entry will be made until the rent is paid; no values have yet been exchanged.)

3 Bought store fixtures from O'Connor & Day for $16,500. Paid by cheque.

3 Bought wrapping paper and twine from Business Warehouse, $145. Paid by cheque.

4   Purchased office supplies for $86.70 from Royal Stationery, sales invoice #223; terms net 30 days.

4   Bought a delivery truck for $12,000 from Canada Auto Sales. Purchase invoice #773, terms net 15 days.

5   Purchased merchandise from Dominion Shoe Co., $2,450. Purchase invoice #523, terms net 10 days.

6   Cash sales, $624.75.

7   Paid salary, $245.

7   Issued a cheque to pay the rent for May.

9   Sold shoes on account to W.A. Crawford, $69.95. Sales invoice #1, terms net 15 days.

10   Cash sales, $924.75.

11   Sales on credit: W.A. Crawford, $47.65; R.G. Dickson, $63.50; W.F. Fuller, $40.00. Sales invoice #2, #3, and #4, terms net 15 days. (Record this as a compound entry.)

13   Acquired additional merchandise on account from Dominion Shoe Co., $1,500. Purchase invoice #587, terms net 30 days.

14   Paid salary, $245.

15   Issued a cheque for $2,450 to Dominion Shoe Co. on account.

16   Cash sales, $1,027.50.

17   Sales on credit: W.F. Fuller, $53.50; R.G. Dickson, $42.40; W.A. Crawford, $39.98. Sales invoices #5, #6, and #7; terms net 15 days.

18   Received a cheque from W.F. Fuller in partial payment of his account, $35.

19   Issued a cheque to Canada Auto Sales, $6,000.

20   Cash sales, $946.98.

21   Paid salary, $245.

23   Paid Dominion Shoe Co. $850 on account.

23   Received cheques on account from: W.F. Fuller, $35.; W.A. Crawford, $69.95; and R.G. Dickson, $63.50.

25   Sales on credit: R.G. Dickson, $72.98; and W.F. Fuller, $44.65. Sales invoices #8 and #9; terms net 15 days.

28   Paid salary, $245.

31   Received a cheque from W.A. Crawford on account, $20.

(c)   Post all transactions to the ledger.

(d)   Prepare a trial balance in proper form.

PRACTICE EXERCISE 6

Jillian Hansen, a bookkeeping trainee, is unable to balance a trial balance she has prepared for Adams & Co. on February 28, 19—, and has asked for your help. Rewrite this trial balance in proper form, correcting all errors.

#	Account	Debit					Credit				
101	Bank	7	4	0	0	00					
104	Government Bonds						5	0	0	0	00
110	Accounts Receivable	13	7	9	5	00					
121	Office Supplies Prepaid	4	4	0	0	00					
125	Insurance Prepaid		7	2	0	00					
150	Land						30	0	0	0	00
160	Office Equipment	15	0	0	0	00					
201	Accounts Payable						10	8	0	0	00
221	Mortgage Payable	20	0	0	0	00					
301	Capital, John Adams						45	0	0	0	00
401	Sales						75	8	7	5	00
410	Interest Revenue		7	0	0	00					
501	Purchases	50	0	4	0	00					
504	Rent Expense						6	0	0	0	00
508	Property Tax Expense	1	2	0	0	00					
511	Salaries Expense	16	0	0	0	00					
515	Interest Expense						1	5	0	0	00
519	Utilities	1	3	2	0	00					
		130	1	2	5	00	174	1	7	5	00

Table title: **Trial Balance for Adams & Co. dated February 28, 19—**

▶ **PRACTICE EXERCISE 7**

Examine the following trial balance for potential errors. Prepare a corrected trial balance in proper form.

December 31, 19— Trial Balance for Timbor Specialties Co.

#	Accounts	Debit					Credit				
105	Bank (overdraft)						15	0	0	0	00
111	A/R Johnson Bros.	11	4	7	0	00					
113	A/R Liston Fuels Ltd.	10	8	6	0	00					
116	Office Supplies Prepaid		3	0	5	00					
118	Packing Supplies Prepaid							4	5	0	00
125	Furniture & Equipment	9	3	7	5	00					
135	Trucks & Vans						28	4	0	0	00
141	Land	50	0	0	0	00					
151	Building	103	0	0	0	00					
204	A/P Dillon Drill-Works	1	5	5	0	00					
208	A/P Royal Rubber							8	8	5	00
303	Capital, Robert Steel						167	5	0	0	00
410	Sales						192	7	6	0	00
420	Interest Revenue		4	2	5	00					
430	Rental Revenue							4	2	3	5	00
510	Purchases	138	7	0	0	00					
520	Advertising Expense	4	3	2	0	00					
525	Business Tax Expense		8	0	0	00					
530	Delivery Expense	1	5	9	0	00					
535	Interest Expense							5	7	5	00
540	Rental Expense (Equipment)	1	1	6	0	00					
545	Salaries Expense	21	3	5	0	00					
				?					?		

► **PRACTICE EXERCISE 8**

Analyze each of the following general journal transactions and write a suitable narrative (memo) for each.

		GENERAL JOURNAL							PAGE	GJ1				

DATE		ACCOUNTS & DESCRIPTION	F.	DEBIT					CREDIT				
19— April	1	Bank		x	x	x	x	xx					
		Prepaid Office Supplies			x	x	x	xx					
		Office Equipment			x	x	x	xx					
		Bank Loan Payable							x	x	x	x	xx
		Capital, Norio Ota							x	x	x	x	xx
	3	Purchases		x	x	x	x	xx					
		Bank							x	x	x	x	xx
	4	Office Furniture		x	x	x	x	xx					
		A/P Sunrise Furniture Co.							x	x	x	x	xx
	6	A/R Susan Little			x	x	x	xx					
		Sales								x	x	x	xx
	10	Rental of Equipment			x	x	x	xx					
		Bank								x	x	x	xx
	10	Salaries Expense		x	x	x	x	xx					
		Bank							x	x	x	x	xx
	14	A/P Sunrise Furniture Co.		x	x	x	x	xx					
		Bank							x	x	x	x	xx
	16	Bank			x	x	x	xx					
		Interest Revenue								x	x	x	xx
	16	Bank		x	x	x	x	xx					
		Sales							x	x	x	x	xx
	18	A/R Packard-Jones Co.			x	x	x	xx					
		A/R Western Glove Ltd.			x	x	x	xx					
		A/R Simon & Sons				x	x	xx					
		Sales							x	x	x	x	xx
	21	Purchases		x	x	x	x	xx					
		A/P Dalhousie Produce							x	x	x	x	xx
	24	Salaries Expense		x	x	x	x	xx					
		Bank							x	x	x	x	xx
	24	Telephone Expense				x	x	xx					
		Bank									x	x	xx
	26	Delivery Expense			x	x	x	xx					
		A/P Speedy Cartage Co.								x	x	x	xx
	28	Mortgage Payable			x	x	x	xx					
		Interest Expense				x	x	xx					
		Bank								x	x	x	xx
	30	Bank			x	x	x	xx					
		A/R Susan Little								x	x	x	xx

THINK ABOUT IT!

1. What is the name of the account used when merchandise is acquired for resale?
2. Which three ledger files might be used in a medium- or large-size business?
3. What is the purpose of a ledger account?
4. What is another name for the Folio column? What is its purpose?
5. Explain posting.
6. In what order are accounts listed on the trial balance?
7. If the totals of the debit and credit columns on the trial balance are equal, does this mean that all accounts are correct? Why?
8. If the trial balance does not balance, where would you look for the errors?
9. Why does the year date appear on all records?
10. Explain the proper procedure for correcting writing errors in financial records.

4

Special Journals

CHAPTER OBJECTIVES

After completing this chapter, you will be able to:

- record purchase transactions in the purchase journal

- record sale transactions in the sales journal

- post from the purchase and sales journals to the general ledger and subsidiary ledgers

- allocate GST on purchase and sales invoices

- prepare a trial balance utilizing control accounts and subsidiary ledgers

IMPORTANT WORDS AND TERMS IN THIS CHAPTER

Accounts Payable	Sales Invoice
Accounts Receivable	Sales Journal
Cash Receipts Journal	Schedule of
Control Account	Accounts Payable
Invoice	Schedule of
Markup & Markdown	Accounts Receivable
Proof (of Equality)	Special Journals
Purchase Invoice	Subsidiary Ledgers
Purchase Journal	

I n Chapters 2 and 3, we learned how to record business transactions in the general journal. By now you can appreciate that the general journal is cumbersome for most daily transactions because many of those transactions are written again and again. How many times did you record a cash sale transaction by debiting Bank and crediting Sales? And how many times did you record the purchase of merchandise on account by debiting Purchases and crediting Accounts Payable? To minimize such repetition, special journals are often created to handle transactions that occur frequently.

These special journals offer several advantages:

1. Special journals reduce the amount of unnecessary writing. This, in turn, reduces time and labour, and minimizes the potential for errors or the omission of necessary details.

2. Special journals provide a means of recording transactions more efficiently and effectively. Specialized columns within these journals capture selected kinds of information, which facilitates posting.

3. Special journals permit a division of labour; that is, they allow two or more employees to record transactions simultaneously rather than only one bookkeeper having access to the journal at any given time.

The most common special journals are the sales journal, the purchase journal, the cash receipts journal, and the cash payments journal. The **sales journal** is used to record sales of merchandise on account, including charges for provincial sales tax (where applicable) and GST (the federal Goods and Services Tax). The **purchase journal** is used to record transactions on account such as expenses incurred and merchandise and assets purchased. The **cash receipts journal** is used to record all money received, including money in the cash register and cheques and money orders received through the mail. The **cash payments journal** is used to record all money paid out (cheques issued).

Each company will design its own special journals to suit the volume of transactions it will record, the nature of the business, and the information needed by the business. To accomplish this, special journals are set up with suitable column headings that reflect the most frequent activities to be recorded. If a particular type of transaction occurs only once in a while, a special column would likely not be established for it.

But the use of special journals does not eliminate the need for the general journal. The general journal will continue to be used for transactions that cannot be recorded in the special journals. Certain transactions will occur that cannot be accommodated by the purchase journal, sales journal, or the cash journals. Such transactions will be recorded in the general journal. The word "general" is important because it distinguishes this journal from the special journals.

The remainder of this chapter will discuss the use of the purchase journal and the sales journal. The cash receipts and cash payments journals will be discussed in detail in Chapter 6.

PURCHASING ON CREDIT

Depending on the size of the company, the purchasing procedure for merchandise and supplies may be long and involved or short and simple. A small business, such as Lance Reed's yard service or Tom Carter's retail store, would have a very simple purchasing procedure based solely on the decisions of the owner. Large companies, particularly factories, have elaborate purchasing procedures that involve purchase requisitions, purchase orders, and purchase invoices. In such cases, the production department would notify the purchasing department of what items it needs; the purchasing department would then contact the supplier to order the goods and would advise the accounting department that the goods have been ordered and to expect an invoice when the goods are delivered. Such a system requires an elaborate routing procedure for its internal paperwork and recordkeeping. Our attention, though, will be on the simple procedures of the small business.

PURCHASE INVOICE

A purchase invoice (Figure 4.1) is the bill received from the vendor or supplier. This invoice is the equivalent of the receipt you would get if you buy goods from a department store on a credit card. It is the store's notification to you that you owe them money for the goods you bought from them. The purchase invoice is checked to see that the goods have, in fact, been received, that all goods are in satisfactory condition, and that the items were charged at the price anticipated.

FROM	Rainbow Supplies	DATE	January 4, 19—
	2009 Jasper Avenue	INVOICE #	29
	Edmonton, AB	F. O. B.	Winnipeg, MB
	T3W 4N6	VIA	Best Transfer Co.
		TERMS	N/30 days
TO	KBC Decorating Co.	YOUR ORDER #	01
	79 Buffalo Place		
	Winnipeg, MB		
	R2W 9V7		

Quantity	Size	Item		Price	
10 cases	4L	C234SG	Latex Interior Paint	@ 72.00/ctn	720.00
10 cases	5L	C235SG	Latex Interior Paint	@ 85.00/ctn	850.00
20 cases	4L	C233	Flat Interior Paint	@ 46.50/ctn	930.00
10 cases	mixed	CM302	Paint Brushes	@ 25.00/case	250.00
10 cases	reg.	RC409	Paint Rollers	@ 25.00/case	250.00
1 only	—	MCD298	Paint Mixer with		
			Colour Dispenser		1500.00
			Subtotal		4500.00
			GST Reg. #123456789		315.00
			Total		4815.00

Figure 4.1   Purchase Invoice

PURCHASE JOURNAL

Once all information has been confirmed, the invoice is recorded in the purchase journal. The purchase journal is used exclusively for purchases on account. As mentioned earlier, the columns used in a purchase journal will vary, depending on the nature of the business and on how frequently certain purchases occur. Some purchase journals might have many columns while others might have only a few. Following is an explanation of the columns that appear in the purchase journal illustrated in Figure 4.2.

Invoice Date. The date shown on the purchase invoice is recorded in this column, rather than the date on which the invoice was received from the supplier. The terms of the invoice (discussed below) are based on the date of the invoice.

Name of Supplier. When goods are purchased on account, a record must be made of the name of the company to which the money is owing. Because only suppliers' names can appear in this column, the term "Accounts Payable" does not have to be written beside each company name.

Invoice Number. The bill received from each supplier will bear an invoice number, identifying the invoice as the source document on which the transaction is based.

Terms. The terms of payment are recorded in the Terms column exactly as shown on the invoice. The most common term allowed by suppliers is net 30 days (or n/30), meaning that the amount owing must be paid within 30 days. Usually, interest is charged on the balance if it remains unpaid after 30 days. Some companies offer incentives to the buyer for early payment by providing terms such as 2/10,n/30, which means that 2% may be deducted from the total of the invoice if it is paid within 10 days; otherwise, the full amount must be paid in 30 days. Other examples of special terms are 3/15,n/45 (3% deducted if paid within 15 days, or full amount due in 45 days); or 3/10,1/20,n/30 (3% deducted if paid within 10 days, or 1% deducted if paid before the 20th day, or full amount due by the 30th day). The exercises throughout this textbook will specify the terms.

Accounts Payable Cr. The total amount of the invoice is recorded in this column, representing the credit side of the transaction (liability increasing). The debit side of the transaction (the item purchased) will be recorded in one of the following columns.

GST-ITC Dr. The amount of GST (Goods and Services Tax) included in the total of the purchase invoice is recorded in this column. This tax is recognized by Revenue Canada as an Input Tax Credit (ITC); that is, it is the amount that the business can credit against (deduct from) the amount payable to the government. (GST will be discussed later in this chapter.)

Purchases Dr. The amount entered in this column is the portion of the invoice total that represents goods purchased for resale. It is not uncommon for an invoice to be allocated to two or more different expense accounts, in which case the amount would be split between two or more columns.

Office Supplies Prepaid Dr. The amount entered here is the portion of the invoice total that represents the purchase of supplies for use within the office, such as pens, pencils, letterhead, envelopes, etc.

Warehouse Supplies Prepaid Dr. The amount entered here is the portion of the invoice total that represents the purchase of supplies used in the warehouse department, such as wrapping paper, tape, shipping labels, etc. It should be noted that a business that does not have a warehouse would not have this column in its purchase journal.

Other Accounts Dr. If all or part of the invoice is for the purchase of items that are not merchandise for resale, office supplies, or warehouse supplies, the amount is recorded in the Other Accounts column; in the case, the name of the asset or expense account is recorded along with the appropriate amount.

Figure 4.2 shows sample transactions for purchases of items on account, demonstrating the advantages of recording such transactions in the purchase journal rather than in the general journal. If each transaction in the general journal is compared with the same entry recorded in the purchase journal, it becomes evident that only one line is required for each transaction in the purchase journal, yet each transaction is a balanced entry. The amount of the invoice entered in the Accounts Payable Cr. column is equal to the amounts entered in the debit columns (GST-ITC Dr., Purchases Dr., Office Supplies Prepaid Dr., Warehouse Supplies Prepaid Dr., or Other Accounts Dr.). Therefore, a balanced entry is recorded. A balanced entry is just as important in the purchase journal as it is in the general journal.

At the end of the operating month, all money columns in the purchase journal are totalled and proved for equal debits and credits. The total of the credit column must be equal to the sum of the debit column totals. Once the journal has been balanced, the totals are ruled with single and double lines, as shown in the illustration.

PROVING DEBITS AND CREDITS

The double-entry system of bookkeeping is based on the principle that for every business transaction the debit entries must equal the credit entries in every journal. When using columnar journals with three or more money columns, it is important to prove that the sum of the totals of the debit columns equals the sum of the totals of the credit columns before any column totals are posted to the ledger. Figure 4.2 shows the proof of the purchase journal, ensuring that all entries are balanced.

POSTING FROM THE PURCHASE JOURNAL

Figure 4.3 illustrates the posting of purchase journal entries to the various ledger accounts.

- The amounts that appear in the Accounts Payable Cr. column will be credited to the individual creditors' accounts in the accounts payable ledger. These should be posted as soon as the transaction is recorded to ensure that the creditors' account balances are kept up to date.

- The total of the GST-ITC column is debited to the GST-ITC account in the general ledger. There is no advantage in posting all the entries in this column if the same result can be accomplished by posting only the total. This one entry saves the repeated postings that would otherwise be necessary if these same transactions were recorded in the general journal.

- The total of the Purchases column is debited to the Purchases account.

GENERAL JOURNAL

PAGE ___GJ1___

DATE		ACCOUNTS NAME AND EXPLANATION	F.	DEBIT	CREDIT
19— Sept.	3	Purchases		8 5 0 60	
		GST–ITC		5 9 54	
		A/P Standard Co.			9 1 0 14
		invoice #16; n/30.			
	6	Purchases		1 6 3 25	
		GST–ITC		1 1 43	
		A/P Manitoba Tire Co.			1 7 4 68
		invoice #75; n/20.			
	17	Warehouse Supplies Prepaid		2 9 0 40	
		GST–ITC		2 0 33	
		A/P Allied Parts Ltd.			3 1 0 73
		invoice #10; n/60.			
	25	Office Supplies Prepaid		7 7 20	
		GST–ITC		5 40	
		A/P K-R Printers			8 2 60
		invoice #303; n/10.			
	30	Advertising Expense		2 5 0 50	
		GST–ITC		1 7 54	
		A/P Canada West Co.			2 6 8 04
		invoice #49; n/30.			

PURCHASE JOURNAL

PAGE ___PJ1___

ACCOUNT CREDIT						**ACCOUNTS DEBIT**							
INVOICE DATE	NAME OF SUPPLIER	INV. NO.	TERMS	F.	ACCOUNTS PAYABLE	GST–ITC	PURCHASES	OFFICE SUP. PREPAID	WHSE. SUPPL. PREPAID	OTHER ACCOUNTS DEBIT			
										ACCOUNT	F.	AMOUNT	
19— Sept. 3	Standard Co.	16	n/30		9 1 0 14	5 9 54	8 5 0 60						
6	Manitoba Tire Co.	75	n/20		1 7 4 68	1 1 43	1 6 3 25						
17	Allied Parts Ltd.	10	n/60		3 1 0 73	2 0 33			2 9 0 40				
25	K-R Printers	303	n/10		8 2 60	5 40		7 7 20					
30	Canada West Co.	49	n/30		2 6 8 04	1 7 54				Advertising		2 5 0 50	
					1 7 4 6 19	1 1 4 24	1 0 1 3 85	7 7 20	2 9 0 40			2 5 0 50	
	Proof: 114.24												
	1013.85												
	77.20												
	290.40												
	_250.50_												
	1746.19												

Figure 4.2 Purchase Entries in the General Journal and in the Purchase Journal

- The total of the Office Supplies Prepaid column is debited to the Offices Supplies Prepaid account.

- The total of the Warehouse Supplies Prepaid column is debited to the Warehouse Supplies Prepaid account.

- The entries that appear under the heading of "Other Accounts" are not related to each other, so they are posted individually.

As before, posting references are recorded in both the purchase journal and the ledger accounts; however, when column totals are posted, the posting references in the purchase journal are written immediately below the totals. (See Figure 4.3.)

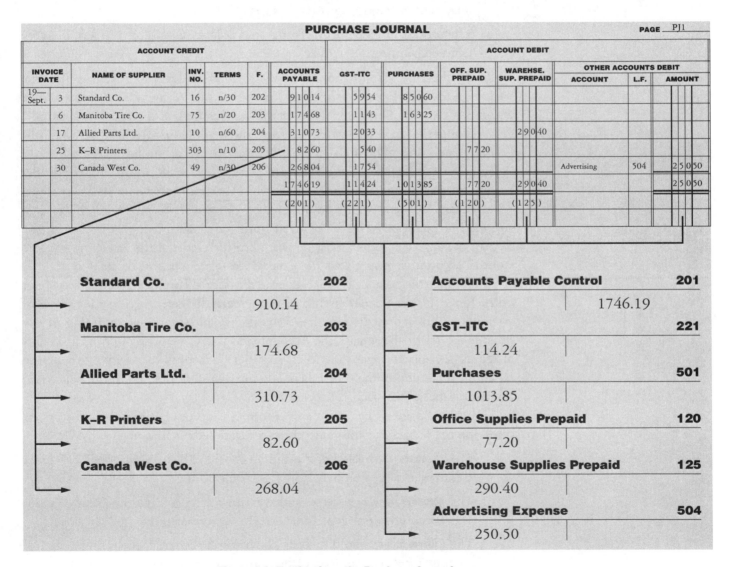

Figure 4.3 Posting from the Purchase Journal

Accounts Payable Control

In a small business where only one employee is hired to keep the books, a single ledger file, called the general ledger, will serve the needs of the business adequately. Chapter 3 showed the general ledger file as the entire group of ledger accounts: all the asset accounts (including a separate account for each customer), all liability accounts (including a separate account for each creditor), the owner's equity accounts, all revenue accounts, and all expense accounts. The trial balance prepared from this ledger was a single list of the accounts and their balances.

Such an arrangement, however, would be impractical for a business with a large number of creditors because:

1. A single large ledger file or book would be too cumbersome for one person to maintain.

2. Only one employee would have access to the ledger accounts at any given time.

3. The trial balance prepared from a single ledger file would be a very long one, perhaps requiring several pages.

4. The process of locating errors in a trial balance would be difficult and very time-consuming.

To divide the work of maintaining the general ledger accounts, as well as the various Accounts Payable (suppliers') accounts, an Accounts Payable Control account is created. This control account takes the place of the individual suppliers' accounts that have been removed from the main ledger (to be kept by another employee), thus allowing the general ledger to remain in balance.

As mentioned earlier, the invoice amounts recorded in the Accounts Payable column of the purchase journal are posted to the credit of the individual suppliers' accounts in the accounts payable ledger. However, because these individual suppliers' accounts have been removed from the general ledger, the total of the Accounts Payable columns must be posted to the credit of the Accounts Payable Control account to ensure that the general ledger remains in balance.

When the trial balance is prepared, the individual suppliers' accounts will not be included in the regular listing of the general ledger; instead, this group of accounts will be represented by the Accounts Payable Control account. Figure 4.4 illustrates a trial balance with the Accounts Payable Control account in the general ledger section and the individual supplier's accounts listed in a supporting schedule. The total of the schedule of accounts payable is equal to the balance in the Accounts Payable Control account.

In a large business that has many customers and/or creditors, it is customary to divide the ledger accounts into three separate ledger files or groups:

1. The **accounts receivable ledger** would contain all the individual customer accounts arranged alphabetically or numerically.

2. The **accounts payable ledger** would contain all the individual creditor (supplier) accounts arranged alphabetically or numerically.

3. The **general ledger** would include all the asset accounts (including a control account for Accounts Receivable), all liability accounts (including a control account for Accounts Payable), the owner's equity accounts, all revenue accounts, and all expense accounts.

Harvey Shortt Promotions
Trial Balance
February 28, 19—

	Account	Debit	Credit
101	Bank	15 7 6 1 60	
104	Accounts Receivable Control	1 0 6 80	
108	Wrapping Supplies Prepaid	4 5 4 00	
111	Store Fixtures	3 8 7 9 50	
115	Equipment	8 4 2 9 50	
201	Accounts Payable Control		4 9 9 0 60
222	Bank Loan Payable		5 0 0 0 00
301	Capital, H. Shortt		22 0 0 0 00
401	Sales		3 7 4 6 70
405	Interest Revenue		3 5 0 00
407	Rental Revenue on Equipment		1 3 4 5 00
501	Purchases	6 3 3 1 90	
503	Freight In	1 3 6 00	
511	Advertising Expense	1 2 7 75	
515	Donations	5 0 00	
519	Miscellaneous Expense	7 4 60	
522	Postage	1 8 70	
526	Salaries Expense	1 8 0 0 00	
533	Telephone Expense	8 3 45	
539	Utilities	1 7 8 50	
		37 4 3 2 30	37 4 3 2 30
	Schedule of Accounts Receivable		
153	Grant, Edward	3 3 95	
156	Hobson, Linda	2 4 70	
159	Lawson, Joe	4 8 15	
		1 0 6 80	
	Schedule of Accounts Payable		
261	Kildonan Lumber Co.		1 8 0 00
265	Neepawa Novelty Co.		4 1 0 60
269	Wholesale Products Ltd.		4 4 0 0 00
			4 9 9 0 60

Figure 4.4   Trial Balance with Schedules

PRACTICE EXERCISE 1

(a)   Set up a purchase journal for the Braus Co. using the headings illustrated in Figure 4.2. The GST-ITC column will not be used in this exercise.

(b)   Open ledger accounts for the following, showing each account as Sheet 1:

Insurance Prepaid, 111; Office Supplies Prepaid, 113; Warehouse Supplies Prepaid, 117; Delivery Equipment, 124; Office Equipment, 127; Office Furniture, 128; Accounts Payable Control, 201; A/P Colville Co., 221;

A/P Dundee Equipment Co., 222; A/P Greene Printers, 223; A/P Harris Trucks Ltd., 224; A/P Nielsens Ltd., 225; A/P Northern Co., 226; A/P Pullack Suppliers, 227; A/P Roberts Furniture Co., 228; A/P Young Insurance Co., 229; Purchases, 501; Advertising Expense, 510.

(c) Record the following transactions in the purchase journal. Post all transactions affecting the accounts payable subsidiary ledger on a daily basis.

19—

May 2 Purchased merchandise from Northern Co., $500; invoice #78 dated May 1; terms net 10 days.

3 Received an invoice for $290 from Pullack Suppliers for the purchase of office supplies and stationery, $120, and supplies for the shipping department, $170; invoice #67 dated May 2; terms net 30 days.

5 Bought furniture for the office, $1,450, from Roberts Furniture Co., invoice #63 dated May 3; terms net 90 days.

6 Received invoice #98 dated May 5 from Colville Co. for $783 for the purchase of merchandise; terms net 10 days.

10 Purchased a typewriter from Dundee Equipment Co. for $750; invoice #27 dated May 8; terms net 60 days.

14 Received invoice #33 dated May 13 from Greene Printers for $90 for advertising material; terms net 20 days.

14 Purchased merchandise, $623, from Northern Co.; invoice #93 dated May 13; terms net 10 days.

15 Purchased a one-year insurance policy from Young Insurance Co. The premium was $175. Invoice #48 was dated yesterday and showed terms of net 10 days.

19 Bought a filing cabinet, $525, from Roberts Furniture Co.; invoice #101 dated May 17; terms net 90 days.

20 Received invoice #174 dated May 18 from Nielsens Ltd. for merchandise purchased, $916; terms net 30 days.

24 Purchased wrapping paper and paper cartons for the warehouse, $230, from Pullack Suppliers; terms net 30 days; invoice #81 dated May 23.

29 Purchased a second-hand truck for the delivery of goods to customers. Harris Trucks Ltd. has sent invoice #21 for $3,000; terms net 90 days.

(d) Total the columns in pencil. Prove equal debits and credits.

(e) After confirming equality, enter the totals in ink. Rule the totals with single and double lines.

(f) Post the total of the Accounts Payable column to the Accounts Payable Control account. Post the other appropriate column totals.

(g) Prepare a trial balance, supported by a schedule of accounts payable. (See Figure 4.4.)

▶ **PRACTICE EXERCISE 2**

Nathan Segal operates the Nu Fashion Shoes & Accessories store in Winnipeg. You are to record the transactions for the month of April in a purchase journal with these headings: Date, Name of Supplier, Invoice No., Terms, Post. Ref., Accounts Payable Cr., Shoe Purchases Dr., Handbag Purchases Dr., Accessories Purchases Dr., Office Supplies Prepaid Dr., and Other Accounts Dr. (with subheadings of Account, Post. Ref., and Amount).

(a)   Set up ledger accounts for the following: Insurance Prepaid, 112; Office Supplies Prepaid, 115; Store Supplies Prepaid, 118; Office Equipment, 130; Store Fixtures, 135; Accounts Payable Control, 220; A/P Best-Fit Wholesalers, 221; A/P Canada Shoe Mfg. Co., 222; A/P Ellie's Belts & Accessories, 223; A/P Harley Equipment Co., 224; A/P Kent Suppliers, 225; A/P Mitchell Insurance Agency, 226; A/P Style-Rite Handbag Co., 227; A/P *The Winnipeg Tribune*, 228; Shoe Purchases, 501; Handbag Purchases, 502; Accessories Purchases, 503; Advertising Expense, 530. All ledger accounts will be marked Sheet 1.

(b)   Record the following transactions in the purchase journal. Be sure to post to the accounts payable subsidiary ledger accounts (creditors' accounts) on a daily basis, including the invoice number and terms in the Memo column. GST will be disregarded for this exercise.

19—

April 2   Purchased fixtures for the store, $800, and furniture and equipment for the office, $1,250, from Harley Equipment Co. Their invoice #47 for $2,050 was dated April 1; terms net 10 days. (Although this is one transaction, it will require two lines in the purchase journal.)

2   Purchased office supplies, $141.50, and packing tape and twine for packaging parcels, $267.35 (Store Supplies), from Kent Suppliers; invoice #94 dated April 2; terms net 10 days.

2   Received invoice #176 dated April 1 for the purchase of a stock of shoes, $1,595, from Canada Shoe Mfg. Co.; terms net 20 days.

3   Received invoice #165 dated April 1 from Style-Rite Handbag Co. for the purchase of handbags, $586; terms of net 10 days.

4   Received invoice #123 dated April 3 from Ellie's Belts & Accessories for the purchase of belts and other accessories, $478; terms net 20 days.

6   Purchased shoes, $489, from Best-Fit Wholesalers; invoice #210 dated April 5; terms net 30 days.

12   Received invoice #120 dated April 11 from *The Winnipeg Tribune* for advertising in the paper for five days. The cost is $275; terms net 30 days.

14   Purchased an additional stock of shoes from Canada Shoe Mfg. Co., $627.30; invoice #237 dated April 13; terms net 20 days.

16 Purchased a one-year insurance policy to cover the stock and building, $530, from Mitchell Insurance Agency; invoice #66 dated April 10; terms net 30 days.

22 Received invoice #198 dated April 21 from Style-Rite Handbag Co. for the purchase of handbags, $495; terms net 10 days.

26 Purchased packaging supplies from Kent Suppliers, $90. Invoice #157 was dated April 26 with terms of net 10 days.

30 Received invoice #190 from Ellie's Belts & Accessories for a special order of belts, $83.75; dated April 30; terms net 20 days.

(c) Total all columns in pencil. Prove the equality of debits and credits.

(d) After confirming equal debits and credits, enter the column totals in ink. Rule the totals with single and double lines.

(e) Post the total of the Accounts Payable column to the credit of the Accounts Payable Control account. Post all other appropriate totals to their respective accounts. All totals will be posted on the last day of the month.

(f) Prepare a trial balance, supported by a schedule of accounts payable. (See Figure 4.4.)

SALES ON CREDIT

In a retail business, a sale is usually made over the counter. It is paid for with cash, a cheque, a credit card, or by charging it to the customer's account. The customer then receives a cash register receipt or a copy of the sales invoice or credit card invoice. In a wholesale business, orders are usually received by mail, by telephone or fax, over the counter, or by travelling sales representatives.

In any situation when the goods are shipped before payment is received, the financial standing and credit rating of each customer is checked by the credit department to ensure that the customer is able to pay the account when it becomes due. After the credit rating is established, a credit limit (the maximum amount that can be charged to the account) is determined for each customer.

Once the order has been filled and shipped, a sales invoice is sent to the customer outlining the contents of the shipment, the value of each item, any additional charges (such as shipping, handling, and taxes), and the total amount due. A sales invoice is shown in Figure 4.5.

In some businesses, these sales invoices are filed in a binder that constitutes the sales journal. When this is the case, posting is made directly from the invoices to the accounts receivable ledger accounts. A notation, much like a folio, would be written directly on the invoice to indicate that it has been posted to the customer's account. Other businesses, however, prefer to use the sales invoice as a source document from which entries are made in a columnar sales journal. Although this method involves copying the information from the invoices into the sales journal, management is able to see at a glance which goods are selling best and to which customers. We will be using the latter method throughout this textbook.

FROM	KBC Decorating Co.		DATE	January 20, 19—
	79 Buffalo Place		INVOICE #	01
	Winnipeg, MB		F.O.B.	Warehouse
	R2W 9V7		VIA	Picked up
			TERMS	Net 30 days
TO	Dayson & Son		YOUR ORDER #	123
	3007 Robin Blvd.			
	Winnipeg, MB			
	R3B 7H7			

2 cases	24-740	Vinyl coated wallpaper	@ 192.00/cs	384.00
6 cases	24-779	Vinyl embossed wallpaper	@ 220.00/cs	1320.00
2 cases	6-977X	Urethane floor coating	@ 180.00/cs	360.00
1 case	RC409	Paint rollers	@ 40.00/cs	40.00
2 cases	48-49X	Oil wood stain	@ 198.00/cs	396.00
		Subtotal		2500.00
		7% GST (Reg. #987654321)		175.00
		7% Manitoba Sales Tax		175.00
		Total		2850.00

Figure 4.5   Sales Invoice

SALES JOURNAL

The sales journal is used for recording all sales of goods and services on account. (Cash sales of merchandise and services will be recorded in a cash receipts journal, which will be discussed in Chapter 6.) The advantages of using the sales journal are the same as those for the purchase journal and for all other special journals:

1. Detailed recording is kept to a minimum.

2. Time is saved during posting.

3. The work of recording and posting can be done by more than one employee (division of labour).

Many businesses use a columnar sales journal tailored to their specific needs, for example, those with two or more departments or those that sell both merchandise and services. Some journals may be set up with many columns, others may have only a few.

Figure 4.6 shows a simple sales journal that might be used by a retail store. Here is a brief description of each column:

Date. The date that appears on the invoice is recorded in this column.

Name of Customer. The name of the customer to whom the merchandise or service was sold is entered in this column. Since only customers' names can be entered in this column, it is not necessary to include the term "Accounts Receivable."

Invoice Number. Sales invoices are usually pre-numbered. To ensure that all invoice numbers are accounted for, they are usually entered in sequential order.

Terms. The terms of sale granted to the customer are entered. If all customers are granted the same terms, such as n/30, this column would be unnecessary.

GENERAL JOURNAL

PAGE GJ17

DATE		ACCOUNT NAME AND EXPLANATION	F.	DEBIT	CREDIT
19— Sept.	1	A/R Trevor Rodin		58 99	
		Sales			51 30
		GST Payable			3 59
		Sales Tax Payable			4 10
		invoice #1; n/10			
	3	A/R Harvey Gray		150 08	
		Sales			130 50
		GST Payable			9 14
		Sales Tax Payable			10 44
		invoice #2; n/30			
	8	A/R Arthur Ward		100 34	
		Sales			87 25
		GST Payable			6 11
		Sales Tax Payable			6 98
		invoice #3; n/20			

SALES JOURNAL

PAGE SJ 11

DATE		NAME OF CUSTOMER	INV. NO.	TERMS	F.	ACCOUNTS REC. DR.	SALES CR.	GST PAYBL. CR. 7%	SALES TAX PAYBL. CR. 8%
19— Aug.	1	Rodin, Trevor	1	n/10		58 99	51 30	3 59	4 10
	3	Gray, Harvey	2	n/30		150 08	130 50	9 14	10 44
	8	Ward, Arthur	3	n/20		100 34	87 25	6 11	6 98
						309 41	269 05	18 84	21 52

Proof: Dr.   Cr.
      309.41   269.05
             21.52
             18.84
      309.41   309.41

Figure 4.6   Sales Entries Recorded in the General Journal and in the Sales Journal

Accounts Receivable Dr. The total amount of the invoice, including provincial sales tax (where applicable) and the GST, is entered in this column. This is the amount that will be posted to the accounts receivable customer's ledger account.

Sales Cr. The amount of the sale, *before taxes*, is entered in this column.

GST Payable Cr. The amount of Goods and Services Tax (GST) charged on the invoice is recorded in this column. The current rate of GST across Canada is 7%.

Sales Tax Payable Cr. The amount of provincial sales tax (if applicable) charged on the sale is recorded in this column.

Just as we saw in the purchase journal, each line recorded in the sales journal is a balanced entry. The debit amount (the total of the invoice recorded in the Accounts Receivable column) must be equal to the credit amounts (the amount of the sale plus the two taxes).

POSTING FROM THE SALES JOURNAL

The procedure for posting entries from the sales journal to the ledger accounts is similar to that discussed earlier for the purchase journal. For the sales journal (Figure 4.7), the amounts that appear in the Accounts Receivable Dr. column are posted to the debit of the individual customers' accounts in the accounts receivable ledger on a daily basis to ensure that these accounts are kept up to date at all times. At the end of the month, after all columns have been totalled and the journal has been proved for equal debits and credits:

- The total of the Accounts Receivable column is posted to the debit of the Accounts Receivable Control account. As was the case with the suppliers' accounts, all the customers' accounts have been removed from the general ledger and have been replaced by the Accounts Receivable Control account, thus ensuring a balanced ledger and a balanced trial balance (as shown in Figure 4.4).

- The total of the Sales column will be posted to the credit of the Sales account.

- The totals of the two tax columns will be posted to the credit of their respective tax accounts.

The individual amounts that are recorded in the Sales column and in the tax columns are not posted—only their totals. There is no point posting these individual amounts if posting only the totals can achieve the same results in the ledger accounts.

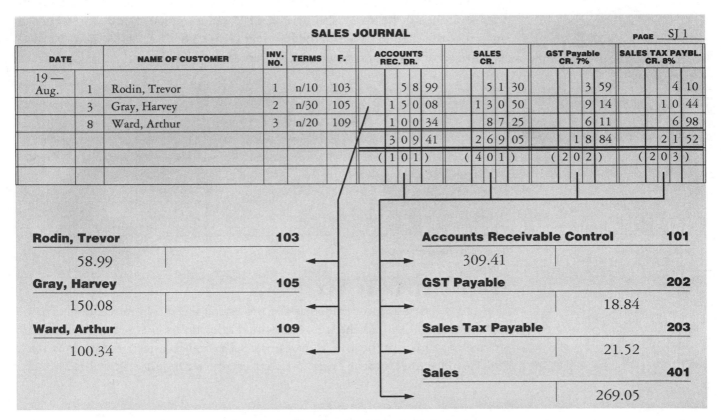

Figure 4.7   Posting from the Sales Journal

GOODS AND SERVICES TAX (GST)

Canada's Goods and Services Tax is charged at a rate of 7% on almost every product and service sold in Canada. The Goods and Services Act stipulates that GST must be calculated on the selling price of the product or service before the provincial sales tax, if any, is applied. The seller is required to show clearly on the sales receipt or invoice the amount of GST charged and the seller's GST registration number.

Because a business pays GST on its purchases of goods, supplies, and services, the purchase journal contains the GST-ITC (Input Tax Credit) Dr. column for recording such taxes paid. The business must also charge GST on the goods and services it sells to its customers; therefore, the sales journal contains the GST Payable column for recording the amount of GST charged on each invoice.

When GST is remitted (sent) to Revenue Canada, the total of the GST-ITC (the GST paid by the business) is deducted from the total of the GST Payable (the GST charged to customers) to determine the amount remitted.

	GST Payable (charged to customers)	$632.07
less:	GST-ITC (paid by the company)	217.53
	GST remitted to Revenue Canada	$414.54

Figure 4.8 shows the general journal entry that is recorded when GST is remitted to Revenue Canada. The debit entry to GST Payable clears the balance of the GST Payable account to zero (much like paying off an accounts payable), making the GST Payable account ready to receive entries for tax collected in the next fiscal period. Similarly, the credit entry to GST-ITC clears the balance of the GST-ITC account to zero, making it ready to receive entries for the tax paid on purchases during the next fiscal period. The credit entry to Bank represents the amount of the cheque issued to the Receiver General of Canada. (A more detailed explanation of GST is provided in Chapter 10.)

April	30	GST Payable			6 3 2 07		
		GST–ITC				2 1 7 53
		Bank				4 1 4 54
		To record remittance of net GST for				
		first fiscal quarter (Jan.–Feb.–Mar.).				

Figure 4.8   Remitting GST

PROVINCIAL SALES TAX

Sales tax is levied and controlled at the provincial level. The percentage of sales tax (see Figure 4.9) and the items on which sales tax is charged will vary from province to province; but, in all cases, the seller must collect it and remit it to the provincial government every month. Certain commodities (gasoline, liquor, and cigarettes) are subject to special excise taxes; therefore, they are exempt from provincial sales tax.

Provincial Sales Tax Rates	
British Columbia	7%
Alberta	none
Saskatchewan	9%
Manitoba	7%
Ontario	8%
Quebec*	8%
New Brunswick*	11%
Nova Scotia*	11%
Prince Edward Island*	11%
Newfoundland & Labrador*	12%
Northwest Territories	none
Yukon Territory	none

* These provinces calculate sales tax on the value of the sale plus the Goods & Services Tax.

Figure 4.9   Provincial Sales Tax Rates (All tax rates are subject to change.)

As seen in the sample sales journal in Figure 4.6, a column is provided for recording the provincial sales tax that is charged on each sales invoice. These taxes collected from the sale of taxable goods or services during the month are posted to the Sales Tax Payable account and held by the company until the middle of the following month when they are remitted to the provincial government. Figure 4.10 shows the entry that would be recorded when the remittance cheque is issued to the government.

May	19	Sales Tax Payable		3 4 1 20		
		Bank			3 4 1 20	
		To record remittance of provincial				
		sales tax on April sales.				

Figure 4.10   Remitting Provincial Sales Tax

MARKUP AND MARKDOWN

The goal of nearly all organizations is to earn a profit. This profit is achieved by selling goods or services for an amount greater than the costs incurred in making such sales. The selling price on all goods bought for resale must be determined in advance. To do this, a cost price is established for each type of merchandise, including freight or other transportation charges, insurance, import duties, brokerage, and a portion of the general operating costs, often called overhead. To this cost, a **markup** is added to provide a return (profit) on the owner's investment.

The amount of markup is the decision of the owner and can vary in many respects. To illustrate the use of markup, assume that the overall cost of merchandise is $30 and that a 60% markup is considered sufficient to provide a reasonable profit. The selling price, then, is $30 + ($30 × 60%) = $48.

Should it become necessary to dispose of all or some of the merchandise quickly, usually at sale or liquidation prices, this reduction of the price is called **markdown**. The usual reasons for marking down goods are:

1. To dispose of slow-moving inventory.

2. To attract customers into the store in the hope that other more expensive items will be sold.

3. To reduce inventory on hand (often at year end).

The above selling price of $48 might then be marked down during a year-end sale. If the price is marked down by 10%, the calculation to determine the new selling price is $48 − ($48 × 10%) = $43.20. If the goods still do not sell, an additional markdown of 15% might be taken. The new selling price, then, becomes $43.20 − ($43.20 × 15%) = $36.72.

The price at which the goods are eventually sold is the basis for calculating GST and provincial sales tax.

ANOTHER WORD ABOUT CONTROL ACCOUNTS

The addition of the Accounts Receivable Control and the Accounts Payable Control accounts to the general ledger has allowed the overall ledger file to be divided into three groups—general ledger accounts, customers' accounts, and suppliers' accounts. A number of advantages are achieved by such a division:

1. More than one employee can work on the ledgers at the same time. The general ledger is usually maintained by the accountant or the head bookkeeper, while the subsidiary ledgers (the customers' and suppliers' accounts) are often maintained by junior employees. When transactions are recorded that affect customers or suppliers, they are posted daily to ensure that the customers' and suppliers' accounts are always up to date.

2. The accounts in the general ledger, including the Accounts Receivable Control account and the Accounts Payable Control account, make this main ledger complete and self-balancing.

3. The balance between the control accounts in the general ledger and the subsidiary accounts provides reasonable assurance that the transactions affecting the customers' and suppliers' accounts have been posted correctly.

4. The total amount owing to the business by its customers and the total amount owed to creditors are clearly visible in the trial balance, which is now structured to represent the three ledger files. (Refer to the trial balance in Figure 4.4.)

Although the most common use of control accounts is for the accounts receivable and accounts payable subsidiary ledgers, control accounts can be used to represent any group of related accounts (see Figures 4.11 and 4.12).

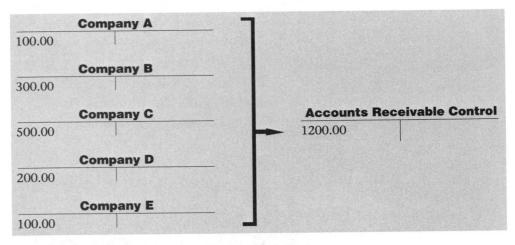

Figure 4.11   Subsidiary Accounts and the Control Account

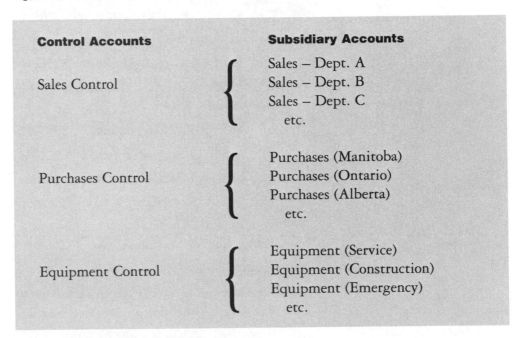

Figure 4.12   Other Uses of the Control Account

PRACTICE EXERCISE 3

The following transactions are to be recorded in the sales journal of Seymours Ltd.

(a) Set up a sales journal (page SJ4) with the following column headings: Date, Name of Customer, Invoice Number, Terms, Folio, Accounts Receivable Dr., Sales Cr., GST Payable Cr., and Sales Tax Payable Cr.

(b) Set up the necessary ledger accounts to which this journal will be posted: Accounts Receivable Control, 110; GST Payable, 220; Sales Tax Payable, 222; Sales, 401. Also, open a ledger account for each of these customers: A/R Beadlor, Terri, 120; A/R Bell, Susan, 121; A/R Grady, Betty, 122; A/R Hardy, Sylvia, 123; A/R Harkness, Kay, 124; A/R Nelson, Marie, 125; A/R Shultz, Edna, 126; A/R Travis, Jane, 127; and A/R Waller, Alison, 128. Assume Sheet 1 for each ledger account.

(c)   All sales invoices are to be numbered consecutively, beginning with #80. Customers are allowed 30 days on all credit sales.

(d)   Add 7% GST and 7% sales tax to all sales. In Manitoba, both GST and sales tax are calculated on the value of the goods. The amounts quoted below represent the value of the goods.

(e)   Post daily to the accounts receivable subsidiary ledger.

19—

May   1   Sold merchandise to Sylvia Hardy, sales invoice #80, $210.25.

      3   Credit sales: Jane Travis, $267.95; Marie Nelson, $141.60; Alison Waller, $242.70.

      5   Sold merchandise to Betty Grady, $155.10.

      6   Credit sales: Jane Travis, $126.90; Betty Grady, $97.20.

      8   Sold merchandise to Susan Bell, $145.30.

     11   Credit sales: Kay Harkness, $258.15; Terri Beadlor, $133.50.

     15   Credit sales: Alison Waller, $239.60; Edna Shultz, $366.55; Marie Nelson, $260.

     18   Sold goods to Sylvia Hardy, $285.15.

     22   Credit sales: Jane Travis, $95.80; Kay Harkness, $65.

     26   Sold merchandise on credit to Alison Waller, $211.65.

     31   Credit sales: Marie Nelson, $275; Susan Bell, $125.30; Edna Shultz, $87.50.

(f)   Prove equal debits and credits.

(g)   Enter the totals and rulings in ink.

(h)   Post the total of the Accounts Receivable column to the Accounts Receivable Control account. Post the other totals appropriately.

(i)   Prepare a trial balance with a schedule of accounts receivable.

▶   **PRACTICE EXERCISE 4**

In the books of Step Into Fashion, you will be recording the sales transactions during April.

(a)   Set up the sales journal (page SJ1) with the following headings: Date, Name of Customer, Invoice No., Terms, Post. Ref., Accounts Receivable Dr., Shoe Sales Cr., Handbag Sales Cr., Accessories Sales Cr.; GST Payable Cr., and Sales Tax Payable Cr.

(b)   Open ledger accounts for: Accounts Receivable Control, 110; A/R Anaka, Beverley, 121; A/R Beaudry, Kay, 122; A/R Blair, Joan, 123; A/R Fraser, Jane, 124; A/R Horvat, Judy, 125; A/R Madill, Anne, 126; A/R Pizl, Darlene, 127; A/R Ritchie, Rose, 128; A/R Scott, Barbara, 129; A/R Stella, Elena, 130; A/R Sutton, Elaine, 131; GST Payable, 221; Sales Tax Payable, 225; Sales—Accessories, 401; Sales—Handbags, 402; Sales—Shoes, 403. All accounts will be shown as Sheet 1.

(c) Record these sales in the sales journal; sales invoices will be numbered consecutively, beginning with #1. Add 7% GST and 7% sales tax to all sales amounts quoted in this exercise. Post to the accounts receivable subsidiary ledger on a daily basis.

19—

April 2 Sold shoes, $65.50, and a handbag, $35.95, to Elaine Sutton; invoice #1, terms net 30 days.

3 Credit sales: Anne Madill, shoes, $44.95, terms net 30 days; Judy Horvat, shoes, $48.95, and accessories, $12.95, terms net 30 days.

5 Sold accessories, $29.75, to Kay Beaudry; terms net 10 days.

8 Sold to Beverley Anaka, shoes, $49.95, and a handbag, $35.75; terms net 30 days.

10 Sold shoes, $64.95, to Jane Fraser; terms net 30 days.

14 Sold a belt and other accessories to Anne Madill, $36.75; terms net 30 days.

16 Sold shoes, $64.95, to Elena Stella; terms net 10 days.

19 Credit sales: Joan Blair, shoes, $75.50, terms net 30 days; Barbara Scott, handbag, $35, and accessories, $27.50, terms net 30 days.

25 Sold to Darlene Pizl, shoes, $61.50, a handbag, $46.50, and accessories, $37.50; terms net 30 days.

28 Sold accessories, $41.25, to Rose Ritchie; terms net 60 days.

30 Sold a handbag to Joan Blair, $47.50; terms net 30 days.

(d) Total the journal in pencil, prove equal debits and credits, and then enter the totals and rulings in ink.

(e) Post the total of the Accounts Receivable column to the debit of the Accounts Receivable Control account. Post the other totals appropriately.

(f) Prepare a trial balance with a schedule of the accounts receivable.

► PRACTICE EXERCISE 5

The following sales and purchases activities are taken from the books of Frank Briggs of Lethbridge, Alberta. Set up appropriate journals as follows:

(a) Sales journal, page SJ3, with these headings: Date, Name of Customer, Invoice No., Terms, Folio, Accounts Receivable Dr., Sales Cr., GST Payable Cr. (No provincial sales tax is recorded in Alberta.) Sales invoices will be numbered consecutively, beginning with #57.

(b) Purchase journal, page PJ3, with these headings: Invoice Date, Name of Supplier, Invoice No., Terms, Folio, Accounts Payable Cr., GST-ITC Dr., Purchases Dr.

(c) Record the following transactions in the appropriate journals. Add 7% GST to all sales. All purchase transaction amounts shown below include 7% GST; therefore, to determine the value of the goods before GST, divide the stated amount by 1.07.

19—

March 3   Bought merchandise from Jake Dyck, $342.40; terms n/30, invoice #79.

5   Sold merchandise to Joan Poyser on invoice #57, $490; terms n/30.

8   Purchased merchandise, $191.53, from Peter Groves; terms n/30, invoice #16.

9   Sold merchandise to Linda Hamm, $340; terms n/30.

11   Sold goods today for $415 to Iris Anderson; terms n/30.

20   Received invoice #25 for $642 from Peter Groves for the purchase of merchandise; terms n/30.

22   Received invoice #85 from Jake Dyck for merchandise, $192.60; terms n/30.

23   Credit sales, terms n/30: Linda Hamm, $225; Joan Poyser, $330; Iris Anderson, $226.

28   Received invoice #40 today for merchandise purchased from Peter Groves, $544.63; terms n/30.

(d)   Total, balance, and rule the journals. (No posting is required.)

▶ **PRACTICE EXERCISE 6**

Westport Merchants Ltd., of St. John's, Newfoundland, has hired you to record the sales and purchases for the month of November.

(a)   Set up a sales journal (page SJ7) with the following headings: Date, Name of Customer, Invoice No., Terms, Post. Ref., Accounts Receivable Dr.,

Sales Cr., GST Payable Cr., Sales Tax Payable Cr. (7% GST and 12% sales tax are to be added to *all* sales of merchandise. In Newfoundland, sales tax is calculated on the combined value of the sale *plus* GST.)

(b)   Set up a purchase journal (page PJ7) with the following headings: Date, Name of Supplier, Invoice No., Terms, Post. Ref., Accounts Payable Cr., GST-ITC Dr., Purchases Dr., Office Supplies Prepaid Dr., Shipping Supplies Prepaid Dr., Other Accounts Dr. (Account, Amount).

(c)   Set up a general journal for those transactions that cannot be accommodated by the special journals. Use page GJ17.

(d)   Record the following transactions in the appropriate journals. (*Hint:* Each transaction will be recorded in only *one* of the journals.)

19—

Nov. 1   James Westport has invested an additional $5,000 into his business.

2   Paid the rent to HG Holdings for November, $450 (includes $29.44 GST); cheque #29.

3   Purchased merchandise from Dunlop Co. invoice #54 dated Nov. 2; terms net 30 days; $1,672.97 (includes $109.45 GST).

3   Bought office supplies from Wilmar Co., invoice #36, terms net 10 days; $101.86 (includes $5.95 GST).

4   Cash sales, $785.

5   Credit sales: (All credit sales are on terms of net 30 days.) Baker Bros., $93.50, invoice #56; Ruth Hill, $50.85, invoice #57; Jack Topper, $72.35, invoice #58. (Continue numbering all sales invoices sequentially.)

6   Purchased office equipment from Office Equipment Suppliers Ltd., terms net 60 days, invoice #87; $1,228.36 (includes $71.75 GST).

7   Purchased merchandise for cash from Blackwell Co., $719.04 (includes $47.04 GST).

7   Bought insurance from General Insurance Co., $450 (GST exempt); terms net 30 days; invoice #26 dated Nov. 6.

8   Credit sales: W.B. Allen, $37.50; Louise Amber, $55.60; Harold Filmore, $29.60.

9   Ran an advertisement in *The Daily Gazette;* invoice #118, terms net 10 days; $149.80 (includes $8.75 GST).

11   Cash sales, $885.50.

12   Purchased merchandise from Burton Co., $790.94 (includes $51.74 GST); invoice #101 dated Nov. 10; terms net 30 days.

13   Issued cheque #31 to Wilmar Co. on account, $101.86.

14   Paid salaries, $2,350 (GST not applicable). Cheques #32, #33, and #34.

15   Bought supplies for the shipping department from Kamtex Supplies Ltd., invoice #98 dated Nov. 15; terms net 10 days; $383.79 (includes $22.42 GST).

18   Cash sales, $931.90.

19   Issued cheque #35 to *The Daily Gazette* on account, $149.80.

23   Credit sales: Brad Parks, $45.75; William Jones, $36.50; Mark Spencer, $25.

24   Purchased merchandise from Dunlop Co., invoice #106 dated Nov. 23; $1,222.37 (includes $79.97 GST); terms net 30 days.

25   Issued cheque #36 for $383.79 to Kamtex Supplies Ltd. on account.

26   Bought wrapping supplies for the shipping department from Kamtex Supplies Ltd., $213.61 *plus* $13.25 GST; invoice #140 dated Nov. 24; terms net 10 days.

27   Bought merchandise from Canada Wholesalers for cash, $659.12 (includes $43.12 GST). Issued cheque #37.

28   Cash sales, $693.50.

29   Paid salaries, $2,350 (GST not applicable). Issued cheques #38, #39, and #40.

30   Credit sales: Baker Bros., $75; Thomas Swain, $55.60; Dale Hogan, $29.90.

(e)   Total, balance, and rule the sales and purchase journals. (No posting is required in this exercise.)

▶ ### PRACTICE EXERCISE 7

Percy Bloomberg opened a retail store called the Bloomberg Family Store, located in Calgary, Alberta, on March 1, 19—.

(a)   Set up a purchase journal (PJ1) with these headings: Invoice Date, Name of Supplier, Invoice No., Terms, Post. Ref., Accounts Payable Cr., GST-ITC Dr., Purchases Dr., Office Supplies Prepaid Dr., Warehouse Supplies Prepaid Dr., Other Accounts (Accounts Dr., Amount).

(b)   Set up the following ledger accounts with account numbers as indicated: Insurance Prepaid, 110; Office Supplies Prepaid, 111; Warehouse Supplies Prepaid, 112; Store & Office Equipment, 123; Accounts Payable Control, 201; A/P Capone Equipment Co., 220; A/P Daily Chronicle, 221; A/P Ecko Wholesalers, 222; A/P Fast Perc Co., 223; A/P Kashta Lumber Co., 224; A/P Kozara Insurance Co., 225; A/P Krane Suppliers, 226; A/P Lees Office Equipment Co., 227; A/P Patton Co., 228; A/P Telec Alarm Services, 229; A/P Walgreen Wholesalers, 230; GST-ITC, 250; Purchases, 501; Advertising, 502.

(c)   Record the following transactions in the purchase journal, posting to the suppliers' ledger accounts on a daily basis.

(d)   The amounts quoted below represent the full amount of the invoice; that is, the value of the goods plus 7% GST. To determine the value of the purchase *before* GST, divide the amount stated by 1.07.

19—

March 1   Purchased counters and shelves from Kashta Lumber Co. on invoice #627 dated March 1; terms net 90 days; $8,774 (Debit Store & Office Equipment).

2   Received invoice #263 dated March 1 from Capone Equipment Co. for the purchase of a cash register; $2,354; terms net 30 days.

3   Purchased packaging supplies, $377.98, from Krane Suppliers on invoice #196 dated March 2; terms net 30 days.

5   Bought a computer, $1,064.65, plus stationery and other office supplies, $236.99, from Lees Office Equipment Co.; invoice #331 dated March 4; terms net 30 days.

6   Placed an advertisement for opening-day specials in the *Daily Chronicle;* $64.68; invoice #899 dated March 6; terms net 10 days.

8   Received invoice #893 from Walgreen Wholesalers for merchandise purchased on March 7, $2,595.95; terms net 30 days.

10   Insurance coverage was purchased from Kozara Insurance Co., $308.16 (GST exempt). Their invoice #287 is dated today; terms net 10 days.

14 Telec Alarm Services installed a fire alarm system at a total invoice cost of $3,210 to be paid in 60 days; invoice #318 dated March 14.

16 Purchased packaging supplies, $237.98, from Krane Suppliers; invoice #326 dated March 15; terms net 30 days.

18 Bought supplies for the office, $193.87, from Lees Office Equipment Co.; invoice #476 dated yesterday carries terms of net 30 days.

23 Bought a coffee maker for use in the store, $89.85. Invoice #532 from Fast Perc Co. is dated today with terms of net 10 days.

26 Purchased a new line of merchandise from Patton Co., $2,395.85; invoice #449 dated March 26; terms net 30 days.

29 Ran an ad in the *Daily Chronicle* advertising the month-end sale, $80.25; invoice #1003 dated March 29; terms net 10 days.

30 Purchased a vacuum cleaner, $488.37, from Ecko Wholesalers; invoice #556 dated March 29; terms net 30 days.

31 Received invoice #2316 dated March 30 from Walgreen Wholesalers for merchandise, $3,697.65; terms net 30 days.

(e) Total, balance, and rule the journal.

(f) Post the total of the Accounts Payable column to the Accounts Payable Control account. Post the other totals appropriately.

(g) Prepare a trial balance with a schedule of accounts payable.

▶ **PRACTICE EXERCISE 8**

C.J. Bach & Sons of Kingston, Ontario, started business on May 1, 19—. Below are the purchasing activities for the month of May.

(a) Set up a purchase journal (PJ1) using these headings: Invoice Date, Account Cr., Invoice Number, Terms, Folio, Accounts Payable Cr., GST-ITC Dr., Purchases Dr., Office & Store Supplies Prepaid Dr., Furniture & Equipment Dr., Other Accounts (Accounts Dr., Amount).

(b) Set up the following ledger accounts, assuming Sheet 1 for each: Insurance Prepaid, 111; Office & Store Supplies Prepaid, 112; Delivery Equipment, 113; Furniture & Equipment, 114; Accounts Payable Control, 201; GST-ITC, 211; Purchases, 501; Advertising, 502; Miscellaneous Expense, 504.

(c) Set up the following creditors' ledger accounts, assuming Sheet 1 for each: A/P City Tribune, 220; A/P Geisbrecht Motors, 221; A/P Genser Furniture Co., 222; A/P Greene Wholesale Co., 223; A/P Katts Equipment Co., 224; A/P Pascoe Electric, 225; A/P Seiko Insurance Co., 226; A/P Stratton Co., 227; A/P Trumpet Stationery Co., 228.

(d) All invoice amounts quoted below *include* 7% GST. The amount of GST included is shown in parentheses.

(e) Record the following transactions for the month of May in a purchase journal, posting to the supplier's ledger accounts on a daily basis.

19—

May   2   Purchased merchandise from Stratton Co., $1,159.35 ($75.85 GST); invoice #108 dated May 1; terms net 10 days.

      3   Purchased office and store supplies from Trumpet Stationery Co., $339.30 ($20.65 GST); invoice #176 dated May 2; terms net 30 days.

      5   Bought furniture for the office from Genser Furniture Co., $4,890.65 ($297.69 GST); invoice #136 dated May 2; terms net 30 days.

      6   Received invoice #189 dated May 5 from Greene Wholesale Co. for $1,738.70 ($113.75 GST) for merchandise; terms net 10 days.

      8   Purchased a typewriter from Katts Equipment Co., $885.75 ($53.92 GST); terms net 60 days. Their invoice #72 is dated May 8.

    10   Goods purchased for resale, $669.55 ($43.80 GST), from Stratton Co.; invoice #341 dated May 9, terms net 10 days.

    12   Bought a filing cabinet from Katts Equipment Co. for $436.25 ($26.55 GST); invoice #103 dated today; terms net 60 days.

    15   Purchased a one-year insurance policy from Seiko Insurance Co., $379.84 (GST exempt). Invoice #148 dated May 14 shows terms of net 30 days.

    16   Received an order of merchandise at a total cost of $1,637.10 ($107.10 GST) from Greene Wholesale Co.; terms net 10 days. The invoice is #237 dated May 15.

    18   Purchased additional office supplies, $124.66 ($7.59 GST), from Trumpet Stationery Co.; invoice #293 dated May 18; terms net 30 days.

    20   Purchased a second-hand delivery truck from Geisbrecht Motors, $5,350 ($325.65 GST). Their invoice #121 carries terms of net 90 days and is dated May 20.

    24   Received an invoice for wrapping paper and cartons, $246.10 ($14.98 GST), from Trumpet Stationery Co.; invoice #333 dated May 23; terms net 30 days.

    26   Bought a stock of merchandise invoiced at $2,824.80 ($184.80 GST) from Stratton Co.; invoice #401 dated May 26; terms net 10 days.

    29   Placed an ad with the *City Tribune* advertising the month-end sale, $80.25 ($4.88 GST); invoice #183 dated May 29; terms net 10 days.

    31   Purchased light bulbs from Pascoe Electric, $40.13 ($2.44 GST); invoice #79 dated May 31; terms net 10 days.

(f)   Total, balance, and rule the journal.

(g) Post the total of the Accounts Payable column to the Accounts Payable Control account. Post all other totals appropriately.

(h) Prepare a trial balance with a schedule of accounts payable.

▶ **PRACTICE EXERCISE 9**

The sales activities of ABC Wholesale Co. of Burnaby, B.C., are detailed below.

(a) Set up a sales journal (SJ1) with the following headings: Date, Name of Customer, Invoice Number, Terms, Folio, Accounts Receivable Dr., Sales—Dept. A Cr., Sales—Dept. B Cr., GST Payable Cr., and Sales Tax Payable Cr.

(b) Set up ledger accounts for each of the following, assuming Sheet 1: Accounts Receivable Control, 105; GST Payable, 210; Sales Tax Payable, 211; Sales—Dept. A, 401; Sales—Dept. B, 402. Also, set up ledger accounts for each of these customers, assuming Sheet 1: A/R Allen, W.B., 120; A/R Baker Co., 121; A/R Bee Company, 122; A/R Bravo Co., 123; A/R Castle Co., 124; A/R Dunlop Co., 125; A/R Fast Co., 126; A/R Lopez, R., 127; A/R Olympus Co., 128; and A/R Post Company, 129.

(c) All invoices will be numbered consecutively beginning with #72. Terms of sale will vary.

(d) Add 7% GST and 7% provincial sales tax to the sale values quoted below. In British Columbia, both GST and sales tax are calculated on the value of the goods.

(e) Record the following transactions in the sales journal, charging the sales amounts quoted to their respective departments, and post daily to the customers' accounts.

19—

Sept. 1 Sold merchandise to Castle Company, $2,472 (Dept. A) on invoice #72; terms net 30 days.

2 Credit sales: Bravo Co., $1,500 (Dept. A); Bee Company, $1,120 (Dept. B). Terms for both invoices, net 30 days.

4 Sold goods to Olympus Co., $3,000 (Dept. A) and $260 (Dept. B); terms net 10 days.

6 Sold on terms of net 30 days: Bee Company, $980 (Dept. B); Dunlop Co., $2,680 (Dept. A); Baker Co., $600 (Dept. A) and $189 (Dept. B).

9 Sold merchandise to R. Lopez $900 (Dept. A) and $425 (Dept. B); terms net 10 days.

11 Sold merchandise to the following customers: Bravo Co., $2,990 (Dept. A), terms 30 days. Fast Co., $5,230 (Dept. A), terms net 60 days; W.B. Allen, $645 (Dept. B), terms net 10 days.

15 Goods were sold to Post Co., $2,500 (Dept. A) and $1,360 (Dept. B); terms net 30 days.

18 Credit sales: Bravo Co., $1,110 (Dept. B), terms net 30 days; Baker Co., $1,395 (Dept. A), terms net 30 days; R. Lopez, $535 (Dept. A); terms net 10 days.

21 Sold merchandise to Fast Co., $1,200 (Dept. A) and $425 (Dept. B); terms net 60 days.

24 Sold goods on credit to: Dunlop Co., $1,173 (Dept. B), terms net 30 days; Olympus Co., $1,700 (Dept. A), terms net 10 days; W.B. Allen, $660 (Dept. A), terms net 10 days.

26 Credit sale to Post Co., $985 (Dept. B); terms net 30 days.

29 Goods were sold to Bee Company, $1,550 (Dept. A) and $810 (Dept. B); terms net 30 days.

(f) Total, balance, and rule the journal.

(g) Post the total of the Accounts Receivable column to the Accounts Receivable Control account. Post the other column totals appropriately.

(h) Prepare a trial balance, supported by a schedule of accounts receivable.

▶ **PRACTICE EXERCISE 10**

Spartan Company of Halifax, Nova Scotia, sells merchandise through its retail store and its catalogue outlet.

(a) Set up a sales journal (SJ1) using the following headings: Date, Name of Customer, Invoice Number, Terms, Folio, Accounts Receivable Dr., Retail Sales Cr., Catalogue Sales Cr., GST Payable Cr., and Sales Tax Payable Cr.

(b) Set up ledger accounts for each of the following: Accounts Receivable Control, 110; GST Payable, 210; Sales Tax Payable, 211; Retail Sales, 401; Catalogue Sales, 402. Also, set up ledger accounts for these customers: A/R Bear, Frederick, 220; A/R Gray, Jane, 221; A/R Harluck, Patrick, 222; A/R Hartman, Sidney, 223; A/R Kipling, Darlene, 224; A/R Kozun, Eva, 225; A/R Miley, Jack, 226; A/R Ritchie, Alison, 227; A/R Singh, Dana, 228; A/R Watko, Bradley, 229. Assume Sheet 1 for all ledger accounts.

(c) All invoices will be numbered sequentially beginning with #1. Terms of sale will vary.

(d) Add 7% GST and 11% provincial sales tax to the selling prices quoted below. In Nova Scotia, sales tax is calculated on the combined value of selling price *plus* GST.

(e) Record the following transactions, charging the appropriate retail or catalogue sales account. Post daily to the customers' accounts.

19—

June 1 Sold merchandise on credit to: Jack Miley, $650 (Retail); terms net 10 days. Sidney Hartman, $327.30 (Retail); terms net 30 days. Jane Gray, $150 (Retail) and $45.50 (Catalogue); terms net 30 days.

  2   Credit sales (10-day terms): Dana Singh, $510.60 (Retail); Jack Miley, $660 (Retail) and $56.55 (Catalogue).

  4   Credit sales (30-day terms) to: Frederick Bear, $85.40 (Catalogue); Jane Gray, $229.65 (Retail); and Alison Ritchie, $60.15 (Catalogue).

  6   Credit sales: Bradley Watko, $811.75 (Retail), terms net 30 days; Darlene Kipling, $136.90 (Catalogue), terms net 10 days; Alison Ritchie, $100 (Retail) and $50 (Catalogue), terms net 30 days.

  8   Sold merchandise to Jane Gray, $165 (Retail) and $135 (Catalogue); terms net 30 days.

 12   Credit sales: Eva Kozun, $295.28 (Retail), terms net 20 days; Sidney Hartman, $450.95 (Retail), terms net 30 days.

 15   Sold merchandise to Patrick Harluck, $95 (Retail) and $30.35 (Catalogue); terms net 30 days.

 19   Sold merchandise on credit to Alison Ritchie, $110 (Catalogue); terms net 30 days.

 24   Sold merchandise on credit: Darlene Kipling, $218.05 (Retail), terms net 10 days; Dana Singh, $95.80 (Retail), terms net 10 days.

 29   Credit sales: Patrick Harluck, $133.26 (Retail), terms net 30 days; Eva Kozun, $220 (Retail) and $55 (Catalogue); terms net 20 days.

(f)   Total, balance, and rule the journal.

(g)   Post the total of the Accounts Receivable column to the Accounts Receivable Control account. Post the other columns appropriately.

(h)   Prepare a trial balance with a schedule of accounts receivable.

▶   **PRACTICE EXERCISE 11**

Sam Wong is the owner and operator of a store in Prince Albert, Saskatchewan, and uses standard sales and purchase journals.

(a)   Set up a sales journal (SJ3) with the headings illustrated in Figure 4.6 and a purchase journal (PJ2) with the headings illustrated in Figure 4.2.

(b)   All sales invoices are to be numbered consecutively beginning with #56. Add 7% GST and 9% sales tax to the sale amounts quoted below. In Saskatchewan, both GST and sales tax are calculated on the selling price of the goods.

(c)   Amounts related to purchases are assumed to include GST unless otherwise stated. The amount of GST included in each invoice is shown in parentheses.

(d)   Record the following transactions in the appropriate journals for the month of March. (No posting is required for this exercise.)

19—

March 2   Purchased merchandise from Spalding Co., $947 ($61.95 GST); invoice #39 dated March 1; terms net 30 days.

3   Bought merchandise from Black & White Co., $772.52 plus 7% GST; terms net 20 days; invoice #79 dated March 3.

4   Credit sales: R. Jones, $183, terms net 30 days; Joan Poyser, $490.25, terms net 30 days; Susan Coulter, $225.35, terms net 10 days.

6   Bought merchandise from Brown Bros. on account, $1,052.85 ($68.88 GST); invoice #127 dated March 5; terms net 10 days.

7   Sold merchandise on credit to Sara King, $218; terms net 30 days.

8   Received invoice #216 from Kachur Wholesalers for merchandise purchased on terms of net 30 days; $1,383.13 plus 7% GST. Their invoice is dated today.

9   Bought a new desk and chair for the office from Interlake Business Equipment Co., $1,875 ($113.15 GST); terms net 60 days; invoice #276 dated March 8.

10   Sold goods on credit to: Linda Hamm, $340.75, terms net 30 days; R. Jones, $356.20, terms net 30 days.

11   Received invoice #187 dated March 10 from Quattrin Stationery for office supplies, $297.95, and wrapping supplies, $424.75; terms net 10 days. The total GST added to these prices is $43.61.

14   Bought merchandise from Brown Bros., $736.55 ($48.19 GST) on invoice #253 dated March 14; terms net 10 days.

17   Credit sales: Susan Coulter, $153.60, terms net 10 days; Sara King, $327.50, terms net 30 days.

20   Received invoice #287 for merchandise purchased from Kachur Wholesalers, $1,495.79 plus 7% GST. The invoice is dated March 18; terms net 30 days.

21   Placed an ad for one week in the *Local News,* $250 ($15.09 GST), terms net 10 days; invoice #367.

22   Purchased merchandise from Black & White Co. on their invoice #134 dated today, $1,580 ($103.36 GST); terms net 20 days.

23   Credit sales (terms net 30 days): Linda Hamm, $225.05; Joan Poyser, $331.89; and Iris Anderson, $226.49.

25   Bought a copier, $1,545.90, and stationery, $260.85, from Interlake Business Equipment Co. on their invoice #412 dated March 24. The total invoice value is $1,806.75 ($109.03 GST) and is due in 90 days. (Only one line is required to record this transaction.)

28   Received invoice #356 dated March 26 from Kachur Wholesalers for merchandise, $1,509.39 ($98.75 GST); terms net 30 days.

30   Credit sales: R. Jones, $169.25, terms net 30 days; Susan Coulter, $110.30, terms net 10 days; Linda Hamm, $175, terms net 30 days; and Sara King, $198.95, terms net 30 days.

(e)   Total, balance, and rule the journals.

▶ **PRACTICE EXERCISE 12**

The following sales journal for a Saskatchewan retailer contains many recording and calculation errors. Examine each line carefully for a variety of recording errors. As you rewrite this journal, consider the following:

(1)   Assume all merchandise sales and service sales are recorded correctly.

(2)   GST is charged on all sales at 7%. Sales tax is charged on all sales at 9%.

(3)   All invoices were to be numbered consecutively, beginning with #471.

SALES JOURNAL   PAGE SJ 16

DATE		ACCOUNT DEBIT	INV. NO.	TERMS	F.	ACCOUNTS REC. DR.	MDSE. SALES CR.	SERVICE SALES CR.	GST PAYBL. CR.	SLS. TX. PAYBL. CR.
19— July	3	Szilard, Joan	471	n/30		267 50	200 00	50 00	17 50	
		Woo, Ross	472	n/30			100 00	200 00	21 00	21 00
		Cosgrove, Patricia	473	n/30		1100 00	1100 00	420 00		
	6	McWhyte, Jill	474	n/30		481 74			28 14	37 80
		Newhouse, Don	475	n/30		207 00	180 00	38 00	12 60	16 00
	11	Turner, Rita	476	n/30		29 00	42 00	40 00	5 60	2 70
		Murphy, Brian	477	n/30			150 00		17 10	17 10
	20	Szilard, Joan	477	n/30		190 00	190 00		3 30	17 10
		Yeung, Danny	479	n/30		575 00	230 00	270 00		
	24	Funk, Peter	480	n/30		575 00	190 00	310 00		45 00
		Carroll, Michael		n/30		217 40		200 00	1 40	18 00
		Fast, Kelly	482	n/30			340 00			
						3454 44	2722 00	1528 00	106 64	174 80

▶ **PRACTICE EXERCISE 13**

Examine each line of this purchase journal for a variety of recording errors. Rewrite this journal, considering the following:

PURCHASE JOURNAL   PAGE PJ6

| INVOICE DATE | | ACCOUNT CREDIT | | | | ACCOUNT DEBIT | | | | | | |
| | | ACCOUNT | INV. NO. | TERMS | F. | ACCOUNTS PAYABLE | MDSE. PURCH. | OFFICE SUPPL. | SHIPPING SUPPL. | OTHER ACCOUNTS DEBIT | | |
										ACCOUNT	F.	AMOUNT
19— Oct.	2	Grummond, S.	417	n/30		427 00	472 00					
		Piccolo, B.	331	n/20		700 00	700 00					
	5	Ranadive, L.	073	n/30		125 00			75 00	Office Supplies		50 00
	8	Cameron, D.	117	n/10			217 00					
	12	Columbus, C.	847	n/30						Office Equipt.		3275 00
	13	Grummond, S.	482	n/30		262 00	226 00					
	17	Shipping Suppl.	114	n/10		75 00				Telson Co. Ltd.		75 00
	20	Deng, G.	221	n/30			145 00		87 00			
	23	Wakefield, B.	21	n/30		820 00				Purchases		802 00
	26	CABC-TV	800	n/10		2100 00			2100 00	Advertising		
	29	Cameron, D.	134	n/10		64 00	64 00					
						4848 00	1543 00	857 00	2262 00			3927 00

(1) Assume all amounts in the debit columns are the correct amounts.

(2) Disregard GST in this exercise.

THINK ABOUT IT!

1. Name the two special journals discussed in this chapter and give a brief explanation of the purpose of each.
2. Give two advantages of using special journals.
3. When recording transactions in the purchase journal, the date of the invoice is recorded rather than the date it is entered. Why?
4. Is the purchase journal used to record only invoices for merchandise purchased for resale? Why?
5. Are cash sales usually recorded in the sales journal? Why?
6. What are the benefits of using a sales journal?
7. Why are sales invoices usually pre-numbered?
8. Are sales tax and GST included in the amount recorded in the Sales account? Why?
9. What are control accounts? In which ledger do they appear?
10. Explain the relationship between the control account and the subsidiary ledger accounts.

5

Introducing KBC Decorating Co.

Henry Martin and John Barker have joined forces to operate a business under the name of KBC Decorating Co., located in the Buffalo Place Industrial Park in Winnipeg, Manitoba. This is a retail operation selling paint, wallpaper, and related supplies. This company will also do service contract work—painting and decorating interiors and exteriors of office buildings, apartment blocks, and private residences. The partners were previously in this same type of work but operated independently from their own homes. They already have some established customers and have bid on several contracts this month. They will hire their former helpers as soon as a contract is awarded to the business.

To form this company, the partners first drew up a partnership agreement that outlined the duties and responsibilities of each partner within the organization. They then located and rented a suitable location at which to operate their business, renting half a building owned by Frank Bailes. These premises include an office and warehouse space with a loading dock.

Because the business is located in an industrial park, and because of the nature of the business, it was not necessary to obtain a business licence; however, the company will be billed for business tax in April, payable in May. Business tax rates are variable, based on the prime rate of the city.

The partners have applied for and received a Manitoba Sales Tax licence. They have also applied for and received a GST (Goods and Services Tax) Registration Number and have elected to remit the GST on a quarterly basis. (GST will be discussed in detail in Chapter 10.)

You have been hired to keep the books for KBC Decorating Co. for the first calendar year. As you progress through the chapters of this textbook, you will LEARN and DO. Each chapter will introduce new topics that you will incorporate into the regular bookkeeping activities of KBC Decorating Co. Just as in any new job, each step will be explained thoroughly before you are asked to put the principle into practice. You will be learning on the job.

All the supplies necessary for keeping the books for KBC Decorating Co. can be found in the package of general supplies that is available with this textbook. All ledger accounts have been pre-printed with the appropriate account names and account numbers. Be sure that the accounts remain in the order given. This will ensure that the ledger is organized and the accounts are easy to locate. The chart of accounts for this ledger has been printed at the end of the textbook for easy reference.

For the January transactions, only the general journal is required. Select the appropriate journal sheet from your supplies and number it GJ1. As you proceed further with this case study in later chapters, you will be referring to this journal page again, so keep it handy.

Using Chapter 2 as a guide, record the following transactions for the month of January in proper general journal form. Add 7% GST and 7% provincial sales tax to all sales.

There are two GST accounts on the books: GST Payable, to record the GST collected on sales (a credit balance); and GST-ITC (Input Tax Credit), to record the GST paid on the purchases of merchandise and assets and for other expenses (a debit balance). The amount of the GST-ITC will be provided for all purchases unless otherwise stated.

All merchandise purchased for resale will be exempt from the Manitoba provincial sales tax under our licence number M2347593.

▶ **JANUARY TRANSACTIONS**

On January 2, Henry Martin invested $20,000 cash (debit Bank); inventory, $8,000; and office furniture and equipment, $2,000. The total of these assets ($30,000) is to be credited to Mr. Martin's Capital account. John Barker has invested $15,000 cash; inventory, $5,000; and a used van (Service Vehicles), $10,000. The total of Mr. Barker's investment is to be credited to his Capital account.

Also on January 2, cheque #1 was issued to Frank Bailes for $2,500 (plus $175 GST) for the January rent. (Provincial sales tax is not charged on rent in Manitoba.) Cheque #2 was issued in payment for advertising in the Saturday issue of the *Winnipeg Free Press,* $500 plus $32.71 GST. Debit Advertising Expense.

Continue recording the following transactions:

Jan. 4 Bought office supplies, $300 plus $19.63 GST; issued cheque #3 for $319.63. (Office Supplies Prepaid)

5 Bought merchandise as follows: paint and supplies, $10,000, wallpaper, $5,000. Issued cheque #4 for $16,050, which includes $1,050 GST.

9 Bought a paint mixer and colour dispenser from Rainbow Supplies, Edmonton, Alberta, $1,500 plus 7% GST. Issued cheque #5. (Tools & Equipment)

10 Cash sales to date: paint and supplies, $3,000; wallpaper, $1,000. (Add 7% GST and 7% sales tax to all sales.)

27 Cash sales to date: paint and supplies, $6,000; wallpaper, $2,000.

30 Paid $1,800 to yourself (the bookkeeper) for the monthly salary (Salaries Expense—Office). Issued cheque #6. GST is not applicable to salaries.

MONTH-END ACTIVITIES

(a) After all journal entries have been recorded, post them to the ledger accounts as described in Chapter 3. (All ledger accounts for KBC Decorating Co. should be neatly arranged in a binder or file so you can access them easily.)

(b)   After all posting is complete, prepare a trial balance as illustrated in Figure 3.3 (Chapter 3).

▶ **FEBRUARY TRANSACTIONS**

February's transactions will require a sales journal and a purchase journal. The sales journal will be numbered SJ1 and the purchase journal will be numbered PJ1. You will continue to use the general journal that was started in January. Also, continue to use the existing ledger accounts.

Set up the sales journal with these headings: Date, Account Dr., Invoice No., Terms, Folio, Accounts Receivable Dr., Sales—Paint & Supplies Cr., Sales—Wallpaper Cr., GST Payable Cr., and Sales Tax Payable Cr.

Set up the purchase journal with these headings: Invoice Date, Account Cr., Invoice No., Terms, Folio, Accounts Payable Cr., Purchases—Paint & Supplies Dr., Purchases—Wallpaper Dr., GST-ITC Dr., and Other Accounts Dr. (with subheadings of Accounts Dr., Folio, and Amount).

Record each of the following transactions in the appropriate journal. Be sure each transaction is recorded as a balanced entry. Post immediately any transaction affecting a customer or a supplier.

Feb.   1   Paid rent for the month to Frank Bailes, $2,500 plus $175 GST. Issued cheque #7 for $2,675.

2   Paid the phone bill from Manitoba Telephone System for January service, $155 plus $10.14 GST; cheque #8. (Telephone Expense)

3   Paid Manitoba Hydro for January service, $160 plus $10.47 GST; cheque #9 (Utilities). Paid Intercity Gas for January heating bill, $350 plus $22.90 GST; cheque #10. (Utilities)

4   Sold paint and supplies to Beavis & Sons, $375 plus taxes. Terms net 30 days; sales invoice #1. This will be the first entry in the sales journal.

7   Purchased from Major Office Supplies, terms n/30, on their invoice #122 dated February 5, stationery worth $250 and warehouse supplies worth $100. Added to the invoice was $22.90 GST. (*Note:* Debit $250 to Office Supplies Prepaid, $100 to Warehouse Supplies Prepaid, and $22.90 to GST-ITC. Although only one invoice was received, this entry will require two lines in the purchase journal. Be sure to charge the total of the invoice to the supplier's account.)

8   Received invoice #87 dated February 5 from Reynolds Paper Co. for the purchase of wallpaper, $600 plus 7% GST. Terms are n/30.

10   Sold to Jay-Mar Co., paint and supplies, $550; terms of n/30, invoice #2. Sold to Dayson & Son, wallpaper, $2,500; terms of n/30, invoice #3. (All sales invoices will be numbered consecutively. Be sure to number all future sales invoices accordingly.)

12   Received invoice #37 dated February 8 from Rainbow Supplies for wallpaper, $350, and paint and supplies, $850, plus GST. Terms are n/30. Sold to S. Miller, paint and supplies, $300; terms n/30.

15   Received invoice #99 dated today from Robinson Insurance Co. for insurance on stock for one year, $600 (GST exempt). Terms are n/30. (Debit Insurance Prepaid.)

19   Remitted the January sales tax to the Provincial Treasurer of Manitoba, cheque #11. (In Manitoba, businesses are entitled to retain a portion of the provincial sales tax collected: 15% of the first $200 and 1% of the balance. KBC Decorating is entitled, therefore, to retain $36.40.) Record this remittance in the general journal: debit Sales Tax Payable for $840, credit Commission Revenue for $36.40, and credit Bank for $803.60.

27   Cash sales to date: paint and supplies, $4,000; wallpaper, $2,000. Add taxes as usual.

28   Paid salary to the bookkeeper, $1,800; cheque #12. (Salaries Expense—Office)

MONTH-END ACTIVITIES

(a)   Total the sales and purchase journals in pencil and prove equal debits and credits. Then, total and rule the journals in ink.

(b)   The transactions affecting customers and suppliers should have been posted on a daily basis; therefore, their accounts should now be up to date. Check to see that all other entries and appropriate totals have been posted, particularly those totals that affect the Accounts Receivable Control account and the Accounts Payable Control account.

(c)   Prepare a trial balance with schedules of accounts receivable and accounts payable as illustrated in Figure 4.11 (Chapter 4).

6

Special Journals Continued

Chapter Objectives

After completing this chapter, you will be able to:

- record cash transactions in the cash receipts and cash payments journals

- post from the cash journals to the general ledger and to subsidiary ledgers

Important Words and Terms in This Chapter

Cash Payments Journal
Cash Receipts Journal
Credit Card
Special Journals

CASH RECEIPTS JOURNAL

The receipt of money is a common transaction on the books of almost any organization, most frequently for the receipt of cash from the sale of goods and services and for cash and cheques received from customers as payment on their accounts. To simplify the recording of such transactions, a cash receipts journal can be designed with special columns to accommodate the most frequently affected accounts. Like the purchase journal and the sales journal, the cash receipts journal requires only a one-line entry for each transaction and yet remains balanced.

CASH RECEIPTS

PAGE ___CR1___

DATE	ACCOUNT CREDIT	MEMO	F.	ACCTS. REC. CR.	SALES DISC. DR.	SALES CR.	GST PAY. CR.	SALES TAX CR.	GENERAL LEDGER CR.	BANK DR.
19— Sept. 1	Capital, G. Greene	invested							2000000	2000000
2	Sales					80000	5600	5600		91200
2	A/R Bell, Harvey	on acct., #15		20000						20000
4	Land	unused parcel							1000000	1000000
8	Sales					150000	10500	10500		171000
12	A/R Dubois, J.P.	on acct., #21		12500						12500
				32500		230000	16100	16100	3000000	3294700
	Proof: 32500									
	230000									
	16100									
	16100									
	3000000									
	3294700									

Figure 6.1   Cash Receipts Journal

All columnar journals are designed to suit the requirements of a particular business. Some may require many columns while others may require only a few. Figure 6.1 illustrates a very basic cash receipts journal. Each column in a special journal captures specific information related to the transaction:

Date. The Date column is used to record the date the transaction occurs.

Account Cr. The same accounts are credited as would have been credited if the same entry were recorded in the general journal. For example, when cash or a cheque is received on account from a customer, the account credited is Accounts Receivable/Customer Name. Therefore, the same entry would be made in the Account Credit column.

Memo. Sometimes called Particulars, this column is used to record all necessary details or explanations that are important to the transaction. These details might include the invoice number to which the payment is to be applied or a notation regarding a refund received for the return of defective goods. Self-explanatory entries, such as cash sale entries, do not require explanations.

Accounts Receivable Cr. When cash is received from a customer on account, the amount is entered in this column and the name of the customer is entered in the Account Cr. column (discussed above). Entries recorded in this column should be posted immediately to the customers' accounts. By posting daily, the balance of each customer's account is kept up to date at all times.

Sales Discount Dr. The purpose of this column will be discussed later.

Sales Cr. Only those entries that represent over-the-counter cash sales of merchandise are recorded in this column. This amount is the selling price *before* GST and provincial sales tax are added. "Sales" or "Cash Sales" would be written in the Account Cr. column.

GST Payable Cr. Like the GST Payable column in the sales journal, this column shows how much GST was charged on the selling price recorded in the Sales Cr. column; that is, 7% of the selling price.

Sales Tax Payable Cr. The applicable provincial sales tax that is charged on the cash sale is recorded in this column. Some provinces will calculate sales tax on the base selling price; others will add the GST to the selling price to determine the base for calculating sales tax. See Figure 4.8 (Chapter 4) to see which provinces use this latter method.

General Ledger Cr. Sometimes called Other Accounts, this column is used to record cash receipt transactions that do not occur frequently. If the transaction does not affect any of the special columns described above because it does not meet the intended purpose of those columns, the amount is recorded in the General Ledger column and the account name is indicated in the Account Cr. column. The transactions entered on September 1 and 4 in Figure 6.1 are examples of this type of entry.

Bank Dr. The amounts recorded in the various credit columns are offset by an equal value in the Bank Dr. column. These debit entries to Bank may be recorded on a line-by-line basis to balance the individual credit entries or they may be represented by only one entry per day to reflect the daily deposit made at the bank.

As discussed in Chapter 2, the account Bank (or Cash) is debited whenever cash is received; therefore, our attention now turns to the credit side of the transaction. When money is received from a customer to be applied against his or her account, the credit entry is to the customer's account, thereby reducing the amount that the customer owes. When money is received for any other reason, the credit entry is to the account that represents that reason. For example, if a cheque is received from John Smith for office space sublet to him, the account credited is Rent Revenue. Or, if money is received for interest earned on a bank investment, the account credited is Interest Revenue (or Interest Earned).

To fully appreciate the advantages of using this special journal, we will look at sample entries as they would appear when recorded in the general journal and again as these same entries would appear in the cash receipts journal. As you review the transactions illustrated in Figure 6.1 and compare them with the same transactions recorded in general journal form illustrated in Figure 6.2, you will see that the debit entry for each is Bank and the credit entry varies to show the reason for the receipt of the cash. It should be noted that regardless of the journal used, the same account is credited.

19— Sept.	1	Bank			20	0	0	0	00					
		Capital, G. Greene									20	0	0	0	00
		To record owner's investment.													
	2	Bank				9	1	2	00						
		Sales										8	0	0	00
		GST Payable											5	6	00
		Sales Tax Payable											5	6	00
		Cash sales for the day.													
	2	Bank				2	0	0	00						
		A/R Bell, Harvey										2	0	0	00
		Received payment on Inv. #15.													
	4	Bank			10	0	0	0	00						
		Land									10	0	0	0	00
		Sold parcel of unused land.													
	8	Bank			1	7	1	0	00						
		Sales									1	5	0	0	00
		GST Payable										1	0	5	00
		Sales Tax Payable										1	0	5	00
		Cash sales for the day.													
	12	Bank				1	2	5	00						
		A/R Dubois, J.P.										1	2	5	00
		Received payment on Inv. #21.													

Figure 6.2   Cash Receipt Transactions in the General Journal

PREPARING FOR POSTING

Before posting the entries from the cash receipts journal, following these preliminary steps will minimize any potential for errors and will simplify the posting process:

1. Total each money column. Pencil figures can be written temporarily at the bottom of each money column.

2. Prove equal debits and credits. The totals of the credit columns are added together and the totals from the debit columns are added together. The total debits and the total credits must be equal if the journal is to be in balance. In the cash receipts journal illustrated in Figure 6.1, a simple proof demonstrates the equality of debits and credits.

3. Total and rule the journal in ink. These permanent totals should be written on the line immediately below the last transaction entry. "Rule" means to draw a single line neatly above the totals and a double line neatly below the totals.

POSTING FROM THE CASH RECEIPTS JOURNAL

To ensure that all information is transferred correctly to the ledgers, the following posting procedure is recommended:

1. **Accounts Receivable Cr.** The individual entries in this column should already have been credited to the customers' accounts in the subsidiary ledgers on a daily basis. The column total is then credited to the Accounts Receivable Control account in the general ledger. This ensures that the total of the Accounts Receivable subsidiary ledger is equal to the balance in the Accounts Receivable Control account. (If necessary, review subsidiary and control accounts discussed in Chapter 4.)

2. **Sales Discount Dr.** The total of this column is debited to the Sales Discount account in the general ledger. (Discounts will be discussed in Chapter 7.)

3. **Sales Cr.** The total of this column is credited to the Sales account in the general ledger. Since this column is for the sole purpose of recording the selling price of the goods sold for cash, only the total is posted, not the individual entries within the column.

4. **GST Payable Cr.** Like the Sales column above, only the total of this column is credited to the GST Payable account, not the individual entries.

5. **Sales Tax Payable Cr.** Only the total is credited to the Sales Tax Payable account.

6. **General Ledger Cr.** The total of this column is *not* posted because it is the sum of a variety of *unrelated* transactions. The individual entries are credited to the accounts named in the Account Cr. column.

7. **Bank Dr.** Only the total of this column is debited to the Bank account in the general ledger. This represents the total amount of cash received during the month.

CREDIT CARDS

Two types of credit cards are commonly used by the buying public: (1) bank credit cards, such as VISA and MasterCard, and (2) nonbank credit cards, issued by department stores, gasoline companies, and other retailers.

A credit card is provided for the customer's convenience in the purchase of goods and services. A credit card number and a credit limit are assigned to each cardholder. The credit limit is established after the customer's credit standing has been investigated. Although the credit cards are issued for use by the customer, they remain the property of the issuing bank or retailer and can be cancelled or recalled at any time.

Credit cards offer a variety of benefits to the customer:

1. The customer need not carry large sums of money.

2. The use of cheque books and means of identification are at a minimum. The credit card itself is a form of identification.

3. Only one statement is received monthly by the customer, detailing all purchases of goods and services during the month.

4. One cheque is issued at month end in payment of the purchases appearing on the statement. This reduces the bank charges on the cheques issued.

The vendor (retailer) also benefits from credit card sales:

1. The amount of cash held on the premises is reduced, thus reducing the potential for theft.

2. The retailer can redeem bank credit card drafts immediately. The retailer's copies of the bank credit card receipts are included in the bank deposit, along with the usual cash and cheques. The bank honours the credit card receipts immediately as if they were cash.

3. There are no losses from uncollectible accounts or bad cheques. Any such losses are sustained by the credit card companies.

4. Investigating customers' credit histories is eliminated. These investigations were conducted by the credit card companies prior to issuing the credit card to the customer.

5. Maintaining an Accounts Receivable ledger is eliminated, along with the task of collecting due and overdue accounts.

When a customer makes a purchase using a bank credit card or a retail credit card, he or she signs a multi-part credit card receipt, one copy of which is a credit card draft. This draft is added to the retailer's daily deposit at the bank. In this respect, the draft is treated as cash; therefore, the retailer records all credit card transactions as cash sales. The credit card company will use the draft as the source document for the detailed billing that will appear on the statement sent to the customer at the end of the month.

For the privilege of honouring bank credit cards, the retailer is charged a fee ranging from 3.5% to 4% of the sale value, depending on the bank or issuing company. This service charge is deducted from the retailer's bank account along with all other service charges on the monthly bank statement.

▶ PRACTICE EXERCISE 1

(a) Set up a cash receipts journal (page CR4) with the following headings: Date, Account Cr., Memo, Folio, Accounts Receivable Cr., Sales Cr., GST Payable Cr., Sales Tax Payable Cr., General Ledger Cr., and Bank Dr.

(b) Record the following transactions on the books of Duscina Industries of Vancouver, B.C., for the month of February, 19—. Add 7% GST and 7% sales tax to all sales. (In British Columbia, both GST and sales tax are calculated on the value of the goods.)

Feb. 1   Received $900 (includes $58.88 GST) from P. Simons for office space sublet to him.

2   Cash sales to date, $1,279 plus taxes.

4   Received $300 from B. Robbins on account.

5   Received a cheque from L. Pierce covering invoice #27 for $230.

6   Received a cheque for interest earned on a short-term investment, $38.

8   Cash sales to date, $1,640 plus taxes.

10   Received a cheque from B. Robbins on account, $250.

12   Cash sales to date, $2,000 plus taxes.

15   Received a cheque from L. Pierce for $400 on account.

18   Cash sales to date, $3,640 plus taxes.

22   Borrowed $15,000 from the bank at a rate of 9.5% interest for two years. (Credit Bank Loan Payable.)

23   David Johnston made a $495 partial payment on account.

27   Cash sales to date, $2,975 plus taxes.

(c)   Total and rule the journal. Prove equal debits and credits.

PRACTICE EXERCISE 2

(a)   Set up a cash receipts journal (page CR7) with the following headings: Date, Account Cr., Memo, Post. Ref., Accounts Receivable Cr., Sales Cr., GST Payable Cr., Sales Tax Payable Cr., General Ledger Cr., and Bank Dr.

(b)   Record the following transactions for Jamieson Specialties located in Halifax, Nova Scotia. Add 7% GST and 11% sales tax to all sales. (In Nova Scotia, sales tax is calculated on the selling price of the goods plus GST.)

19—

May   1   Received a cheque for $1,350 (includes $88.32 GST) from Jack Spano for office space sublet to him.

2   Cheques were received on account from B. Parker, $325 on invoice #816, and Dale Barclay, $215 on invoice #802.

3   Jack Cole sent a cheque for $625 as a partial payment on sales invoice #822 dated April 17.

5   Received a cheque from Peter Greene, $404.91, on his overdue account of $396 plus interest for three months at 9% per annum (per year). A two-line entry is required for this transaction.

8   Cash sales for the week, $2,890.65 plus taxes.

8   A cheque was received on account from Andrew Richer, $196.75 for invoice #835.

12   Borrowed $9,000 from the bank for one year with interest at 9% per annum. (Credit Bank Loan Payable.) (Interest will not be recorded until the first loan payment is made.)

15   Cash sales for the week, $3,133.20 plus taxes.

20   Received cheques from Alison Clements on invoice #831, $84.50, and Adam Jones on invoice #833, $40.75.

22   Cash sales for the week, $2,923.70 plus taxes.

25   Sold an old typewriter to Grace Foster for cash, $250. Both GST and sales tax will be charged on the sale of this asset. Because this is

not the sale of usual merchandise, $250 is recorded in the General Ledger column, not in the Sales column.

29   Cash sales for the week, $3,286.15 plus taxes.

31   Received notice from the bank that interest earned on a term investment has been deposited into the business's account, $410. (Interest Revenue)

(c)   Total and rule the journal. Prove equal debits and credits.

CASH PAYMENTS JOURNAL

Also known as the cash disbursements journal, the cash payments journal is used to record all payments of money. To provide an adequate record of these payment transactions, all payments should be made by cheque. Therefore, the payments journal can be thought of as a form of cheque book.

The cheque stub is the source document from which the information is recorded in the cash payments journal, so the stub should be completed before the cheque is separated and mailed. The cheque stub shows the date of the transaction, the amount of the cheque, and the name of the company or person to whom the cheque was issued. A sample cheque and stub are shown in Figure 6.3.

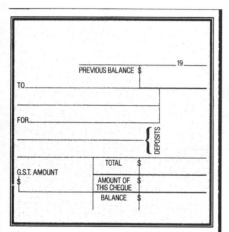

Figure 6.3   Sample Cheque with Stub

Cheques are legal proof of payment; therefore, they should be written very carefully to prevent fraud and alterations. Spoiled cheques should be voided, but not destroyed. These will be filed along with the cancelled cheques that are returned from the bank.

As with all special journals, the cash payments journal may be specifically designed to meet the needs of the particular company. Here is a brief explanation of the columns that appear in the cash payments journal illustrated in Figure 6.4.

Date. The Date column is used for recording the date on which the transaction occurs; that is, the date on which the cheque was written or the payment was made.

Account Dr. The name of the account affected (debited) by this transaction is entered in this column. For example, if the cheque is issued to pay the rent, Rent Expense is the account debited; therefore, Rent Expense is the account name entered in this column.

					CASH PAYMENTS					PAGE CP11
DATE	**ACCOUNT DEBIT**	**MEMO**	**F.**	**ACCTS. PAY. DR.**	**PURCH. DISC. DR.**	**PURCH. DR.**	**GST–ITC DR.**	**GEN. LED. DR.**	**BANK CR.**	**CH. NO.**
19— Jan. 2	Rent Expense	for January					49 07	700 93	750 00	1
3	Purchases					185 00	12 95		197 95	2
4	A/P Manitoba Motors	on acct.		400 00					400 00	3
6	A/P Packards Ltd.	on acct.		75 00					75 00	4
10	Mortgage Payable							500 00		
	Interest Expense	on mtg.						150 00	650 00	DM
12	Office Supplies Prepaid	stationery					2 45	35 00	37 45	5
				475 00		185 00	64 47	1385 93	2110 40	
	Proof:	475 00								
		185 00								
		64 47								
		1385 93								
		2110 40								

Figure 6.4   Cash Payments Journal

Memo. Sometimes called Particulars, this column is used to record all necessary details or explanations that are important to the transaction. These details might include the invoice number for which a payment has been made or a notation regarding a refund given for the return of defective goods.

Accounts Payable Dr. When cheques are issued to creditors (suppliers), the amount is entered in this column and the name of the creditor is entered in the Account Dr. column. Entries affecting accounts payable should be posted immediately to the creditors' accounts in the Accounts Payable subsidiary ledger. By posting daily, the balance of each creditor's account is kept up to date at all times.

Purchase Discounts Cr. Purchase discounts will be discussed in Chapter 7.

Purchases Dr. Only those entries that represent cash purchases of goods for resale, including C.O.D. orders, are recorded in this column. "Purchases" or "Cash Purchases" would be written in the Account Dr. column. If provincial sales tax is paid on the merchandise, this tax is included in the amount entered in this column.

GST-ITC Dr. The amount of GST (if any) included in the total payment is entered in this column.

General Ledger Dr. Sometimes called Other Accounts, this column is used to record payment transactions that cannot be recorded in any of the previous money columns because it does not meet the intended purpose of those columns. The amount recorded in this column includes any provincial taxes paid. The name of the specific account to be debited is written in the Account Dr. column.

Bank Cr. The amount of the cheque is entered here. This credit amount offsets the debit entry (or entries) on the same line.

Cheque No. The number appearing on the cheque is recorded in this column. The procedure for recording transactions in the cash payments journal is similar to that of the cash receipts journal. Because money is being paid out, the credit entry is always to Bank. The debit entry, then, is to the name of the company to which the cheque is issued when payment is made on account or to the account that represents why the cheque is issued. For example, if a cheque is issued to

ABC Suppliers Ltd. as payment on account, the account debited is Accounts Payable/ABC Suppliers Ltd. Or, if a cheque is issued for the payment of a membership fee, the debit entry is to Membership Expense.

Examine the sample payment entries that appear in the general journal illustrated in Figure 6.5 and compare them with the same transactions in the cash payments journal illustrated in Figure 6.4. You will see that the credit entry for each transaction is Bank and that the debit entry will vary depending on the reason for the payment.

19— Jan.	2	Rent Expense		7 0 0 93	
		GST–ITC		4 9 07	
		Bank			7 5 0 00
		Paid January rent; allocated GST.			
		Issued cheque #1.			
	3	Purchases		1 8 5 00	
		GST–ITC		1 2 95	
		Bank			1 9 7 95
		Bought mdse. from Winnipeg Wholesalers Ltd;			
		cheque #2.			
	4	A/P Manitoba Motors		4 0 0 00	
		Bank			4 0 0 00
		Paid on account; cheque #3.			
	6	A/P Packards Ltd.		7 5 00	
		Bank			7 5 00
		Paid on account; cheque #4.			
	10	Mortgage Payable		5 0 0 00	
		Interest Expense		1 5 0 00	
		Bank			6 5 0 00
		Paid mortgage and interest.			
	12	Office Supplies Prepaid		3 5 00	
		GST–ITC		2 45	
		Bank			3 7 45
		Bought stationery; cheque #5.			

Figure 6.5   Cash Payment Transactions in the General Journal

In the cash payments journal, just as in any other journal, you can see that each entry is balanced. Each transaction calls for one or more debit amounts being offset by an equal amount in the credit column. Because each entry is balanced, the journal itself is in balance. A simple proof shows the equality of debits and credits recorded in this journal.

PREPARING FOR POSTING

The steps followed in preparing to post from the cash payments journal are the same as those explained for the cash receipts journal:

1. Total the columns in pencil.

2. Prove equal debits and credits.

3. Total and rule the journal in ink.

POSTING FROM THE CASH PAYMENTS JOURNAL

To be sure that all information is transferred to the ledger accounts correctly, follow this procedure for each column:

1. **Accounts Payable Dr.** The individual entries are debited to the creditors' accounts in the subsidiary ledger on a daily basis. The total of the column is debited to the Accounts Payable Control account in the general ledger. The total of all the subsidiary Accounts Payable accounts will then agree with the balance in the Accounts Payable Control account.

2. **Purchase Discounts Cr.** The total of this column is credited to the Purchase Discounts account in the general ledger.

3. **Purchases Dr.** Only the total of this column is debited to the Purchases account in the general ledger.

4. **General Ledger Dr.** The individual entries in this column are debited to the accounts named in the Account Dr. column. The total is *not* posted because it represents transactions that have nothing in common.

5. **Bank Cr.** The total of this column is credited to the Bank account in the general ledger.

PRACTICE EXERCISE 3

(a) Record the following transactions for the Dennis Hayward Co. of Lethbridge, Alberta, during the month of November, 19—, in a cash payments journal (page CP6) with these headings: Date, Account Dr., Memo, Folio, Accounts Payable Dr., GST-ITC Dr., Purchases Dr., General Ledger Dr., Bank Cr., and Cheque No.

The first cheque to be issued will be #111. Number all cheques sequentially. Account for the GST as required according to the information provided below.

19—

Nov. 1   Paid rent for November, $700 (includes $45.79 GST). Cheque #111.

3   Paid for a one-year insurance policy on stock, $325 (GST exempt).

4   Purchased merchandise, $115 plus 7% GST.

5   Paid D. Buchanan for invoice #72 dated October 8, $300.

8   Paid Tracy Franks for invoice #39, $441.

10   Bought merchandise from Litz Bros., $301 plus GST; C.O.D.

11   Paid the October telephone bill, $179 plus GST.

15   Paid salaries for November 1–15, $3,200 (GST not applicable).

17   Bought letterhead and other stationery for general office use, $124.50 plus GST.

20   Paid Lance Courier for delivering merchandise to a customer, $45 (includes $2.94 GST). (Delivery Expense)

23   Paid Donald Plant on account, invoice #447, $390.

27   Paid the water bill, $65 (GST exempt).

30   Paid salaries for November 16–30, $3,200.

(b)   Total, balance, and rule the journal.

▶ PRACTICE EXERCISE 4

These transactions will be recorded in the books of Jamieson & Sons of Edmonton, Alberta, during the month of May.

(a)   Set up a cash payments journal (page CP2) using the following headings: Date, Account Dr., Memo, Post. Ref., Accounts Payable Dr., GST-ITC Dr., Purchases Dr., Salaries Expense Dr., General Ledger Dr., Bank Cr., and Cheque No. All cheques issued are numbered sequentially, beginning with #20.

(b)   Record these transactions, accounting for GST as required according to the information provided.

19—

May   1   Issued cheque #20 for $800 (includes $52.34 GST) to Smith Agency for the May rent.

2   Cheques are issued to Parks Ltd., $185.90, and J. Temple & Co., $203.15, as payment on invoices #2822 and #417 respectively.

3   Bought merchandise from Apex Ltd., $390.85 plus 7% GST.

4   Issued a cheque for $18 plus GST to ABC Truckers for merchandise delivered to warehouse. (Freight In)

4   Bought office supplies, $42.50, and warehouse supplies, $64.85, from Wilson's Ltd. Add 7% GST. (Only one cheque was issued.)

6   Purchased a typewriter for the office, $805 plus GST, from Interlake Equipment Co.

9   Paid invoices dated April 10 to R. Cruise & Co., $287.30 on invoice #221, and Bailey & Sons, $123.10 on invoice #810.

10   Purchased a second-hand delivery truck for $2,500 plus 7% GST. Total cost $2,675.

10   Bought gasoline for the delivery truck, $45 (includes $2.94 GST). (Truck Expense)

14   Paid the gas bill for the month, $34 plus GST.

15   Paid salaries: sales representative, $650, and bookkeeper, $600. (GST does not apply to salaries.) Separate cheques are to be issued.

20 Paid $368.25 plus GST for goods purchased for resale, from Apex Ltd.

23 Bought coffee, cream, and sugar for the office, $13.20 (GST exempt). (Miscellaneous Expense)

25 Issued cheques to creditors on account, as follows: Mack Bros., $65.25 on invoice #041; and Forrest & Co., $118.90 on invoice #1002.

31 Paid salaries: sales representative, $650, and bookkeeper, $600.

31 Issued a cheque to Provincial Hydro for electricity bill, $293.65 plus GST.

(c) Total, balance, and rule the journal.

▶ PRACTICE EXERCISE 5

The following cash receipt and cash payment activities are to be recorded on the books of Roblin Fashions of Kenora, Ontario.

(a) Set up a cash receipts journal (page CR3) with the following headings: Date, Account Cr., Memo, Folio, Accounts Receivable Cr., Sales Cr., GST Payable Cr., Sales Tax Payable Cr., General Ledger Cr., and Bank Dr. (Add 7% GST and 8% provincial sales tax to all sales. Both taxes are based on the selling price of the goods.)

(b) Set up a cash payments journal (page CP5) with the following headings: Date, Account Dr., Memo, Folio, Accounts Payable Dr., Purchases Dr., GST-ITC Dr., General Ledger Dr., Bank Cr., and Cheque No. (All payments will be made by cheque, beginning with #180.)

(c) Record these transactions for the month of July, 19—:

19—

July 3 Paid $650 (includes $42.52 GST) to Jakeman & Co. for rent.

4 Received $372.40 from J. Thom in full payment of invoice #636.

5 Paid Keast Fashions $1,274 on invoice #73.

6 Cash sales, $1,770 plus taxes.

9 Paid the water bill, $160.50 (GST exempt).

10 Bought a special order of merchandise from Harrop Formals, $453.60 plus $31.75 GST; terms C.O.D.

11 Paid Chase Manufacturing $1,000 on invoice #083.

12 Received cheques from J. Thom for $220; A. Stephanow for $315; and Debbie Andres for $170. These payments cover invoices #647, #648, and #649 respectively.

15 Paid salaries for July 1–15, $1,500 (GST not applicable).

15 Cash sales, $2,990 plus taxes.

16 Bought merchandise, $92 ($6.02 GST included), from Taylor Fashion Suppliers.

17   Received a cheque from Debbie Andres for $269.50 to settle sales invoice #645 dated June 15.

19   Cash sales, $2,001 plus taxes.

21   Paid phone bill, $52.92 plus $3.43 GST.

24   Bought supplies for the office, $374.33 ($22.79 GST included).

26   Cash sales, $2,475 plus taxes.

31   Paid salaries for July 16–31, $1,500.

(b)   Total, balance, and rule both journals.

► ### PRACTICE EXERCISE 6

Mid-West Co. of Saskatoon, Saskatchewan, uses multi-column special journals for cash receipts and cash payments. Your job is to record these transactions appropriately.

(a)   Set up a cash receipts journal (page CR7) with these headings: Date, Account Cr., Memo, Post. Ref., Accounts Receivable Cr., Sales Cr., GST Payable Cr., Sales Tax Payable Cr., General Ledger Cr., and Bank Dr.

(b)   Set up a cash disbursements journal (page CD9) with these headings: Date, Account Dr., Memo, Post. Ref., Accounts Payable Dr., GST-ITC Dr., Purchases Dr., Salaries Dr., General Ledger Dr., Bank Cr., and Cheque No. All payments are made by cheque, beginning with #48.

Note: Add 7% GST and 9% sales tax to all sales. Both taxes are based on the selling price of the goods.

19—

Nov.   1   Tom Middleton, the owner, invested an additional $22,000 and deposited this money immediately in the bank.

1   Purchased Government of Canada savings bonds for cash, $8,000. (Debit Gov't of Canada Bonds.) GST does not apply to the purchase of government bonds. Issued cheque #48.

2   Paid the November rent, $650 (includes GST).

3   Purchased merchandise from Spaulding Co., $885 plus GST; terms C.O.D.

4   Received $565.30 from Janice Brown in settlement of invoice #725.

5   Sold a piece of unused land for cash, $5,000 plus GST.

6   Cash sales, $988.50 plus taxes.

6   Received cheques on account from: John Kingston, $87.60 on invoice #732; Peter Calder, $125.30 on invoice #735; and Jill Smith, $55 on invoice #730.

7   Paid for advertising in the *Weekly News,* $50 plus both taxes.

7   Received $223.50 from Michael Gray for his overdue account. Included is $23.50 of overdue interest (two entries required).

9 Paid $295 for a one-year fire insurance policy (GST exempt). (Insurance Prepaid)

10 Cash sales, $1,020.40 plus taxes.

10 Purchased a second-hand truck. Paid $6,600 plus both taxes. (Debit Delivery Equipment for the value of the truck plus the provincial sales tax.)

10 Issued a cheque for $48.50 (includes 7% GST) to Atlas Service Centre for gas and oil for the delivery truck. (Delivery Expense)

11 Issued cheques on account to T. Kindle Co., $365.50 on invoice #3307; Medland Bros., $210.75 on invoice #411; and Lakeview Co., $330.70 on invoice #036.

13 Received cheques on account from: John Cameron, $175.95 on invoice #736; Ben Nixon, $250 on invoice #737; and Marie Simpson, $65 on invoice #740.

15 Paid salaries, $1,525 (GST not applicable).

15 Remitted October sales tax to the Provincial Treasurer, $673.80.

16 Bought office supplies, $129.60 (includes $7.82 GST).

16 Rented unused office space to Ted King Studios. Received their cheque for $1,250 (includes GST). (Rental Revenue)

18 Purchased merchandise to fill a special order, $35.60 plus GST.

20 Issued a cheque for $1,225 plus taxes to Woods Equipment Co. for a new cash register.

22 Cash sales, $1,123.95 plus taxes.

25 Paid $136.20 plus taxes to Taper Supply Co. for wrapping supplies for the shipping department. (Shipping Supplies)

26 Received cheques on account from: Donald O'Connor, $78.25 for invoice #739; W.B. Dallard, $220 for invoice #741; and James Starr, $41.80 for invoice #742.

27 Paid telephone bill, $37.20 plus taxes.

28 Issued a cheque for $50 plus taxes to the *Weekly News* for month-end advertising.

29 Cash sales, $735.75 plus taxes.

29 Sold old cash register to Betty Clements for cash, $250 plus taxes.

30 Paid salaries, $1,525.

(c) Total, balance, and rule the journals.

▶ **PRACTICE EXERCISE 7**

The cash activities for the Spalding Co., a retail store operating in Alberta, are detailed below.

(a) Set up a cash receipts journal (CR3) with these headings: Date, Account

Cr., Memo, Post. Ref., Accounts Receivable Cr., Sales Cr., GST Payable Cr., General Ledger Cr., and Bank Dr.

(b)   Set up a cash payments journal (CP4) with these headings: Date, Account Dr., Memo, Post. Ref., Accounts Payable Dr., GST-ITC Dr., Purchases Dr., Salaries Dr., General Ledger Dr., Bank Cr., and Cheque No.

(c)   The following general ledger accounts should be opened immediately with balances forward on June 1 as indicated: Bank, #101, $10,559.10 (debit); Accounts Receivable Control, #110, $1,247.45 (debit); Office Supplies Prepaid, #111, $195.25 (debit); Warehouse Supplies Prepaid, #112, $154.75 (debit); Delivery Equipment, #118, $9,000 (debit); Office Equipment, #120, $650 (debit); Accounts Payable Control, #201, $1,806.55 (credit); GST Payable, #210; GST-ITC, #211; Capital, Jack Spalding, #301, $20,000 (credit); Sales, #401; Interest Revenue, #410; Rent Revenue, #420; Purchases, #501; Advertising Expense, #510; Delivery Expense, #520; Rent Expense, #530; Salaries, #540; Telephone Expense, #550; and Utilities, #560.

(d)   Open the following customers' ledger accounts: Bell, Henry, #150, $468.30; Stuart, Tom, #151, $197.45; Watson, Jim, #152, $326.45; Wright, Jack, #153, $255.25.

(e)   Open the following creditors' ledger accounts: Blair Mfg. Co., #250, $275; Central Wholesale Ltd., #251, $496.10; Kelly Distributors, #252, $384.95; Kendall Equipment Co., #253, $650.50.

(f)   Record the following transactions in the appropriate journals. All payments are to be made by cheque, beginning with #35. All entries affecting the customers' and creditors' accounts are to be posted daily. Add 7% GST to all sales and purchases, unless otherwise stated. (*Note:* When GST is included in the given amount, multiply the amount by 7/107 to determine the amount of GST.)

19—

June   1   Jack Spalding has invested an additional $5,000 in his business.

1   Issued cheque #35 to Leipsic Agency for June rent, $600. This amount includes 7% GST.

2   Received $250 (including GST) for office space sublet to Jack Newman.

2   Purchased merchandise, $865.30 plus GST.

4   Issued a cheque, $400, to Kendall Equipment Co. as partial payment on balance owing as of June 1.

6   Bought office supplies, $205 plus GST, from Victoria Suppliers.

7   Cash sales for the week, $985.90 plus GST.

7   Received a cheque from Jack Wright for the balance owing on June 1.

8   Paid $48 (includes GST) for gas and oil for the delivery truck. (Delivery Expense)

10   Purchased a new typewriter for the office, $722.25 (includes GST).

12   Sold the old typewriter to Bill Mason, $250 plus GST. He has paid by personal cheque.

14   Cash sales for the week, $1,146.35 plus GST.

14   Received $200 from Henry Bell as partial payment on his June 1 balance.

15   Paid salaries, $3,000. (GST is not applicable.)

16   Purchased merchandise, $500 plus GST. Terms C.O.D.

17   Issued a cheque to Local Press for advertising, $93.09 (includes GST).

18   Paid the amount owing on June 1 to Blair Mfg. Co., $275.

21   Received $150 from Jim Watson on account.

21   Paid telephone bill, $29.45 plus GST.

21   Cash sales for the week, $1,220.60 plus GST.

22   Purchased wrapping supplies and twine, $69.50 plus GST, from Riordon Suppliers Ltd. (Warehouse Supplies Prepaid)

23   Issued a cheque for $200 to Kelly Distributors on account.

26   Paid the electricity bill by cheque, $263.85 (includes GST). (Utilities)

28   Cash sales for the week, $980.75 plus GST.

30   Received notice from the bank that interest earned on a term deposit has been deposited in the business's account, $65. All banking transactions are exempt from GST.

30   Paid salaries, $3,000.

(g)   Total, balance, and rule each journal.

(h)   Complete the postings. Post column totals rather than individual entries where applicable.

(i)   Prepare a trial balance with schedules of accounts receivable and accounts payable.

▶ ## PRACTICE EXERCISE 8

Rewrite this cash receipts journal, correcting all recording errors. Consider the following:

(1)   In the event of a discrepancy in amounts, assume the Accounts Receivable and Sales amounts to be correct.

(2)   7% GST and 8% sales tax are charged on all sales. Both taxes are based on the selling price.

(3)   Assume that daily deposits are to be recorded; that is, only one debit entry to the Bank column per day.

(4)   Total all columns and prove equal debits and credits.

CASH RECEIPTS JOURNAL PAGE CR4

DATE	ACCOUNT CREDIT	MEMO	F.	ACCTS. REC. CR.	SALES CR.	GST PAY. CR.	SALES TAX CR.	GEN. LED. CR.	BANK DR.
19— Aug. 4	Swift, Oliver	on acct.		387 20					378 20
5	Sales				2340 00	168 30	187 20		
	Funk, Daniel	on acct.						275 00	2970 50
9	Rental Revenue	office space				105 00		1500 00	1605 00
12	O'Connor, David	on acct.		471 00					
	Bakos, David	on acct.		321 00					321 00
16	Sales				4114 50	288 02	329 16		4731 68
18	Western Produce	on acct.		200 00					200 00
	Abdul, Marie	on acct.				390 00		390 00	590 00
23	Office Equipment	old computer				31 50	36 00	450 00	
24	Sales				1920 00				2208 00
26	Leimones, John	on acct.		339 00			18 00		339 00
31	Sales				2500 00	17 50	200 00		2875 00
				5511 70	9100 00	505 32	191 36		16218 38

▶ **PRACTICE EXERCISE 9**

Rewrite the following cash payments journal, correcting all errors. Disregard GST. In the event of a discrepancy in amounts, assume the error is in the Bank column. Total all columns and prove equal debits and credits.

CASH PAYMENTS JOURNAL PAGE CP11

DATE	ACCOUNT DEBIT	MEMO	F.	ACCTS. PAY. DR.	PURCH. DR.	ADVERT. DR.	SALARIES DR.	GEN. LED. DR.	BANK CR.	CH. NO.
19— Feb. 1	Rent Expense	Feb. rent						2100 00	2000 00	104
3	Utilities	hydro bill		287 00					287 00	
	Utilities	water bill						165 00	156 00	
	paid phone bill	telephone exp.						96 00	96 00	
5	Liston Links	on acct.			219 00				219 00	
10	Mortgage Payable			340 00						
	Interest Expense	on mtg.		170 00					510 00	
14	Salaries	Feb 1–14						3820 00	3820 00	
17	Calvin Long	on acct.		327 00					372 00	
	Advertising	newspaper				144 00			140 00	
22	Sales Tax Payable	remittance		834 00					834 00	
23	Purchases	C.O.D.			440 00					
	Liston Links	on acct.		216 00						
	Zimmer Ltd.	on acct.						1312 00	1969 00	
26	Purchases	C.O.D.							420 00	
28	Salaries	Feb 15–28						3820 00	3280 00	
				2174 00	659 00	144 00		11313 00	14624 00	

THINK ABOUT IT!

1. What is the purpose of a cash receipts journal? of a cash payments journal?
2. How is time saved by using special journals?
3. How is the Bank balance determined from the totals of the cash receipts and cash payments journals?
4. Does the Bank Dr. column in the cash receipts journal have an entry on every line? Why or why not?
5. Are the totals of the General Ledger columns in the cash receipts and cash payments journals posted? Explain.
6. Explain why spoiled cheques cannot be simply thrown away.
7. Explain how a journal is ruled properly.
8. Why is it important to prove that the totals of a columnar journal are in balance?
9. If a transaction cannot be accommodated in any of the special journals, where will it be recorded?
10. Why should all cash receipts be deposited daily?

► MARCH TRANSACTIONS: KBC DECORATING CO.

KBC Decorating Co. has been awarded three contracts by Gluting Properties. The first contract (Job #1) is for painting and decorating the remodelled suites in an apartment building. Work will start April 1 and is to be completed on April 30. Job #2 covers painting and decorating offices in a small building, to start May 1 and to be completed June 15. Job #3 is for painting the exterior of apartment buildings between June 16 and June 30.

Because of these new contracts, KBC Decorating will hire three painting and decorating personnel whom the owners have hired in the past. Tony Asfour, Dale Campbell, and Rudy Wenzel will start work on Job #1 on April 1 at starting salaries of $2,400 per month.

In March, however, all four special journals will be used: sales journal (SJ2), purchase journal (PJ2), cash receipts journal (CR1), and cash payments journal (CP1). Use the same headings in the sales and purchase journals as were used last month. The general journal will not be used this month.

The cash receipts journal will require these headings: Date, Account Cr., Memo, Folio, Accounts Receivable Cr., Sales Discounts Dr., Sales—Paint & Supplies Cr., Sales—Wallpaper Cr., GST Payable Cr., Sales Tax Payable Cr., General Ledger Cr., and Bank Dr.

The cash payments journal will require these headings: Date, Account Dr., Memo, Folio, Accounts Payable Dr., Purchase Discounts Cr., GST-ITC Dr., General Ledger Dr., Bank Cr., and Cheque No.

Record the following transactions for March, considering these special notes:

(a) Add 7% GST and 7% sales tax to all sales, except sales of service to which only GST is added.

(b) The last sales invoice was #4; therefore, the next invoice to be issued this month is #5. The last cheque issued was #12; therefore, the next to be issued is #13.

(c)   All cash transactions are to be recorded in the cash receipts and cash payments journals.

(d)   Post all transactions affecting customers' and suppliers' accounts on a daily basis.

19—

Mar. 1   Paid March rent, $2,500 plus $175 GST. Paid the phone bill for February services, $160 plus $10.47 GST. Paid the February hydro bill, $180 plus $11.78 GST. Paid Intercity Gas for the February heating bill, $420 plus $27.48 GST.

2   Paid Major Office Supplies on invoice #122. Check their ledger account for the correct amount. Received purchase invoice #52 dated February 28 from Coleman Industries for paint, $5,000 plus $350 GST; terms n/30.

4   Received payment on sales invoice #1 from Beavis & Sons, $427.50. Cash sales to date: paint and supplies, $800, and wallpaper, $1,200.

5   Paid Reynolds Paper Co. for invoice #87. Check their ledger account for the correct amount.

8   Bought scaffolding from Rainbow Supplies, $10,000 plus $700 GST; invoice #45 dated March 1, terms n/60. (Tools & Equipment) The scaffolding will be delivered on March 30.

9   Received invoice #92 dated March 5 from Reynolds Paper Co. for wallpaper, $1,500 plus $105 GST; terms n/30.

10   Paid Rainbow Supplies the balance owing on invoice #37. See their ledger account for the correct amount.

11   Cash sales to date: paint and supplies, $1,500, and wallpaper, $500.

12   Received payment on sales invoice #2 from Jay-Mar Co.; from Dayson & Son on invoice #3; and from S. Miller on invoice #4.

15   Sold to the following customers on terms of n/30: Beavis & Sons, paint and supplies, $1,000, and wallpaper, $1,000. Jay-Mar Co., paint, $1,200, and wallpaper, $1,000. Dayson & Son, paint, $1,500, and wallpaper, $500.

16   Purchased a 1991 GMC half-ton truck from Standard Motors for $15,000 plus $981.30 GST (Service Vehicles). Paid Robinson Insurance Co. for registration and insurance on the truck, $600 (GST exempt). Debit Delivery Expense for these truck-related costs.

17   Paid Robinson Insurance Co. for their invoice #99.

19   Remitted the sales tax collected in February by recording the following entry in the cash payments journal: First, debit Sales Tax Payable $680.75 (the amount is entered in the General Ledger column). Next, write Commission Revenue in the Account Dr. column and enter ($34.81) in the General Ledger column. Notice that this amount is entered in brackets to denote that it is a credit value in a debit column. Finally, enter the amount of the cheque,

$645.94, in the Bank column and assign an appropriate cheque number. To ensure that the Commission Revenue is posted correctly, you might wish to post it now. (Remember: $34.81 is a credit value, not a debit.)

20   Bought warehouse supplies, $150 plus $9.81 GST, from Schick Hardware. Issued a cheque.

28   Cash sales to date: paint and supplies, $1,200, and wallpaper, $1,500.

30   Paid office salaries, $1,800.

MONTH-END ACTIVITIES

(e)   Prove equal debits and credits in each journal. Total and rule the journals in ink. (*Note:* When totalling the cash payments journal, remember that the bracketed amount in the General Ledger column is a credit value; therefore, it must be subtracted from the other values in that column.)

(f)   Post all remaining transactions and appropriate totals.

(g)   Prepare a trial balance with schedules of accounts receivable and accounts payable.

7

Credit Notes and Cash Refunds

CHAPTER OBJECTIVES

After completing this chapter, you will be able to:

- record adjustments on sales and purchases for goods returned or damaged, including adjustments to GST and sales tax

- record discounts for early payment of account

IMPORTANT WORDS AND TERMS IN THIS CHAPTER

Cash Refunds
C.O.D. (Cash on Delivery)
Credit Note
Credit Terms
Purchase Discounts
Purchase Returns & Allowances
Sales Discounts
Sales Returns & Allowances

....

As a company sells merchandise to its customers, it will either receive immediate payment in cash (a cash sale) or record an account receivable to be collected in the near future (a credit sale). As discussed in Chapters 4 and 6, the balance in the Sales account represents the total of all goods sold—cash sales plus credit sales. However, other factors are taken into consideration when computing the actual amount of sales, such as (1) unsatisfactory goods that have been returned by customers (returns), and (2) price adjustments made for defective goods that the customer has decided to keep (allowances). These two factors reduce the amount of total revenue earned by the business.

SALES RETURNS & ALLOWANCES

Returns and allowances on goods sold can be handled in two ways: (1) if the anticipated number of returns and allowances is small, debit entries can be made directly to the Sales account; or (2) if a large number of returns and allowances are expected, such adjustments can be recorded to an account called **Sales Returns & Allowances** rather than to the Sales account. This method will show both the total sales and the total amount of returns and allowances in separate accounts. The percentage relationship between total returns and allowances and total sales will be of interest to the owner of the business because such a comparison may point out a level of customer dissatisfaction, which might result in a loss of customers, or an inferior quality of merchandise purchased for resale, possibly making it necessary to look for a new supplier.

Sales Returns & Allowances is an account used by the seller to record price adjustments allowed to customers on either cash sales or credit sales. Cash refunds would be given on sales made originally for cash, and credit notes would be issued for allowances made on credit sales. A **credit note** (Figure 7.1) is the source document used to initiate the journal entry to reduce the amount owing by the customer and to reduce the amount of the sale.

Figure 7.2 illustrates the general journal entries to record a cash sale and the refund (including the adjustment to taxes) given to the customer when damaged goods were returned. The customer paid cash for the goods at the time of the sale; therefore, the cash is refunded when the goods are returned or the price is adjusted. Depending on the method of adjustment used, either Sales or Sales Returns & Allowances will be debited when the refund is recorded. This refund will normally appear in the cash payments journal.

Figure 7.3 shows the general journal entry to record the sale of merchandise on account and the entry to record a credit note issued when the goods were returned. Because the customer had bought the goods on credit, he or she cannot expect to receive a cash refund when goods are returned. Instead, the seller will adjust the customer's account. Either Sales or Sales Returns & Allowances can be debited in the adjustment entry, depending on the method used. Entries for credit notes will normally appear in the general journal.

CREDIT NOTE

ROMANICK COMPANY LTD.

1122 Main Street North

Dauphin, Manitoba

TO	Leslie Rousseau	**DATE**	17 March 19—
	277–10th Avenue	**INVOICE #**	24
	Brandon, MB		
	R1W 2N6	**ACCOUNT #**	21162-301

Quantity	Size	Item		Price	
2 dozen	16mm	X3347T	Grapple Grommets	@ 16.40/doz	$32.80
7 each	10mm	L448SG	Filber Flanges	@ 11.00/ea	$77.00
20 boxes		R233E	Winkle Wing-Nuts	@ 46.50/box	$930.00
			Subtotal		$1039.80
			GST Reg. #123456789		72.79
			Sales Tax 7%		72.79
			Total		$4815.00

Figure 7.1   Credit Note

19— Sept.	2	Bank			5 7 0 00			
		Sales				5 0 0 00		
		GST Payable				3 5 00		
		Sales Tax Payable				3 5 00		
		Cash sales for the day.						
	6	Sales (or Sales Returns & Allowances)			3 0 00			
		GST Payable			2 10			
		Sales Tax Payable			2 10			
		Bank				3 4 20		
		Refund to cash customer; adjusted to taxes.						

Figure 7.2   Issuing a Refund on Cash Sales

19— Sept.	2	A/R Bell, Harvey			4 5 6 00			
		Sales				4 0 0 00		
		GST Payable				2 8 00		
		Sales Tax Payable				2 8 00		
		Sale on account; terms n/30.						
	6	Sales (or Sales Returns & Allowances)			3 5 00			
		GST Payable			2 45			
		Sales Tax Payable			2 45			
		A/R Bell, Harvey				3 9 90		
		Issued credit note for goods returned; taxes adjusted.						

Figure 7.3   Issuing a Credit Note on Credit Sales

Since the original credit entry to the Sales account would *increase* total revenues, a debit to Sales or Sales Returns & Allowances will *decrease* the total revenues. For example,

Total Sales	$15,450.00
less: Sales Returns & Allowances	850.00
Net Sales	$14,600.00

PURCHASE RETURNS & ALLOWANCES

A retailer that purchases merchandise for resale to its customers also could encounter shortages or damaged goods in the shipments it receives, or could request an allowance on the price. These adjustments will have the effect of decreasing the amount of Purchases. If these adjustments to Purchases do not occur frequently, they may be recorded by reversing the original transaction, as follows:

19— June		3	Purchases						1	0	7	00			
			GST–ITC							7	00				
			A/P LMN Company										1	1	4	00
			Bought merchandise on account.													
		6	A/P LMN Company						5	7	00				
			Purchases										5	3	50
			GST–ITC											3	50
			Received credit note for goods returned.													

Other companies will prefer to use the **Purchase Returns & Allowances** account rather than to credit the Purchases account directly (Figure 7.4). Using the Purchase Returns & Allowances account will show the total amount of goods that required adjustments. Returns can prove to be very expensive and time-consuming and should be kept to a minimum. Excessive returns might indicate an inefficiency of the purchasing department or the need to buy from a more dependable supplier.

The Purchases account is used only for merchandise purchased for resale; therefore, the Purchase Returns & Allowances account is used for adjustments allowed only on merchandise. When adjustments are made on items that are *not* for resale (assets or other expenses), the original account debited when the items were purchased must be credited when the adjustment is recorded. This applies to both cash purchases and credit purchases of nonmerchandise items (Figure 7.5).

SALES DISCOUNTS

Most businesses rely on the prompt collection of cash from customers in order to pay their own bills, including the purchase of more inventory for resale or the acquisition of additional assets. Therefore, they might offer special terms on credit sales to encourage their customers to pay promptly. Prompt collections reduce the risk of a customer's account balance becoming uncollectible; but, more importantly, the cash collected can be used for the purchase of additional merchandise and for meeting the ongoing cash requirements for paying bills.

Credit terms differ from one company to another and sometimes even within the same company. They may vary according to the type of customer, the volume of purchases made by the customer, and the ability of the customer to pay the account. A common term of credit is net 30 days (usually written as *n/30*), meaning that the full amount of the invoice is due in 30 days.

19— July	2	Purchases				8 0 2 50				
		GST–ITC				5 2 50				
		Bank						8 5 5 00		
		Bought mdse. from Canadian Wholesalers.								
	6	Bank				5 7 00				
		Purchase Returns & Allowances						5 3 50		
		GST–ITC						3 50		
		Received refund from Canadian Wholesalers for goods returned;								
		taxes adjusted.								
Aug.	2	Purchases				3 2 1 00				
		GST–ITC				2 1 00				
		A/P Red River Co.						3 4 2 00		
		Bought mdse. on terms n/30.								
	8	A/P Red River Co.				6 8 40				
		Purchase Returns & Allowances						6 4 20		
		GST–ITC						4 20		
		Received credit note for shortage on shipment from Red								
		River Co.; taxes adjusted.								

Figure 7.4 Refunds and Credit Notes on Merchandise

19— May	3	Office Supplies				4 2 80				
		GST–ITC				2 80				
		Bank						4 5 60		
		Bought stationery from R. Eatton Co.								
	9	Bank				1 1 40				
		Office Supplies						1 0 70		
		GST–ITC						70		
		Received a refund from R. Eatton Co. for supplies returned.								
	23	Office Equipment				3 2 1 00				
		GST–ITC				2 1 00				
		A/P Seele Office Store						3 4 2 00		
		Bought typewriter; terms n/60.								
	29	A/P Seele Office Store				8 5 50				
		Office Equipment						8 0 25		
		GST–ITC						5 25		
		Received credit note for overcharge on typewriter; adjusted taxes.								

Figure 7.5 Refunds and Credit Notes for Nonmerchandise Items

Other terms or combinations of terms will sometimes be offered, such as, 2/10,n/30; or 1/20,n/60; or 3/5,n/15. The term 2/10,n/30 means the customer may deduct 2% from the amount of the invoice (or, alternatively, of the pre-tax price of the goods) if the payment is made within 10 days of the invoice date; otherwise, the payment for the full amount of the invoice is due in 30 days. The 2% discount is referred to as a cash discount and is recorded in the cash receipts journal as a debit entry to the **Sales Discounts** account. Sales discounts *decrease* the sales revenue; therefore, like Sales Returns & Allowances, they are recorded as debit entries.

To illustrate the use of sales discounts, we will assume that on January 6, merchandise is sold to Jack Harper for $500 (plus taxes) with terms of 2/10,n/30 on invoice #16. The entry to record this sale is:

19— Jan.	6	A/R Harper, Jack			5 7 0 00		
		Sales				5 0 0 00
		GST Payable				3 5 00
		Sales Tax Payable				3 5 00
		Invoice # 16; terms 2/10, n/30.				

Let us further assume that on January 16, Mr. Harper is able to take advantage of the 2% discount and pay off his invoice. If the 2% discount is based on the full amount of the invoice, he will deduct $570 × 2% = $11.40 and will send a cheque for $570 − $11.40 = $558.60. If, on the other hand, the 2% discount is based on the selling price of the goods ($500), he will deduct $500 × 2% = $10, in which case he will send a cheque for $570 − $10 = $560. Whether the discount is based on the full value of the invoice or on the value of the goods (not including the taxes), the journal entry to record this receipt of cash is essentially the same. The following general journal entry assumes the discount was based on the full amount of the invoice:

19— Jan.	16	Bank			5 5 8 60		
		Sales Discounts			1 1 40	
		A/R Harper, Jack				5 7 0 00
		Received in full of Invoice #16				
		less 2% discount.				

The difference of $11.40 between the amount of the invoice ($570) and the amount actually received to settle the invoice in full ($558.60) is debited to Sales Discounts. An important point to remember is that the discount will always appear on the same side of the journal entry as Bank because it must account for the difference between the amount of the invoice being paid off and the amount actually received.

The receipt of cash would, of course, be recorded in the cash receipts journal, as illustrated in Figure 7.6. Notice that it is still a balanced entry—debits equal credits.

To show the effect of these entries on Jack Harper's account in the accounts receivable subsidiary ledger, Figure 7.7 shows the sale on January 6 and the

CASH RECEIPTS										PAGE	CR1
DATE	ACCOUNT CREDIT	MEMO	F.	ACCTS. REC. CR.	SALES DISC. DR.	SALES CR.	GST PAY. CR.	GENERAL LEDGER CR.	BANK DR.		
19— Jan. 16	A/R Harper, Jack	on acct. - 2%	126	5 7 0 00	1 1 40				5 5 8 60		

Figure 7.6   Recording Receipts in the Cash Receipts Journal

receipt of cash on January 16. Although only $558.60 was actually received from him, the full amount of the invoice ($570 recorded in the Accounts Receivable Cr. column) is posted to the subsidiary ledger in order to clear this invoice. The amount of the discount is not recorded in the customer's account unless the book-keeper sees a need for noting the discount in the Memo column.

ACCOUNT A/R Harper, Jack   ACCT. NO. 126

Oak Bluff, Manitoba   SHEET NO.   1

DATE		MEMO	DISC. DATE	F.	✓	DEBIT	✓	CREDITS	✓	DR. CR.	BALANCE
19— Jan.	6	#16 2/10, n/30	Jan. 16	SJ4		5 7 0 00				Dr.	5 7 0 00
	16	on acct. - 2%		CR2				5 7 0 00			Ø

Figure 7.7   Jack Harper's Account

You will notice too that in the Discount Date column a notation is made of the date on which the discount will expire on invoice #16. In this case, the discount expires 10 days after the date of the invoice, on January 16.

PURCHASE DISCOUNTS

The recording of purchase discounts is virtually the same as that of sales discounts. A cash discount taken when offered by one of the suppliers of merchandise is recorded as a **Purchase Discount**. Taking advantage of such special terms will reduce the cost of the merchandise.

Assume that $9,000 worth of merchandise was purchased on December 4 from A.C. Suppliers Ltd. on terms of 2/10,n/30. To take advantage of the 2% discount, the invoice must be paid within the 10-day discount period. Figure 7.8 shows both the purchase transaction and the payment of the invoice in general journal form. The 2% discount, in this case, is based on the value of the goods

19— Dec.	4	Purchases		9 0 0 0 00	
		GST–ITC		6 3 0 00	
		A/P A.C. Suppliers			9 6 3 0 00
		Bought mdse. on Invoice #15; terms 2/10, n/30.			
	6	A/P A.C. Suppliers		9 6 3 0 00	
		Purchase Discounts			1 8 0 00
		Bank			9 4 5 0 00
		Paid Invoice #15 less 2 % discount based on value of goods.			

Figure 7.8   Purchase and Payment with Discount

rather than on the total invoice value ($9,000 × 2% = $180). Notice that the credit to Purchase Discounts recognizes the difference between the amount of the original invoice ($9,630) and the amount of the payment ($9,450) made to settle the invoice. This payment entry, of course, would appear in the cash payments journal as illustrated in Figure 7.9.

		CASH PAYMENTS									PAGE CP1	
DATE	ACCOUNT DEBIT	MEMO	F.	ACCTS. PAY. DR.	PURCH. DISC. CR.	PURCH. DR.	GST–ITC DR.	GEN. LED. DR.	BANK CR.	CH. NO.
19— Dec. 4	A/P A.C. Suppliers Ltd.	on inv. #15 -2%		9630 00	180 00				9450 00	10

Figure 7.9   Discounts in the Cash Payments Journal

If, however, the above payment has *not* yet been made and A.C. Suppliers Ltd. has issued a credit note for $100 plus GST for an overcharge on the invoice, the sequence of entries would be as shown in Figure 7.10. When the discount is calculated on December 14, it is based on the current (net) value of the invoice ($8,900), not on the original value before the credit note was applied.

19— Dec.	4	Purchases			9 0 0 0 00				
		GST–ITC			6 3 0 00				
		A/P A.C. Suppliers				9 6 3 0 00			
		Invoice #15; terms 2/10, n/30.							
	7	A/P A.C. Suppliers			1 0 7 00				
		Purchase Returns & Allow. (or Purchases)				1 0 0 00			
		GST–ITC				7 00			
		Received credit note for overcharge on Invoice #15.							
	14	A/P A.C. Suppliers			9 5 2 3 00				
		Purchase Discounts				1 7 8 00			
		Bank				9 3 4 5 00			
		Paid Invoice #15 less credit note and 2% discount on							
		value of goods ($8900).							

Figure 7.10   Purchase, Return, and Payment with Discount

Purchase Discounts, like Purchase Returns & Allowances, will have the effect of *decreasing* the Purchases account. However, if discounts are taken on items other than merchandise, such as Office Equipment or Office Supplies, the original asset or expense account charged will be reduced directly. Figure 7.11 illustrates the purchase of computers on terms of 2/10,n/30 and the subsequent payment that takes advantage of the eligible discount. Notice that the discount is deducted directly from the asset, Office Equipment.

19— Jan.	13	► Office Equipment				3	4	7	7	50					
		GST–ITC				2	2	7	50						
		A/P BD Business Systems									3	7	0	5	00
		Bought two computers, invoice #55, $3250 plus taxes;													
		terms 2/10, n/30.													
	23	A/P BD Business Systems				3	7	0	5	00					
		► Office Equipment											6	5	00
		Bank									3	6	4	0	00
		Paid invoice #55 less 2 % discount on $3250.													

Figure 7.11　Discounts on Nonmerchandise Items

CASH ON DELIVERY (C.O.D.)

Goods shipped C.O.D. are treated as cash purchases, so the transaction is entered in the cash payments journal when the invoice and the goods are received. These goods will not be released by the delivery driver until the buyer has paid for them by writing a cheque. Shipments are usually sent C.O.D. to customers who are not known by the seller or to those who have an unacceptable credit rating. In short, C.O.D. transactions are *cash* transactions.

► ## PRACTICE EXERCISE 1

Complete this chart by filling in the blanks and totalling the columns where shown. Prove the totals. (Remember: The discount, if eligible, is calculated on the net invoice value; that is, on the value *after* the credit note is deducted.)

Date of Invoice	Amount of Invoice	Terms	Discount Date	Credit Notes	Date Cash Received	Discount Amount	Amount Received
Jan. 3	$428.97	2/10, n/30	_____		Jan. 12	_____	_____
Jan. 5	230.25	n/30	_____	$30.25	Jan. 31	_____	_____
Jan. 7	97.80	1/10, n/20	_____	7.80	Jan. 17	_____	_____
Jan. 9	137.75	3/20, n/30	_____		Jan. 30	_____	_____
Jan. 12	396.85	2/10, n/30	_____	9.25	Jan. 21	_____	_____
Jan. 15	186.95	2/15, n/30	_____		Jan. 31	_____	_____
Jan. 19	73.80	1/10, n/30	_____	8.00	Jan. 29	_____	_____
Jan. 23	265.85	2/5, n/15	_____		Jan. 28	_____	_____
Jan. 24	50.65	n/20	_____		Feb. 13	_____	_____
Jan. 29	150.00	2/10, n/30	_____	10.00	Feb. 8	_____	_____
Totals							

► ## PRACTICE EXERCISE 2

Record the following transactions in a general journal (GJ7), complete with appropriate explanations. Returns and allowances on purchases and sales of merchandise are to be recorded in the Purchase Returns & Allowances and Sales

Returns & Allowances accounts. Disregard GST and sales tax on both sale and purchase transactions.

19—

Jan. 3   Bought merchandise from Caldwell Co., $360; invoice #498, terms n/10.

4   Sold merchandise to J.D. North, $175; invoice #105, terms n/15.

4   Purchased a typewriter from Centre Equipment Co., $895; invoice #323, terms n/30.

5   J.D. North returned goods worth $25; a credit note was issued.

5   Invoice #323 received from Centre Equipment Co. shows an overcharge of $50; received a credit note today. (*Hint:* This is *not* an adjustment on merchandise; therefore, the overcharge must be charged against the account originally debited.)

6   Purchased merchandise from Stone Co., $165. Paid by cheque #74.

6   Merchandise worth $30 purchased from Caldwell Co. on invoice #498 was of poor quality; received a credit note.

7   Cash sales for the week, $767.25.

8   A customer who bought goods for cash returned $16 worth and was refunded the money.

10   Bought merchandise, $285, from Brill Mfg. Co. Paid by cheque #75.

11   Returned $15 worth of merchandise bought on January 10. Received a cash refund.

13   Issued a cheque to Caldwell Co. to cover invoice #498 of January 3, less the credit note.

14   Cash sales for the week, $635.60.

16   Sold merchandise to John Trent, $198; terms n/30, invoice #129.

17   Issued a credit note to John Trent for a shortage in shipment on invoice #129, $18.

19   Received a cheque from J.D. North to cover the sale dated January 4, less the credit note.

19   Sold an old typewriter to Mary Hestor for cash, $250.

▶ **PRACTICE EXERCISE 3**

Record the following transactions in the general journal, complete with detailed memos. Returns and allowances on sales and purchases of merchandise are to be charged directly back to the original Purchases and Sales accounts. Add 7% GST and 7% sales tax to all sales, both taxes based on the value of the goods as quoted here.

19—

Oct. 1 Sold merchandise to Jack Ryan, $465; invoice #10, terms n/20.

2 Purchased office supplies from Pico Stationery Co., $96.30 plus $6.30 GST; invoice #57, terms n/30.

2 Cash sales, $700.

3 Granted an allowance to Jack Ryan for minor defects discovered in the merchandise sold to him on October 1, $60 plus taxes.

4 Received a credit note from Pico Stationery Co. for office supplies returned on invoice #57, $10.70 plus $0.70 GST.

5 A cash customer reported a shortage on a sale of October 2. We have issued a refund for $12 plus taxes; cheque #82.

10 Purchased merchandise from Steele Co., $468.95 (includes $30.68 GST); invoice #81, terms n/10.

10 Cash sales, $675.

12 Bought a desk and chair for the office from Ward Equipment Co., $1,395.55 (includes $85.69 GST); invoice #94, terms n/10.

12 Received a credit note from Steele Co. for damaged goods received on their invoice #81, $16.95 (includes $1.11 GST).

15 Bought advertising material from Selkirk Printers, $62.15 (includes $3.82 GST); invoice #97, terms n/30.

20 Issued cheque #83 to Steele Co. for the amount due on invoice #81 less the credit note.

21 Received a cheque from Jack Ryan to cover the invoice of October 1 less the allowance of October 3.

22 Paid the amount due to Ward Equipment Co. on invoice #94; cheque #84.

25 Purchased merchandise, $824.90 (includes $53.97 GST), from Selzer Co. Paid by cheque #85.

26 Returned merchandise purchased on October 25 and received a refund, $22.60 (includes $1.48 GST).

31 Issued a cheque to cover the amount owing to Pico Stationery Co. on invoice #57 less credit note; cheque #86.

▶ **PRACTICE EXERCISE 4**

Prepare general journal entries on page GJ8 for the following transactions, paying special attention to credit notes and discounts on sales and purchases. Returns and allowances on purchases and sales of merchandise are to be recorded in the Purchase Returns & Allowances and Sales Returns & Allowances accounts. Add 7% GST and 10% sales tax to all sales and to all adjustments to sales. Sales tax will be based on the value of the goods *plus* GST. All eligible discounts are to be calculated on the balance of the unpaid invoice. (Use T-accounts, if necessary, for customers' and creditors' accounts to keep track of sales, purchases, and credit notes.)

19—

May   1   Bernard Lundy, the owner, has invested additional assets into his business: cash, $18,000; delivery equipment, $16,000; and office equipment, $11,000.

1   Purchased merchandise from Brown Wholesalers, $698.36 (includes $45.69 GST). Issued cheque #47.

2   Sold merchandise to J.B. Watt, $95.80; invoice #41, terms 2/10,n/30.

3   Received a cheque from Henry Bell on invoice #30, $136.80 less 2% discount.

3   Received a cash refund for damaged goods purchased on May 1, $18.36 (includes $1.20 GST).

4   Sent a credit note for $5.80 plus taxes to J.B. Watt for a shortage on the invoice dated May 2.

4   Cash sales, $423.89.

5   Bought office supplies from Chang Stationery, $72.84 plus $4.61 GST. Paid by cheque #48.

5   A cash customer, Frank Hoyle, returned $16 (plus taxes) worth of unwanted merchandise; refunded the cash.

6   Purchased merchandise from Post Co., $367.25 (includes $24.03 GST); invoice #844; terms 1/10,n/30.

6   Returned office supplies purchased on May 5, $11.77 (includes $0.70 GST). Received a cash refund.

8   Sold merchandise to B.A. Guest, $137.85; invoice #42, terms 2/5,n/20.

10   Bought a computer for the office, $1,088.73 (includes $64.75 GST), from Burton Equipment Co.; invoice #386, terms n/30.

11   Discovered an overcharge on the purchase of the above computer and received a credit note for $55.35 plus $3.50 GST.

12   Received a cheque from J.B. Watt for the invoice dated May 2. (Check for credit notes and eligible discounts.)

13   Purchased merchandise from Bravo Co., $592.30 (includes $38.75 GST); invoice #226, terms 2/10,n/30.

14   Cash sales, $737.15.

16   Issued a cheque to Post Co. for goods purchased on May 6.

16   The invoice of May 13 showed an overcharge of $19.15 plus $1.34 GST; applied for an adjustment and received a credit note.

18   Received a cheque from B.A. Guest for the invoice dated May 8.

18   Purchased merchandise from Sawyer Co., $410.20 (includes $26.84 GST); invoice #727, terms n/30.

20   Returned defective merchandise to Sawyer Co. and received a credit note, $15.20 (includes $0.99 GST).

22   Issued cheque #49 to Bravo Co. in payment of the invoice dated May 13.

24   Purchased wrapping supplies from Consumer Box Co., $193.73 plus $12.25 GST; invoice #369, terms n/10. (Shipping Supplies Prepaid)

25   Cash sales, $902.65.

27   Credit sales (invoices #43, #44, #45; terms 2/10,n/30): Joyce Dunn, $156.35; George Russell, $122.95; Kathy Mills, $73.80. Record this as a compound entry.

28   Issued cheque #50 for $41.20 (includes $2.45 GST) to the *Community News Journal* for advertising.

30   Paid manager's salary, $2,550; cheque #51 to T. Ong (GST not applicable).

▶ **PRACTICE EXERCISE 5**

Record general journal entries for the following transactions. All returns and allowances on purchases and sales of merchandise are to be charged directly back to the original Purchases and Sales accounts. Add 7% GST and 7% sales tax (based on the value of goods) to all sales and adjustments to sales. (Use T-accounts, if necessary, for customers' and creditors' accounts to keep track of sales, purchases, and credit notes.)

19—

Sept.   1   Sold $1,427 worth of merchandise to Reimer Packaging Co.; invoice #472, terms 2/10,n/30.

4   Reimer Packaging Co. has returned damaged goods sold to them on invoice #472. Credit note #042 has been issued for $215 plus taxes.

8   Bought merchandise from QSL Products, $2,775.90 (includes $181.60 GST); invoice #8060, terms 2/10,n/30.

9   Bought a computer system from Computer Solutions Ltd., $3,870.30 (includes $237.65 GST); invoice #A4073, terms n/30.

11   Received a partial payment from Reimer Packaging Co. on invoice #472, $500.

13   Over-the-counter cash sales, $24,729.

15   Asked QSL Products for a price adjustment because of poor-quality goods received on invoice #8060. They have sent a credit note for $456 (includes $29.83 GST).

16   Returned one of the computer terminals to Computer Solutions Ltd. (invoice #A4073). A credit note was received for $775.75 plus $50.75 GST.

18   Made payment to QSL Products for the balance owing on invoice #8060; cheque #211. The discount will be calculated on the balance of the unpaid invoice.

21   Gave cash refunds to customers who have returned damaged merchandise, $392 plus taxes.

26   Received the balance owing on invoice #472 from Reimer Packaging Co.

30   Paid the balance owing on account to Computer Solutions Ltd.; cheque #212.

► PRACTICE EXERCISE 6

(a) Set up a cash receipts journal (CR2) with the following headings: Date, Account Cr., Memo, Folio, Accounts Receivable Cr., Sales Discounts Dr., General Ledger Cr., Bank Dr.

(b) Set up a cash payments journal (CP2) with the following headings: Date, Account Dr., Memo, Folio, Accounts Payable Dr., Purchase Discounts Cr., General Ledger Dr., Bank Cr., Cheque Number.

(c) Record these transactions in the cash journals. Refunds on merchandise will be charged to Sales Returns & Allowances and Purchase Returns & Allowances. All payments will be made by cheque, beginning with #16.

19—

Nov.   4   Paid Mitchell Fabrics for invoice #367, $629.50 less 2% discount.

6   Paid Robinson Ltd. $419 for invoice #112, which had terms of n/30.

8   Received payment from Sellers & Shaw for sales invoice #665, $1,821 less 3% discount.

8   Gave a refund of $64.90 plus 7% GST to a customer who returned defective goods.

9   Received a cheque from William Wight to cover sales invoice #649, $355 less 3% discount.

12   Wrote a cheque for $318.01 to pay Walton Fixtures Ltd. for invoice #9029; have taken a discount of $6.49.

14   Received a refund for unwanted merchandise returned to the supplier, $52.50 plus $3.68 GST.

14   Received a money order for $325.50 from Cambridge Auto Sales for the balance owing on invoice #683.

17   A customer returned merchandise sold to him last week; refunded $71.40 plus 7% GST.

20   Issued a cheque to The Stationery Store for invoice #1012, $730.60. The invoice was dated November 2 and carried terms of 2/10,n/30.

24   Issued a cheque for $220.50 to pay Dahl Services for invoice #0039; have taken the 2% discount.

25   Received a $601.40 cheque from Peter Seung to settle invoice #694. He has already deducted the 3% discount.

30   Received a refund for the overcharge on an order of letterhead and envelopes for the office, $40 plus 7% GST.

(d)   Total and rule the journals as usual. Prove equal debits and credits.

THINK ABOUT IT!

1. Today you purchased merchandise on an invoice that carries terms of 2/10,n/30. Would you receive a cash refund if you return part of the order tomorrow? Why or why not?

2. If you had purchased merchandise for cash, would you receive a credit note if defective goods were returned? Why or why not?

3. Some businesses prefer to record returns and allowances in specific accounts set up for that purpose, such as Purchase Returns & Allowances and Sales Returns & Allowances. Why?

4. Why do some businesses record returns and allowances directly to the Sales or Purchases accounts?

5. When it is necessary to record the return of defective office supplies, which account is credited? Why?

6. What is the meaning of the term *2/20,n/60?* of the term *3/5,1/20,n/45?*

7. An invoice for $320 dated January 27 carries terms of 2/10,n/30. If the invoice is paid on February 6, can the discount still be taken? If so, how much?

8. In which of the five journals discussed so far would a C.O.D. purchase be recorded? a C.O.D. sale? Why?

▶ APRIL TRANSACTIONS: KBC DECORATING CO.

The three painters hired for the painting and decorating service have started work on Job #1. The client has agreed to a price of $19,000 to be paid upon the completion of the project on April 30. Because this job is in a high-risk category, the Workers Compensation Board has been contacted by phone to arrange for coverage for the three employees. The rate in this category for a new company is $7.68 per $100 of salary. The premium for the remaining nine months of this year will be $4,974.64. KBC Decorating must remit half of the amount ($2,488.32) upon receipt of the Workers Compensation billing in approximately two weeks' time. The balance is to be paid by the end of August. Premiums for Workers Compensation coverage are GST exempt.

The transactions for April will be recorded in the same manner as those in March. This month, however, the purchase journal will not be required because adequate inventories of paint, wallpaper, and related supplies are on hand. The general journal will be required.

Chapter 7 has dealt with the use of the Sales Returns & Allowances account for adjustments on sales of merchandise and the Purchase Returns & Allowances account for adjustments on purchases of merchandise. Because KBC Decorating Co. uses three sales accounts and two purchases accounts, any adjustments to sales and purchases of merchandise will be charged directly back to the original sales and purchases accounts. For example, if a customer returns defective wallpaper, a debit entry will be recorded to Sales—Wallpaper rather than to Sales Returns & Allowances. This same procedure will apply to any adjustments to purchases.

Record the following transactions in the appropriate journals:

19—

April 1   Paid rent for April, $2,500 plus $175 GST. Paid Reynolds Paper $1,605 on their invoice #92.

4   Paid the hydro bill for March, $190 plus $12.43 GST. Paid the March heating bill, $450 plus $29.44 GST.

8   Paid the phone bill for March, $200 plus $13.08 GST. Paid the City of Winnipeg water bill for January, February, and March, $180. (Water bills are GST exempt.)

9   Cash sales to date: paint and supplies, $3,000; wallpaper, $2,500.

10   Gave a refund of $43.32 to C. Kell for the return of one can of paint (wrong colour) purchased April 9. This entry will be made in the cash payments journal: debit Sales—Paint & Supplies $38, debit GST Payable $2.66, and debit Sales Tax Payable $2.66. A cheque was issued for $43.32.

12   Received payment on March sales invoices from Beavis & Sons, Jay-Mar Co., and Dayson & Son.

12   Filed the quarterly GST Tax Return, which covers January, February, and March. Since the amount of GST paid on purchases (the balance in the GST-ITC account) is greater than the amount collected from customers (the balance in the GST Payable account), KBC Decorating will receive a refund for the difference. The following entry is to be recorded in the general journal: debit GST Payable $2,423.75 and credit GST-ITC for the same amount. When posted, this entry will clear the GST Payable account to zero and will leave a balance of $1,696.84 (the amount of the refund) in the GST-ITC account. This balance will be cleared from the GST-ITC account when the refund cheque is received from Revenue Canada.

15   Credit sales on terms of 2/10,n/30 were made to the following customers: Edna Morton, paint and supplies, $1,500, and wallpaper, $1,800. S. Wilkinson, paint and supplies, $1,200, and wallpaper, $1,400. K. Young Painting, paint and supplies, $700, and wallpaper, $900. S. Miller, paint and supplies, $850, and wallpaper, $750.

16   Received a statement from the Workers Compensation Board for $4,976.64 covering the period April 1 to December 31. Issued a cheque for $2,488.32 (half the premium now due). Debit Workers Compensation Expense. The balance is payable by August 31.

18   Gave a credit note to Edna Morton for the return of one roll of damaged wallpaper: $20 for the wallpaper, $1.40 for GST, and $1.40 for sales tax. The total of the credit note is $22.80. (This

entry is recorded in the general journal. Be sure to post the amount of the credit note to the Accounts Payable Control account as well as to Edna Morton's account.)

19   Paid the Provincial Treasurer of Manitoba for the sales tax collected in March. Refer to the entry recorded in the cash payments journal on March 19 and record a similar entry as follows: Sales Tax Payable $903, Commission Revenue $37.03, Bank $865.97.

22   Took a certified cheque for $107 to the post office for postage added to the postage meter machine. This amount includes $7 GST. Charge Postage Expense.

23   Received a credit note from Reynolds Paper Co. on their invoice #92 for defective wallpaper. The value of the wallpaper is $15 and the adjustment to GST-ITC is $1.05; the credit note total is $16.05.

24   Received payments on account from S. Wilkinson, K. Young Painting, and S. Miller for sales made to them on April 15. They have each earned a 2% discount for early payment. In the cash receipts journal, write each of their names in the Account Cr. column. Next, write the full amount of each invoice in the Accounts Receivable Cr. column. (The amounts of the invoices can be found in their ledger accounts. For example, the invoice value being paid by Wilkinson is $2,964.) Now, calculate the 2% discount on the value of the goods only, not including taxes. Enter this amount in the Sales Discounts column. (The amount of the goods sold to Wilkinson before the taxes were added was $2,600; therefore, 2% of $2,600 is $52.) Finally, enter the amount received from the customer in the Bank column. Wilkinson sent a cheque for $2,964 − $52 = $2,912. (*Note:* To determine the value of the sale *before* taxes, you may look at the sale as it was recorded in the sales journal; however, always be sure to consult the customer's ledger account first to see if any partial payments or credit notes apply to the invoice being settled.)

28   Paid Rainbow Supplies for the amount owing on invoice #45. Paid Coleman Industries for invoice #52.

30   Cash sales to date: paint and supplies, $2,600, and wallpaper, $2,700. Bought office supplies, $120 plus $7.85 GST; C.O.D.

30   Paid office salaries, $1,800, and service salaries, $7,200. Only one cheque will be issued for $9,000. The bank will issue separate cheques to the employees through their payroll service.

30   The cheque from Gluting Properties for the completion of Job #1 has not yet arrived. Their clerk mailed the cheque rather than sending it by courier. No entry will be recorded until the cheque arrives.

MONTH-END ACTIVITIES

(a)   Total and rule the journals in ink. Prove equal debits and credits in all journals.

(b)   Post to the ledger accounts as usual, including all appropriate totals.

(c)   Prepare a trial balance, complete with schedules of accounts receivable and accounts payable.

8

Freight and Petty Cash

CHAPTER OBJECTIVES

After completing this chapter, you will be able to:

- record transactions for freight charges on merchandise and nonmerchandise items

- record the establishment, maintenance, and reimbursement of the petty cash fund using both the general journal and the cash payments journal

IMPORTANT WORDS AND TERMS IN THIS CHAPTER

Cash Over or Short
Delivery Expense
Duty & Brokerage
Freight In
Petty Cash
Reimbursing Petty Cash
Transportation Charges

FREIGHT IN

When goods are purchased for resale, the supplier may or may not cover the cost of delivering the goods. If not, the buyer will pay these shipping costs, whether directly to the supplier or to an independent courier/shipper.

Freight In (or Transportation In) is the account on the buyer's books in which the cost of transporting the incoming merchandise is recorded. Transportation costs contribute to the total cost of goods purchased for resale and, along with all other costs, are taken into consideration when setting the selling prices of goods and services.

The Freight In account is used to record such transportation costs on *merchandise* only. Using this separate account allows management to track the necessary information for controlling costs and making decisions, such as whether to order in small quantities or in carloads, or which mode of transportation would be more economical.

Here is the journal entry to record the payment of freight costs on merchandise. The amount charged to Freight In includes any provincial sales tax charged by the shipper. Any GST added to the freight bill is charged to GST-ITC.

19— May	16	Freight in						3 8 52				
		GST–ITC						2 52				
		Bank								4 1 04		
		Paid freight bill on an order of merchandise:										
		Freight 36.00										
		7% GST 2.52										
		7% PST 2.52										
		Total 41.04										

If freight charges have been included by the supplier on the purchase invoice, the following journal entry would be recorded to show the portion of the invoice that represents the actual goods and the portion that represents the freight:

19— May	16	Purchases						5 4 0 00				
		Freight In						1 7 12				
		GST–ITC						3 8 92				
		Bank								5 9 6 04		
		Bought merchandise on terms C.O.D. plus freight charges:										
		Merchandise 540.00										
		Freight 16.00										
		7% GST × 556.00 38.92										
		7% PST × 16.00 1.12										
		Total 596.04										

Transportation costs on *incoming* shipments of merchandise to the retailer should not be confused with the costs incurred by the retailer for transporting merchandise to its own customers. Transportation charges on deliveries of merchandise to customers are debited to **Delivery Expense**. Whether the retailer uses its own delivery truck or hires the services of a courier, the Delivery Expense account is charged.

19—											
May	20	Delivery Expense			2	5	15				
		GST–ITC				1	65				
		Bank							2	6	80
		Paid Zippy Courier for delivery of order to customer:									
		Courier charge 23.50									
		7% GST 1.65									
		7% PST 1.65									
		Total 26.80									

DUTY & BROKERAGE

Until recently, many goods imported into Canada have been subject to import duties and tariffs imposed by the federal government. Although such tariffs are gradually being eliminated in North America as a result of the Canada/U.S. Free Trade Agreement and the North American Free Trade Agreement, other tariffs exist on goods imported from other countries around the world.

When imported goods are subject to import duties and related federal taxes, whether the goods are imported from the United States or any other country, these additional costs are debited to an account called **Duty & Brokerage**. The word "brokerage" refers to the fees that are incurred for the services of a customs broker who will handle the importation of foreign goods. The appropriate amount of GST applicable on the value of imported goods and the GST on the broker's fee are also paid to the broker who will then forward the tax to the government on the purchaser's behalf. As discussed previously, the GST is debited to the GST-ITC account as an input tax credit against the GST collectible from customers when the goods are sold.

19—											
May	22	Duty & Brokerage			8	1	00				
		GST–ITC			4	3	47				
		Bank							1	2	4	47
		Paid brokerage fees on imported goods, plus									
		GST on fees (7% of $81) and GST on									
		imported goods (7% of $540).									

Figure 8.1 illustrates a statement showing how the freight and duty and brokerage costs contribute to the total cost of goods purchased for resale.

As mentioned already, Freight In is the cost of transporting incoming merchandise and is part of the total cost of goods purchased. If, however, freight or other express charges are paid on items that are *not* for resale, these charges should not be included in the Freight In account. Instead, they are charged directly to the asset or expense account that was debited when the item was originally purchased. For example, if transportation charges are paid on an order of office supplies, the account debited is Office Supplies Prepaid. Or, if shipping is paid on the delivery of advertising brochures, the account debited is Advertising Expense.

Cost of Goods Purchased for Resale:								
Purchases						11 2 5 1 30	
Add: Freight In	6 8 1 50					
Duty & Brokerage	4 2 4 60		1 1 0 6 10	
Total Cost of Goods						12 3 5 7 40	

Figure 8.1   Total Cost of Merchandise for Resale

To illustrate further, assume that $35 was paid to ABC Trucking Co. for the delivery of a second-hand word processor recently purchased for use in the office. The cost of the word processor is $900. The shipping charges will be added directly to the cost of the equipment as shown here:

19— May	25	Office Equipment		9 0 0 00	
		Bank			9 0 0 00
		Bought word processor.			
	25	Office Equipment		3 5 00	
		Bank			3 5 00
		Paid for delivery costs on word processor.			

Although both entries are dated May 25, it is necessary to issue two separate cheques since two different companies are involved; therefore, two separate entries are required.

► PRACTICE EXERCISE 1

Prepare general journal entries on page GJ9 for the following transactions related to purchases, transportation and delivery charges, and duty and brokerage. Include suitable memos for each entry. Add 7% GST and 8% sales tax to all sales (both taxes based on the selling prices quoted). GST is included in the purchase prices quoted and is shown in parentheses. All payments are made by cheque, beginning with #73.

19—

Sept.   1   Bought merchandise from Bright Co., $625.30 ($40.91 GST); invoice #292, terms n/30.

2   Sold merchandise to John Cabot, $240.10; invoice #66, terms n/30.

2   Paid transportation charges to Apex Carriers on goods received from Bright Co., $13.50 ($0.82 GST); cheque #73.

3   Issued a cheque for $9.78 ($0.60 GST) to Fast Courier Service for delivering merchandise to John Cabot.

4   Purchased store fixtures from J. Sparling Ltd., $1,380 ($84 GST). Paid by cheque.

4   Paid ABC Truckers $32.20 ($1.96 GST) for delivering the store fixtures to the store.

6   Purchased merchandise, $960, from Fielding Co. of Fargo, North Dakota, U.S.A. The import broker has billed an additional $221.28, which includes the applicable GST ($77.28) on the imported merchandise and on their brokerage fee. Also, special freight and handling charges were paid, $102.72 ($6.25 GST). Since separate cheques are issued, record these as separate entries. (All amounts here are expressed in Canadian funds. Most imported goods are subject to GST.)

8   Purchased merchandise worth $189.75 ($12.41 GST) from Burton Co.; terms C.O.D.

9   Bought office supplies from Royal Stationery, $110.40 ($6.72 GST); invoice #B273, terms n/30.

9   Paid freight charges to Apex Carriers on goods purchased on Sept. 8, $14.38 ($0.88 GST).

11   The office supplies purchased from Royal Stationery were delivered today by Fast Courier Service. Paid shipping charges of $13.80 ($0.84 GST).

13   Purchased a computer for the office, $1,025 from the Better Computer Co. of Grand Forks, North Dakota, U.S.A. Also paid brokerage fees, $236.26 (includes $82.51 GST on the computer and on the broker's fee); and freight charges to RK Transport, $145.52 ($8.86 GST). (*Note:* The Duty & Brokerage account is used to record import duties and brokerage fees on merchandise only.) All amounts here are quoted in Canadian funds. Issue separate cheques for these items.

17   Purchased a delivery truck from Grand Auto Sales of Oshawa, Ontario. Issued a cheque for $17,250 ($1,050 GST).

17   Paid transportation charges to CP Rail on the truck, $341.55 ($20.79 GST). These charges are to be added to the cost of the truck.

18   Paid service bill at Gerry's Garage for the truck, $56.75 ($3.45 GST).

20   Bought advertising material from Prairie Printers, $74.75 ($4.55 GST). Issued a cheque.

21   Paid courier charges to Fast Courier Service on the advertising material, $6.10 ($0.37 GST).

27   Received invoice #3691 for $43.73 ($2.66 GST) from Speedy

Cartage Co. covering transportation costs for merchandise delivered from a supplier, Casey Bros.; terms net 10 days.

28   Sold merchandise to Thomas Kaatz, $647, on invoice #67, terms net 30 days.

29   Issued a cheque for $32.20 ($1.96 GST) to Speedy Cartage Co. for delivering the goods sold to Thomas Kaatz yesterday.

▶ **PRACTICE EXERCISE 2**

Prepare general journal entries for the following transactions related to freight and duty/brokerage charges. Provide suitable detailed explanations (memos) for each transaction. All payments are made by cheque, beginning with #101.

19—

Jan.   3   Bought merchandise on account from Kelsey Equipment Company of Dallas, Texas, $7,230 (Canadian funds); invoice #421, terms n/30.

5   Paid cheque #101 for duty and brokerage charges on the goods imported from Texas, $1,666.52 (includes $582.02 GST on imported merchandise and on related broker's fees).

6   Paid Acme Transport for transporting the merchandise from Texas, $372 (includes $8.56 GST for the Canadian portion of the paid distance).

12   Bought a computer system from Quality Computer Solutions Ltd. of Boston, Mass., $8,200 (Canadian funds); invoice #83647, terms n/45.

17   Paid brokerage charges on the computer system imported from Quality Computer Solutions, $1,670.75 (includes $660.01 GST on computer and brokerage fee).

20   Paid Lowell Delivery Service for the local shipping charges for the computer system, $39 (includes $2.37 GST).

What would the balance be in the Equipment account, assuming a zero opening balance, if the above entries had been posted? Why?

PETTY CASH

The importance of enforcing proper control over cash transactions requires that all money received be deposited in the bank daily and that all payments be made by cheque. However, every business will have expenditures of such small amounts that it would be inconvenient and impractical to issue cheques for such trivial amounts. These expenditures might include purchases of small quantities of office supplies or payments to the courier driver for express charges. Such small cash payments, often for amounts under $20 or $25, can best be made from a petty cash fund.

ESTABLISHING THE FUND

The amount of the **petty cash fund** (often $50 or $100) is determined by management based on its experience and its anticipated needs. The amount established must be considered sufficient to provide petty cash disbursements for a reasonable period, such as two weeks or one month. A cheque is issued and charged to a general ledger account called Petty Cash. This account will remain open indefinitely with a debit balance equal to the total amount of the fund. A change in the base fund will occur only if the amount of the existing fund is considered insufficient to cover the anticipated expenditures for the specified period. The fund will be increased to an appropriate amount (or decreased if the fund is excessive).

The petty cashier, the employee who controls the petty cash fund, cashes the cheque and places the money in a drawer or till for safekeeping. He or she ensures that the fund is used only for the purpose for which it was intended; therefore, only the petty cashier has access to the money. When payments are made from the fund, the petty cashier fills out a **petty cash voucher** (Figure 8.2) for each expenditure. This voucher contains information as to the amount of the expenditure, the date of the payment, the name of the person to whom the cash was paid, the purpose of the expenditure, the account to be debited, and all necessary signatures (the person who received the cash and the person who approved the payment of the expenditure).

No. 1   **Amount $** _____

PETTY CASH VOUCHER

                                                             Date: _____

Paid to _____

For _____

Charge to _____

KBC DECORATING CO.

Approved by _____

Received by _____

Figure 8.2   Petty Cash Voucher

The signed vouchers for the petty cash expenditures are placed in the petty cash drawer to represent the amount that has been paid out. The total of the vouchers plus the balance of the cash in the drawer should equal the original amount of the fund. When the fund is nearly exhausted, a summary of the expenditures is prepared and given to the accountant who issues a cheque for the total of the expenditures in order to reimburse (replenish) the fund. (See Figure 8.3.)

Just as for the special journals discussed so far, the petty cash sheet or book contains multiple columns to suit the needs of that particular business. These special columns are set up to simplify the recording of frequently recurring expenditures.

The expenditures will be posted to the ledger accounts using one of the following methods:

Method 1. The petty cash sheet or book is used as a journal. In this method, the total of each column is posted to the debit of the appropriate expense account in the general ledger. Expenses for items that cannot be allocated to the special columns are entered in the "Other Accounts" column and require individual postings to the ledger accounts. The Bank account is credited for the total amount of the reimbursement in the cash payments journal when the reimbursing cheque is issued.

Method 2. The petty cash sheet or book is used as a summary sheet from which the expenditures are transferred to the cash payments journal and a cheque is issued to reimburse the fund for the total petty cash expenditures. The amounts are then posted from the cash payments journal to the debit of the expense accounts. Method 2 will be used throughout this textbook.

PETTY CASH SHEET   PAGE

Amount in Petty Cash Fund Account _____   **DISTRIBUTION OF PAYMENTS**

19— DATE	EXPLANATION	VO. #	AMOUNT PD. OUT	GST– ITC	OFFICE SUPP.	POSTAGE EXP.	WHSE. SUPP.	MISC. EXP.	OTHER ACCTS.	AMOUNT
	Total paid out		$							
	Cash on hand		$							
			$							
	Reimbursement cheque required		$			Cheque # _____				

Figure 8.3   Petty Cash Summary Sheet

To illustrate how petty cash works, we have established a petty cash fund on October 1 for $75. The opening entry in general journal format follows, while Figure 8.6 shows the same entry in the cash payments journal.

19— Oct.	1	Petty Cash Fund			7 5 00	
		Bank				7 5 00
		Issued cheque to establish petty cash fund.				

The following petty cash transactions were recorded during the month of October. Notice in Figure 8.4 that the recording of petty cash transactions is similar to the recording of transactions in the purchase journal. The amount of GST (if any) included in the cost is recorded in the GST-ITC column and the balance of the amount is allocated to one of the special columns or to the Other Accounts column.

Oct.	2	Bought a stamp pad for office use	$ 3.75
	4	Paid for window cleaning	16.05
	8	Paid express on incoming merchandise	5.62
	11	Bought paper and twine for shipping room	7.76
	16	Paid express on advertising material	4.49
	19	Bought merchandise to fill a special order	8.03
	24	Paid express on shipping supplies	7.44
	29	Bought cups for the soft-drink machine	2.68
	30	Bought a printer ribbon	7.22

The voucher number of each expenditure is clearly recorded and all money columns are totalled and balanced to ensure accuracy of the petty cash sheet.

PETTY CASH SHEET

PAGE 1

Amount in Petty Cash Fund Account __75.00__

DISTRIBUTION OF PAYMENTS

19— DATE	EXPLANATION	VO. #	AMOUNT PD. OUT	GST-ITC	OFFICE SUPPL.	POSTAGE EXP.	WHSE. SUPPL.	MISC. EXP.	OTHER ACCTS.	AMOUNT
Oct 2	stamp pad	1	3 75	25	3 50					
4	window cleaning	2	16 05	1 05				15 00		
8	express charges	3	5 62	37					Freight in	5 25
11	paper and twine	4	7 76	51			7 25			
16	express on advertising	5	4 49	29					Advertising	4 20
19	special order	6	8 03	53					Purchases	7 50
24	express	7	7 44	49			6 95			
29	cups	8	2 68	18				2 50		
30	printer ribbon	9	7 22	47		6 75				
	Total paid out		$ 63 04	4 14	10 25		14 20	17 50		16 95
	Cash on hand		$ 11 96							
			$ 75 00							
	Reimbursement cheque required		$ 63 04	Cheque # __101__						

Figure 8.4   Petty Cash Sheet

REIMBURSING THE FUND

When most or all of the petty cash money has been spent, it must be replenished so that similar expenditures can be made in the future. Reimbursement of the fund can be made at any time, though most often at the end of the month in order to recognize the expenditures as expenses incurred during the month just ended. In a small business, however, such a need to charge the expenses to the month in which they were incurred is not of significance; the fund, then, will be reimbursed, only whenever the need arises.

Figure 8.5 illustrates the reimbursement entry as it would appear in the general journal. Each column total is debited to its respective expense account and the total amount spent is credited to Bank (or Cash) to represent the cheque issued to replace the money spent. However, because this transaction involves the issuance of a cheque, the entry will normally be recorded in the cash payments journal, as illustrated in Figure 8.6.

When the reimbursement is recorded in the cash payments journal, the petty cash expenses are distributed to the appropriate columns, taking advantage of special columns, if available. Since the Purchases and GST-ITC can be accommodated by the special columns available, they need not be named in the Account Dr. column. The amount of the reimbursing cheque is entered in the Bank Cr. column on the same line as the last petty cash entry, thus completing a balanced journal entry.

19— Oct.	31	GST–ITC				4 14		
		Office Supplies Prepaid			1 0 25			
		Warehouse Supplies Prepaid			1 4 20			
		Miscellaneous Expense			1 7 50			
		Freight In			5 25			
		Advertising Expense			4 20			
		Purchases			7 50			
		Bank					6 3 04	
		Cheque #101 to reimburse petty cash.						

Figure 8.5   Reimbursing Petty Cash (General Journal)

CASH PAYMENTS   PAGE ___CP3

DATE		ACCOUNT DEBIT	MEMO	F.	ACCTS. PAY. DR.	PURCH. DISC. CR.	PURCH. DR.	GST-ITC DR.	GEN. LED. DR.	BANK CR.	CH. NO.
19— Oct.	1	Petty Cash	to establish						7 5 00	7 5 00	60
	31	Office Supplies Prepaid					7 50	4 14	1 0 25		
		Warehouse Supplies Prepaid							1 4 20		
		Miscellaneous Expense	to reimburse						1 7 50		
		Freight In	Petty Cash						5 25		
		Advertising Expense							4 20	6 3 04	101

Figure 8.6   Reimbursing Petty Cash (Cash Payments Journal)

CASH OVER OR SHORT

When goods or services are sold for cash, the cash register or cash drawer is started with a fund (called a float) from which to make change. At the end of the day, the cash in the drawer, minus the float, should equal the total cash received as shown on the cash register tape. Figure 8.7 shows the calculation at the end of the work day. If the amount of cash differs from the reading on the cash register tape, this difference is recorded in an account called **Cash Over or Short**.

Cash overages are recorded as *credit* entries to the Cash Over or Short account while shortages are recorded as *debit* entries. Figure 8.8 shows how both shortages and overages are recorded in the cash receipts journal. These entries ensure that the amount recorded as the day's receipts of cash does, in fact, match the amount actually deposited. A shortage reduces the amount being deposited, so it must be deducted from the sales figure by showing the amount in parentheses in the General Ledger column. The use of parentheses is the means of recording amounts to be deducted, necessary to determine the amount of the day's entry to the Bank column. Figure 8.9 shows the entries in the cash receipts journal posted to the Cash Short or Over account.

If the cash shortages are greater than the cash overages at the end of the operating year, the Cash Over or Short account will have a debit balance and will be treated as an expense. But if the cash overages are greater than the cash shortages, the Cash Over or Short account will have a credit balance and will be treated as revenue.

Example 1: Cash Shortage

Total cash in cash drawer (end of day)	5	2	0	00
Deduct Float		2	5	00
Net cash sales for the day	4	9	5	00
Reading on cash register tape	5	0	0	00
Cash Shortage			5	00

Example 2: Cash Overage

Total cash in cash drawer (end of day)	5	3	5	00
Deduct Float		2	5	00
Net cash sales for the day	5	1	0	00
Reading on cash register tape	5	0	0	00
Cash Overage			1	0	00

Figure 8.7 Calculating Cash Shortage & Cash Overage

CASH RECEIPTS

PAGE CR1

DATE		ACCOUNT CREDIT	MEMO	F.	ACCTS. REC. CR.	SALES DISC. DR.	CASH SALES CR.	GENERAL LEDGER CR.	BANK DR.
19— Feb.	16	Sales	daily sales				5 0 0 00		
	16	Cash Over or Short	cash overage	575				1 0 00	5 1 0 00
	23	Sales	daily sales				5 0 0 00		
	23	Cash Over or Short	cash shortage	575				(5 00)	4 9 5 00

Figure 8.8 Cash Shortages and Overages (Cash Receipts Journal)

ACCOUNT	Cash Over or Short										ACCT. NO.	575

SHEET NO. ____1____

DATE		MEMO	DISC. DATE	F.	✓	DEBIT	✓	CREDITS	✓	DR. CR.	BALANCE
19— Feb.	25	shortage		CR1		5 00				Dr.	5 00
	27	overage		CR1				1 0 00		Cr.	5 00

Figure 8.9   Cash Over or Short Account

▶ PRACTICE EXERCISE 3

Holloway Bros. has a petty cash fund of $125. The following items were paid from this fund during the month of August.

(a) Enter these payments on a petty cash sheet, beginning with voucher #44. The amount of GST included in the price, if any, is shown in parentheses.

19—

Aug.   6   Broom for the warehouse, $12.57 ($0.82).

8   Coffee and creamer, $6.25.

9   Delivery of special order of office supplies, $7.49 ($0.49).

12   Typewriter ribbon for the office, $7.06 ($0.46).

14   Special order of merchandise, $11.13 ($0.73).

15   Delivery of special sale brochures, $23.01 ($1.51).

16   Masking tape for the warehouse, $5.89 ($0.39).

20   Donation to the Special Olympics, $10.

22   Marking pens for the office, $6.96 ($0.46).

24   Postage due, $4.69 ($0.31).

(b) Total the petty cash sheet and prove equal debits and credits. Calculate the cash on hand.

(c) Prepare a general journal (GJ22) entry to reimburse the fund at month end. Cheque #101 was issued.

(d) Prepare a cash payments journal (CP12) entry to reimburse the fund at month end. Cheque #101 was issued.

▶ PRACTICE EXERCISE 4

Record the following transactions on a petty cash sheet. All petty cash vouchers will be numbered sequentially, beginning with #1. Add 7% GST to all amounts, unless otherwise stated. There is no provincial sales tax.

19—

Nov.   1   Cheque #101 has been issued for $135 to establish the fund.

1   Purchased stationery for the office, $5.95.

3   Paid $2 for the delivery of the above stationery.

4   Paid $10 for a special order of merchandise.

4   Paid $1.50 for the delivery of the above special order of merchandise by courier.

5   Bought sugar and cream for the staff kitchen, $4.50 (GST exempt).

6   Paid $6.45 for minor repairs to the office typewriter. (Debit Repair Expense)

6   Paid ABC Courier for delivering merchandise to a customer, $3.15.

7   Bought wrapping paper and twine for the warehouse, $7.65.

10   Paid for the printing of advertising leaflets, $18.25.

12   Bought stamps to mail the advertising leaflets, $4.30.

17   Paid $7.65 for the delivery of incoming merchandise.

21   Contributed $10 to the Heart & Stroke Foundation (GST not applicable).

25   Bought postage stamps for the office, $21.50. (Subtotal the Petty Cash Sheet and cross-check the subtotals for equal debits and credits. Carry the subtotals to the top line of the next Petty Cash Sheet.)

27   Bought cleaning supplies, $10.30.

28   Paid express charges for the delivery of a new office chair, $5.

30   Paid freight charges on incoming merchandise, $6.40.

(a)   Total all columns and prove equal debits and credits.

(b)   Prepare a general journal entry for the establishment of the fund on November 1 and a compound entry for the reimbursement of the fund on November 30. Use cheque #149.

▶ PRACTICE EXERCISE 5

(a)   Set up a petty cash sheet for the month of June. The balance in the fund on May 31 was $33.38. Cheque #61 was issued on May 31 to reimburse the fund for $66.62. All vouchers are numbered in sequence beginning with #41.

(b)   Enter these transactions on the petty cash sheet. Assume that all amounts *include* 7% GST. To calculate the value before GST, divide the amount by 1.07. Assume there is no provincial sales tax.

19—

June   1   Paid express charges for delivery of the company's new typewriter, $8.83.

2   Paid freight charges on incoming merchandise, $7.81.

6   Bought stationery and supplies for the office, $5.55.

8   Paid Speedy Courier for delivering merchandise to a customer, Hank Bell, $8.

12   Bought stamps for the office, $9.63.

14   Purchased coffee cups for the staff room, $2.09.

17   Purchased packaging and tape for the warehouse, $9.65.

17   Paid express charges on the delivery of the packaging and tape, $1.85.

21   Bought straws for the soft-drink machine, $1.67.

23   Bought stamps for mailing advertising material, $7.46.

26   Purchased merchandise to fill a special order, $10.53.

29   Gave a donation to the Cancer Society, $10 (GST not applicable).

(c)   Total the columns and prove equal debits and credits.

(d)   Prepare the general journal entry on page GJ19 to reimburse the petty cash fund. The reimbursing cheque is #97 dated June 30.

PRACTICE EXERCISE 6

(a)   Select a petty cash sheet from the working papers and cross out these column headings: GST-ITC, Office Supplies, Postage, Warehouse Supplies, and Miscellaneous Expense. Then read through the following petty cash transactions to determine which accounts are charged frequently. Enter *only two* new column headings to accommodate these frequent expenses. All other charges will be recorded in the Other Accounts column.

(b)   Enter the opening transaction for petty cash in the general journal (CJ22), and record the rest of the transactions on your newly designed petty cash sheet. (Disregard GST in this exercise.)

19—

Oct.   1   The amount to establish the fund is $200. Issued cheque #287.

1   Coffee, cream, and sugar for the staff room, $17.41.

3   Pens and pencils for the office, $8.90.

3   To Speedy Courier for transporting merchandise to us from ABC Suppliers Ltd., $6.95.

4   Contribution to the Heart Fund, $20.

6   Tape and labels for the office, $16.47.

8   Stamps for general mailings, $8.40.

9   To Speedy Courier for freight on merchandise from Dexter Industries, $12.29.

13   Delivery of promotional brochures, $9.60.

14   Straws for soft drink machine, $3.20.

15   Special order of letterhead and envelopes, $26.30.

19   Stamps for mailing promotional brochures to customers, $12.45.

23   Printer ribbons for the office computer, $8.92.

24   Delivery of merchandise to a customer, $11.19. (Subtotal the Petty Cash Sheet and cross-check the subtotals for equal debits and credits. Carry the subtotals to the top line of the next Petty Cash Sheet.)

25   Delivery of merchandise from a supplier, $17.50.

28   Paper for the fax machine, $6.25.

(c)   Prepare a general journal entry on October 31 to reimburse the petty cash fund. Use cheque #309.

THINK ABOUT IT!

1.   For what purpose is the Freight In account used?
2.   Name the account used to record the cost of delivering merchandise to customers.
3.   When is the Duty & Brokerage account used?
4.   When would freight charges *not* be debited to the Freight In account?
5.   If the total of the cash in the cash register does not agree with the total recorded on the cash register tape, how is the difference recorded on the books?
6.   Discuss the advantage of using a petty cash fund.
7.   What entry would be recorded to *increase* the amount in the petty cash fund? to *decrease* the fund?
8.   When reimbursing the petty cash fund, which accounts are debited? Why? Which account is credited? Why?

▶ MAY TRANSACTIONS: KBC DECORATING CO.

The contract work for Gluting Properties (Job #1) was completed yesterday, April 30, and the painters are now working on Job #2 (painting and decorating the offices of the Canada Building). This job must be completed by June 15. The contract is worth $30,000, with half the amount payable on May 22 and the balance on June 15.

Record the following transactions as usual:

19—

May   1   Paid the rent, $2,500 plus $175 GST. Received payment for Job #1 from Gluting Properties, $19,000 plus GST. (Credit Sales—Service.) Received payment of $3,739.20 from Edna Morton for the balance due on invoice #8. (She is not eligible for the discount.) Received a cheque for $1,696.84 from Revenue Canada for the refund claimed on the GST return filed for the first quarter. (Credit GST-ITC.)

2   Received invoice #110 dated May 1 from Reynolds Paper Co. for wallpaper, $3,000 plus 7% GST; terms 2/10,n/30.

3   Paid the phone bill for April, $225 plus $14.72 GST. Paid the bill from Intercity Gas, $350 plus $22.90 GST.

4   Received invoice #63 dated May 3 from Coleman Industries, terms 2/10,n/30, for paint and supplies, $1,800, and wallpaper, $1,700, plus $245.00 GST. Received from Rainbow Supplies invoice #60 dated May 3 for paint and supplies, $1,200, and wallpaper, $1,400, plus $182 GST; terms 2/10,n/30.

7   Received invoice #1224 dated May 4 from Minnesota Decor & Supply of Minneapolis, Minnesota, for a special order of wallpaper, $800 (Canadian funds). Terms n/30.

   Border Brokers Ltd. cleared the shipment at the port of entry, paying any fees such as GST on KBC's behalf. They have billed KBC for their services. The bill from them is for $96.66, payable on receipt, for the following: brokerage fees, $38, and GST, $58.66 (7% of $838).

   For these transactions, record the usual entry in the purchase journal for the invoice from Minnesota Decor. (Do not record the GST in the purchase journal.) Next, in the cash payments journal, record the cheque issued to Border Brokers Ltd. for their fees and the GST (debit Duty & Brokerage $38, debit GST-ITC $58.66, and credit Bank $96.66).

   Finally, record the cheque issued to Consolidated Freight for $47.94 (includes $2.94 GST) for the transportation charges on this shipment. (Debit Freight In.)

8   Paid the hydro bill, $180 plus $11.78 GST. Bought warehouse supplies, $300 plus $19.63 GST; terms C.O.D. (Debit Warehouse Supplies Prepaid.)

9   Cash sales to date: paint and supplies, $2,850, and wallpaper, $2,150.

11 Issued a cheque to Reynolds Paper for invoice #110 less the eligible 2% discount. First, the discount is calculated on the value of the goods, not including the taxes; therefore, $3,000 × 2% = $60 discount. In the cash payments journal, enter the discount ($60) in the Purchase Discounts column. Next, enter the balance of Reynolds Paper's account ($3,193.95) in the Accounts Payable column. We must enter this balance rather than the amount of the invoice because we are taking into consideration the previous debit balance of $16.05 that created this lower balance. By posting only $3,193.95, we will clear the account to zero.

12 Paid Coleman Industries for invoice #63 and Rainbow Supplies for invoice #60. Calculate the discount based on the pre-tax value of the goods.

19 Paid the April sales tax. Look back to the entry recorded in the cash payments journal in March. The total tax collected in April was $1,388.94 and commission is $41.89.

22   Received from Gluting Properties $15,000 plus 7% GST as the first instalment on Job #2.

24   Credit sales on terms of 2/10,n/30 to the following customers: Dayson & Son, paint and supplies, $1,100, and wallpaper, $900. Beavis & Sons, paint and supplies, $800, and wallpaper, $700. Jay-Mar Co., paint and supplies, $1,150, and wallpaper, $850. S. Wilkinson, paint and supplies, $800, and wallpaper, $500.

27   Bought additional insurance on stock from Robinson Insurance, $500. Received their invoice #120 dated May 25, terms n/30.

28   Paid the business tax for the current year, $850 (GST not applicable). (Debit Business Tax Expense.)

29   Cash sales to date: paint and supplies, $3,200, and wallpaper, $2,800.

31   Paid office salaries, $1,800, and service salaries, $7,200. (Only one cheque is issued for the total.) Established a petty cash fund for $50. The cheque is made payable to yourself as the cashier. (Debit Petty Cash Fund.)

MONTH-END ACTIVITIES

(a)   Balance all journals by proving equal debits and credits. Total and rule the journals.

(b)   Post all remaining transactions and totals as required.

(c)   Prepare a complete trial balance, including schedules of accounts receivable and accounts payable.

Bank Reconciliation

CHAPTER OBJECTIVES

After completing this chapter, you will be able to:

- reconcile the Bank account in the general ledger with the bank statement

- prepare a bank reconciliation statement and resulting journal entries

IMPORTANT WORDS AND TERMS IN THIS CHAPTER

Bank Errors	Debit Memo
Bank Charges	Interest Expense
Bank Reconciliation	NSF (Non-Sufficient
Bank Statement	Funds)
Cancelled Cheques	Outstanding Cheques
Certified Cheque	Outstanding Deposit
Credit Memo	

When a business deposits all cash receipts daily and makes all payments by cheque, a permanent double record is maintained of all cash transactions. One record is maintained by the bank (by means of the bank statement) and the other record is kept by the company (in the cash journals). In theory, it is logical to expect that the balances of these two independent records should be equal. However, in reality, the cash balance shown on the company's records is seldom equal to the balance reported by the bank on the bank statement. At the end of the month, the bookkeeper will reconcile the bank account in an effort to determine the reasons for this difference and to bring the two sets of records into agreement.

Cancelled cheques are issued cheques that have been cleared by the bank and charged back to the issuing company's bank account. The cancelled cheques are returned to the client, sorted in the order that they appear on the bank statement. In addition to the cancelled cheques, the bank will include notices of other charges (such as loan or mortgage payments) and credits (such as interest deposits) that had not been mailed to the client before the end of the month.

Outstanding cheques are cheques that have been issued, and entered in the cash payments journal, but have not yet been cashed by the companies to which they were issued and have not been cleared through the company's bank account. These outstanding cheques have reduced the cash book balance because the entries are recorded in the cash journal, but they have not yet reduced the balance in the bank account.

Outstanding deposits are cash and cheques received on the last day of the month and recorded in the cash receipts journal, but deposited too late to be included on that same month's bank statement. These deposits have increased the cash book balance but have not yet increased the balance in the bank account.

Certified cheques are guaranteed by the bank to the effect that the issuer of the cheque has sufficient funds in the account to cover the cheque when presented for payment. Because the bank will immediately withdraw the amount of the certified cheque from the issuing company's account at the time the cheque is certified, a certified cheque cannot be outstanding.

NSF (Non-Sufficient Funds) cheques are those cheques issued for an amount greater than the balance in the chequing account. All cheques received in the normal course of daily business are recorded in the cash receipts journal and are included as usual in the daily deposit. Occasionally, the bank will "bounce" (or dishonour) a customer's cheque because the customer did not have sufficient funds in the account to cover the cheque. This dishonoured cheque is then returned by the customer's bank to the business's bank and the amount is deducted from the business's account (debit memo). The business must then charge the amount back to the customer by debiting Accounts Receivable and crediting Bank in the cash payments journal. Because the cheque was originally deposited to the Bank account through an entry in the cash receipts journal, it must be taken out of the Bank account by means of an entry in the cash payments journal, even though a cheque has not been issued. Instead of a cheque number, "DM" is written in the Cheque Number column to indicate that this payment was the result of a debit memo.

Figure 9.1 shows this transaction as it would appear if recorded in the general journal and as it would appear in the cash payments journal. It is important to note that the debit entry to Accounts Receivable is recorded in the General Ledger Dr. column, not in the Accounts Payable Dr. column. The amount must then be posted to both the Accounts Receivable Control account in the general ledger and the customer's account in the accounts receivable subsidiary ledger. This double-posting ensures the equality between the control account and the subsidiary ledger.

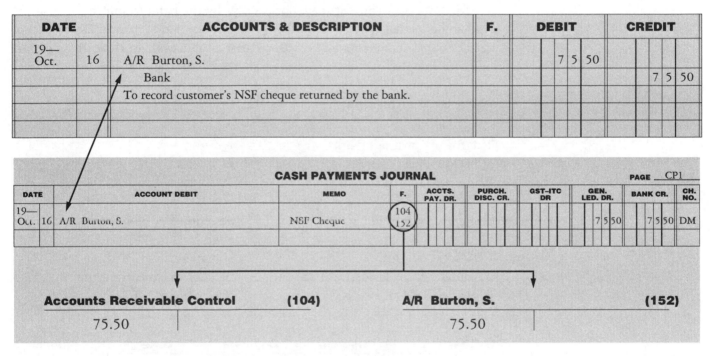

Figure 9.1   Recording an NSF Cheque

BANK STATEMENT

At the end of each month, the company will receive from the bank a statement of the banking transactions that occurred during the month (see Figure 9.2), accompanied by the company's cancelled cheques. The statement shows the balance in the account at the beginning of the month, the deposits made, the cheques paid, any other charges and credits (indicated by debit memos and credit memos), and the balance at the end of the month.

Credit memos (or credit slips) are notices sent by the bank during the month to inform the company of transactions that have *increased* the balance in the bank account. They are the source documents for recording these transactions in the cash receipts journal. (For illustration purposes, the credit memo transactions are shown here in general journal form.) Such transactions might include interest earned on investments or a recently negotiated bank loan deposited by the bank to the business's account.

19— June	30	Bank				1	6	0	00					
		Interest Revenue									1	6	0	00
		Credit memo for interest earned and deposited.												
	30	Bank												
		Bank Loan Payable				5	0	0	0	00				
		Credit memo for bank loan deposited to business account.									5	0	0	0	00

If such transactions should take place near the end of the month, the credit memos will be mailed along with the bank statement. Those credit memos received after the end of the month will require an adjustment on the bank reconciliation with all other discrepancies (discussed later in this chapter).

Debit memos (or debit slips) are notices sent by the bank to inform the company of amounts that have *decreased* the balance of the bank account. Debit memos are the source documents for recording these transactions in the cash payments journal. Examples include bank service charges, NSF cheques, and loan or mortgage payments. Debit memos received after the end of the month will also require an adjustment in the bank reconciliation.

The Royal Canadian Bank
3000 Pembina Highway
Winnipeg, MB R2G 1W1

Statement of Account with:

KBC Decorating Co.
79 Buffalo Place Industrial Park
Winnipeg, MB R3C 7K9

Account No. 654-789-7
Page 1
Statement date: 30 June 19—
Balance forward from previous statement: $8,292.96

Cheques	Cheques	Deposits	Date	Balance
950.00		1,309.04	June 1	8,652.00
		541.08	2	9,193.08
1,800.00	140.00	1,057.04	3	
140.00			3	8,170.12
50.00	86.20	2,898.81	8	10,932.73
506.00 D/M	70.00		9	10,356.73
50.00	275.00	438.38	10	10,470.11
23.00		1,737.53	15	12,184.64
		864.24	17	13,048.88
		2,255.54	25	15,304.42
452.75		775.64	26	15,627.31
578.08 D/M			30	15,049.23

Figure 9.2 Bank Statement

19—										
June	30	Bank Charges				1 5 00				
		Bank							1 5 00
		Debit memo for monthly service charges.							
	30	A/R Customer				5 6 00				
		Bank							5 6 00
		Debit memo for customer's cheque returned NSF.							

Bank charges (or service charges) are the amounts deducted by the bank each month to cover the expense of maintaining the bank account. The amount of the service charges will vary depending on the bank, on the balance in the account, and on the number of transactions processed. Bank accounts with large balances are sometimes free from bank service charges. The debit memos for the bank charges and for other charges not represented by cheques will be sent to the depositor along with the bank statement and the cancelled cheques at the end of the month. These might include charges for printing cheques, rental fees for safety deposit boxes, and interest charged on a mortgage or bank loan.

BANK ERRORS

The most common errors made by the bank are those that result from charging a cheque to the wrong bank account, or recording an incorrect amount in the company's account. A cheque charged to the business's account in error would reduce the bank balance, so it should be added back to the bank statement balance when preparing the bank reconciliation. A deposit made to the business's account in error will increase the bank balance, so it should be deducted from the bank statement balance when preparing the bank reconciliation. Once aware of the error, the bank will make the necessary correction. An advice notice is usually sent by the bank to the company when the account has been adjusted. Bank errors have no effect on the company's journals; therefore, the adjustment will be shown only on the bank reconciliation statement.

CASH BOOK ERRORS

Although bank errors now occur infrequently because of computerized banking, writing errors within a company's own records are common enough to warrant special attention. For example, the amount written on a cheque might be correct, but an error can be made when recording the cheque in the cash payments journal. Such errors are usually transposed figures ($89 recorded as $98) or misplaced decimal points, called slides ($132 recorded as $1.32). These errors would be revealed when the cancelled cheques returned with the bank statement are checked against the entries recorded in the cash payments journal.

▌ Example 1.

Cheque #67 was issued to Gordon Bros. for $89 as full settlement of the account; however, the payment was recorded incorrectly on page 6 of the cash payments journal as $98. Since $9 more than necessary was deducted from the Bank account on the business's books, a correcting entry is required to add the $9 difference back into the Bank account:

19— June	30	Bank		9	00		
		A/P Gordon Bros.				9	00
		To correct error in CP6 (cheque #67) for $89 recorded as $98.					

▌ Example 2.

Cheque #76 for $132 issued to A. Dudeck & Co. on account was incorrectly recorded as only $1.32 on page 7 of the cash payments journal. Since the entry in the cash payments journal is not enough to fully cover the actual amount of the cheque issued, an additional $132–$1.32 or $130.68 must be deducted. The correcting entry is:

19— June	30	A/P A. Dudeck & Co.		1	3	0	68				
		Bank							1	3	0	68
		To correct error in CP7 (cheque #76).									

RECONCILING THE BANK ACCOUNT

Often, transactions will appear on the company books but have not yet been recorded by the bank. These usually include outstanding cheques (cheques that have been issued but have not yet been cashed) and outstanding deposits (usually night deposits that are not processed by the bank until the next day). Other transactions may appear on the bank statement that have not yet been recorded in the company's cash books. These will include usual bank service charges, customers' NSF cheques that have been returned, other bank charges and credits (debit memos and credit memos), and other reconciling items (errors corrected by the bank and errors made on the company's records).

Bank reconciliation is the process of accounting for the discrepancies between the cash book records and the bank statement, and to determine the correct bank balance. The following steps are performed to accomplish this:

1. Compare the cancelled cheques, debit memos, and credit memos with the items recorded on the bank statement. Place check marks beside the items that agree. An unchecked item on the bank statement would indicate a likely bank error, such as someone else's cheque charged to the business's account by mistake. Such errors would have reduced the bank balance; therefore, when doing the bank reconciliation, we will add these amounts back to the bank statement balance.

2. Compare the deposits listed on the bank statement with the deposits recorded in the cash receipts journal. Place a check mark beside each item that agrees. Unchecked items in the cash receipts journal are usually outstanding deposits. "OS" (outstanding) should be written beside each unchecked item. Since the bank was not aware of the outstanding deposits at the time the statement was printed, we will add them to the bank statement balance. An amount in the deposit column on the bank statement that does not have a corresponding amount in the cash receipts journal

would likely indicate a bank error, usually a cheque credited to the business's account by mistake; therefore, we will have to deduct this erroneous deposit from the bank statement balance.

3. Arrange the cancelled cheques in numerical order and compare them with the entries recorded in the cash payments journal, placing check marks beside items that agree. Unchecked items in the cash payments journal are outstanding cheques. "OS" should be written beside each unchecked item. Since these cheques had not yet cleared the bank by the time the statement was printed, they will be deducted from the bank statement balance.

4. Deduct from the cash book balance (the balance in the Bank account in the general ledger) any debit memos issued by the bank for items not recorded in the cash payments journal, such as NSF cheques and bank charges.

5. Add to the cash book balance any credit memos issued by the bank that have not yet been recorded in the cash receipts journal.

6. Prepare a bank reconciliation statement (discussed below).

7. Prepare the necessary journal entries for the items that appear on the bank statement but have not yet been recorded in the cash books.

Reconciling items, then, are of two kinds:

1. Adjustments for items recorded on the bank statement unknown to the depositor, such as NSF cheques, bank charges, and interest charges on a bank loan or mortgage. These items require an adjustment in the business's books.

2. Adjustments for items recorded in the cash books that are unknown to the bank, such as outstanding cheques and outstanding deposits. These items do not require an adjustment since they are already recorded in the business's books.

BANK RECONCILIATION STATEMENT

To illustrate the bank reconciliation procedure, we will assume that the October bank statement received by Parkdale Company shows a balance of $5,338.40. The Bank account in the general ledger, however, shows a balance of $4,968.80. The purpose of the bank reconciliation is to point out why there is a difference of $369.60 between the two balances and to identify the items that caused that difference. Here is a list of the reconciling items. As each item is explained, locate it on the bank reconciliation statement in Figure 9.3.

1. A deposit of $301.90 was made through the night depository on October 31. The bank, therefore, did not receive it on time for the October 31 bank statement. If this deposit had been made on time, the amount would have been added to the statement balance by the bank; therefore, it must be added to the statement balance in the reconciliation statement.

2. A credit memo issued by the bank on October 30 for $65 is listed in the deposit column on the bank statement. This credit memo represents interest earned on investments. Since this item has not yet been recorded on Parkdale's books, it must be added to the cash book balance on the reconciliation statement.

Parkdale Company
Bank Reconciliation Statement
October 31, 19—

Bank Statement Balance						5	3	3 8	40
Add: Bank Error		6	4	20					
Outstanding Deposits	3	0	1	90			3 6	6	10
						5	7	0 4	50
Deduct: Outstanding Cheques									
#602	1	1	8	50					
#684	1	1	0	00					
#692	3	1	4	45					
#696	2	1	5	00			7 5	7	95
						4	9	4 6	55
Adjusted Balance									
Cash Book (General Ledger) Balance						4	9	6 8	80
Add: Interest Revenue								6 5	00
						5	0	3 3	80
Deduct: Bank Charges		1	5	00					
Error on Cheque #680		2	7	00					
NSF Cheque (L.D. Peters)		4	5	25				8 7	25
Adjusted Balance						4	9	4 6	55

Figure 9.3 Bank Reconciliation Statement (Adjusted Balance Method)

3. Several cheques issued in September and October have not yet cleared through the bank and are considered outstanding:

Date	Cheque #	Amount
Sept. 10	602	$118.50
Oct. 19	684	110.00
Oct. 29	692	314.45
Oct. 30	696	215.00

When these cheques eventually clear the account, they will reduce the statement balance; therefore, they must be deducted from the statement balance in the reconciliation statement.

4. No entry has been made in the books for an NSF cheque (originally received from L.D. Peters and deposited) that was returned by Peters's bank on October 30, $45.25. Since the bank has already deducted the amount of this bad cheque from Parkdale's account, the amount will have to be deducted from the Bank account in the general ledger. Therefore, it is shown as a deduction from the cash book balance in the reconciliation statement.

5. Cheque #680, issued October 18 for $96 to pay the telephone bill, was recorded on the cheque stub and in the cash payments journal as only $69. The cheque was cleared by the bank and was included in the cancelled cheques on October 31. Because an additional $27 must be deducted from the Bank account in the general ledger in order to fully cover this cheque,

it is shown as a deduction from the cash book balance in the reconciliation statement.

6.   A debit memo issued by the bank on October 31 for the usual monthly service charge of $15 was included with the cancelled cheques on October 31. This amount has not yet been recorded on the books, so it is shown as a deduction from the cash book balance.

7.   Cheque #364 for $64.20 issued to Greene Bros. was listed among the cheques on the bank statement and was included with the cancelled cheques. This cheque, however, was not issued by Parkdale Company. Because the bank cleared someone else's cheque through Parkdale's account, they will correct their error by redepositing the amount; therefore, Parkdale will show this as an addition to the bank statement balance on the reconciliation.

The bank reconciliation statement illustrated in Figure 9.3 shows that an adjusted balance of $4,946.55 would have been the amount available in the account if all reconciling items had been cleared or recorded by the close of business on October 31.

To bring Parkdale Company's records up to date, journal entries affecting the Bank account are necessary to make up the difference between the present balance in the Bank account ($4,968.80) and the adjusted balance of $4,946.55.

As you can see, every reconciling transaction is recorded either as a debit to the Bank account or as a credit to the Bank account. To save time in recording and posting these transactions, it is easier to combine the four preceding entries into one compound journal entry. The net effect on the Bank account (the difference between all debit entries to the Bank account and all credit entries to the Bank account) is a credit entry of $22.25.

19—Oct.	31	Bank				6 5 00			
		Interest Revenue						6 5 00	
		To record interest deposited by the bank.							
	31	A/R Peters, L.D.				4 5 25			
		Bank						4 5 25	
		To record NSF cheque returned by the bank.							
	31	Bank Charges				1 5 00			
		Bank						1 5 00	
		To record service charges deducted by the bank.							
	31								
		Telephone Expense				2 7 00			
		Bank						2 7 00	
		To correct error in CP7 for cheque #680 entered							
		as $69 instead of $96 ($96 − $69=$27).							

19— Oct.	31	A/R Peters, L.D.			4 5 25		
		Bank Charges			1 5 00		
		Telephone Expense			2 7 00		
		Bank				2 2 25	
		Interest Revenue				6 5 00	
		To record items from bank reconciliation that have not yet					
		been recorded.					

▶ **PRACTICE EXERCISE 1**

From the information that follows, prepare a Bank Reconciliation Statement for Lennox & Morton Consulting showing the adjusted bank balance (see Figure 9.3) for June 30, 19—.

The bank statement dated June 30 shows a balance of $10,462.85. The Bank account in the general ledger, on the other hand, shows a balance of $9,897.30. Cheques that have been issued but do not appear on the bank statement are: #56, $166.50; #61, $175.40; #74, $236.25; #75, $348.75. On June 30, a late deposit of $361.35 was made but does not appear on the bank statement.

▶ **PRACTICE EXERCISE 2**

On April 30, the Bank account in the general ledger of Warren Company showed a balance of $8,596.50. On May 31, the total of the Bank Dr. column of the cash receipts journal was $15,766.90 and the total of the Bank Cr. column of the cash payments journal was $11,947.60.

(a)   Calculate the balance that would appear in the Bank account in the general ledger on May 31.

The May 31 bank statement showed a balance of $12,532.85. The outstanding cheques were determined to be #701 for $402.50, #723 for $89.60, #729 for $127.85 and #730 for $118.35. A late deposit of $621.25 did not appear on the bank statement.

(b)   Prepare a bank reconciliation statement for Warren Company showing the adjusted bank balance on May 31, 19—. (Refer to Figure 9.3 if necessary.)

▶ **PRACTICE EXERCISE 3**

The following information concerns the banking activities of Gen Gaber & Associates on March 31, 19—.

The balance on the March bank statement received today is $5,900. The balance in the Bank account in the general ledger is $7,750. The cash receipts journal showed that a deposit of $1,500 was outstanding. The cash payments journal showed that these cheques had not yet cleared the bank: #77 for $75; #81 for $125; #82 for $100; and #84 for $50.

A debit memo was enclosed with the bank statement showing that a pre-authorized bank loan payment of $500 plus interest of $200 had been deducted from Gaber's account. These entries have not yet been recorded on the books.

Prepare a bank reconciliation statement for March 31, 19—, and a compound general journal entry to record those items not yet recorded on Gaber's books.

► PRACTICE EXERCISE 4

The Bank account in the general ledger of A & P Distributors Ltd. shows a balance of $5,224.50 on February 28, 19—. The balance on the bank statement of the same date is $4,992.25. The following information has been determined:

1. These cheques recorded in the cash payments journal have not yet been cleared by the bank on February 28: #221, $123; #223, $150.60; #227, $226.75; #229 (certified on February 26), $102.85; #230, $73.65; and #231, $90.

2. On February 28, cheques from customers were received and were deposited through the night depository, $830.40.

3. A credit memo for $93 received from the bank for interest earned on Canada Savings Bonds has been credited to A&P Distributors' account; it has not been recorded in the cash receipts journal as of February 28.

4. Cheque #218 issued for the purchase of office supplies, $63, was incorrectly entered in the cash payments journal as $36.

5. A cheque for $67.85, received from Paul Ward, a customer, and included in the February 25 deposit, was returned today by the bank marked NSF.

6. A $17 debit memo was included with the bank statement to cover service charges. It has not yet been recorded in the cash payments journal.

7. Cheque #890 for $47 was included in the bundle of cancelled cheques returned with the bank statement. This cheque belongs to another company but the bank has charged it to A&P Distributors' account by mistake.

From the above information, prepare a bank reconciliation statement for February 28 and a compound general journal entry for those items not yet recorded on the books.

► PRACTICE EXERCISE 5

The following information pertains to the banking activities of the D & N Appliance Co.:

1. The Bank account in the general ledger shows a balance of $5,232.65 on November 30, 19—.

2. The November bank statement shows a balance of $4,907.20.

3. Cheques received from customers on November 30 came too late to be deposited on that date. The total of these cheques is $535.75.

4. Cheque #155 issued for $34.75 had been recorded incorrectly in the cash payments journal as $43.75. This cheque was issued to pay the freight on incoming merchandise.

5. A cross-check of the cash payments journal entries and the cancelled cheques reveals that these cheques in November are still outstanding: #140, $182.50; #161, $47.80; #170, $200.25; #172, $95.25. Also, cheque #178 for $580, which was certified two weeks ago, has not yet been returned by the bank.

6. Among the cancelled cheques returned by the bank is cheque #501 for $210 issued by N & D Appliance Repair Co. but charged in error to the account of D & N Appliance Co.

7. A debit memo for $25 included with the November bank statement represents a charge for the safety deposit box rental.

8. The bank statement shows a service charge of $19.50 identified by a debit memo received with the bank statement.

9. A cheque received from a customer, Jack Miller, for $70 was returned by the bank marked NSF and charged back to D & N Appliance Co.'s account on November 29.

From the above information, prepare a bank reconciliation statement showing the adjusted balance. Also, prepare a compound general journal entry to record those items from the reconciliation that have not yet been recorded on the books.

▶ **PRACTICE EXERCISE 6**

In the books of Bill's Refrigeration Co., the cash transactions for the month of June were as follows:

1. On June 1, the Bank account in the general ledger showed a balance of $12,951.71.

2. On June 30, the Bank Dr. column in the cash receipts journal showed a total of $45,142.25.

3. On June 30, the Bank Cr. column in the cash payments journal showed a total of $36,470.85.

4. Cash received on June 30 was deposited in the night depository after regular banking hours, $4,567.10; therefore, it was not recorded by the bank on the June statement.

5. The June bank statement showed a balance on June 30 of $19,115.59.

6. Included with the June statement was a debit memo from the bank for services charges, $20.65.

7. A comparison of the paid cheques (returned by the bank) with the entries in the cash payments journal reveals that cheque #121 issued for $153 on June 25 as payment of a utility bill had been entered in the journal as $135.

8. An examination of the cancelled cheques returned by the bank reveals that four cheques issued in June have not yet been paid by the bank: #131, $861.24; #134, $625.50; #139, $311.80; #145, $139.69.

9. Included with the June bank statement was a $200 cheque marked NSF.

This cheque was originally received from our customer, Victor Abbot, and deposited on June 26.

10. A credit memo included with the June statement indicates that $360 in interest earned on a term deposit was credited to the company's account on June 30.

From the above information:

(a) Prepare a bank reconciliation on June 30.

(b) Prepare a compound general journal entry for the reconciling items not yet recorded in the cash books.

▶ ## PRACTICE EXERCISE 7

The information necessary for the preparation of the bank reconciliation statement for Blackwell Co. is listed below:

1. The Bank balance in the general ledger on March 31 is $18,260.77.

2. The bank statement balance on March 31 is $19,305.29.

3. Accompanying the bank statement on March 31 are:

   (i) B. Sather's cheque for $181, which was returned by the bank marked NSF.

   (ii) A debit memo for the safety deposit box rental, $45.

   (iii) A debit memo for bank service charges, $30.31.

   (iv) A credit memo for interest earned on a short-term investment, $235.

4. Cash received on March 31 was not deposited until April 1, $1,958.47.

5. Cheques outstanding on March 31 were as follows: #182 for $1,811.05; #186 for $1,303; and #187 for $16.25.

6. A cheque for $250 was charged to Blackwell Co.'s account in error. (It was drawn on the Blackdale Corp.'s account.)

7. A cheque for $160 received on account from Jack Martin was recorded in the cash receipts journal as $16 by mistake.

From this information:

(a) Prepare a bank reconciliation statement.

(b) Prepare a compound general journal entry to record all items not yet recorded in the cash books.

▶ ## PRACTICE EXERCISE 8

The following information is provided from the financial records of the Joshua Charles Corporation on March 31, 19—:

1. The Bank balance in the general ledger shows $192, but the balance on the bank statement dated March 31 is $631.85.

2. A comparison of the cash journals with the bank statement shows that these cheques have not yet cleared the bank: #461, $391.40; #479,

$523.25; #480 certified for $883.78; and #488, $322.10.

3. Cheque #454 for $132.79 to pay a utility bill was entered in the cash payments journal as $123.79 by mistake.

4. Cheques totalling $230.50 received from customers late on the 31st were deposited through the night depository and, therefore, were too late to appear on the March statement.

5. The following items appear on the bank statement, but not on the books:

(i) a cheque returned marked NSF, $48.90, given on account by Dillon Cordell and deposited on April 14;

(ii) a loan payment, $269.35, and interest on the loan, $120.35;

(iii) regular monthly bank service charges, $18.50.

6. A cheque written on someone else's account was charged to the business account in error, $100.30. The bank has been notified of their error. They have promised to correct this error in time for the next statement.

From this information:

(a) Prepare a bank reconciliation statement on March 31, 19—.

(b) Prepare a compound general journal entry to record those items not yet recorded on the books.

▶ **PRACTICE EXERCISE 9**

(a) Prepare a bank reconciliation statement on August 31 from the information taken from the books of KRA Enterprises. To assist you with this task, the following documents have been provided: the bank reconciliation statement prepared last month (Figure 9.4a), the cash receipts and cash payments journals for August (Figures 9.4b and 9.4c), and the bank statement dated August 31 (Figure 9.4d).

Follow these steps carefully:

1. Compare the outstanding deposit and cheques listed on last month's reconciliation statement with the deposits and cheques listed on the August bank statement. If these items appear on the bank statement, place a check mark beside each of these amounts on the bank statement since they are no longer outstanding.

2. Check the August deposits in cash receipts journal against the deposits listed on the bank statement. Write "O/S" beside any deposits in the journal that do not appear on the bank statement. These are the outstanding deposits to be shown on this month's bank reconciliation.

3. Check the August cheques and debit memos in the cash payments journal against the cheques listed on the bank statement. Write "O/S" beside any payments in the journal that do not have corresponding amounts on the statement. These are the outstanding cheques to be shown on this month's bank reconciliation.

4. These items were received with the bank statement at the end of August

(i) Credit memo for $250 for interest earned on a term deposit.

(ii) Debit memo for $40 for the rental of a safety deposit box.

(iii) Debit memo for $120 for an NSF cheque from Janet Long.

(b) Prepare the general journal entry necessary to record the items not yet recorded on the books.

KRA Enterprises
Bank Reconciliation
July 31, 19—

Balance per bank statement		14 0 7 2 50
Add: Outstanding Deposit		1 1 2 9 34
		15 2 0 1 84
Deduct: Outstanding Cheques		
#85	9 5 0 00	
#86	1 5 0 0 00	2 4 5 0 00
Balance per books		12 7 5 1 84

Figure 9.4a Bank Reconciliation Statement for KRA Enterprises

KRA ENTERPRISES
CASH RECEIPTS JOURNAL
PAGE ___CR6___

DATE	ACCOUNT CREDIT	MEMO	F.	ACCTS. REC. CR.	SALES DISC. DR.	SALES PAINT CR.	SALES WALLPAPER CR.	SALES SUNDRIES CR.	GST PAYABLE CREDIT	SALES TAX CR.	GENERAL LEDGER CR.	BANK DR.
19— Aug. 4	Rental Revenue	Clear-View	412						1 3 0 84		1 8 6 9 16	2 0 0 0 00
5	Dorn & Son	on a/c -2%	151	5 8 1 01	1 1 62							
	Beaver & Sons	on a/c -2%	150	2 8 1 41	5 63							
	Cash Sales					1 6 0 0 00	1 8 0 0 00	2 2 0 00	2 5 3 40	2 5 3 40		4 9 7 1 97
13	Sales—Service	to date	404						1 4 3 92		2 0 5 6 08	2 2 0 0 00
17	Cash Sales					1 4 0 0 00	1 1 5 0 00	4 0 0 00	2 0 6 50	2 0 6 50		3 3 6 3 00
19	Beaver & Sons	on a/c	150	1 4 6 0 55								
	Dayton Co.	on a/c	151	1 9 6 3 45								
	Jasper Co.	on a/c	152	9 6 3 00								4 3 8 7 00
27	Cash Sales					1 2 0 0 00	1 1 5 0 00	3 5 0 00	1 8 9 00	1 8 9 00		
	Dorn & Son	on a/c	151	5 0 0 00								3 5 7 8 00
28	E. Morgan	on a/c -2%	154	9 4 1 60	1 8 83							
	S. Wikinson	on a/c -2%	155	1 0 3 6 40	2 0 73							
	K. Yeung	on a/c -2%	156	7 4 9 00	1 4 98							
	Sales—Service								5 2 34		7 4 7 66	3 4 7 2 46
				8 4 7 6 42	7 1 79	4 2 0 0 00	4 1 0 0 00	9 7 0 00	9 7 6 00	6 4 8 90	4 6 7 2 90	23 9 7 2 43
				(1 0 4)	(4 1 5)	(4 0 1)	(4 0 2)	(4 0 3)	(2 2 0)	(2 1 0)		(1 0 1)

Figure 9.4b Cash Receipts Journal for KRA Enterprises

KRA ENTERPRISES
CASH PAYMENTS JOURNAL

PAGE ___CP6___

DATE		ACCOUNT DEBIT	MEMO	F.	ACCTS. PAY. DR.	PURCH. DISC. CR.	GST–ITC DR	GEN. LED. DR.	BANK CR.	CH. NO.
19—Aug.	4	Telephone		531			11 41	1 74 41	1 85 82	87
		Utilities	electricity	534			1 40	21 40	22 80	88
		Utilities	hydro	534			5 39	82 39	87 78	89
		Mortgage Payable	Aug. paymt.	214				3 13 50		
		Interest on Mtg.	on above	523				1 00 00	1 3 13 50	DM
		Freight In		506			3 15	48 15	51 30	90
		Duty & Brokerage	duty & fees	505			6 02	85 98	92 00	91
	5	Postage		526			7 00	1 00 00	1 07 00	92
	11	Freight In	CP Freight	506			2 29	32 71	35 00	93
	12	Donations	Red Cross	520				50 00	50 00	94
	14	Bank Loan Payable	Pd. off loan	202				8 5 00 00		
		Int. & Bank Chgs.	on above	522				32 60	8 5 32 60	DM
	19	Sales Tax Payable	for July	210				1 2 17 30	1 2 17 30	95
	26	Business Tax Exp.	City of Wpg.	513				8 00 00	8 00 00	96
	27	Miscellaneous Exp.		524				16 90		
		Postage	to reimburse	526			22	3 10		
		Advertising	petty cash	510			1 96	29 96	52 14	97
	28	Salaries—Office		528				9 50 00	9 50 00	98
		Salaries—Service		529				1 5 00 00	1 5 00 00	99
		Colfield Industries	on a/c -2%	250	1 6 00 00	3 2 00			1 5 68 00	100
		Rayburn Suppliers	on a/c -2%	254	8 20 00	1 6 40			8 03 60	101
		Spencer Stationers	on a/c -2%	257	2 2 00 00				2 2 00 00	102
		Drawings (Krause)		302				2 0 00 00	2 0 00 00	103
		Drawings (Allen)		304				2 0 00 00	2 0 00 00	104
		Int. & Bank Chgs.	bank stmt.	522				42 00	42 00	DM
					4 6 20 00	4 8 40	3 8 84	19 0 00 40	23 6 10 84	
					(201)	(504)	(222)		(101)	

Figure 9.4c KRA Enterprises, Cash Payments Journal

The Royal Canadian Bank
3000 Pembina Highway
Winnipeg, MB
R2G 1W1

Statement of Account with:

KRA Enterprises
70 Buffalo Place
Winnipeg, MB   ACCOUNT NUMBER   BALANCE FORWARD
R3C 7JB   654-789-7   14,072.50

Cheques	Cheques	Cheques	Deposits	Date	BALANCE
950.00	1,500.00		1,129.34	Aug. 4	12 751.84
	MTG 1313.50		2,000.00	4	13 438.34
185.82	87.78	22.80	4,971.97	5	18 113.91
92.00				6	18 021.91
35.00			2200.00	13	20 186.91
LP8532.60				14	11 654.31
45.00	107.00		3363.00	17	14 859.01
50.00	800.00		4387.00	19	18 396.01
1,217.30	SDB 40.00	RTD 120.00	3578.00	27	20 596.71
52.14	950.00	1500.00	ID 250.00	28	18 344.57
2000.00	2000.00	SC 42.00			14 302.57

EXPLANATIONS OF SYMBOLS
Transactions are identified by the following symbols
MTG - Mortgage Payment   RTD - Returned Item
SC - Service Charge   LP - Loan Payment
SDB - Safe Deposit Box Payment   ID - Interest Deposit

Figure 9.4d   Statement of Account with KRA Enterprises

THINK ABOUT IT!

1. Does the balance on the bank statement usually agree with the balance in the business's books? Why?
2. What are the two chief differences between the bank statement balance and the Bank account balance in the ledger?
3. When is the bank balance reconciled?
4. Name two items that accompany the bank statement when it is sent to the customer.
5. What is an outstanding cheque?
6. What is a certified cheque? Is a certified cheque listed as an outstanding cheque? Why or why not?
7. What is an NSF cheque?
8. What are bank charges? What do they cover? In what account on a business's books would they be recorded?

▶ JUNE TRANSACTIONS: KBC DECORATING CO.

The service employees are still working on Job #2, which must be completed by June 15. They will then start on Job #3, painting the stucco and trim on small apartment buildings.

Mr. Bailes, the owner of the building rented by KBC Decorating Co., has contacted Mr. Martin and Mr. Barker to offer them the opportunity to buy the building. Mr. Bailes plans to retire to Kelowna, B.C. After some negotiations, a price has been agreed upon and the partners will take ownership of the building on July 1 and will receive rent from the other tenant, Clear-Vu Windows. (This will not affect the June transactions.)

Set up the usual journals and a petty cash sheet. Record the following transactions:

19—

June 1 Paid the rent, $2,500 plus $175 GST. Gave a donation of $50 to the War Amps of Canada (debit Donations). GST is not applicable on donations.

2 In April, KBC Decorating applied for credit cards from Shell Canada and has now received a billing from them for purchases made during May, $350. This amount includes $22.90 GST. A cheque was issued to pay the bill. (Debit Delivery Expense.)

2 Received invoice #19 dated May 29 from Spencer Stucco for stucco paint, $5,000 plus $350 GST; terms 2/10,n/30.

3 Received payment on the May 24 invoices as follows: Beavis & Sons, invoice #13; Dayson & Son, invoice #12; Jay-Mar Co., invoice #14; and S. Wilkinson, invoice #15. They have all earned the 2% discount. (Remember, the discount is taken only on the value of the goods, not including taxes.)

3 Received a debit memo from the bank for $32 for May service charges. Debit Bank Charges & Interest in the cash payments journal. Since no cheque was issued, write "DM" in the Cheque No. column to indicate that the source document for this transaction is the bank's debit memo.

5 Paid the phone bill for May, $230 plus $15.05 GST. Paid Minnesota Decor Supply on invoice #1224, $800, Canadian funds with a U.S. bank draft. The bank deducted this amount from the account by means of a debit memo. Disregard currency exchange on this transaction. Assume the service charge for the bank draft will be included in the month-end bank service charge.)

7 Paid these utilities for May services: Intercity Gas, $150 plus $9.81 GST; and hydro, $170 plus $11.12 GST.

8 Paid Spencer Stucco in full for invoice #19 less the 2% discount. All eligible discounts on sales and purchase invoices will be calculated on the value of the goods *before* taxes are added, unless instructed otherwise.

9 Payments from petty cash were: postage, $3.50 plus $0.25 GST; paper coffee cups, $7.50 plus $0.49 GST; tape for the warehouse, $9.50 plus $0.62 GST; a can of turpentine, $14.50 plus $0.95 GST (debit Purchases—Paint & Supplies). These items will be entered on the petty cash sheet.

12 Received invoice #21 from Tranborg & Noble for power paint rollers, $600 (debit Tools & Equipment); paint and supplies, $240; and wallpaper, $500. Added to the invoice was $87.66 GST. Terms are 2/10,n/30.

15 Received the balance owing on Job #2 from Gluting Properties, $15,000 plus 7% GST.

16 The painters have now started on Job #3, stucco work and painting the trim on small apartment buildings. This contract is to be completed by June 30. The total contract price due at completion is $20,000 plus GST.

17 Took a certified cheque to the post office to refill the postage meter machine, $107. This amount includes $7 GST.

18 Received invoice #69 dated June 16 from Coleman Industries for paint and supplies, $2,200, and wallpaper, $1,200, on usual terms. Added to the invoice was $238 GST. Cash sales to date: paint and supplies, $2,200, and wallpaper, $1,500.

19 Remitted the provincial sales tax collected in May: total collected, $1,246; commission, $40.46. (Refer, if necessary, to the entry recorded on this date last month.) Paid Tranborg & Noble for invoice #21. Paid Robinson Insurance in full for invoice #120.

22 Payments from the petty cash fund: postage due, $4 plus $0.28 GST; coffee for the office, $5 (GST exempt). Issued a cheque to reimburse the petty cash fund. Refer to Figure 8.6 (Chapter 8).

26 Paid Coleman Industries for invoice #69 less the 2% discount. Cash sales to date: paint and supplies, $2,200, and wallpaper, $3,700.

29 The partners have each invested an additional $5,000 into the business due to the anticipated purchase of the property on July 2. (Credit each partner's Capital account.)

29 Credit sales (usual terms): S. Miller, paint and supplies, $800, and wallpaper, $300. Edna Morton, paint and supplies, $1,700, and wallpaper, $1,500. Wm. Zelisko Enterprises, paint and supplies, $900, and wallpaper, $430.

30 Paid office salaries, $1,800, and service salaries, $7,200. (Only one cheque is issued.) Job #3 is now complete. Received a cheque for $20,000 plus GST.

MONTH-END ACTIVITIES

(a) Balance all journals as usual.

(b) Post all remaining transactions and appropriate column totals. Prepare a trial balance with schedules.

10

Goods and Services Tax

CHAPTER OBJECTIVES

After completing this chapter, you will be able to:

- calculate and record the net GST to be remitted to government based on the GST collected and the GST paid

- file a GST tax return

IMPORTANT WORDS AND TERMS IN THIS CHAPTER

GST (Goods & Services Tax)
GST-ITC (Input Tax Credit)

··········

Canada's Goods and Services Tax (known generally as **GST**) was introduced on January 1, 1991, to replace the 13.5% Manufacturers' Sales Tax. Although the present GST rate of 7% is lower than the tax it replaced, GST is charged on a much wider range of goods, and is chargeable on services as well. Both the rate and the range of goods and services on which GST must be charged are subject to change at the federal government's discretion.

Some goods and services are classified as *zero-rated*; that is, no GST is charged to the customer when the good or service is sold. These include goods exported from Canada, sales to provincial governments, and sales to Indians living on reserves. If any GST was paid when these goods were acquired for resale, it may be claimed as an input tax credit.

Other goods and services are classified as *GST exempt,* including food, water utility costs, and financial services.

REGISTERING FOR GST

Each business that sells goods and services subject to GST must register with the Regional Excise Office of Revenue Canada by filing the Goods and Services Tax Registration Form (see Figure 10.1), which identifies the name and location of the business, the nature of the business, and the province(s) in which it will conduct its commercial activities. A nine-digit GST Registration Number, such as R123456789, is then assigned to the business; this number must be quoted on its sales invoices and receipts that show a charge for GST.

As well, a GST Election for Reporting Period form (see Figure 10.2) is filed to determine the reporting period (monthly, quarterly, or annually) selected for filing the GST Tax Return. The reporting period is determined in part by the amount of taxable sales and revenues. For example, a monthly reporting period is mandatory if GST-taxable sales and revenues exceed $6 million annually. A quarterly reporting period may be elected if annual GST-taxable sales and revenues are under $6 million. A yearly reporting period may be elected if such taxable revenues are $500,000 or less.

FILING THE GST RETURN

Prior to the end of each GST reporting period, Revenue Canada will mail a GST Tax Return form (see Figure 10.3) to the business. This return must be completed, signed, and returned with the appropriate remittance within one month after the end of the reporting period. For example, a GST Return form covering the first quarter of the year (January, February, and March) must be filed by the end of April.

Revenue Canada
Customs and Excise

Revenu Canada
Douanes et Accise

COMPLETE AND MAIL THIS COPY

Protected (when completed)

GOODS AND SERVICES TAX REGISTRATION FORM
(see instructions on reverse before completing)
This form is prescribed by the Minister of National Revenue under the Excise Tax Act.

OFFICE USE ONLY

R

This form also constitutes an application for registration for all specified provincial/territorial consumption taxes that Revenue Canada, Customs and Excise is authorized to administer.

1. Full Legal Business or Organization Name
KBC Decorating Co.

2. Trade Name (if different from above)

3. Mailing Address
79 Buffalo Place Industrial Park
Winnipeg, MB
R2W 9V7

4. Name of Contact Person within the Business or Organization
Henry Q. Martin

Title

5. Telephone No. *(204) 555-0131*

6. Language Preference ☑ English ☐ French

If the information above is incomplete or incorrect, complete items 1 to 3.

7. Annual GST-taxable Sales and Revenues (includes zero-rated sales and revenues)

$ _____

(see instruction 8(d) if you are a partner or a branch)

* If $30,000 or less and you do not wish to be registered, go to item 8.
* If $30,000 or less and you wish to be registered, go to item 9.
* If greater than $30,000 go to item 9 (GST registration required).

GST REGISTRATION NOT REQUIRED (check appropriate box and complete Certification below)

8. I have read the Registration booklet and understand that my business or organization is not required to be registered because **(check only one)**

(a) ☐ GST-taxable sales and revenues did not exceed $30,000 in the past twelve months (taxi/limousine operators are excluded as explained in the booklet).

(b) ☐ I do not conduct any commercial activity subject to the Goods and Services Tax.

(c) ☐ Operations ceased as of   Year   Month

(d) ☐ I am a partner in a partnership or operate a branch of a business or organization which is registered separately for GST.

▶ _____
Name of partnership, business or organization

(e) ☐ Other (briefly specify the reason):

▶ _____

GST REGISTRATION REQUIRED

9. Year End for Income Tax Purposes
(If you are a corporation, provide your fiscal year end.)

Month *Dec.* | Day *31*

10. Briefly describe your major and secondary business activities.
Retail Paint and Wallpaper

11. For Office Use Only

12. Effective Date of Registration
Y   M   D
9 x | *0 1* | *0 1*

13. Enter the numbers which apply to your operation.

Taxation Corp. Acc. No. or Social Insurance No.
601-010-199

Payroll Deduction Account No. (only one)

Custom Importer No. (only one)

14. Check **only** if you are considered to be one of the following entities.

1 ☐ Government, Municipality
2 ☐ Registered Charity
3 ☐ Non-profit Organization
4 ☐ "Listed" Financial Institution
5 ☐ University, School Board, Hospital
6 ☐ Joint Venture Operator (not a partnership)
7 ☐ Non Resident Charging Admission Directly to Spectators/Attenders
8 ☐ Non Resident engaged in Commercial Activity(ies) in Canada
9 ☐ Taxi/Limousine Operator

15. Check the boxes to indicate the province(s)/territory(ies) in which you engage in commercial activities and/or maintain a permanent establishment:

	Commercial Activity	Permanent Establishment		Commercial Activity	Permanent Establishment		Commercial Activity	Permanent Establishment		Commercial Activity	Permanent Establishment
Alberta	☐	☐	New Brunswick	☐	☐	Nova Scotia	☐	☐	Quebec	☐	☐
British Columbia	☐	☐	Newfoundland	☐	☐	Ontario	☐	☐	Saskatchewan	☐	☐
Manitoba	☑	☑	Northwest Territories	☐	☐	Prince Edward Island	☐	☐	Yukon Territory	☐	☐

16. Please check the appropriate box.   1 ☐ Sole Proprietorship   2 ☑ Partnership   3 ☐ Corporation   99 ☐ Other (specify):

CERTIFICATION

I hereby certify that the information given on this form, and in any document attached, is true, correct and complete in every respect to the best of my knowledge and that I am authorized to sign on behalf of the person named above.

Name and Title of Authorized Person (print)
Henry Q. Martin

Signature of Authorized Person

Y   M   D
9 x | *0 1* | *0 1*

Personal information provided on this form is protected under the provisions of the Privacy Act and is maintained in Personal Information Bank RCC/P-PU-065.

GST 1E (92/02)   Disponible en français GST 1F

Canada

Figure 10.1   GST Registration Form

Source: Revenue Canada—Custom, Excise and Taxation. Reproduced with permission of the Minister of Supply and Services Canada.

Revenue Canada
Customs and Excise

Revenu Canada
Douanes et Accise

PROTECTED when completed
PROTÉGÉ une fois rempli

REPORTING PERIOD - PÉRIODE DE DÉCLARATION
ELECTION FOR REPORTING PERIOD - CHOIX VISANT LA PÉRIODE DE DÉCLARATION
(Sections 245-251 of the Excise Tax Act - Articles 245 à 251 de la Loi sur la taxe d'accise)

This form is prescribed by the Minister of National Revenue under the Excise Tax Act - Cette formule est prescrite par le ministre du Revenu national en vertu de la Loi sur la taxe d'accise

A • IDENTIFICATION - RENSEIGNEMENTS

Full Legal Name - Raison sociale au complet
KBi Decorating Co.

GST Registration No.
N° d'inscription aux fins de la TPS
125 205 427

Trading Name (if different from above) - Nom commercial (si différent de la raison sociale)

Mailing Address - Adresse postale
79 Buffalo Place Industrial Park

City - Ville
Winnipeg

Province
Manitoba

Postal Code - Code postal
R2W 9V7

Contact Person - Personne ressource
Henry Q. Martin

Title - Titre

Tel. No. - N° de tél.
(204) 555 - 0131

B • ELIGIBILITY - ADMISSIBILITÉ

Reporting Period Election Rules (except listed financial institutions; refer to instructions)
Règles concernant le choix visant la période de déclaration (à l'exception des institutions financières désignées, voir les renseignements)

Total GST-Taxable Revenues Total des recettes assujettis à la TPS	Assigned Période attribuée	Options Available Choix possibles
Exceed $6,000,000 Supérieur à 6 000 000 $	Monthly mensuelle	None aucun
Exceed $500,000 to $6,000,000 Excède 500 000 $ à 6 000 000 $	Quarterly trimestrielle	(i) Monthly (ii) Quarterly (i) mensuel (ii) trimestriel
$500,000 or less 500 000 $ ou moins	Quarterly trimestrielle	(i) Monthly (ii) Quarterly (iii) Annual with Quarterly Instalment Payments (i) mensuel (ii) trimestriel (iii) annuel avec versement d'acomptes provisionnels

STEP / ÉTAPE 1 Current Reporting Period:
Période de déclaration courante :   ▶ ☐ Monthly Mensuelle   ☑ Quarterly Trimestrielle   ☐ Annual Annuelle

STEP / ÉTAPE 2 Annual GST-Taxable Sales and Revenues:
Ventes et recettes annuelles assujetties à la TPS :

For Year Ended
Pour l'année se terminant le   Y-A   M   D-J

Registrant's - de l'inscrit   ▶ $ **350,000**

Associates' - de ses associés   ▶ $ _____

Total   ▶ $ **350,000**

STEP / ÉTAPE 3 Compare the total calculated in Step 2 to the table above to ensure that the registrant is eligible for the election. The registrant may select any option on that line.
Comparez le total calculé à l'étape 2 au tableau précédent pour s'assurer que l'inscrit est admissible au choix. L'inscrit peut choisir n'importe quelle des options apparaissant sur cette ligne.

C • ELECTION - CHOIX

The registrant elects to file returns on the following basis:
L'inscrit choisit de présenter des déclarations sur une base :   ▶ ☐ Monthly Mensuelle   ☑ Quarterly Trimestrielle   ☐ Annual Annuelle

(If you choose an annual reporting period please also submit the instalment base calculation with this form.)
(Si vous choisissez une période de déclaration annuelle, veuillez joindre le calcul de la base des acomptes provisionnels à la présente formule.)

First fiscal year to which election applies: (e.g., from Jan. 1, 1991 to Dec. 31, 1991)
Premier exercice auquel le choix s'applique : (par exemple du 1er janv. 1991 au 31 déc. 1991)   ▶ from / du Y-A **9x** M **01** D-J **01** to / au Y-A **9x** M **12** D-J **31**

DECLARATION - DÉCLARATION

I certify that the information given on this form is true, correct and complete to the best of my knowledge and that I am authorized to sign on behalf of the electing registrant.

J'atteste que les renseignements fournis sont, au meilleur de ma connaissance, vrais et exacts sous tous les rapports, et que je suis autorisé à signer au nom de l'inscrit qui exerce un choix.

Name (Please print) - Nom (En majuscules)
Henry Q. Martin

Signature

Date   Y-A **9x**   M **01**   D-J **01**

Personal information provided on this form is protected under the provisions of the Privacy Act and is maintained in Personal Information Bank RCC/P-PU-065
Les renseignements personnels fournis dans cette formule sont protégés en vertu de la Loi sur la protection des renseignements personnels et sont conservés dans le Répertoire des renseignements personnels RND P-PU-065

GST 20 (91/05)

Canada

Figure 10.2   GST Election for Reporting Period

Source: Revenue Canada—Custom, Excise and Taxation. Reproduced with permission of the Minister of Supply and Services Canada.

Revenue Canada
Customs, Excise and Taxation

Revenu Canada
Accise, Douanes et Impôt

GOODS AND SERVICES TAX RETURN (NON-PERSONALIZED)

Working Copy

Disponible en français

PROTECTED when completed

GST Account Number	Reporting Period From: To:	Due Date
GST Contact Name		Telephone Number

INSTRUCTIONS

1. This form provides general instructions for your convenience and guidance only. The instructions do not replace the provisions of the Excise Tax Act and Regulations. For further information or assistance, please consult the *Guide to the GST Tax Return for Registrants* or contact your local Revenue Canada Office.
2. Copy the amounts from the shaded boxes on the working copy to the corresponding boxes in the lower portion. Ensure that your numbers are printed in the boxes as illustrated. Identify a negative number with a minus sign in the separate box. See example below.

   - 1 2 3 4 5 6 7 8 9 0 1

3. Enter your GST account number, if you have one, and the reporting period, in the boxes provided in the lower portion on the front side of the return.
4. Enter your complete name, mailing address, name of contact person and telephone number, in the boxes provided in the lower portion on the reverse side of the return.
5. KEEP THE TOP PORTION. This is your working copy. It and any other information used in preparing your return are subject to audit and must be retained for verification purposes.
6. A balance of less than $1 will neither be charged nor refunded.
7. Do not staple or use paper clips.
8. See reverse for line-by-line completion instructions.

Personal information provided on this form is protected under the provisions of the Privacy Act and is maintained in Personal Information Bank RCC/P-PU-065.

REPORTING PERIOD SUMMARY

Sales & Other Revenue	101	00
Total Purchases	102	00

TAX CALCULATIONS

GST Collected and GST Collectible	103			
Adjustments	104			
Total GST and Adjustments for Period (Add Lines 103 and 104)			→	105
Input Tax Credits (ITC's)	106			
Adjustments	107			
Total ITC's and Adjustments (Add Lines 106 and 107)			→	108
NET TAX (Subtract Line 108 from Line 105)				109

OTHER CREDITS IF APPLICABLE

Paid by Instalments	110			
Rebates	111			
Total Other Credits (Add Lines 110 and 111)			→	112
BALANCE (Subtract Line 112 from Line 109)				113

REFUND CLAIMED	114
PAYMENT ENCLOSED	115

Detach and Return Lower Portion

Revenue Canada
Customs, Excise and Taxation

Revenu Canada
Accise, Douanes et Impôt

GOODS AND SERVICES TAX RETURN (NON-PERSONALIZED)

GST Account Number

Reporting Period From: To:

Sales & Other Revenue	101	0 0	Total GST and Adjustments for Period	105
Total Purchases	102	0 0	Total ITC's and Adjustments	108
Paid by Instalments	110		NET TAX	109
Rebates	111		REFUND CLAIMED	114
			PAYMENT ENCLOSED	115

I hereby certify that the information given in this return and in any documents attached is, to the best of my knowledge, true, correct and complete in every respect and that I am authorized to sign on behalf of the registrant.

Authorized Signature Date / /

For GST Use Only

GST 62E (93/04) IT IS A SERIOUS OFFENCE TO MAKE A FALSE RETURN. *PLEASE DO NOT WRITE BELOW THIS LINE*

⑈0006 201 11⑈ ⑆01903⑉117⑆ 96

Figure 10.3 GST Tax Return

Source: Revenue Canada—Custom, Excise and Taxation. Reproduced with permission of the Minister of Supply and Services Canada.

Locate the following lines on the GST Tax Return as each is explained:

Line 101—Sales and Other Revenue. The amount entered on this line represents the total sales of all GST-taxable goods and services (excluding provincial sales tax and GST collected) during the reporting period. Zero-rated goods and services must be included in this amount. Sales exempt from GST are not included in this amount.

Line 102—Total Purchases. This amount is the value of goods and services acquired or imported for use or resale during the reporting period. This amount includes any provincial sales tax paid, but not GST. (The amounts on lines 101 and 102 are rounded to the nearest dollar when reported on the GST return.)

Line 103—GST Collected and Collectible. This amount is the total GST charged to customers on the sales of goods and services during the reporting period. The balance in the GST Payable account at the end of the reporting period is the amount that is recorded on this line.

Line 104—GST Adjustments. Occasionally, adjustments must be made for recognizing GST other than for amounts collected from customers during the reporting period. An example is when a customer's account was previously written off, because it was assumed to be uncollectible and an adjustment was made at that time for the GST no longer collectible, but the account (or a portion of it) has now been recovered. The amount of the payment received from the customer is considered to include GST, which must now be reported.

Line 105—Total GST and Adjustments for Period. This amount is the total of lines 103 and 104.

Line 106—Input Tax Credits (ITCs). The **GST-ITC** amount is the total GST paid on the purchases of goods and services during the reporting period, including any GST tax credits not claimed in earlier reporting periods. This amount is usually the balance in the GST-ITC account.

Line 107—Input Tax Credit Adjustment. Any adjustments to GST-ITC are shown on line 107. An example is GST reported on a sale to a customer in a previous reporting period that is now assumed to be uncollectible. Since the GST charged at the time of the sale can no longer be collected, the company may record this lost GST as an ITC adjustment, thus reducing the net GST to be remitted. (See also Line 104 above.)

Line 108—Total ITCs and Adjustments. This amount is the total of lines 106 and 107.

Line 109—Net Tax. The difference between line 105 and line 108 is entered on line 109. If the amount is negative, a minus sign is written in the box located to the left of the amount.

Line 110—Paid by Instalments. If the company has chosen to file the GST return only once yearly, the total amount of instalment payments made during the year covered by the return is entered on line 110. If the total GST collected in the operating year is less than $1,000, the GST owing may be remitted only once a year.

Line 111—Rebates. Any rebate amounts to be claimed are entered on this line. The appropriate rebate application must accompany the GST return.

Line 112—Total Other Credits. This amount is the total of lines 110 and 111.

Line 113—Balance. The difference between line 109 and line 112 is entered on this line. If the amount is negative, a minus sign is written in the box located to the left of the amount.

Line 114—Refund Claimed. If the amount entered on line 113 is a negative amount, it is entered on this line in order to claim the refund.

Line 115—Payment Enclosed. If the amount on line 113 is a positive amount, it is entered on this line. A cheque for this amount must accompany the GST return when it is filed. A balance of less than $1 on lines 114 or 115 is neither payable nor refunded.

REMITTING GST

The net amount of GST may be remitted to Revenue Canada in one of the following ways:

1. by making payment to any chartered bank or participating financial institution;

2. by mailing the return and the remittance cheque to the GST Processing Centre or to any Revenue Canada Excise Office; or

3. by delivering it to any Revenue Canada Excise Office.

The net amount of GST referred to above is generally the difference between the GST charged to customers on all taxable sales and revenues and the amount of GST paid to suppliers for the acquisition of assets and expenses that were necessary to generate the sales and revenues. If, for example, a total of $1,500 in GST was paid on the purchase of merchandise, supplies, and services during the fiscal quarter and a total of $2,300 in GST was collected from customers during the same fiscal quarter, the net amount of GST remitted is $2,300–$1,500 = $800.

Figure 10.4 shows how the remittance of GST would be recorded in general journal form and how the same entry would be recorded in the cash payments journal. The debit entry to GST Payable and the credit entry to GST-ITC will clear the balances of these two accounts to zero. The accounts are then ready to receive transactions for the next reporting period.

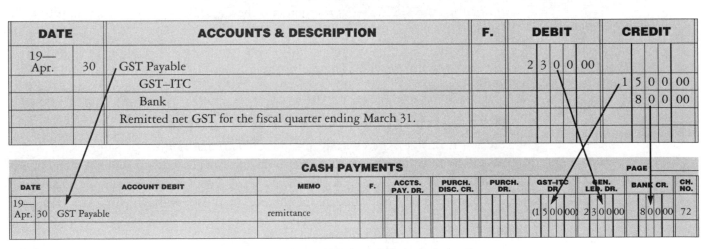

Figure 10.4   Remitting GST (Cash Payments Journal)

PENALTIES AND INTEREST

A penalty of 6% per year plus interest at a prescribed rate are charged on:

1. the total unpaid balance from the day following the due date of the return to the day the amount is remitted; and

2. late or insufficient instalments.

The annual penalty charge and the prescribed interest charges are compounded daily.

NOTICE OF ASSESSMENT

After the GST Return has been received and processed by Revenue Canada, a Notice of Assessment will be issued if (a) Revenue Canada has adjusted any of the amounts on the return; or (b) a rebate has been claimed; or (c) the business is entitled to a refund. The Notice of Assessment serves to confirm the information presented by the company and accepted by Revenue Canada based on the GST return that was filed.

KEEPING RECORDS

Revenue Canada does not require that receipts and supporting documents be submitted with the GST Tax Return; however, such receipts and documents must be kept for six years from the end of the period to which they apply. All regular financial books and records must also be kept in the event a Revenue Canada Excise auditor requests them.

EARLY PAYMENT DISCOUNTS OFFERED TO CUSTOMERS

If a business offers a discount to a customer as an encouragement for early payment, such a discount does not affect the amount of GST charged and collected on the invoice. For example, if $100 worth of goods are sold to a customer, $100 × 7% = $7 GST would be added to the invoice; therefore, the customer is billed $107. Although the customer may take advantage of a 2% discount for early payment, the GST amount remains at $7. The customer would then pay $100 + $7 GST − $2 discount = $105.00.

Late payment charges that may have been added to a customer's account are not subject to GST; therefore, such late charges do not affect the amount of GST remitted.

Volume discounts offered to customers represent a change in the selling price of the goods or service. Therefore, the GST is then calculated on this reduced price.

PROMOTIONAL GIFTS AND FREE SAMPLES

When a business gives away promotional items as gifts or samples, it is not required to collect the GST that would have been charged had the goods been sold. However, any GST paid by the business when the goods were purchased can be claimed as an input tax credit; that is, the business may deduct the GST paid on these items from the GST collected on its regular sales when determining the net amount of GST for remittance.

DEPOSITS ON GOODS AND SERVICES

A deposit received from a customer toward the sale of merchandise or services does not affect the amount of GST charged. GST is calculated on the selling price of the goods, whether a deposit is paid or not. However, if the customer withdraws the order, thus forfeiting the deposit, the amount of the deposit is then assumed to include GST. If a customer orders $700 worth of goods and pays

$150 as a deposit, and subsequently cancels the order, the forfeited deposit of $150 is considered to include 7% GST ($150 × 7/107 = $9.81), which must be reported.

SALES TO ABORIGINALS

Special rules apply when making sales to Aboriginals, Aboriginal bands, band-empowered entities, and tribal councils. Most sales to Aboriginals made on reserves or delivered to reserves are treated as zero-rated. The purchase order must certify that the goods are being acquired for band activities. Sales made to non-Aboriginals living on the reserve, or to Aboriginals living off the reserve, are GST taxable.

IMPORTED ITEMS

Goods imported into Canada are subject to GST, except zero-rated goods and those specified as "nontaxable importations" under the GST legislation. Examples of nontaxable importations include medals, trophies, and other prize items; goods imported by a charity that have been donated to it; and warranty replacement parts.

GST is collected at 7% on taxable goods and is calculated on the duty-and-excise-tax-paid value of the goods. The importer is responsible for paying the GST at the same time as paying the duties. The GST paid can then be claimed as an input tax credit.

CALCULATING GST AND PROVINCIAL SALES TAX

In Chapter 4, the application of GST and provincial sales tax was discussed briefly. In all provinces, GST must be calculated on the value of the good or service before the provincial sales tax, if any, is calculated. Provincial sales tax is then calculated on either the value of the good or service (the selling price) or the combined value of the good or service plus GST. Figure 10.5 shows the provincial sales tax rates across Canada and identifies which provinces calculate sales tax on the value of the goods or services plus GST.

Provincial Sales Tax Rates	
British Columbia	7%
Alberta	none
Saskatchewan	9%
Manitoba	7%
Ontario	8%
Quebec*	8%
New Brunswick*	11%
Nova Scotia*	11%
Prince Edward Island*	11%
Newfoundland & Labrador*	12%
Northwest Territories	none
Yukon Territory	none

* These provinces calculate sales tax on the value of the sale plus the Goods & Services Tax.

Figure 10.5   Provincial Sales Tax Rates

All provinces from Ontario west to British Columbia, except Alberta (which has no provincial sales tax), calculate the provincial sales tax on the value of the good or service. For example, in Ontario a product or service selling for $100 is taxed as follows:

Value of good or service	$100.00
7% GST on $100.00	7.00
8% sales tax on $100.00	8.00
Total paid by customer	$115.00

All provinces from Quebec east to the Maritimes, including Newfoundland/Labrador, calculate the provincial sales tax on the combined value of the good or service plus GST. In these provinces, the same product or service selling for $100, for the moment assuming the same tax rate, is taxed as follows:

Value of good or service	$100.00
7% GST on $100.00	7.00
	107.00
8% sales tax on $107.00	8.56
Total paid by customer	$115.56

Some provinces permit companies to retain a small commission on the provincial sales tax collected as compensation for their efforts in collecting and remitting the tax to the provincial government. In Manitoba, for instance, companies may retain 15% on the first $200 of tax collected and 1% on the balance over $200. If the total remittance is $3 or less, the company is permitted to keep this small amount. Commissions retained by the company are typically credited to a Commissions Earned account.

In Ontario, the commission on provincial sales tax is based on a scale as follows:

- on $20 tax collected or less, the entire amount may be retained by the company;

- on $20.01 to $400 tax collected, a commission of $20 is retained;

- on $400 tax or more, 5% of the tax may be retained.

The maximum commission retained by Ontario companies is $1,500 for a 12-month period ending March 31.

GST on Purchases

Just as a company must charge its customers GST on the sales of goods and services, the company itself also pays GST on its purchases of goods, supplies, and services, including rent, utilities, furniture, and equipment. The GST paid on such expenditures is recorded as an input tax credit (GST-ITC), which is deducted from the GST collected from customers in determining the amount of GST to be remitted to Revenue Canada.

For example, in Alberta, a company buys an item for resale:

Price of hedge clipper	$100.00
7% GST paid	7.00
Total cost	$107.00

The company then sells the same item to its own customer:

Price of hedge clipper	$140.00
7% GST charged	9.80
Customer pays	$149.80

When remitting the GST to the government, the GST Tax Return filed by the company would show the GST collected from customer ($9.80) and the GST input tax credit ($7). The amount remitted, then, is $9.80 – $7.00 = $2.80.

▶ ## PRACTICE EXERCISE 1

Using the following information, complete a GST Tax Return for the Winslow-Trail Company (GST Reg. No. R555789000) for the fiscal quarter July 1 to September 30, 19—. This return is due by October 31, 19—.

(1)   Total sales for the fiscal reporting period are $23,560.39.

(2)   Total purchases of supplies and merchandise for resale are $14,221.78.

(3)   The balance in the GST Payable account at the end of the reporting period is $1,649.23.

(4)   The balance in the GST-ITC account at the end of the reporting period is $849.55.

(5)   A customer's account has been determined to be uncollectible because the customer has declared bankruptcy. The amount of GST applicable to the sales made to the customer was $42.19 and was reported as collectible on the GST return for the last reporting period. Since this GST will not be collected, an adjustment will be required on this GST return.

Sign your name and title (General Manager) and date this return October 27, 19—.

▶ ## PRACTICE EXERCISE 2

Prepare a GST Tax Return from the following information:

(1)   The company name is Nelson Office Products and the Registration Number is R345678900. The return covers the reporting period of April 1 to June 30, 19—.

(2)   Purchases of merchandise and supplies for the fiscal period are $22,419.38; the total GST paid on these purchases is $1,421.66.

(3)   Total sales for the fiscal period are $24,720.44 (before taxes); the GST collected from customers during this period is $1,730.43.

(4)   A customer's balance was written off last quarter as uncollectible because the customer had not been heard from for some time. When the GST return was filed for that quarter, a GST adjustment was made for the tax not collected. The customer, however, has since made a partial payment of $500 on the account. To calculate the portion of this payment that must be considered to be GST received and payable, multiply this payment by 7/107.

Indicate the due date of this return. Sign your own name and title (Accounts Manager) and date this return July 29, 19—.

▶ ### PRACTICE EXERCISE 3

The R.A.M. Software Company files a GST Tax Return on an annual basis. Their GST Registration Number is R987000001. Complete a GST return for one year ending July 31, 19—, based on the following information:

(1)   A total of $103,487.71 GST was collected on sales of $1,478,395.12.

(2) $35,204.03 GST was paid on assets and expenses acquired at a value of $543,112.78.

(3) $60,000 GST has been paid in instalments so far. No rebates are being claimed.

(4)   Enter the due date of this return. Sign your own name and title (Office Manager) and date this return August 22, 19—.

▶ ### JULY TRANSACTIONS: KBC DECORATING CO.

The purchase of the property by KBC Decorating Co. has taken place. KBC has arranged with the other tenant, Clear-Vu Windows, to make their rental payments to KBC at the same monthly rate, $2,500 plus GST.

KBC has been awarded a new decorating contract from Homes Moderne for painting the exterior, and doing some interior decorating, of two large senior citizens' homes. This contract (Job #4) will be completed by July 31 at a price of $21,000 plus GST.

Set up all usual journals, including the petty cash sheet, and record these transactions:

19—

July   2   KBC has been in negotiations with the bank for a mortgage on the purchase of the building from Frank Bailes. The papers were signed today for a 12-year mortgage at 12% interest with payments to be made at the beginning of each month, the first due on August 1. (You will be reminded when to make these mortgage payments.) The bank has deposited the mortgage money to KBC's account, $100,000. KBC has received the bank's credit memo. Make an entry for these proceeds in the cash receipts journal, crediting Mortgage Payable. A cheque is now issued to Frank Bailes for the purchase price of the property. Make an entry in the cash payments journal, debiting Building for $100,000 and Land for $40,000. Two lines are required for this transaction, but only one cheque was issued.

       2   KBC has also taken over the insurance on the property and has issued another cheque to Mr. Bailes for $1,500 for the unexpired portion of the premium for the insurance policy (July 1 to December 31). (Debit Insurance Prepaid).

2 Received a cheque from Clear-Vu Windows for their July rent, $2,500 plus GST. (Credit Rental Revenue.)

4 Received invoice #127 from Reynolds Paper Co. dated July 2 with terms 2/10,n/30 for paint and supplies, $4,000, and wallpaper, $4,200 (plus $574 GST). Received invoice #80 from Rainbow Supplies (same date and terms) for paint and supplies, $2,000, and wallpaper, $4,000 (plus $420 GST). Major Office Supply has sent us their invoice #150 dated July 2 for office furniture, $2,000 plus $130.84 GST; terms n/30.

5 Payments from petty cash: postage due, $3.10 plus $0.22 GST; coffee, cream, and sugar, $8.90 (GST exempt); deodorizer for the washrooms, $6.50 plus $0.43 GST; and a ruler for the office, $1.50 plus $0.10 GST.

7 Paid the water bill for April, May, and June, $200 (GST exempt). Paid Shell Oil for their monthly statement, $340 (includes $22.24 GST).

8 Received payments in full for the June 29 invoices: S. Miller, Edna Morton, and Wm. Zelisko Enterprises. These customers have taken advantage of the eligible discounts.

10 Received the bank statement today containing cancelled cheques. We are now ready to reconcile our bank account with the statement balance of $57,406.25. Follow each step carefully:

Step 1. Check each deposit on the bank statement (Figure 10.6) against those in the Bank column of your June cash receipts journal. If any deposits in the cash receipts journal do not have a corresponding entry on the statement, write "O/S" (outstanding) beside that amount in the journal. Only one deposit has not appeared on the statement: $21,400.00 received on June 30 but deposited too late to be recorded on the June bank statement.

Step 2. Check each cheque amount shown on the bank statement against those in the Bank column of your June cash payments journal. Mark the cheque outstanding (O/S) if it does not have a corresponding amount on the statement. Only two cheques have not yet cleared the bank and are therefore outstanding: #65 for $500 and #67 for $3,570.

Step 3. A debit memo was received with the bank statement. This debit memo covers the bank charges for June, $30.15, but has not yet been recorded in the books.

Step 4. Prepare a bank reconciliation statement based on the information determined from steps 1 to 3. See Figure 9.3 (Chapter 9) for the suggested format.

Step 5. Make an entry in the cash payments journal for the bank charges deducted on the statement. Debit Bank Charges & Interest, $30.15, dated July 10. When this entry is posted, both the bank statement and the Bank account will agree.

12 Paid Reynolds Paper Co. for invoice #127, $8,774 less 2% of the value of the goods ($8,200). Paid Rainbow Supplies for invoice #80, $6,420 less 2% of $6,000.

The Royal Canadian Bank
3000 Pembina Highway
Winnipeg, MB
R3M 4W8

Statement of Account with:

KBC Decorating Co.
79 Buffalo Place Industrial Park
Winnipeg, MB
R2W 9V7

Account No. 654-789-7
Page 1
Statement date: 30 June 19—

Balance Forward: $34,329.37

Cheques	Cheques	Deposits	Date	Balance
2,675.00	350.00	7,616.00	June 3	38,920.37
245.05	50.00		7	38,625.32
	32.00DM		9	38,593.32
800.00	181.12		10	37,612.20
159.81	5,250.00		12	32,202.39
		16,050.00	15	48,252.39
107.00		4,218.00	18	52,363.39
1,205.54	1,400.86		22	49,756.99
46.59		6,726.00	26	56,436.40
		10,000.00	29	66,436.40
9,000.00	30.15DM		30	57,406.25

DM = Debit Memo

Figure 10.6　Bank Statement (KBC Decorating Co.)

13　Paid the hydro bill, $75 plus $4.91 GST. Paid the Intercity Gas bill, $50 plus $3.27 GST. Paid the phone bill, $250 plus $16.35 GST.

14　Cash sales to date: paint and supplies, $2,000, and wallpaper, $1,400.

19　Paid the June provincial sales tax: total collected, $1,066.10; KBC's commission, $38.66. Paid from petty cash: markers for the warehouse, $5.70 plus $0.37 GST; postage due, $6 plus $0.42 GST; coffee, tea, and hot chocolate, $10 (GST exempt).

19　Reimbursed the petty cash. Total and balance the petty cash sheet, then record the reimbursement entry in the cash payments journal as shown in Figure 8.6 (Chapter 8).

27　The quarterly GST return is to be filled out and taken to the bank along with the cheque for the net remittance. Make this entry in the cash payments journal: debit GST Payable for $8,531.04 in the general ledger column and credit GST-ITC for ($1,979.47) in the GST-ITC column. (Note that the amount credited to GST-ITC must be shown in brackets because it is a credit amount written in a debit column.) Credit Bank for the difference between the two amounts, $6,551.57. (See Figure 10.5 for an example of this entry.) When posted, these two entries will have the effect of clearing the GST accounts at the end of June. Prepare the GST Tax Return for the second fiscal quarter. To determine the amount of sales for line 101 of the return, add up the sales posted to the Sales ledger accounts during April, May, and June. To determine the total amount of purchases, add up the purchases posted to the Purchases accounts during April to June. (For the sake of simplicity, we will ignore the purchases of other expenses and assets during this fiscal period.)

28 Received the following invoices (terms 2/10,n/30): #32 from Spencer Stucco for $7,000 plus $490 GST for paint and supplies; and #11 from Tranborg & Noble for paint, $1,000, and wallpaper, $800 (plus $126 GST). Both invoices were dated July 26.

28 KBC has decided that its petty cash fund is not sufficient to meet the monthly needs and is increasing it today to $100. Make an entry in the cash payments journal, debiting Petty Cash for the amount necessary to increase the fund to $100.

29 Credit sales to these customers: Beavis & Sons, paint, $900, and wallpaper, $800. Dayson & Son, paint, $1,400, and wallpaper, $600. Jay-Mar Co., paint, $800, and wallpaper, $200. S. Wilkinson, paint and supplies, $1,000, and wallpaper, $800. All sales are with the usual terms.

31 Paid Major Office Supplies for invoice #150. Cash sales to date: paint and supplies, $1,800, and wallpaper, $1,000. Paid the monthly salaries: office, $2,000 (the bookkeeper has been given a salary increase); service, $7,200. Received payment for Job #4, $21,000 plus GST.

Month-End Activities

(a) Prove equal debits and credits in all journals as usual, and then post the appropriate entries and totals to the ledger accounts.

(b) Prepare a trial balance with schedules.

Partnerships

CHAPTER OBJECTIVES

After completing this chapter, you will be able to:

- record investments and withdrawals by the owner(s) of the business

- calculate a reasonable estimate of the interim profit or loss generated from business activities

IMPORTANT WORDS AND TERMS IN THIS CHAPTER

Articles of Partnership
Dissolution of Partnership
Drawings (Withdrawals)
Limited Life
Liquidation of Partnership
Mutual Agency
Noncash Assets
Unlimited Liabilities

From a customer's perspective, one business is like any other business—they may market different products or services, but a business is a business! Although this simplistic view may on the surface be essentially true, each business will fall into one of three types of organization: (1) proprietorship, (2) partnership, or (3) corporation.

A **proprietorship** is a business owned by one person. Because only the owner is responsible for all decisions and actions taken in the operation of the business, it is considered a proprietorship.

A **partnership** is a business owned by two or more persons who have combined their financial resources and expertise. Their decisions and actions would generally be made jointly, and each would share in the profits made or losses generated by the partnership. KBC Decorating Co. is a partnership—owned and operated by its two partners, Henry Martin and John Barker.

A **corporation** is a business that operates under a government charter. Its ownership is divided into shares or stocks that are usually bought and sold through a stock exchange. Although only large, well-known companies (such as IBM and Air Canada) are often thought of as corporations, small private corporations also exist with only a few people sharing ownership. The difference between four people forming a partnership and the same four people forming a corporation is a legal difference. The corporation must have a government charter permitting it to operate; the partnership does not.

THE PARTNERSHIP

In Canada, each province has its own partnership legislation that provides fundamental rules specifying the terms and conditions under which a partnership may operate. These terms and conditions are spelled out in the **articles of partnership**—an agreement or contract intended to protect the rights of each partner. Such a partnership contract outlines:

1. The name, location, and nature of the business.

2. The names, duties, and rights of each partner within the scope of operations. Some partners may be granted the right to make all ongoing operating decisions while other partners may be just financial backers (not taking a direct hand in the day-to-day operations).

3. The amount of capital to be invested by each partner and an evaluation of noncash assets invested or withdrawn by each partner. All partners may not have equal investment in the business; some may contribute only cash and other assets while others may contribute valuable expertise.

4. The method of sharing profits and losses. Often, profits and losses are shared in proportion to the capital investment by each partner; however,

other factors may also determine how much profit can be claimed. An example is a partner who, because of his or her special skills or abilities, is able to attract additional clients to the business.

5. The amount of cash each partner is allowed to withdraw from the partnership.

6. A provision for insurance on the lives of partners, with the surviving partners (or the partnership itself) named as the beneficiaries.

7. The accounting period to be used (a calendar year or a fiscal year).

8. An annual audit by a public auditor.

9. A provision for settling disputes by arbitration.

10. A provision for **dissolution of the partnership** (the method of computing the equity value of a retiring or deceased partner or when the business ceases to exist).

11. A provision for liquidating the partnership (the method of sharing any deficiency in a partner's Capital account by the other partners).

A partnership arrangement provides a number of advantages to the owners:

1. A partnership provides an opportunity to bring additional capital into the business that might otherwise not be available to a sole owner.

2. A partnership provides an opportunity to combine special skills and talents.

3. A partnership is generally easier and less expensive to form than a corporation.

4. A partnership is not a separate legal entity, so it does not pay income tax on its earnings as does a corporation. Each partner pays income tax on his or her share of the business's net income.

5. A partnership can operate more flexibly and with more freedom from government regulations.

6. The partners may withdraw funds and make business decisions without having to hold formal meetings.

There are also disadvantages to a partnership arrangement that must be considered:

1. **Limited life**: A partnership ceases to exist when a partner dies or withdraws from the partnership, or when a new partner is added. In such an event, the business continues under a new partnership agreement reflecting the change in ownership. The general public is usually unaware that such a change in ownership has occurred.

2. **Unlimited liability**: Each partner is personally responsible for all the debts incurred by the business. If, however, the partner is deemed to be a "limited partner," the partnership contract would specify the limited extent to which he or she can be held liable for the business's debts.

3. **Mutual agency**: Each partner acts as an agent or representative of the partnership and can enter into contracts for the purchase and sale of goods and

services. Once such contracts have been entered into, all other partners are bound by the terms of the contracts.

PARTNERSHIP ACCOUNTING

Overall, partnership accounting is virtually the same as accounting for a single proprietorship. However, to accurately detail the investments into the partnership by the various partners, a separate Capital account would be maintained for each partner as well as a separate Drawings account for each.

Another distinctive feature of partnership accounting is the division of the net income or loss in a ratio specified in the partnership contract. Because partners often contribute different amounts of assets and personal services to the business, the contract will usually provide for "salaries" to be paid to each partner as a means of compensation for the time and effort spent on business activities. Such "salaries" are recorded in the partners' **Drawings** accounts rather than in the Salaries account. Because the partner is actually withdrawing part of what he or she had originally invested, the total of owner's equity must be reduced by the amount of the withdrawal. The Salaries account is an operating expense for recording salaries paid to employees. Partners cannot be employees of their own businesses.

Whenever a new partner contributes assets other than cash into a partnership, the fair market value (the equivalent value that would be realized if these assets were to be sold today) should be assigned to these assets at the date of transfer to the partnership. The noncash assets of the existing partner(s) should also be revalued to reflect the present market value of such assets.

To illustrate the formation of a partnership, Richard Adams and David Crane, operating separate retail stores, decided to form a partnership by combining their two businesses, effective January 1. Separate entries will be recorded for each partner's investment and a separate Capital account is opened for each partner. The noncash assets are recorded at their fair market value.

Figure 11.1 shows the general journal entries recorded for the assets and liabilities invested by both Adams and Crane. The net Capital investment by Adams is determined by applying the accounting equation discussed in Chapter 2: Assets – Liabilities = Equity. The total of the Adams's assets ($190,000) minus the liability ($40,000) equals Capital of $150,000.

A similar calculation is made to determine the net Capital investment made by Crane: assets ($170,000) minus the liability ($20,000) equals Capital ($150,000).

▶ PRACTICE EXERCISE 1

On June 1, 19—, Arthur Blair and Adam Storey, who had been operating competing retail stores, decided to form a partnership by merging their two businesses.

Arthur Blair has contributed Cash, $30,000; Accounts Receivable, $50,000; Inventory, $80,000; and Accounts Payable, $20,000.

Adam Storey has contributed Cash, $10,000; Land, $40,000; Building, $90,000; Inventory, $60,000; and Accounts Payable, $60,000.

DATE		ACCOUNTS & DESCRIPTION	F.	DEBIT	CREDIT
19— Jan.	2	Bank		10 0 0 0 00	
		Land		50 0 0 0 00	
		Building		90 0 0 0 00	
		Inventory		40 0 0 0 00	
		Accounts Payable			40 0 0 0 00
		Capital, R. Adams			150 0 0 0 00
		To record investment by R. Adams in the partnership			
		of Adams & Crane.			
	2	Bank		30 0 0 0 00	
		Accounts Receivable		60 0 0 0 00	
		Inventory		80 0 0 0 00	
		Accounts Payable			20 0 0 0 00
		Capital, D. Crane			150 0 0 0 00
		To record investment by D. Crane in the partnership			
		of Adams & Crane.			

Figure 11.1   Investments in a Partnership

Prepare a compound general journal entry to record each partner's investment in Blair & Storey. Be sure to balance each journal entry and provide suitable explanations.

PRACTICE EXERCISE 2

Prepare the general journal entries to open the books of the partnership of Smith & Mann Grocery on January 1, 19—.

John Smith has invested Cash, $12,000; Store Fixtures, $8,000; Delivery Truck, $9,000; and Bank Loan, $5,000.

Charles Mann has invested Inventory, $10,000; Store Equipment, $7,000; and sufficient cash to give him an *equal* interest in the partnership. (*Hints:* An equal interest in the partnership means that Mann will have the same net capital investment as John Smith's. To compute the amount of cash invested, work backwards from the Capital value to arrive at the amount that will balance the entry.)

**PARTNERS'
DRAWINGS
ACCOUNTS**

Drawings reduces the amount of equity by reducing the owner's Capital. Drawings is the partner's personal account into which are recorded withdrawals of assets (cash, merchandise, supplies, etc.) during the year. Since the partners have each contributed to the business, each is entitled to withdraw assets from the business.

To continue the previous example with Richard Adams and David Crane, we will assume that the following transactions have taken place during the year and have already been recorded, as shown in Figure 11.2, and have been posted to the Drawings account for each partner (Figure 11.3).

March	15	Richard Adams withdrew $2,000 cash.
July	31	David Crane took a used typewriter from the business for his own use at a cost of $500 (including $35 GST). When non-merchandise items, such as typewriters, computers, and office supplies, are withdrawn by the owner, an adjustment must be made to the GST-ITC account.
August	3	Richard Adams withdrew merchandise worth $90 plus $6.30 GST for his personal use. Because the buyer and the seller cannot be the same person, the Sales account cannot be credited in this transaction. The merchandise was withdrawn at *cost* price, so it should be deducted from the account in which the cost of the merchandise was originally recorded; that is, Purchases. This disposal of goods is still subject to GST as if the goods were sold; therefore, $6.30 is charged to the GST Payable account.
November 30		Paid David Crane's home telephone bill of $35 by issuing a company cheque.

DATE		ACCOUNTS & DESCRIPTION	F.	DEBIT					CREDIT				
19— Mar.	15	Drawings, R. Adams	303	2	0	0	0	00					
		Bank							2	0	0	0	00
		Withdrew $2,000 from partnership funds for personal use.											
Jul.	31	Drawings, D. Crane	304		5	0	0	00					
		Office Equipment								4	6	5	00
		Took used typewriter for personal use.									3	5	00
Aug.	3	Drawings, R. Adams	303			9	6	30					
		Purchases									9	0	00
		Withdrew merchandise for own use.										6	30
Nov.	30	Drawings, D. Crane	304			3	5	00					
		Bank									3	5	00
		Paid D. Crane's home telephone bill from											
		partnership funds.											

Figure 11.2   Withdrawal Transactions for Adams, Crane

The Drawings account continues to receive the various transactions involving the owners' withdrawals of assets throughout the year. At year end, the balance in the Drawings account will be cleared so that the account is ready to receive withdrawal activities in the new financial year. The procedure for closing the Drawings accounts will be discussed in detail in Chapter 17.

ACCOUNT _Drawings, Richard Adams_ ACCT. NO. _303_

SHEET NO. _1_

DATE		MEMO	DISC. DATE	F.	✓	DEBIT	✓	CREDIT	✓	DR. CR.	BALANCE
19—Mar.	15	withdrew funds		J1		2 0 0 0 00				Dr	2 0 0 0 00
Aug.	3	withdrew merchandise		J1		9 6 30					2 0 9 6 30

ACCOUNT _Drawings, David Crane_ ACCT. NO. _304_

SHEET NO. _1_

DATE		MEMO	DISC. DATE	F.	✓	DEBIT	✓	CREDIT	✓	DR. CR.	BALANCE
19—Jul.	31	typewriter		J1		5 0 0 00				Dr	5 0 0 00
Nov.	30	phone bill		J1		3 5 00					5 3 5 00

Figure 11.3   Drawings Accounts for Adams, Crane

▶ **PRACTICE EXERCISE 3**

Record each of the following transactions in general journal form, complete with suitable memos. Adjust GST in these transactions as indicated.

1. Ms. Rita Jackson, the owner of a grocery store, withdrew merchandise for her own use.

2. Issued a cheque for $65.81 to the Provincial Telephone Co. to pay the company telephone bill, $43 plus $2.81 GST, and the owner's home telephone bill, $20.

3. The owner has given you the receipt for a bouquet of flowers sent to her husband. The amount was paid with company funds, $25.

4. The owner took a used typewriter, valued at $225 plus GST, from the business for use at home.

5. Issued a cheque for $500 to Ms. Jackson for personal use.

6. Received an invoice for $63.84 from Manitoba Supply Co. for the purchase of office supplies on terms of n/30. The owner took $15 (plus $0.98 GST) worth of the supplies for her own use.

7. Paid the owner's dry cleaning bill, $15.50, by issuing a company cheque.

8. The owner withdrew merchandise ($50 plus GST) and cash ($125) for personal use.

9. Issued a cheque for $424.60 to the City Gas Co. to cover the company's heating bill, $330.60 (includes $20.30 GST), and the Jacksons's home heating bill, $94.

10. Issued a cheque to pay the business's hydro bill, $54.72 (includes $3.36 GST).

11.   The owner withdrew $15 from the petty cash box for lunch money.

12.   The owner took stationery for personal use at home, $9.12 (includes $0.56 GST).

► ### PRACTICE EXERCISE 4

The following transactions are from the records of Campbell & Stewart Co. Record these investments and withdrawals by the partners in a general journal, and then post the appropriate entries to their respective Capital accounts and Drawings accounts.

19—

Jan.   4   Peter Campbell invested $17,500 cash and a computer system worth $8,500.

Jan.   4   Brian Stewart invested $4,000 cash, $6,200 in receivables, and $12,000 in merchandise.

Feb.   10   Peter Campbell withdrew $500 cash.

Feb.   20   Brian Stewart withdrew $400 cash and $300 (includes $19.63 GST) worth of merchandise for his own use.

Apr.   16   Brian Stewart used $900 of company funds to pay personal debts.

Jun.   21   Peter Campbell invested an additional $12,000 cash. Brian Stewart withdrew $2,000 cash.

Jul.   4   Peter Campbell gave his home utility bill, $150, to the bookkeeper and asked that it be paid with company funds.

Aug.   10   Brian Stewart invested $3,000 cash and a truck valued at $7,500.

Oct.   1   The partners withdrew $1,000 each.

► ### PRACTICE EXERCISE 5

Set up compound general journal entries for the following investment and withdrawal:

(a)   On July 15, Willie Silva, owner of Redwood Shrubs, made an investment of $5,000 cash, a delivery truck valued at $10,000, inventory of $8,500, nursery tools and equipment worth $15,000, and a bank loan of $18,000.

(b)   On September 10, John Rundquist, owner of Belmont Florists, withdrew $900 cash and $100 (plus GST) worth of merchandise for his own use. Also, his home utility bills were paid with a company cheque, $125.

► ### PRACTICE EXERCISE 6

Robert Chappel is starting a new business on June 1, 19—, by investing these assets and liabilities: cash, $16,600; equipment, $19,600; supplies, $800; a debt owing to Temple Office Equipment Ltd., $15,000; and a bank loan, $10,000.

(a)   Record a compound general journal entry for Robert Chappel's investment.

(b) Assume that David Church will join Chappel in a partnership by investing sufficient cash to give him an *equal* interest in the business. Record Church's investment on June 1.

(c) Assume that David Church will invest enough cash to give him a *25%* share in the business. Record Church's investment on June 1.

▶ **PRACTICE EXERCISE 7**

From the following T-accounts, prepare the general journal entries based on the keyed entries provided:

Cash	
	640.00 (a)
	300.00 (b)
	400.00 (d)
	75.00 (e)

Supplies	
	25.00 (b)
	90.00 (d)
	50.00 (e)

Drawings, R. Chappel	
(a) 640.00	
(c) 300.00	
(e) 125.00	

Drawings, D. Church	
(b) 325.00	
(d) 690.00	

Purchases	
	300.00 (c)
	200.00 (d)

INTERIM PROFIT & LOSS

Earning a profit is the main objective of virtually every business organization. The profit represents how much "better off" the business is as a result of its regular sales activities. Although an accurate measurement of profit is required at each year end for income tax purposes, management is often interested in the interim profit or loss position as a reasonable estimate of its success and cost efficiency during the short term. Interim profit or loss is often calculated monthly, quarterly, or semi-annually (every six months).

By regularly estimating the profitability of the company's operations, trends can be observed that could affect management's decisions. A period of rising profits might prompt management to pursue expansion plans or to take on additional employees. On the other hand, a period of decreasing profits might lead to management's decision to lay off staff or to delay the construction of a new building.

THE INTERIM STATEMENT

Figure 11.4 illustrates a sample interim statement of profit or loss after three months of operations for the T.J. Barr Company. Because the interim statement is prepared only for management's use, its structure may take a variety of forms. The illustration lists the accounts and their balances in essentially the order in which they appear on the trial balance.

T.J. Barr Company Interim Statement of Profit (For Management Use Only) for three months ending March 31, 19—										
	EXPENSES DEBIT					REVENUES CREDIT				
Inventory, January 1, 19—	144	5	0	0	00					
Interest Revenue						6	1	0	0	00
Rent Revenue						3	5	0	0	00
Sales						558	0	0	0	00
Sales Returns & Allowances	40	0	0	0	00					
Sales Discounts	16	0	0	0	00					
Purchases	331	0	0	0	00					
Purchase Returns & Allowances						28	0	0	0	00
Purchase Discounts						7	0	0	0	00
Freight In	10	0	0	0	00					
Advertising Expense	5	0	0	0	00					
Insurance Expense (b)	1	0	0	0	00					
Interest Expense	4	9	5	0	00					
Office Supplies Expense (c)		4	5	0	00					
Salaries Expense	85	0	0	0	00					
Telephone Expense	9	0	0	0	00					
Utilities Expense	3	0	0	0	00					
Inventory, March 31, 19— (a)						139	0	0	0	00
Subtotals	649	9	0	0	00	742	1	0	0	00
Interim Profit	92	2	0	0	00					
	742	1	0	0	00	742	1	0	0	00

Figure 11.4   Interim Statement of Profit/Loss (Informal)

Figure 11.5 shows the same information arranged more formally. In this format, the revenues are grouped to show the total earnings for the three-month period; the expenses are similarly grouped to show total operating costs. The difference between these two categories represents the net profit (or loss) for the period. Regardless of the format used for an interim statement, the information presented is the same.

PREPARING THE INTERIM STATEMENT

Most of the figures for the interim profit/loss statement are taken directly from the latest trial balance. These include all sales and purchase account balances, as well as other operating expenses, such as utilities, advertising, telephone, etc. Other revenues and expenses must be calculated to represent that portion of the revenue or expense applicable to the period covered by the interim statement.

For example, if $240 worth of office supplies was purchased during the past three months, and only $50 worth of these supplies is still on hand, the estimated value of supplies considered to have been "consumed" (used up) during the period is $240 − $50 = $190. The portion consumed, $190, is recognized as an expense for this period while the unused portion, $50, will be recognized as an expense in a future period.

T.J. Barr Company
Interim Statement of Profit
(For Management Use Only)
For three months ending March 31, 19—

Revenue:										
Sales	558	0	0	0	00					
Sales Returns & Allowances	(40	0	0	0	00)					
Sales Discounts	(16	0	0	0	00)					
Interest Revenue	6	1	0	0	00					
Rent Revenue	3	5	0	0	00					
Total Revenue						511	6	0	0	00
Operating Expenses:										
Inventory, January 1, 19—	144	5	0	0	00					
Inventory, March 31, 19—	(139	5	0	0	00)					
Purchases	331	0	0	0	00					
Purchase Returns & Allowances	(28	0	0	0	00)					
Purchase Discounts	(7	0	0	0	00)					
Freight In	10	0	0	0	00					
Advertising Expense	5	0	0	0	00					
Insurance Expense	1	0	0	0	00					
Interest Expense	4	9	5	0	00					
Office Supplies Expense		4	5	0	00					
Salaries Expense	85	0	0	0	00					
Telephone Expense	9	0	0	0						
Utilities Expense	3	0	0	0						
Total Expenses						419	4	0	0	00
Interim Profit						92	2	0	0	00

Figure 11.5 Interim Statement of Profit/Loss (Formal)

In another example, a 12-month insurance policy was purchased three months ago at a cost of $1,440. The portion of this cost that is considered to be "consumed" is $1,440 × 3/12 = $360. Therefore, only $360 is recognized as the expense for the interim period; the remaining $1,080 will eventually be consumed but will not be recognized during the current period.

Similarly, if $50,000 has been invested in a 90-day term deposit at a rate of 7.5%, the interest earned at the end of the first month is approximately $310. This amount is considered to be a revenue earned during the interim period even though the amount has not yet been paid to the company by the bank.

Usually, interim statements of profit or loss are based on reasonable estimates of the revenue and expense values since such statements are prepared only for internal use. Any account balances considered to be trivial are often ignored since they would have a negligible effect on the net profit or loss.

T.J. Barr Company's trial balance dated March 31, 19—, from which the interim statement of profit and loss was prepared, is illustrated in Figure 11.6. A comparison of the figures in both the trial balance and the interim statement will reveal that not all values were taken directly from the trial balance:

T.J. Barr Company
Trial Balance
March 31, 19—

ACCOUNT NAME	DEBIT					CREDIT				
Bank	20	0	0	0	00					
Canada Savings Bonds	10	0	0	0	00					
Accounts Receivable	66	0	0	0	00					
Inventory (January 2, 19—)	144	5	0	0	00					
Insurance Prepaid	4	0	0	0	00					
Office Supplies Prepaid	1	8	0	0	00					
Land	35	0	0	0	00					
Building	90	0	0	0	00					
Accounts Payable						70	0	0	0	00
Mortgage Payable						12	0	0	0	00
Capital, Richard Barr						190	6	5	0	00
Interest Revenue						6	1	0	0	00
Rental Revenue						3	5	0	0	00
Sales						558	0	0	0	00
Sales Returns & Allowances	40	0	0	0	00					
Sales Discounts	16	0	0	0	00					
Purchases	331	0	0	0	00					
Purchase Returns & Allowances						28	0	0	0	00
Purchase Discounts						7	0	0	0	00
Freight In	10	0	0	0	00					
Advertising Expense	5	0	0	0	00					
Interest Expense	4	9	5	0	00					
Salaries Expense	85	0	0	0	00					
Telephone Expense	9	0	0	0	00					
Utilities	3	0	0	0	00					
	875	2	5	0	00	875	2	5	0	00

Figure 11.6   Trial Balance (T.J. Barr Company)

(a) The value of merchandise inventory at the beginning of the year, $144,500, is recognized as an expense because it represents the value of the goods purchased prior to the beginning of this period and, therefore, contributes to the cost of operating the business during this period. The inventory on hand at the end of the three-month period is estimated to be $139,500, which represents unsold goods to be carried into the next period. This value is shown in the Revenue column on the interim statement in Figure 11.4 only to distinguish it as a negative expense.

(b) The insurance policy (Insurance Prepaid) was purchased three months ago; therefore, approximately one-quarter of the cost can be recognized as an expense for this three-month period ($1,000) and is recorded on the interim statement.

(c) An estimate of the value of office supplies used up during the period is $450. This amount is shown on the interim statement.

The adjusted amounts discussed in points (a), (b), and (c) above are not formally recognized on the books of T.J. Barr Company; therefore, no journal entries are recorded for these adjustments. They are reasonable estimates determined solely for the purpose of preparing the interim statement.

▶ **PRACTICE EXERCISE 8**

Bel Air Flying Service started operations on December 1, 19—. After its first month of business, the following trial balance was prepared and the additional information was determined for the purpose of preparing an interim statement of profit or loss. Prepare a suitable interim statement.

Bel Air Flying Service
Trial Balance
December 31, 19—

ACCOUNT NAME	DEBIT	CREDIT
Cash	29 8 5 0 00	
Rent Costs Prepaid	12 0 0 0 00	
Insurance Prepaid	15 6 0 0 00	
Maintenance Costs Prepaid	7 5 0 0 00	
Spare Parts Inventory	19 0 0 0 00	
Aircraft	240 0 0 0 00	
Capital, Tom Jackson		325 9 2 0 00
Passenger Revenue Earned		63 3 3 0 00
Advertising Expense	1 8 0 0 00	
Fuel Expense	24 6 0 0 00	
Salaries Expense	38 9 0 0 00	
	389 2 5 0 00	389 2 5 0 00

The following additional information has been determined on December 31 but has not been recorded on the books.

(1) One month's worth of the rent paid in advance is now recognized as an expense, $1,000.

(2) One month's worth of the insurance paid in advance is now recognized as an expense, $1,300.

(3) Interlake Air Services provides the aircraft maintenance work for Bel Air at a cost of $2,500 per month. Bel Air has paid for three months in advance; therefore, one month's worth of the prepaid maintenance is now recognized as an expense.

▶ **PRACTICE EXERCISE 9**

From the following trial balance and supporting information, prepare a suitable interim statement of profit or loss for the period of three months ending July 31, 19—.

Additional information:

(1) Estimated inventory of the supplies on hand, $900.

(2) Estimated inventory of merchandise on hand, $600 (this amount will be shown as a negative expense by deducting it from the Purchases value on the interim statement).

(3) Three months' worth of the rent contract has expired ($1,000 per month).

Charles–Sydney Enterprises
Trial Balance
July 31, 19—

ACCOUNT NAME	DEBIT					CREDIT				
Bank	2	5	0	0	00					
Accounts Receivable	4	1	0	0	00					
Supplies Prepaid	2	1	0	0	00					
Rent Prepaid	12	0	0	0	00					
Furniture & Equipment	18	7	5	0	00					
Accounts Payable						9	5	0	0	00
Bank Loan Payable						14	0	0	0	00
Capital, Joshua Charles						30	0	0	0	00
Sales						24	2	5	0	00
Service Revenue						18	4	0	0	00
Purchases										
Advertising Expense	12	9	0	0	00					
Bank Charges	1	5	0	0	00					
Delivery Expense		1	0	0	00					
Salaries & Wages	2	1	0	0	00					
Utilities	38	4	0	0	00					
	1	7	0	0	00					
	96	1	5	0	00	96	1	5	0	00

▶ **PRACTICE EXERCISE 10**

From the following trial balance and additional information, prepare an interim statement of profit or loss for the four months ending April 30, 19—. Use a set-up similar to the informal statement in Figure 11.4.

Additional information:

(1) $700 of the prepaid supplies was consumed in the four-month period.

(2) $500 of the prepaid insurance is considered to have expired during the four-month period.

(3) The estimated value of merchandise in inventory on April 30 is $57,230.

Westport Company
Trial Balance
April 30, 19—

ACCOUNT NAME	DEBIT					CREDIT				
Bank	9	0	0	0	00					
Accounts Receivable	35	0	0	0	00					
Inventory, Jan. 2, 19—	62	0	0	0	00					
Supplies Prepaid	3	5	4	0	00					
Insurance Prepaid	1	5	2	0	00					
Land	40	0	0	0	00					
Buildings	90	0	0	0	00					
Equipment	75	1	0	0	00					
Accounts Payable						37	6	2	0	00
Mortgage Payable						30	0	0	0	00
Capital, Leslie Parker						190	0	0	0	00
Rental Revenue						5	8	0	0	00
Sales						396	2	0	0	00
Sales Returns & Allowances	8	0	0	0	00					
Sales Discounts	5	8	0	0	00					
Purchases	232	0	0	0	00					
Purchase Returns & Allowances						4	0	0	0	00
Purchase Discounts						1	6	8	0	00
Transportation-In	9	6	4	0	00					
Advertising Expense	3	5	0	0	00					
Delivery Expense	2	5	0	0	00					
Interest Expense	12	0	0	0	00					
Property Tax Expense	2	0	0	0	00					
Salaries & Wages	53	2	3	0	00					
Selling Commission Expense	17	4	7	0	00					
Telephone Expense		8	0	0	00					
Utilities	2	2	0	0	00					
	665	3	0	0	00	665	3	0	0	00

THINK ABOUT IT!

1. Name and explain the three common types of business organization.
2. Explain two advantages of forming a partnership. What is a significant disadvantage of forming a partnership?
3. When an owner invests assets into the business, which accounts are debited? Which accounts are credited?
4. What is the purpose of the Drawings account? How does it differ from the Salaries account?
5. Name three items that might be charged to the owner's Drawings account.
6. If the owner withdraws merchandise for personal use, what account is credited? Why?
7. If the owner withdraws stationery and other general office supplies for personal use, what account is credited? Why?
8. When can an interim statement of profit/loss be prepared?

9. What are the advantages of preparing an interim statement of profit/loss rather than waiting until the end of the financial year?

▶ **AUGUST TRANSACTIONS: KBC DECORATING CO.**

KBC has received confirmation that a contract (Job #5) has been awarded to it and will require two months to complete (August 1 to September 30). This contract involves painting barns, outbuildings, the house, corrals, and fences at the Rancho Riding Stables located outside Winnipeg. The price has been set at $40,000 plus GST, half to be paid on August 30 and the balance upon completion at the end of September.

19—

Aug. 1 Received a cheque from Clear-Vu Windows for August rent, $2,500 plus GST. Received a debit memo from the bank for the first payment on the mortgage. This entry will require two lines in the cash payments journal. First, debit Mortgage Payable for $313.50 (the amount of principal repayment). Next, debit Interest on Mortgage for $1,000. The total amount of the payment is $1,313.50 in the Bank column. Since no cheque was issued, write "DM" (debit memo) in the Cheque No. column.

1 Payments from petty cash: date stamp for the office, $13.50 plus $0.89 GST; postage due, $2.80 plus $0.20 GST; freight on merchandise, $17.25 plus $1.12 GST; parking fees (Miscellaneous Expense), $6 plus $0.39 GST; twine for the warehouse, $9 plus $0.59 GST.

5 Paid Spencer Stucco and Tranborg & Noble for the July invoices, less the eligible 2% discount. Paid Shell Oil for the statement received, $450 plus $29.44 GST.

6 Paid these bills: hydro, $70 plus $4.58 GST; gas, $45 plus $2.94 GST; and phone, $275 plus $17.99 GST.

7 Received payment on the July 24 invoices: #19, #20, #21, and #22. Check for eligible discounts.

10 Cash sales: paint and supplies, $1,950, and wallpaper, $1,350.

11 Received the bank statement and cancelled cheques for July. Complete a bank reconciliation statement using the following information: The July 31 bank statement shows a balance of $19,875.64. These items do not appear on the statement: the deposit of July 31, $25,662; cheque #80 for $6,425.58; and cheque #82 for $2,130.84. A bank charge of $32 plus $15 for the rental of a safety deposit box were shown as deducted from the account but these items have not yet been recorded on the books. Record and post the necessary entry that results from this bank reconciliation.

12 Payments from petty cash: postage due, $3.20 plus $0.22 GST; office supplies, $6.50 plus $0.43 GST; delivery expense, $10 plus $0.70 GST.

13 Sales on terms of 2/10,n/30: William Zelisko Enterprises, paint and supplies, $1,000, and wallpaper, $600. K. Young Painting, paint and supplies, $200, and wallpaper, $400. Dayson & Son, paint and supplies, $1,200, and wallpaper, $700. S. Miller, paint and supplies, $700, and wallpaper, $500.

14 Refilled the postage meter machine, $100 plus GST. Bought from Minnesota Decor Supply on their invoice #1290, terms n/30, wallpaper, $1,400 (Canadian funds). Do not add GST to this order; GST will be paid by the broker, who will then bill KBC.

19 Remitted the July provincial sales tax: total collected, $889; commission, $36.89; net remitted, $852.11.

22 Cash sales: paint and supplies, $2,100, and wallpaper, $1,010. Donated $100 to the Wheelchair Olympics.

23 Received invoice #39 from Mitchell Advertising dated August 22 for $800 plus $52.34 GST for a newspaper advertisement; terms n/30. Received invoice #77 from Coleman Industries (terms 2/10,n/30) dated August 22 for paint and supplies, $4,000, and wallpaper, $200, plus $294 GST. Received payment on the August 13 invoices (#23, #25, and #26).

28 Purchased a forklift from Powell Equipment for use in the warehouse. Issued a cheque. Debit Tools & Equipment for $5,400 (which includes the cost of the forklift, $5,000, and the sales tax, $350, and their delivery cost, $50); debit GST-ITC for $327.10; and credit Bank for the total. The forklift will be delivered August 31.

30 Cash sales: paint and supplies, $900, and wallpaper, $500. Payments from petty cash: postage due, $4.60 plus $0.32 GST; special purchase of paint brushes, $20 plus $1.31 GST. Reimburse the petty cash fund.

30 Received payment on invoice #24 from K. Young Painting, which has missed the discount date.

31 Received partial payment from Rancho Riding Stables for Job #5, $20,000 plus GST.

31 Paid Workers Compensation Board for the remaining premium, $2,488.32 (GST not applicable); debit Workers Compensation Expense. Paid office salary, $2,000, and the service salaries, $7,200.

31 The partners have each agreed to withdraw $3,000 per month, in lieu of salaries, for living expenses. Cheques will be issued to them on the last working day of each month. The entries are as follows: In the cash payments journal, debit Drawings, H. Martin for $3,000 and debit Drawings, J. Barker for $3,000. (The Drawings' accounts are used to record all withdrawals by the owners.)

MONTH-END ACTIVITIES

(a)   Prove equal debits and credits in all journals as usual, and then post the appropriate entries and totals to the ledger accounts.

(b)   Prepare a trial balance with schedules of accounts receivable and accounts payable.

C H A P T E R

12

Payroll

CHAPTER OBJECTIVES

After completing this chapter, you will be able to:

- calculate and record payroll for employees in hourly, piecework, salary, commission, and salary/commission payroll systems, including using government deduction tables

- complete payroll records and employee earnings records

IMPORTANT WORDS AND TERMS IN THIS CHAPTER

Canada Pension Plan (CPP)
Compulsory Deductions
Employee Earnings Record
Gross Earnings (Gross Pay)
Income Tax
Payroll Record
Unemployment Insurance (UI)
Voluntary Deductions
Workers Compensation

··········

Salaries and wages constitute a significant portion of the total cost of operating a business. The employer not only pays a salary or wage to the employees but also contributes to the federal government's Canada Pension and Unemployment Insurance plans, as well as to company pension plans, medical plans, and Workers Compensation.

Because salaries and wages represent such a large part of total operating expenses, and because of the many federal and provincial laws pertaining to the administration of payroll, each company is required to maintain detailed payroll information not only for its own internal purposes but also for its employees and for Revenue Canada. The employer's payroll system must include all the pertinent input data, such as social insurance numbers, the number of regular hours worked, overtime hours worked, pay rates, and payroll taxes. As well, it must produce accurate paycheques, payroll records, withholding statements, and reports to government agencies. Such payroll records are also used for determining employees' vacation time and pay, sick leaves, and retirement pensions.

EMPLOYEES VS. INDEPENDENT CONTRACTORS

Both employees and independent contractors are hired by the employer under a contract of service; however, the relationship between the employer and these two groups differs considerably.

Employees are hired on a full- or part-time basis and are placed on the regular payroll; their salaries or wages are subject to payroll deductions. In addition, the employer has the right to direct and supervise the performance of the employees and impose performance standards on them.

Independent contractors, on the other hand, are not controlled or supervised by the employer. They are paid a fee for their services rather than a wage or salary, and such fees are not subject to payroll deductions. A carpenter, for example, might be contracted to build shelves in the store, or an accountant might be hired at year end to prepare the company's financial statements.

THE PAYROLL PROCESS

CALCULATIONS

The method of calculating an employee's gross pay will depend on the nature of that employee's work, such as a factory worker paid on an hourly basis or an office employee earning a fixed monthly salary. **Gross pay** refers to the value earned by the employee before any deductions are taken. Here are some of the most commonly used payroll methods:

1. **Hourly Payroll**: Employees are paid on the basis of the number of hours worked per day or per week. A record of the number of hours worked is compiled from the time card (see Figure 12.1) stamped in a time clock by

the employee. From each time card, the regular and overtime hours are calculated. If the employee works under a union contract, such a contract might require that he or she be paid time-and-a-half for hours worked in excess of eight hours in any single day or for hours worked in excess of 40 hours in a week. Contracts will vary in this respect.

As shown in Figure 12.1, Ron Davies has clocked 40 regular hours and two overtime hours during the current work week. His regular pay is $1,000 ($25 per hour × 40 regular hours worked) and the overtime pay is $75 ($37.50 per hour × 2 overtime hours worked). The total gross pay is $1,000 + $75 = $1,075.

WEEK ENDING   January 8   19 9—

NO.   103
NAME   Ronald Davies

	Morning IN	Noon OUT	Noon IN	Night OUT	Extra IN	Extra OUT	TOTAL HOURS
M	7:55	12:00	12:29	4:30	5:00	7:02	8 + 2
T	8:00	12:00	12:30	4:30			8
W	8:01	12:01	12:30	4:31			8
T	8:00	12:00	12:30	4:30			8
F	7:58	12:00	12:28	4:30			8
S							

TOTAL TIME   40 + 2 = 42   HRS.
RATE   25.00 / 37.50
TOTAL WAGES FOR WEEK $ 1075.00

Figure 12.1   Time Card

Reductions in pay for an employee arriving late for work will be handled according to the policies of the company and the nature of the work. Some companies do not impose a penalty for lateness unless 15 minutes or more is involved. In a manufacturing business or on an assembly line, for example, a penalty might be imposed even if the worker is only a minute or two late, which might result in 15 to 30 minutes of pay deducted as a penalty.

2. **Piecework Payroll**: Employees are paid for the number of pieces they produce during a pay period. In a piecework payroll system, the employer sees an increase in production under less supervision, but may have to sacrifice quality for quantity. The incentive for the employee is an increase in earnings, resulting from the increase in production.

A factory employee might be paid $0.50 for each of the first 500 pieces produced, $0.60 for each of the next 250 pieces, and $0.65 for each piece over 750 that is completed. The more productive the employee is, the more he or she is paid.

3. **Salary Payroll**: The salaried employee is paid a fixed amount for a specific pay

period, usually weekly, bi-weekly (every two weeks), semi-monthly (twice per month), or monthly.

4. **Commission Payroll**: Commission employees, such as car salespeople and real estate brokers, are paid on an incentive basis similar to that of the piece-work payroll. This employee is paid a commission based on sales (usually a fixed percentage of either the number of units sold or the value of the goods or services sold), such as 7% of all sales recorded during the month. Some employees are paid on an escalating commission scale as an added incentive, such as 7% on the first $5,000 of sales and 8% on all sales over $5,000.

5. **Salary–Commission Payroll**: These employees are paid a straight weekly or monthly salary plus a commission on the total sales recorded for the pay period; for example, $400 a week plus 5% commission on sales. This is sometimes known as the guaranteed pay method. An employee might earn a high commission on sales during peak sales periods but would have to depend on the basic salary of $400.00 per week when sales are low.

DEDUCTIONS

In Figure 12.1, we determined that the gross pay for Ron Davies is $1,075. However, this amount will not be paid to him because deductions must be withheld from the gross pay. These deductions are remitted to the government by the employer on Ron's behalf. **Compulsory deductions** are those to which every employee must contribute, including income tax, Canada Pension Plan contributions, and Unemployment Insurance premiums.

1. **Federal Income Tax**: The **income tax** category (Claim Code) for each employee is determined from a TD1 Tax Exemption Return (Figure 12.2), which is completed and signed by the employee when he or she begins employment with the company. Ron Davies's claim code is determined to be Code 5. If the employee is entitled only to the basic personal exemption, however, the TD1 form is not required. The basic exemption is the minimum claim for exemption by all taxpayers. In the 1993 tax year, the basic exemption was $6,456, but the amount changes each year.

    The amount of income tax to be deducted is determined by looking up the employee's gross pay in the Income Tax Deduction Table, found in the booklet of Payroll Deduction Tables issued by Revenue Canada each year.

2. **Canada Pension Plan (or Quebec Pension Plan) (CPP/QPP)**: For the purposes of calculating payroll in this textbook, we will be referring to the Canada Pension Plan; however, the Quebec Pension Plan is similar. **Canada Pension Plan** came into effect on January 1, 1966, requiring every employee in Canada to contribute to the plan 1.8% of the year's pensionable earnings. An equal amount is contributed by the employer. The contribution rate has increased several times over the years—the latest to 2.5% on January 1, 1993. All employees from age 18 to 70 who are in pensionable employment and who are not currently receiving a Canada or Quebec Pension Plan retirement or disability pension are required to contribute

Revenue Canada   Revenu Canada
Taxation   Impôt

page 1

TD1(E)
Rev. 93

1993 Personal Tax Credit Return

Family name (Please print)	Usual first name and initials	Employee number
DAVIES	Ronald	103

Address		Social insurance number
17 President Lane	For non-residents only / Country of permanent residence	6 0 9 4 3 2 0 1 7

	Postal code		Date of birth
Winnipeg MB	R3R 0Y8		Day 1 2 Month 1 0 Year 1 9 6 2

You have to complete this form if:
- you have a new employer (or payer);
- your status changed since the last time you filled out this form; or
- you claimed three or more dependent children when you filled out this form for the 1992 taxation year.

Income includes: salary, wages, commissions, and any other remuneration; superannuation or pension benefits including an annuity payment made under a superannuation or pension fund or plan; Unemployment Insurance benefits, including training allowances; and payments under registered retirement income funds or registered retirement savings plans.

Instructions
Please fill out this form so your employer (or payer) will know how much tax to deduct regularly from your pay. Regular deductions will help you avoid having a balance to pay when you file your income tax return. If you do not fill out this form, tax will be deducted from your pay using only the basic personal amount of $6,456 (item 2 below) as the amount of your personal tax credit claim.

Give the completed form to your employer or payer. If you are a pensioner who receives Canada Pension Plan benefits, or Old Age Security or Guaranteed Income Supplement payments, please send the completed form to your Health and Welfare Canada regional office.

Need help?
If you need help to complete this form, see the additional information on page 2 under "Notes to employees and payees." If you still need help, ask your employer (or payer), or call the Source Deductions section of your local taxation office.

---

1. **Are you a non-resident of Canada?** (See note 1 on page 2.)   Yes ☐ No ☐
   - If Yes – answer the next question.
   - If No – go to item 2.

   If you are a non-resident, will you be including less than 90% of your 1993 total world income when figuring out the taxable income you earned in Canada?   Yes ☐ No ☐
   - If Yes – enter claim code 0 in the box at line 16, then sign and date the form at item 19.
   - If No – go to item 2.

2. **Basic personal amount.** Everyone may claim this amount, then go to item 3.   ▶ $ 6,456 2.

3. **Are you supporting your spouse with whom you live?** (See note 2 on page 2. Common-law relationships could qualify.)   Yes ☒ No ☐
   - If Yes – figure out your claim amount below.
   - If No – go to item 4.

   Claim amount calculation:
   Identify whether the amount in A, B, or C will be your spouse's net income for 1993. Enter the claim amount at line 3, then go to item 4. (See notes 2, 3, and 4 on page 2.)
   Note: A spouse claimed here cannot be claimed again at item 6.

   A) spouse's net income under $538 – enter $5,380 at line 3
   B) spouse's net income between $538 and $5,918 – figure out your claim amount in the box to the right. →→→
   C) spouse's net income over $5,918 – enter $0 at line 3

	$ 5,010
Minus: Spouse's net income( )	
Enter this amount at line 3 $	

   ▶ 5918 3.

4. **Do you have any dependants who will be under 19 at the end of 1993?**   Yes ☐ No ☐
   - If Yes – indicate how many in the box at line 4, then go to item 5.
   - If No – go to item 5.

   ☐ 4.

5. **Are you single, divorced, separated, or widowed and supporting a dependent relative who lives with you?** (See note 5 on page 2.)   Yes ☐ No ☐
   - If Yes – answer the next question.
   - If No – go to item 6.

   Is that dependent relative either your parent or grandparent?   Yes ☐ No ☐
   - If Yes – figure out the amount of that dependant's net income for 1993, then go to the claim amount calculation for line 5.
   - If No – answer the next question.

   Was that dependent relative under 19 at the end of 1993?   Yes ☐ No ☐
   - If Yes – figure out the amount of that dependant's net income for 1993, then go to the claim amount calculation for line 5.
   - If No – answer the next question.

   Is that dependent relative 19 or older and infirm?   Yes ☐ No ☐
   - If Yes – figure out the amount of that dependant's net income for 1993, then go to the claim amount calculation for line 5.
   - If No – answer the next question.

   Claim amount calculation:
   Identify whether the amount in A, B, or C will be your dependant's net income for 1993. Calculate the claim amount for each dependant separately, and enter the total claim amount at line 5, then go to item 6. (See note 4 on page 2 to figure out net income.)
   Note: A dependant claimed here cannot be claimed again at item 6.

   A) net income under $538 – enter $5,380 at line 5.
   B) net income between $538 and $5,918 – figure out your claim amount in the box to the right. →→→
   C) net income over $5,918 – enter $0 at line 5.

Minus:	$ 5,918
Dependant's net income ( )	
Enter this amount at line 3 $	

   ▶ 5.

6. **If you are supporting a dependent relative who is 18 or older and infirm, identify whether the amount in A, B, or C will be that dependant's net income for 1993 and enter the claim amount at line 6,** then go to item 7. (See note 3 on page 2 to figure out net income.)
   Note: A dependant claimed at line 3 or 5 cannot be claimed again at line 6.

   A) dependant's net income under $2,690 – enter $1,583 at line 6.
   B) dependant's net income between $2,690 and $4,273 – figure out your claim amount in the box to the right. →→→
   C) dependant's net income over $4,273 – enter $0 at line 6.

Minus:	$ 4,273
Dependant's net income ( )	
Enter this amount at line 6 $	

   ▶ 6.

7. **Do you receive eligible pension income?** (See note 6 on page 2.)   Yes ☐ No ☐
   - If Yes – enter your eligible pension income OR $1,000 (whichever is less) at line 7, then go to item 8.
   - If No – go to item 8.

   ▶ 7.

8.   Total (Add lines 2, 3, and 5 to 7, then enter the amount at line 8.) Please enter this amount at line 9 on page 2. ▶ $ 12 374 8.

Figure 12.2 Personal Tax Credit Return

Source: Revenue Canada—Custom, Excise and Taxation. Reproduced with permission of the Minister of Supply and Services Canada.

9.

Total (from line 8 on page 1.) ► $ *12 374* 9. page 2

10. Will you be 65 or older at the end of 1993?
- If Yes – enter $3,482 at line 10, then go to item 11.
- If No – go to item 11.

Yes ☐ No ☒   ►_____ 10.

11. Are you a person with a disability? (See note 7 below.)
- If Yes – enter $4,233 at line 11, then go to item 12.
- If No – go to item 12.

Yes ☐ No ☒   ►_____ 11.

12. Are you a student?
- If Yes – figure out your claim amount below, then go to item 13.
- If No – go to item 13.

Yes ☐ No ☒

– Claim **tuition fees** paid for courses you take in 1993 at a university, college, or certified education institution. $_____

– Claim an **education amount** of $80 for each month or part month in 1993 that you will be enrolled full-time in a qualifying educational program at a university, college, or a school offering job retraining courses or correspondence courses. (Part-time students who are eligible for the disability tax credit, or who have written certification from a medical doctor that they are disabled, can also claim this credit.) $_____

– If you expect to receive scholarships, fellowships, or bursaries in 1993, subtract the amount by which they exceed $500 from your tuition fees and education amount. $(_____)

Total (Enter the amount at line 12.) $_____ ►_____ 12.

13. Are you claiming unused pension income, age, disability, tuition fees, or education amounts transferred from your spouse or dependants? (See notes 2 and 8 below.)
- If Yes – figure out your claim amounts below.
- If No – go to item 14.

Yes ☐ No ☐

– If your **spouse receives eligible pension income**, you can claim any unused balance of your spouse's eligible pension amount to a maximum of $1,000. (See note 6 below.) ► $_____

– If your **spouse will be 65 or older** in 1993, you can claim any unused balance of your spouse's age amount to a maximum of $3,482. ► $_____

– If your **spouse or dependant is disabled**, you can claim any unused balance of that person's disability amount to a maximum of $4,233. (See note 7 below.) ► $_____

– If you are supporting a **spouse or dependant who is attending a university, college, or a certified educational institution**, you can claim the unused balance of that person's tuition fees and education amount to a maximum of $4,000. (See note 8 below.) ► $_____

Total (Enter the amount at line 13.) $_____ ►_____ 13.

14. Total claim amount – Add lines 9 to 13, then enter the amount at line 14. ► $ *12 374* 14.

15. Is your estimated total income for 1993 less than your total claim amount at line 14?
- If Yes – enter E in the box at line 16, and tax will **not** be deducted from your pay, then go to item 17.
- If No – go to item 16.

Yes ☐ No ☐

16. Claim code – Match your total claim amount at line 14 with the table below to determine your claim code, and enter this code in the box to the right. If you already have a code in the box, go to item 17. ☐ *5* 16.

17. Do you want to increase the amount of tax to be deducted from your salary or from other amounts paid to you such as pensions, commissions, etc.? (See note 9 below.)
- If Yes – enter the amount of additional tax you wish to have deducted from each payment at line 17.
- If No – go to item 18.

Yes ☐ No ☒   ► $_____ 17.

18. Will you be living in the Yukon Territory, Northwest Territories, or another designated area for more than six months in a row beginning or ending in 1993?
- If Yes – claim $7.50 **basic residency amount** for each day you live in a designated area; and an **additional residency amount** of $7.50 for each day you live in and maintain a "dwelling" in that designated area, if you are the only person within that dwelling during that period claiming the **basic residency amount**. The maximum amount you can claim depends on the category of your designated area. (See note 10 below.) Enter the amount at line 18.
- If No – go to item 19.

Yes ☐ No ☒   ► $_____ 18.

19. I certify that the information given in this return is correct and complete.

Signature *Ronald Davies*   Date *January 1, 199x*

If your status changes, complete a new return within seven days. It is an offence to make a false return.

Notes to employees and payees

1.   If you are in doubt about your **non-resident** status, contact the Source Deductions section of your local taxation office. If you are a non-resident, and you will be including 90% or more of your 1993 total world income when determining the taxable income you earned in Canada, you can claim personal amounts. For more information, contact your local taxation office.

2.   A **spouse** includes a common-law spouse (that is a person of the opposite sex with whom you cohabit in a conjugal relationship.) To be considered common-law spouses, the two individuals have to have had such a relationship for at least 12 months, or be the natural or adoptive parents of the same child.

3.   If you **marry** during the year, or enter into a common-law relationship as described in note 2, your spouse's net income includes the income earned before and during marriage.

4.   **Net income,** for tax withholding purposes, is the total annual income from all sources including salary, pensions, Old Age Security, Unemployment Insurance, Workers' Compensation, and social assistance payments, minus annual deductions for registered pension plan and registered retirement savings plan contributions.

5.   A **dependant** is an individual who is dependent on you for support and is either under 19 at the end of 1993, or 19 or older and physically or mentally infirm. This includes a child, grandchild, parent, grandparent, brother, sister, aunt, uncle, niece, or nephew (including in-laws). Except in the case of a child or grandchild, this individual must also be living in Canada.

6.   **Eligible pension income** includes pension payments received from a pension plan or fund as a life annuity, and foreign pension payments. It does not include payments from the Canada or Quebec Pension Plan, Old Age Security, Guaranteed Income Supplement, or lump-sum withdrawals from a pension fund.

7.   To claim a **disability amount,** an individual has to be severely impaired (mentally or physically) in 1993, and have a Disability Tax Credit Certificate. Such an impairment has to markedly restrict the individual's daily living activities. The impairment has to have lasted, or be expected to last for a continuous period of at least 12 months.

8.   Your spouse or dependants have to first use any applicable pension income, age, disability, tuition fee, and education amounts to reduce their federal tax to zero before you are entitled to use any balance of these amounts.

9.   You may find it convenient to deduct additional tax at line 17 for other income you receive that has little or no tax deducted from it. (e.g. Unemployment Insurance benefits, Old Age Security payments, or investment or rental income. If you want to change this extra deduction later, you have to fill out a new Form TD1.

10.   "Dwelling" means a self-contained domestic establishment and includes a house, apartment, or similar place where you sleep and eat. It does **not** include a bunkhouse, dormitory, hotel room, or a boarding house room. For more information, including a list, and the categories of designated areas, and instructions for figuring out the amount of tax that should be deducted, see the Northern Residents Deductions Tax Guide, available at any taxation office.

1993 claim codes	
Total claim amount	Claim code
Over – Not over	
No claim amount	0
$ 0 – $6,456	1
6,456 – 8,037	2
8,037 – 9,619	3
9,619 – 11,202	4
11,202 – 12,783	⑤
12,783 – 14,364	6
14,364 – 15,946	7
15,946 – 17,527	8
17,527 – 19,109	9
19,109 – 20,693	10
20,693 – and over	X
No tax withholding required	E

Cette formule existe aussi en français.

Figure 12.2   Personal Tax Credit Return Continued

to this government pension plan. The Payroll Deduction Tables from Revenue Canada contain the appropriate tables for determining the CPP contributions. The basic exemption per person for Canada Pension in 1993 was $3,300 (or $63.46 per week). The exemption and maximum payable can change from year to year.

3. **Unemployment Insurance (UI)**: The **Unemployment Insurance** fund is administered by the Canadian government to provide benefits for limited periods of unemployment and for maternity leave. The premiums are paid by most employees at a rate of 3% of insurable earnings to a maximum of $22.35 per week (assuming 1993 rates). For income under $745.00 per week, the UI premium can be determined by using the Payroll Deduction Tables. The employer is also required to contribute to UI at a rate of 1.4 times the amount deducted from employees.

4. **Other Deductions**: In addition to the compulsory deductions discussed above, **voluntary deductions** are often authorized by the employee for such items as accident and life insurance, company pension plans, registered retirement savings plans (RRSPs), and Canada Savings Bonds. Union dues, on the other hand, are a compulsory deduction if the employee is a member of a union.

   Most life insurance companies offer group insurance plans that may cover not only life insurance but also health benefits for employees unable to work due to illness. This may also include semi-private hospital coverage, vision care, ambulance fees, and dental insurance.

   In addition to the amount deducted from the employee, the employer will contribute to some of the voluntary plans, depending on the type of plan.

To continue our example with Ron Davies's time card, the weekly earnings calculated is $1,075 (gross pay). To calculate the amount he will receive on his paycheque (net pay), we must determine the income tax, unemployment insurance, Canada Pension Plan, and group health insurance deductions.

First, we will determine the amount of income tax by using Code 5 on the *weekly* income tax table (Figure 12.3). Look for the range of remuneration into which his gross pay ($1,075) falls. The range is $1,065 to $1,077. You will see that the amount of tax is $311.15.

Next, we will find the amount of Canada Pension Plan contribution using the table in Figure 12.4. Again, look for the range of remuneration into which the gross pay ($1,075) falls. Here the range is $1,072.86 to $1,082.85. The contribution is $25.36.

Now, we will determine the amount of the Unemployment Insurance premium from the UI table in Figure 12.5. Again, look for the appropriate range of remuneration ($1,074.84 to $1,075.16) and read the UI deduction of $32.25. However, the bottom of the UI table indicates that the maximum amount that can be deducted on a weekly pay is $22.35; therefore, only $22.35 is deducted from Ron Davies's gross pay.

In addition to these compulsory deductions, a voluntary deduction has been made for life, health, and dental insurance using a family rate of $18.

Manitoba
Tax Deductions
Weekly (52 pay periods a year)

Manitoba
Retenues d'impôt
Hebdomadaire (52 périodes de paie par année)

C-3

Weekly pay / Rémunération hebdomadaire		If the employee's claim code from form TD1 is / Si le code de demande de l'employé selon la formule TD1 est										
		0	1	2	3	4	5	6	7	8	9	10
From / De	Less than / Moins que	Deduct from each pay / Retenez sur chaque paie										
457.-	465.	124.45	91.70	78.65	70.65	62.65	53.65	37.00	28.95	20.95	14.90	9.55
465.-	473.	126.60	93.85	80.95	72.95	64.95	55.95	39.30	31.30	23.25	16.20	10.85
473.-	481.	128.75	96.00	83.30	75.25	67.25	58.25	41.60	33.60	25.60	17.55	12.20
481.-	489.	130.90	98.15	85.60	77.60	69.55	60.60	43.90	35.90	27.90	19.90	13.50
489.-	497.	133.05	100.30	87.90	79.90	71.90	62.90	46.25	38.20	30.20	22.20	14.85
497.-	505.	135.20	102.50	90.20	82.20	74.20	65.20	48.55	40.55	32.50	24.50	16.15
505.-	513.	137.35	104.65	92.55	84.50	76.50	67.50	50.85	42.85	34.85	26.80	17.85
513.-	521.	139.50	106.80	94.85	86.85	78.80	69.85	53.15	45.15	37.15	29.15	20.15
521.-	529.	141.65	108.95	97.15	89.15	81.10	72.15	55.50	47.45	39.45	31.45	22.45
529.-	537.	143.80	111.10	99.45	91.45	83.45	74.45	57.80	49.80	41.75	33.75	24.75
537.-	545.	145.95	113.25	101.80	93.75	85.75	76.75	60.10	52.10	44.10	36.05	27.10
545.-	553.	148.10	115.40	104.10	96.10	88.05	79.10	62.40	54.40	46.40	38.40	29.40
553.-	561.	150.25	117.55	106.40	98.40	90.35	81.40	64.75	56.70	48.70	40.70	31.70
561.-	569.	152.40	119.70	108.70	100.70	92.70	83.70	67.05	59.05	51.00	43.00	34.00
569.-	577.	155.10	122.40	111.60	103.55	95.55	86.55	69.90	61.90	53.90	45.85	36.90
577.-	585.	158.45	125.75	115.10	107.10	99.05	90.00	73.35	65.30	57.30	49.30	40.30
585.-	593.	161.90	129.20	118.70	110.65	102.65	93.45	76.75	68.75	60.75	52.70	43.75
593.-	601.	165.30	132.60	122.25	114.25	106.25	96.85	80.20	72.20	64.15	56.15	47.15
601.-	609.	168.75	136.05	125.85	117.85	109.85	100.30	83.60	75.60	67.60	59.60	50.60
609.-	617.	172.20	139.45	129.45	121.45	113.40	103.70	87.05	79.05	71.00	63.00	54.00
617.-	625.	175.60	142.90	133.05	125.00	117.00	107.15	90.50	82.45	74.45	66.45	57.45
625.-	633.	179.05	146.30	136.60	128.60	120.60	110.55	93.90	85.90	77.90	69.85	60.90
633.-	641.	182.45	149.75	140.20	132.20	124.20	114.00	97.35	89.30	81.30	73.30	64.30
641.-	649.	185.90	153.20	143.80	135.80	127.80	117.45	100.80	92.75	84.75	76.75	67.75
649.-	657.	189.40	156.65	147.45	139.45	131.40	120.95	104.25	96.25	88.25	80.20	71.25
657.-	665.	192.85	160.15	151.10	143.10	135.05	124.40	107.75	99.75	91.70	83.70	74.70
665.-	673.	196.35	163.65	154.75	146.75	138.70	127.90	111.20	103.20	95.20	87.20	78.20
673.-	681.	199.85	167.10	158.40	150.35	142.35	131.45	114.80	106.75	98.75	90.75	81.75
681.-	689.	203.30	170.60	162.00	154.00	146.00	135.10	118.40	110.40	102.40	94.40	85.40
689.-	697.	206.80	174.10	165.65	157.65	149.65	138.75	122.05	114.05	106.05	98.00	89.05
697.-	705.	210.25	177.55	169.30	161.30	153.25	142.35	125.70	117.70	109.70	101.65	92.70
705.-	713.	213.75	181.05	172.95	164.95	156.90	146.00	129.35	121.35	113.30	105.30	96.30
713.-	721.	217.25	184.50	176.60	168.55	160.55	149.65	133.00	124.95	116.95	108.95	99.95
721.-	729.	220.70	188.00	180.20	172.20	164.20	153.30	136.65	128.60	120.60	112.60	103.60
729.-	737.	224.20	191.50	183.85	175.85	167.85	156.95	140.25	132.25	124.25	116.20	107.25
737.-	745.	227.70	194.95	187.50	179.50	171.45	160.55	143.90	135.90	127.90	119.85	110.90
745.-	753.	231.20	198.45	191.20	183.15	175.15	164.25	147.60	139.55	131.55	123.55	114.55
753.-	761.	234.75	202.00	194.90	186.85	178.85	167.95	151.30	143.25	135.25	127.25	118.25
761.-	769.	238.30	205.55	198.60	190.55	182.55	171.65	155.00	146.95	138.95	130.95	121.95
769.-	777.	241.80	209.10	202.30	194.30	186.25	175.35	158.70	150.70	142.65	134.65	125.65
777.-	785.	245.35	212.65	206.00	198.00	189.95	179.05	162.40	154.40	146.35	138.35	129.35
785.-	793.	248.90	216.20	209.70	201.70	193.65	182.75	166.10	158.10	150.05	142.05	133.05
793.-	801.	252.45	219.75	213.40	205.40	197.35	186.45	169.80	161.80	153.80	145.75	136.80
801.-	809.	256.00	223.30	217.10	209.10	201.05	190.15	173.50	165.50	157.50	149.45	140.50
809.-	817.	259.55	226.85	220.80	212.80	204.80	193.90	177.20	169.20	161.20	153.15	144.20
817.-	825.	263.10	230.35	224.50	216.50	208.50	197.60	180.90	172.90	164.90	156.85	147.90
825.-	833.	266.65	233.90	228.20	220.20	212.20	201.30	184.60	176.60	168.60	160.60	151.60
833.-	841.	270.15	237.45	231.90	223.90	215.90	205.00	188.30	180.30	172.30	164.30	155.30
841.-	849.	273.70	241.00	235.65	227.60	219.60	208.70	192.05	184.00	176.00	168.00	159.00
849.-	857.	277.25	244.55	239.35	231.30	223.30	212.40	195.75	187.70	179.70	171.70	162.70
857.-	865.	280.80	248.10	243.05	235.00	227.00	216.10	199.45	191.40	183.40	175.40	166.40
865.-	873.	284.35	251.65	246.75	238.70	230.70	219.80	203.15	195.15	187.10	179.10	170.10
873.-	881.	287.90	255.20	250.45	242.45	234.40	223.50	206.85	198.85	190.80	182.80	173.80
881.-	889.	291.45	258.70	254.15	246.15	238.10	227.20	210.55	202.55	194.50	186.50	177.50
889.-	897.	295.00	262.25	257.85	249.85	241.80	230.90	214.25	206.25	198.20	190.20	181.25

Figure 12.3   Income Tax Table

C-4

Manitoba	Manitoba
Tax Deductions	Retenues d'impôt
Weekly (52 pay periods a year)	Hebdomadaire (52 périodes de paie par année)

Weekly pay Rémunération hebdomadaire		If the employee's claim code from form TD1 is Si le code de demande de l'employé selon la formule TD1 est										
From De	Less than Moins que	0	1	2	3	4	5	6	7	8	9	10
		Deduct from each pay Retenez sur chaque paie										
897.-	909.	299.40	266.70	262.50	254.45	246.45	235.55	218.90	210.85	202.85	194.85	185.85
909.-	921.	304.75	272.00	268.00	260.00	251.95	241.10	224.45	216.40	208.40	200.40	191.40
921.-	933.	310.05	277.35	273.30	265.30	257.30	246.65	230.00	222.00	213.95	205.95	196.95
933.-	945.	315.35	282.65	278.65	270.60	262.60	252.20	235.55	227.55	219.50	211.50	202.50
945.-	957.	320.65	287.95	283.95	275.95	267.90	257.75	241.10	233.10	225.10	217.05	208.10
957.-	969.	326.00	293.30	289.25	281.25	273.25	263.30	246.65	238.65	230.65	222.60	213.65
969.-	981.	331.30	298.60	294.60	286.55	278.55	268.60	252.20	244.20	236.20	228.20	219.20
981.-	993.	336.60	303.90	299.90	291.90	283.85	273.95	257.75	249.75	241.75	233.75	224.75
993.-	1005.	341.95	309.20	305.20	297.20	289.20	279.25	263.35	255.30	247.30	239.30	230.30
1005.-	1017.	347.25	314.55	310.55	302.50	294.50	284.55	268.90	260.85	252.85	244.85	235.85
1017.-	1029.	352.55	319.85	315.85	307.85	299.80	289.90	274.45	266.45	258.40	250.40	241.40
1029.-	1041.	357.90	325.15	321.15	313.15	305.15	295.20	280.00	272.00	263.95	255.95	246.95
1041.-	1053.	363.20	330.50	326.50	318.45	310.45	300.50	285.55	277.55	269.55	261.50	252.55
1053.-	1065.	368.50	335.80	331.80	323.80	315.75	305.85	291.10	283.10	275.10	267.05	258.10
1065.-	1077.	373.85	341.10	337.10	329.10	321.10	311.15	296.65	288.65	280.65	272.60	263.65
1077.-	1089.	379.15	346.45	342.45	334.40	326.40	316.45	302.20	294.20	286.20	278.20	269.20
1089.-	1101.	384.45	351.75	347.75	339.75	331.70	321.75	307.80	299.75	291.75	283.75	274.75
1101.-	1113.	389.80	357.05	353.05	345.05	337.05	327.10	313.35	305.30	297.30	289.30	280.30
1113.-	1125.	395.10	362.40	358.40	350.35	342.35	332.40	318.90	310.90	302.85	294.85	285.85
1125.-	1137.	400.40	367.70	363.70	355.70	347.65	337.70	324.45	316.45	308.40	300.40	291.40
1137.-	1149.	405.95	373.25	369.25	361.25	353.20	343.30	330.25	322.25	314.20	306.20	297.20
1149.-	1161.	412.00	379.15	375.10	367.10	359.10	349.15	336.35	328.35	320.35	312.30	303.35
1161.-	1173.	418.05	385.00	381.00	373.00	364.95	355.05	342.45	334.45	326.45	318.45	309.45
1173.-	1185.	424.10	390.90	386.85	378.85	370.85	360.90	348.60	340.55	332.55	324.55	315.55
1185.-	1197.	430.15	396.75	392.75	384.75	376.70	366.75	354.70	346.70	338.65	330.65	321.65
1197.-	1209.	436.20	402.65	398.60	390.60	382.60	372.65	360.80	352.80	344.80	336.75	327.80
1209.-	1221.	442.25	408.50	404.50	396.50	388.45	378.50	366.95	358.90	350.90	342.90	333.90
1221.-	1233.	448.30	414.50	410.40	402.35	394.35	384.40	373.05	365.05	357.00	349.00	340.00
1233.-	1245.	454.35	420.55	416.40	408.25	400.20	390.25	379.15	371.15	363.15	355.10	346.15
1245.-	1257.	460.40	426.60	422.45	414.20	406.10	396.15	385.25	377.25	369.25	361.25	352.25
1257.-	1269.	466.45	432.65	428.50	420.25	411.95	402.00	391.40	383.35	375.35	367.35	358.35
1269.-	1281.	472.45	438.70	434.55	426.30	418.00	407.90	397.50	389.50	381.45	373.45	364.45
1281.-	1293.	478.50	444.75	440.60	432.35	424.05	413.85	403.60	395.60	387.60	379.55	370.60
1293.-	1305.	484.55	450.80	446.65	438.40	430.10	419.90	409.75	401.70	393.70	385.70	376.70
1305.-	1317.	490.60	456.85	452.70	444.45	436.15	425.95	416.05	407.80	399.80	391.80	382.80
1317.-	1329.	496.65	462.90	458.75	450.50	442.20	432.00	422.30	414.05	405.90	397.90	388.95
1329.-	1341.	502.70	468.95	464.80	456.55	448.25	438.05	428.60	420.35	412.05	404.00	395.05
1341.-	1353.	508.75	475.00	470.85	462.60	454.30	444.10	434.90	426.60	418.35	410.15	401.15
1353.-	1365.	514.80	481.05	476.90	468.65	460.35	450.15	441.20	432.90	424.65	416.35	407.25
1365.-	1377.	520.85	487.10	482.95	474.70	466.40	456.20	447.45	439.20	430.90	422.65	413.40
1377.-	1389.	526.90	493.15	489.00	480.75	472.45	462.25	453.75	445.50	437.20	428.95	419.70
1389.-	1401.	532.95	499.20	495.05	486.80	478.50	468.30	460.05	451.75	443.50	435.20	426.00
1401.-	1413.	539.00	505.25	501.10	492.80	484.55	474.35	466.10	457.80	449.55	441.25	432.25
1413.-	1425.	545.05	511.30	507.15	498.85	490.60	480.40	472.15	463.85	455.60	447.30	438.55
1425.-	1437.	551.10	517.35	513.20	504.90	496.65	486.45	478.15	469.90	461.65	453.35	444.85
1437.-	1449.	557.15	523.40	519.25	510.95	502.70	492.50	484.20	475.95	467.70	459.40	451.10
1449.-	1461.	563.20	529.40	525.30	517.00	508.75	498.55	490.25	482.00	473.75	465.45	457.15
1461.-	1473.	569.25	535.45	531.35	523.05	514.80	504.60	496.30	488.05	479.75	471.50	463.20
1473.-	1485.	575.30	541.50	537.40	529.10	520.85	510.65	502.35	494.10	485.80	477.55	469.25
1485.-	1497.	581.35	547.55	543.45	535.15	526.90	516.70	508.40	500.15	491.85	483.60	475.30
1497.-	1509.	587.40	553.60	549.50	541.20	532.95	522.75	514.45	506.20	497.90	489.65	481.35
1509.-	1521.	593.45	559.65	555.55	547.25	539.00	528.80	520.50	512.25	503.95	495.70	487.40
1521.-	1533.	599.50	565.70	561.60	553.30	545.05	534.85	526.55	518.30	510.00	501.75	493.45
1533.-	1545.	605.55	571.75	567.60	559.35	551.05	540.90	532.60	524.35	516.05	507.80	499.50
1545.-	1557.	611.60	577.80	573.65	565.40	557.10	546.90	538.65	530.40	522.10	513.85	505.55

Figure 12.3   Income Tax Table Continued

Source: Revenue Canada—Custom, Excise and Taxation. Reproduced with permission of the Minister of Supply and Services Canada.

B-6   **Canada Pension Plan Contributions – Cotisations au Régime de pensions du Canada**

Weekly (52 pay periods) – Hebdomadaire (52 périodes de paie)

$639.26 – 3342.85

Pay Rémunération From – De	To – À	CPP RPC	Pay Rémunération From – De	To – À	CPP RPC	Pay Rémunération From – De	To – À	CPP RPC	Pay Rémunération From – De	To – À	CPP RPC
639.26	639.65	14.40	1272.86	1282.85	30.36	1992.86	2002.85	48.36	2712.86	2722.85	66.36
639.66	640.05	14.41	1282.86	1292.85	30.61	2002.86	2012.85	48.61	2722.86	2732.85	66.61
640.06	640.45	14.42	1292.86	1302.85	30.86	2012.86	2022.85	48.86	2732.86	2742.85	66.86
640.46	640.85	14.43	1302.86	1312.85	31.11	2022.86	2032.85	49.11	2742.86	2752.85	67.11
640.86	641.25	14.44	1312.86	1322.85	31.36	2032.86	2042.85	49.36	2752.86	2762.85	67.36
641.26	641.65	14.45	1322.86	1332.85	31.61	2042.86	2052.85	49.61	2762.86	2772.85	67.61
641.66	642.05	14.46	1332.86	1342.85	31.86	2052.86	2062.85	49.86	2772.86	2782.85	67.86
642.06	642.45	14.47	1342.86	1352.85	32.11	2062.86	2072.85	50.11	2782.86	2792.85	68.11
642.46	642.85	14.48	1352.86	1362.85	32.36	2072.86	2082.85	50.36	2792.86	2802.85	68.36
642.86	652.85	14.61	1362.86	1372.85	32.61	2082.86	2092.85	50.61	2802.86	2812.85	68.61
652.86	662.85	14.86	1372.86	1382.85	32.86	2092.86	2102.85	50.86	2812.86	2822.85	68.86
662.86	672.85	15.11	1382.86	1392.85	33.11	2102.86	2112.85	51.11	2822.86	2832.85	69.11
672.86	682.85	15.36	1392.86	1402.85	33.36	2112.86	2122.85	51.36	2832.86	2842.85	69.36
682.86	692.85	15.61	1402.86	1412.85	33.61	2122.86	2132.85	51.61	2842.86	2852.85	69.61
692.86	702.85	15.86	1412.86	1422.85	33.86	2132.86	2142.85	51.86	2852.86	2862.85	69.86
702.86	712.85	16.11	1422.86	1432.85	34.11	2142.86	2152.85	52.11	2862.86	2872.85	70.11
712.86	722.85	16.36	1432.86	1442.85	34.36	2152.86	2162.85	52.36	2872.86	2882.85	70.36
722.86	732.85	16.61	1442.86	1452.85	34.61	2162.86	2172.85	52.61	2882.86	2892.85	70.61
732.86	742.85	16.86	1452.86	1462.85	34.86	2172.86	2182.85	52.86	2892.86	2902.85	70.86
742.86	752.85	17.11	1462.86	1472.85	35.11	2182.86	2192.85	53.11	2902.86	2912.85	71.11
752.86	762.85	17.36	1472.86	1482.85	35.36	2192.86	2202.85	53.36	2912.86	2922.85	71.36
762.86	772.85	17.61	1482.86	1492.85	35.61	2202.86	2212.85	53.61	2922.86	2932.85	71.61
772.86	782.85	17.86	1492.86	1502.85	35.86	2212.86	2222.85	53.86	2932.86	2942.85	71.86
782.86	792.85	18.11	1502.86	1512.85	36.11	2222.86	2232.85	54.11	2942.86	2952.85	72.11
792.86	802.85	18.36	1512.86	1522.85	36.36	2232.86	2242.85	54.36	2952.86	2962.85	72.36
802.86	812.85	18.61	1522.86	1532.85	36.61	2242.86	2252.85	54.61	2962.86	2972.85	72.61
812.86	822.85	18.86	1532.86	1542.85	36.86	2252.86	2262.85	54.86	2972.86	2982.85	72.86
822.86	832.85	19.11	1542.86	1552.85	37.11	2262.86	2272.85	55.11	2982.86	2992.85	73.11
832.86	842.85	19.36	1552.86	1562.85	37.36	2272.86	2282.85	55.36	2992.86	3002.85	73.36
842.86	852.85	19.61	1562.86	1572.85	37.61	2282.86	2292.85	55.61	3002.86	3012.85	73.61
852.86	862.85	19.86	1572.86	1582.85	37.86	2292.86	2302.85	55.86	3012.86	3022.85	73.86
862.86	872.85	20.11	1582.86	1592.85	38.11	2302.86	2312.85	56.11	3022.86	3032.85	74.11
872.86	882.85	20.36	1592.86	1602.85	38.36	2312.86	2322.85	56.36	3032.86	3042.85	74.36
882.86	892.85	20.61	1602.86	1612.85	38.61	2322.86	2332.85	56.61	3042.86	3052.85	74.61
892.86	902.85	20.86	1612.86	1622.85	38.86	2332.86	2342.85	56.86	3052.86	3062.85	74.86
902.86	912.85	21.11	1622.86	1632.85	39.11	2342.86	2352.85	57.11	3062.86	3072.85	75.11
912.86	922.85	21.36	1632.86	1642.85	39.36	2352.86	2362.85	57.36	3072.86	3082.85	75.36
922.86	932.85	21.61	1642.86	1652.85	39.61	2362.86	2372.85	57.61	3082.86	3092.85	75.61
932.86	942.85	21.86	1652.86	1662.85	39.86	2372.86	2382.85	57.86	3092.86	3102.85	75.86
942.86	952.85	22.11	1662.86	1672.85	40.11	2382.86	2392.85	58.11	3102.86	3112.85	76.11
952.86	962.85	22.36	1672.86	1682.85	40.36	2392.86	2402.85	58.36	3112.86	3122.85	76.36
962.86	972.85	22.61	1682.86	1692.85	40.61	2402.86	2412.85	58.61	3122.86	3132.85	76.61
972.86	982.85	22.86	1692.86	1702.85	40.86	2412.86	2422.85	58.86	3132.86	3142.85	76.86
982.86	992.85	23.11	1702.86	1712.85	41.11	2422.86	2432.85	59.11	3142.86	3152.85	77.11
992.86	1002.85	23.36	1712.86	1722.85	41.36	2432.86	2442.85	59.36	3152.86	3162.85	77.36
1002.86	1012.85	23.61	1722.86	1732.85	41.61	2442.86	2452.85	59.61	3162.86	3172.85	77.61
1012.86	1022.85	23.86	1732.86	1742.85	41.86	2452.86	2462.85	59.86	3172.86	3182.85	77.86
1022.86	1032.85	24.11	1742.86	1752.85	42.11	2462.86	2472.85	60.11	3182.86	3192.85	78.11
1032.86	1042.85	24.36	1752.86	1762.85	42.36	2472.86	2482.85	60.36	3192.86	3202.85	78.36
1042.86	1052.85	24.61	1762.86	1772.85	42.61	2482.86	2492.85	60.61	3202.86	3212.85	78.61
1052.86	1062.85	24.86	1772.86	1782.85	42.86	2492.86	2502.85	60.86	3212.86	3222.85	78.86
1062.86	1072.85	25.11	1782.86	1792.85	43.11	2502.86	2512.85	61.11	3222.86	3232.85	79.11
1072.86	1082.85	25.36	1792.86	1802.85	43.36	2512.86	2522.85	61.36	3232.86	3242.85	79.36
1082.86	1092.85	25.61	1802.86	1812.85	43.61	2522.86	2532.85	61.61	3242.86	3252.85	79.61
1092.86	1102.85	25.86	1812.86	1822.85	43.86	2532.86	2542.85	61.86	3252.86	3262.85	79.86
1102.86	1112.85	26.11	1822.86	1832.85	44.11	2542.86	2552.85	62.11	3262.86	3272.85	80.11
1112.86	1122.85	26.36	1832.86	1842.85	44.36	2552.86	2562.85	62.36	3272.86	3282.85	80.36
1122.86	1132.85	26.61	1842.86	1852.85	44.61	2562.86	2572.85	62.61	3282.86	3292.85	80.61
1132.86	1142.85	26.86	1852.86	1862.85	44.86	2572.86	2582.85	62.86	3292.86	3302.85	80.86
1142.86	1152.85	27.11	1862.86	1872.85	45.11	2582.86	2592.85	63.11	3302.86	3312.85	81.11
1152.86	1162.85	27.36	1872.86	1882.85	45.36	2592.86	2602.85	63.36	3312.86	3322.85	81.36
1162.86	1172.85	27.61	1882.86	1892.85	45.61	2602.86	2612.85	63.61	3322.86	3332.85	81.61
1172.86	1182.85	27.86	1892.86	1902.85	45.86	2612.86	2622.85	63.86	3332.86	3342.85	81.86
1182.86	1192.85	28.11	1902.86	1912.85	46.11	2622.86	2632.85	64.11			
1192.86	1202.85	28.36	1912.86	1922.85	46.36	2632.86	2642.85	64.36			
1202.86	1212.85	28.61	1922.86	1932.85	46.61	2642.86	2652.85	64.61			
1212.86	1222.85	28.86	1932.86	1942.85	46.86	2652.86	2662.85	64.86			
1222.86	1232.85	29.11	1942.86	1952.85	47.11	2662.86	2672.85	65.11			
1232.86	1242.85	29.36	1952.86	1962.85	47.36	2672.86	2682.85	65.36			
1242.86	1252.85	29.61	1962.86	1972.85	47.61	2682.86	2692.85	65.61			
1252.86	1262.85	29.86	1972.86	1982.85	47.86	2692.86	2702.85	65.86			
1262.86	1272.85	30.11	1982.86	1992.85	48.11	2702.86	2712.85	66.11			

* For earnings above this amount, see the calculation method in the *Employers' Guide to Payroll Deductions.*

* Si la rénumération de votre employé dépasse ce montant, reportez-vous au *Guide de l'employeur – Retenues sur la paie.*

Figure 12.3   Income Tax Table Continued

Source: Revenue Canada—Custom, Excise and Taxation. Reproduced with permission of the Minister of Supply and Services Canada.

B-60   Unemployment Insurance Premiums — Cotisations à l'assurance-chômage

Pay Rémunération From – De	To – À	UI premium Cotisation à l'A-C	Pay Rémunération From – De	To – À	UI premium Cotisation à l'A-C	Pay Rémunération From – De	To – À	UI premium Cotisation à l'A-C	Pay Rémunération From – De	To – À	UI premium Cotisation à l'A-C
576.17	576.49	17.29	600.17	600.49	18.01	624.17	624.49	18.73	648.17	648.49	19.45
576.50	576.83	17.30	600.50	600.83	18.02	624.50	624.83	18.74	648.50	648.83	19.46
576.84	577.16	17.31	600.84	601.16	18.03	624.84	625.16	18.75	648.84	649.16	19.47
577.17	577.49	17.32	601.17	601.49	18.04	625.17	625.49	18.76	649.17	649.49	19.48
577.50	577.83	17.33	601.50	601.83	18.05	625.50	625.83	18.77	649.50	649.83	19.49
577.84	578.16	17.34	601.84	602.16	18.06	625.84	626.16	18.78	649.84	650.16	19.50
578.17	578.49	17.35	602.17	602.49	18.07	626.17	626.49	18.79	650.17	650.49	19.51
578.50	578.83	17.36	602.50	602.83	18.08	626.50	626.83	18.80	650.50	650.83	19.52
578.84	579.16	17.37	602.84	603.16	18.09	626.84	627.16	18.81	650.84	651.16	19.53
579.17	579.49	17.38	603.17	603.49	18.10	627.17	627.49	18.82	651.17	651.49	19.54
579.50	579.83	17.39	603.50	603.83	18.11	627.50	627.83	18.83	651.50	651.83	19.55
579.84	580.16	17.40	603.84	604.16	18.12	627.84	628.16	18.84	651.84	652.16	19.56
580.17	580.49	17.41	604.17	604.49	18.13	628.17	628.49	18.85	652.17	652.49	19.57
580.50	580.83	17.42	604.50	604.83	18.14	628.50	628.83	18.86	652.50	652.83	19.58
580.84	581.16	17.43	604.84	605.16	18.15	628.84	629.16	18.87	652.84	653.16	19.59
581.17	581.49	17.44	605.17	605.49	18.16	629.17	629.49	18.88	653.17	653.49	19.60
581.50	581.83	17.45	605.50	605.83	18.17	629.50	629.83	18.89	653.50	653.83	19.61
581.84	582.16	17.46	605.84	606.16	18.18	629.84	630.16	18.90	653.84	654.16	19.62
582.17	582.49	17.47	606.17	606.49	18.19	630.17	630.49	18.91	654.17	654.49	19.63
582.50	582.83	17.48	606.50	606.83	18.20	630.50	630.83	18.92	654.50	654.83	19.64
582.84	583.16	17.49	606.84	607.16	18.21	630.84	631.16	18.93	654.84	655.16	19.65
583.17	583.49	17.50	607.17	607.49	18.22	631.17	631.49	18.94	655.17	655.49	19.66
583.50	583.83	17.51	607.50	607.83	18.23	631.50	631.83	18.95	655.50	655.83	19.67
583.84	584.16	17.52	607.84	608.16	18.24	631.84	632.16	18.96	655.84	656.16	19.68
584.17	584.49	17.53	608.17	608.49	18.25	632.17	632.49	18.97	656.17	656.49	19.69
584.50	584.83	17.54	608.50	608.83	18.26	632.50	632.83	18.98	656.50	656.83	19.70
584.84	585.16	17.55	608.84	609.16	18.27	632.84	633.16	18.99	656.84	657.16	19.71
585.17	585.49	17.56	609.17	609.49	18.28	633.17	633.49	19.00	657.17	657.49	19.72
585.50	585.83	17.57	609.50	609.83	18.29	633.50	633.83	19.01	657.50	657.83	19.73
585.84	586.16	17.58	609.84	610.16	18.30	633.84	634.16	19.02	657.84	658.16	19.74
586.17	586.49	17.59	610.17	610.49	18.31	634.17	634.49	19.03	658.17	658.49	19.75
586.50	586.83	17.60	610.50	610.83	18.32	634.50	634.83	19.04	658.50	658.83	19.76
586.84	587.16	17.61	610.84	611.16	18.33	634.84	635.16	19.05	658.84	659.16	19.77
587.17	587.49	17.62	611.17	611.49	18.34	635.17	635.49	19.06	659.17	659.49	19.78
587.50	587.83	17.63	611.50	611.83	18.35	635.50	635.83	19.07	659.50	659.83	19.79
587.84	588.16	17.64	611.84	612.16	18.36	635.84	636.16	19.08	659.84	660.16	19.80
588.17	588.49	17.65	612.17	612.49	18.37	636.17	636.49	19.09	660.17	660.49	19.81
588.50	588.83	17.66	612.50	612.83	18.38	636.50	636.83	19.10	660.50	660.83	19.82
588.84	589.16	17.67	612.84	613.16	18.39	636.84	637.16	19.11	660.84	661.16	19.83
589.17	589.49	17.68	613.17	613.49	18.40	637.17	637.49	19.12	661.17	661.49	19.84
589.50	589.83	17.69	613.50	613.83	18.41	637.50	637.83	19.13	661.50	661.83	19.85
589.84	590.16	17.70	613.84	614.16	18.42	637.84	638.16	19.14	661.84	662.16	19.86
590.17	590.49	17.71	614.17	614.49	18.43	638.17	638.49	19.15	662.17	662.49	19.87
590.50	590.83	17.72	614.50	614.83	18.44	638.50	638.83	19.16	662.50	662.83	19.88
590.84	591.16	17.73	614.84	615.16	18.45	638.84	639.16	19.17	662.84	663.16	19.89
591.17	591.49	17.74	615.17	615.49	18.46	639.17	639.49	19.18	663.17	663.49	19.90
591.50	591.83	17.75	615.50	615.83	18.47	639.50	639.83	19.19	663.50	663.83	19.91
591.84	592.16	17.76	615.84	616.16	18.48	639.84	640.16	19.20	663.84	664.16	19.92
592.17	592.49	17.77	616.17	616.49	18.49	640.17	640.49	19.21	664.17	664.49	19.93
592.50	592.83	17.78	616.50	616.83	18.50	640.50	640.83	19.22	664.50	664.83	19.94
592.84	593.16	17.79	616.84	617.16	18.51	640.84	641.16	19.23	664.84	665.16	19.95
593.17	593.49	17.80	617.17	617.49	18.52	641.17	641.49	19.24	665.17	665.49	19.96
593.50	593.83	17.81	617.50	617.83	18.53	641.50	641.83	19.25	665.50	665.83	19.97
593.84	594.16	17.82	617.84	618.16	18.54	641.84	642.16	19.26	665.84	666.16	19.98
594.17	594.49	17.83	618.17	618.49	18.55	642.17	642.49	19.27	666.17	666.49	19.99
594.50	594.83	17.84	618.50	618.83	18.56	642.50	642.83	19.28	666.50	666.83	20.00
594.84	595.16	17.85	618.84	619.16	18.57	642.84	643.16	19.29	666.84	667.16	20.01
595.17	595.49	17.86	619.17	619.49	18.58	643.17	643.49	19.30	667.17	667.49	20.02
595.50	595.83	17.87	619.50	619.83	18.59	643.50	643.83	19.31	667.50	667.83	20.03
595.84	596.16	17.88	619.84	620.16	18.60	643.84	644.16	19.32	667.84	668.16	20.04
596.17	596.49	17.89	620.17	620.49	18.61	644.17	644.49	19.33	668.17	668.49	20.05
596.50	596.83	17.90	620.50	620.83	18.62	644.50	644.83	19.34	668.50	668.83	20.06
596.84	597.16	17.91	620.84	621.16	18.63	644.84	645.16	19.35	668.84	669.16	20.07
597.17	597.49	17.92	621.17	621.49	18.64	645.17	645.49	19.36	669.17	669.49	20.08
597.50	597.83	17.93	621.50	621.83	18.65	645.50	645.83	19.37	669.50	669.83	20.09
597.84	598.16	17.94	621.84	622.16	18.66	645.84	646.16	19.38	669.84	670.16	20.10
598.17	598.49	17.95	622.17	622.49	18.67	646.17	646.49	19.39	670.17	670.49	20.11
598.50	598.83	17.96	622.50	622.83	18.68	646.50	646.83	19.40	670.50	670.83	20.12
598.84	599.16	17.97	622.84	623.16	18.69	646.84	647.16	19.41	670.84	671.16	20.13
599.17	599.49	17.98	623.17	623.49	18.70	647.17	647.49	19.42	671.17	671.49	20.14
599.50	599.83	17.99	623.50	623.83	18.71	647.50	647.83	19.43	671.50	671.83	20.15
599.84	600.16	18.00	623.84	624.16	18.72	647.84	648.16	19.44	671.84	672.16	20.16

Note: The following are the maximum amounts you can deduct for each pay period.
Remarque : Vous trouverez ci-dessous la cotisation maximale que vous pouvez retenir pour chaque période de paie.

Weekly	Hebdomadaire	22.35	10 pay periods a year	10 périodes de paie par année	116.22
Biweekly	Aux deux semaines	44.70	13 pay periods a year	13 périodes de paie par année	89.40
Semimonthly	Bimensuel	48.42	22 pay periods a year	22 périodes de paie par année	52.83
Monthly	Mensuel	96.85			

Figure 12.4   Canada Pension Plan Contribution Table

Source: Revenue Canada—Custom, Excise and Taxation. Reproduced with permission of the Minister of Supply and Services Canada.

Unemployment Insurance Premiums — Cotisations à l'assurance-chômage   B-61

Pay Rémunération From – De	To – À	UI premium Cotisation à l'A-C	Pay Rémunération From – De	To – À	UI premium Cotisation à l'A-C	Pay Rémunération From – De	To – À	UI premium Cotisation à l'A-C	Pay Rémunération From – De	To – À	UI premium Cotisation à l'A-C
672.17 -	672.49	20.17	696.17 -	696.49	20.89	720.17 -	720.49	21.61	744.17 -	744.49	22.33
672.50 -	672.83	20.18	696.50 -	696.83	20.90	720.50 -	720.83	21.62	744.50 -	744.83	22.34
672.84 -	673.16	20.19	696.84 -	697.16	20.91	720.84 -	721.16	21.63	744.84 -	745.16	22.35
673.17 -	673.49	20.20	697.17 -	697.49	20.92	721.17 -	721.49	21.64	745.17 -	745.49	22.36
673.50 -	673.83	20.21	697.50 -	697.83	20.93	721.50 -	721.83	21.65	745.84 -	745.83	22.37
673.84 -	674.16	20.22	697.84 -	698.16	20.94	721.84 -	722.16	21.66	745.84 -	746.16	22.38
674.17 -	674.49	20.23	698.17 -	698.49	20.95	722.17 -	722.49	21.67	746.17 -	746.49	22.39
674.50 -	674.83	20.24	698.50 -	698.83	20.96	722.50 -	722.83	21.68	746.50 -	746.83	22.40
674.84 -	675.16	20.25	698.84 -	699.16	20.97	722.84 -	723.16	21.69	746.84 -	747.16	22.41
675.17 -	675.49	20.26	699.17 -	699.49	20.98	723.17 -	723.49	21.70	747.17 -	747.49	22.42
675.50 -	675.83	20.27	699.50 -	699.83	20.99	723.50 -	723.83	21.71	747.50 -	747.83	22.43
675.84 -	676.16	20.28	699.84 -	700.16	21.00	723.84 -	724.16	21.72	747.84 -	748.16	22.44
676.17 -	676.49	20.29	700.17 -	700.49	21.01	724.17 -	724.49	21.73	748.17 -	748.49	22.45
676.50 -	676.83	20.30	700.50 -	700.83	21.02	724.50 -	724.83	21.74	748.50 -	748.83	22.46
676.84 -	677.16	20.31	700.84 -	701.16	21.03	724.84 -	725.16	21.75	748.84 -	749.16	22.47
677.17 -	677.49	20.32	701.17 -	701.49	21.04	725.17 -	725.49	21.76	749.17 -	749.49	22.48
677.50 -	677.83	20.33	701.50 -	701.83	21.05	725.50 -	725.83	21.77	749.50 -	749.83	22.49
677.84 -	678.16	20.34	701.84 -	702.16	21.06	725.84 -	726.16	21.78	749.84 -	750.16	22.50
678.17 -	678.49	20.35	702.17 -	702.49	21.07	726.17 -	726.49	21.79	750.17 -	750.49	22.51
678.50 -	678.83	20.36	702.50 -	702.83	21.08	726.50 -	726.83	21.80	750.50 -	750.83	22.52
678.84 -	679.16	20.37	702.84 -	703.16	21.09	726.84 -	727.16	21.81	750.84 -	751.16	22.53
679.17 -	679.49	20.38	703.17 -	703.49	21.10	727.17 -	727.49	21.82	751.17 -	751.49	22.54
679.50 -	679.83	20.39	703.50 -	703.83	21.11	727.50 -	727.83	21.83	751.50 -	751.83	22.55
679.84 -	680.16	20.40	703.84 -	704.16	21.12	727.84 -	728.16	21.84	751.84 -	752.16	22.56
680.17 -	680.49	20.41	704.17 -	704.49	21.13	728.17 -	728.49	21.85	752.17 -	752.49	22.57
680.50 -	680.83	20.42	704.50 -	704.83	21.14	728.50 -	728.83	21.86	752.50 -	752.83	22.58
680.84 -	681.16	20.43	704.84 -	705.16	21.15	728.84 -	729.16	21.87	752.84 -	753.16	22.59
681.17 -	681.49	20.44	705.17 -	705.49	21.16	729.17 -	729.49	21.88	753.17 -	753.49	22.60
681.50 -	681.83	20.45	705.50 -	705.83	21.17	729.50 -	729.83	21.89	753.50 -	753.83	22.61
681.84 -	682.16	20.46	705.84 -	706.16	21.18	729.84 -	730.16	21.90	753.84 -	754.16	22.62
682.17 -	682.49	20.47	706.17 -	706.49	21.19	730.17 -	730.49	21.91	754.17 -	754.49	22.63
682.50 -	682.83	20.48	706.50 -	706.83	21.20	730.50 -	730.83	21.92	754.50 -	754.83	22.64
682.84 -	683.16	20.49	706.84 -	707.16	21.21	730.84 -	731.16	21.93	754.84 -	755.16	22.65
683.17 -	683.49	20.50	707.17 -	707.49	21.22	731.17 -	731.49	21.94	755.17 -	755.49	22.66
683.50 -	683.83	20.51	707.50 -	707.83	21.23	731.50 -	731.83	21.95	755.50 -	755.83	22.67
683.84 -	684.16	20.52	707.84 -	708.16	21.24	731.84 -	732.16	21.96	755.84 -	756.16	22.68
684.17 -	684.49	20.53	708.17 -	708.49	21.25	732.17 -	732.49	21.97	756.17 -	756.49	22.69
684.50 -	684.83	20.54	708.50 -	708.83	21.26	732.50 -	732.83	21.98	756.50 -	756.83	22.70
684.84 -	685.16	20.55	708.84 -	709.16	21.27	732.84 -	733.16	21.99	756.84 -	757.16	22.71
685.17 -	685.49	20.56	709.17 -	709.49	21.28	733.17 -	733.49	22.00	757.17 -	757.49	22.72
685.50 -	685.83	20.57	709.50 -	709.83	21.29	733.50 -	733.83	22.01	757.50 -	757.83	22.73
685.84 -	686.16	20.58	709.84 -	710.16	21.30	733.84 -	734.16	22.02	757.84 -	758.16	22.74
686.17 -	686.49	20.59	710.17 -	710.49	21.31	734.17 -	734.49	22.03	758.17 -	758.49	22.75
686.50 -	686.83	20.60	710.50 -	710.83	21.32	734.50 -	734.83	22.04	758.50 -	758.83	22.76
686.84 -	687.16	20.61	710.84 -	711.16	21.33	734.84 -	735.16	22.05	758.84 -	759.16	22.77
687.17 -	687.49	20.62	711.17 -	711.49	21.34	735.17 -	735.49	22.06	759.17 -	759.49	22.78
687.50 -	687.83	20.63	711.50 -	711.83	21.35	735.50 -	735.83	22.07	759.50 -	759.83	22.79
687.84 -	688.16	20.64	711.84 -	712.16	21.36	735.84 -	736.16	22.08	759.84 -	760.16	22.80
688.17 -	688.49	20.65	712.17 -	712.49	21.37	736.17 -	736.49	22.09	760.17 -	760.49	22.81
688.50 -	688.83	20.66	712.50 -	712.83	21.38	736.50 -	736.83	22.10	760.50 -	760.83	22.82
688.84 -	689.16	20.67	712.84 -	713.16	21.39	736.84 -	737.16	22.11	760.84 -	761.16	22.83
689.17 -	689.49	20.68	713.17 -	713.49	21.40	737.17 -	737.49	22.12	761.17 -	761.49	22.84
689.50 -	689.83	20.69	713.50 -	713.83	21.41	737.50 -	737.83	22.13	761.50 -	761.83	22.85
689.84 -	690.16	20.70	713.84 -	714.16	21.42	737.84 -	738.16	22.14	761.84 -	762.16	22.86
690.17 -	690.49	20.71	714.17 -	714.49	21.43	738.17 -	738.49	22.15	762.17 -	762.49	22.87
690.50 -	690.83	20.72	714.50 -	714.83	21.44	738.50 -	738.83	22.16	762.50 -	762.83	22.88
690.84 -	691.16	20.73	714.84 -	715.16	21.45	738.84 -	739.16	22.17	762.84 -	763.16	22.89
691.17 -	691.49	20.74	715.17 -	715.49	21.46	739.17 -	739.49	22.18	763.17 -	763.49	22.90
691.50 -	691.83	20.75	715.50 -	715.83	21.47	739.50 -	739.83	22.19	763.50 -	763.83	22.91
691.84 -	692.16	20.76	715.84 -	716.16	21.48	739.84 -	740.16	22.20	763.84 -	764.16	22.92
692.17 -	692.49	20.77	716.17 -	716.49	21.49	740.17 -	740.49	22.21	764.17 -	764.49	22.93
692.50 -	692.83	20.78	716.50 -	716.83	21.50	740.50 -	740.83	22.22	764.50 -	764.83	22.94
692.84 -	693.16	20.79	716.84 -	717.16	21.51	740.84 -	741.16	22.23	764.84 -	765.16	22.95
693.17 -	693.49	20.80	717.17 -	717.49	21.52	741.17 -	741.49	22.24	765.17 -	765.49	22.96
693.50 -	693.83	20.81	717.50 -	717.83	21.53	741.50 -	741.83	22.25	765.50 -	765.83	22.97
693.84 -	694.16	20.82	717.84 -	718.16	21.54	741.84 -	742.16	22.26	765.84 -	766.16	22.98
694.17 -	694.49	20.83	718.17 -	718.49	21.55	742.17 -	742.49	22.27	766.17 -	766.49	22.99
694.50 -	694.83	20.84	718.50 -	718.83	21.56	742.50 -	742.83	22.28	766.50 -	766.83	23.00
694.84 -	695.16	20.85	718.84 -	719.16	21.57	742.84 -	743.16	22.29	766.84 -	767.16	23.01
695.17 -	695.49	20.86	719.17 -	719.49	21.58	743.17 -	743.49	22.30	767.17 -	767.49	23.02
695.50 -	695.83	20.87	719.50 -	719.83	21.59	743.50 -	743.83	22.31	767.50 -	767.83	23.03
695.84 -	696.16	20.88	719.84 -	720.16	21.60	743.84 -	744.16	22.32	767.84 -	768.16	23.04

Note: The following are the maximum amounts you can deduct for each pay period.
Remarque : Vous trouverez ci-dessous la cotisation maximale que vous pouvez retenir pour chaque période de paie.

Weekly	Hebdomadaire	22.35	10 pay periods a year	10 périodes de paie par année	116.22
Biweekly	Aux deux semaines	44.70	13 pay periods a year	13 périodes de paie par année	89.40
Semimonthly	Bimensuel	48.42	22 pay periods a year	22 périodes de paie par année	52.83
Monthly	Mensuel	96.85			

Figure 12.5   Unemployment Insurance Premium Table

Unemployment Insurance Premiums – Cotisations à l'assurance-chômage   B-65

Pay Rémunération From – De	To – À	UI premium Cotisation à l'A-C	Pay Rémunération From – De	To – À	UI premium Cotisation à l'A-C	Pay Rémunération From – De	To – À	UI premium Cotisation à l'A-C	Pay Rémunération From – De	To – À	UI premium Cotisation à l'A-C
1056.17	1056.49	31.69	1080.17	1080.49	32.41	1104.17	1104.49	33.13	1128.17	1128.49	33.85
1056.50	1056.83	31.70	1080.50	1080.83	32.42	1104.50	1104.83	33.14	1128.50	1128.83	33.86
1056.84	1057.16	31.71	1080.84	1081.16	32.43	1104.84	1105.16	33.15	1128.84	1129.16	33.87
1057.17	1057.49	31.72	1081.17	1081.49	32.44	1105.17	1105.49	33.16	1129.17	1129.49	33.88
1057.50	1057.83	31.73	1081.50	1081.83	32.45	1105.50	1105.83	33.17	1129.50	1129.83	33.89
1057.84	1058.16	31.74	1081.84	1082.16	32.46	1105.84	1106.16	33.18	1129.84	1130.16	33.90
1058.17	1058.49	31.75	1082.17	1082.49	32.47	1106.17	1106.49	33.19	1130.17	1130.49	33.91
1058.50	1058.83	31.76	1082.50	1082.83	32.48	1106.50	1106.83	33.20	1130.50	1130.83	33.92
1058.84	1059.16	31.77	1082.84	1083.16	32.49	1106.84	1107.16	33.21	1130.84	1131.16	33.93
1059.17	1059.49	31.78	1083.17	1083.49	32.50	1107.17	1107.49	33.22	1131.17	1131.49	33.94
1059.50	1059.83	31.79	1083.50	1083.83	32.51	1107.50	1107.83	33.23	1131.50	1131.83	33.95
1059.84	1060.16	31.80	1083.84	1084.16	32.52	1107.84	1108.16	33.24	1131.84	1132.16	33.96
1060.17	1060.49	31.81	1084.17	1084.49	32.53	1108.17	1108.49	33.25	1132.17	1132.49	33.97
1060.50	1060.83	31.82	1084.50	1084.83	32.54	1108.50	1108.83	33.26	1132.50	1132.83	33.98
1060.84	1061.16	31.83	1084.84	1085.16	32.55	1108.84	1109.16	33.27	1132.84	1133.16	33.99
1061.17	1061.49	31.84	1085.17	1085.49	32.56	1109.17	1109.49	33.28	1133.17	1133.49	34.00
1061.50	1061.83	31.85	1085.50	1085.83	32.57	1109.50	1109.83	33.29	1133.50	1133.83	34.01
1061.84	1062.16	31.86	1085.84	1086.16	32.58	1109.84	1110.16	33.30	1133.84	1134.16	34.02
1062.17	1062.49	31.87	1086.17	1086.49	32.59	1110.17	1110.49	33.31	1134.17	1134.49	34.03
1062.50	1062.83	31.88	1086.50	1086.83	32.60	1110.50	1110.83	33.32	1134.50	1134.83	34.04
1062.84	1063.16	31.89	1086.84	1087.16	32.61	1110.84	1111.16	33.33	1134.84	1135.16	34.05
1063.17	1063.49	31.90	1087.17	1087.49	32.62	1111.17	1111.49	33.34	1135.17	1135.49	34.06
1063.50	1063.83	31.91	1087.50	1087.83	32.63	1111.50	1111.83	33.35	1135.50	1135.83	34.07
1063.84	1064.16	31.92	1087.84	1088.16	32.64	1111.84	1112.16	33.36	1135.84	1136.16	34.08
1064.17	1064.49	31.93	1088.17	1088.49	32.65	1112.17	1112.49	33.37	1136.17	1136.49	34.09
1064.50	1064.83	31.94	1088.50	1088.83	32.66	1112.50	1112.83	33.38	1136.50	1136.83	34.10
1064.84	1065.16	31.95	1088.84	1089.16	32.67	1112.84	1113.16	33.39	1136.84	1137.16	34.11
1065.17	1065.49	31.96	1089.17	1089.49	32.68	1113.17	1113.49	33.40	1137.17	1137.49	34.12
1065.50	1065.83	31.97	1089.50	1089.83	32.69	1113.50	1113.83	33.41	1137.50	1137.83	34.13
1065.84	1066.16	31.98	1089.84	1090.16	32.70	1113.84	1114.16	33.42	1137.84	1138.16	34.14
1066.17	1066.49	31.99	1090.17	1090.49	32.71	1114.17	1114.49	33.43	1138.17	1138.49	34.15
1066.50	1066.83	32.00	1090.50	1090.83	32.72	1114.50	1114.83	33.44	1138.50	1138.83	34.16
1066.84	1067.16	32.01	1090.84	1091.16	32.73	1114.84	1115.16	33.45	1138.84	1139.16	34.17
1067.17	1067.49	32.02	1091.17	1091.49	32.74	1115.17	1115.49	33.46	1139.17	1139.49	34.18
1067.50	1067.83	32.03	1091.50	1091.83	32.75	1115.50	1115.83	33.47	1139.50	1139.83	34.19
1067.84	1068.16	32.04	1091.84	1092.16	32.76	1115.84	1116.16	33.48	1139.84	1140.16	34.20
1068.17	1068.49	32.05	1092.17	1092.49	32.77	1116.17	1116.49	33.49	1140.17	1140.49	34.21
1068.50	1068.83	32.06	1092.50	1092.83	32.78	1116.50	1116.83	33.50	1140.50	1140.83	34.22
1068.84	1069.16	32.07	1092.84	1093.16	32.79	1116.84	1117.16	33.51	1140.84	1141.16	34.23
1069.17	1069.49	32.08	1093.17	1093.49	32.80	1117.17	1117.49	33.52	1141.17	1141.49	34.24
1069.50	1069.83	32.09	1093.50	1093.83	32.81	1117.50	1117.83	33.53	1141.50	1141.83	34.25
1069.84	1070.16	32.10	1093.84	1074.16	32.82	1117.84	1118.16	33.54	1141.84	1142.16	34.26
1070.17	1070.49	32.11	1094.17	1094.49	32.83	1118.17	1118.49	33.55	1142.17	1142.49	34.27
1070.50	1070.83	32.12	1094.50	1094.83	32.84	1118.50	1118.83	33.56	1142.50	1142.83	34.28
1070.84	1071.16	32.13	1094.84	1095.16	32.85	1118.84	1119.16	33.57	1142.84	1143.16	34.29
1071.17	1071.49	32.14	1095.17	1095.49	32.86	1119.17	1119.49	33.58	1143.17	1143.49	34.30
1071.50	1071.83	32.15	1095.50	1095.83	32.87	1119.50	1119.83	33.59	1143.50	1143.83	34.31
1071.84	1072.16	32.16	1095.84	1096.16	32.88	1119.84	1120.16	33.60	1143.84	1144.16	34.32
1072.17	1072.49	32.17	1096.17	1096.49	32.89	1120.17	1120.49	33.61	1144.17	1144.49	34.33
1072.50	1072.83	32.18	1096.50	1096.83	32.90	1120.50	1120.83	33.62	1144.50	1144.83	34.34
1072.84	1073.16	32.19	1096.84	1097.16	32.91	1120.84	1121.16	33.63	1144.84	1145.16	34.35
1073.17	1073.49	32.20	1097.17	1097.49	32.92	1121.17	1121.49	33.64	1145.17	1145.49	34.36
1073.50	1073.83	32.21	1097.50	1097.83	32.93	1121.50	1121.83	33.65	1145.50	1145.83	34.37
1073.84	1074.16	32.22	1097.84	1098.16	32.94	1121.84	1122.16	33.66	1145.84	1146.16	34.38
1074.17	1074.49	32.23	1098.17	1098.49	32.95	1122.17	1122.49	33.67	1146.17	1146.49	34.39
1074.50	1074.83	32.24	1098.50	1098.83	32.96	1122.50	1122.83	33.68	1146.50	1146.83	34.40
1074.84	1075.16	32.25	1098.84	1099.16	32.97	1122.84	1123.16	33.69	1146.84	1147.16	34.41
1075.17	1075.49	32.26	1099.17	1099.49	32.98	1123.17	1123.49	33.70	1147.17	1147.49	34.42
1075.50	1075.83	32.27	1099.50	1099.83	32.99	1123.50	1123.83	33.71	1147.50	1147.83	34.43
1075.84	1076.16	32.28	1099.84	1100.16	33.00	1123.84	1124.16	33.72	1147.84	1148.16	34.44
1076.17	1076.49	32.29	1100.17	1100.49	33.01	1124.17	1124.49	33.73	1148.17	1148.49	34.45
1076.50	1076.83	32.30	1100.50	1100.83	33.02	1124.50	1124.83	33.74	1148.50	1148.83	34.46
1076.84	1077.16	32.31	1100.84	1101.16	33.03	1124.84	1125.16	33.75	1148.84	1149.16	34.47
1077.17	1077.49	32.32	1101.17	1101.49	33.04	1125.17	1125.49	33.76	1149.17	1149.49	34.48
1077.50	1077.83	32.33	1101.50	1101.83	33.05	1125.50	1125.83	33.77	1149.50	1149.83	34.49
1077.84	1078.16	32.34	1101.84	1102.16	33.06	1125.84	1126.16	33.78	1149.84	1150.16	34.50
1078.17	1078.49	32.35	1102.17	1102.49	33.07	1126.17	1126.49	33.79	1150.17	1150.49	34.51
1078.50	1078.83	32.36	1102.50	1102.83	33.08	1126.50	1126.83	33.80	1150.50	1150.83	34.52
1078.84	1079.16	32.37	1102.84	1103.16	33.09	1126.84	1127.16	33.81	1150.84	1151.16	34.53
1079.17	1079.49	32.38	1103.17	1103.49	33.10	1127.17	1127.49	33.82	1151.17	1151.49	34.54
1079.50	1079.83	32.39	1103.50	1103.83	33.11	1127.50	1127.83	33.83	1151.50	1151.83	34.55
1079.84	1080.16	32.40	1103.84	1104.16	33.12	1127.84	1128.16	33.84	1151.84	1152.16	34.56

Note: The following are the maximum amounts you can deduct for each pay period.
Remarque : Vous trouverez ci-dessous la cotisation maximale que vous pouvez retenir pour chaque période de paie.

Weekly	Hebdomadaire	22.35	10 pay periods a year	10 périodes de paie par année	116.22
Biweekly	Aux deux semaines	44.70	13 pay periods a year	13 périodes de paie par année	89.40
Semimonthly	Bimensuel	48.42	22 pay periods a year	22 périodes de paie par année	52.83
Monthly	Mensuel	96.85			

Figure 12.5   Unemployment Insurance Premium Table Continued

Source: Revenue Canada—Custom, Excise and Taxation. Reproduced with permission of the Minister of Supply and Services Canada.

The deductions from Ron Davies's pay, then, are:

Income Tax	$311.15
Canada Pension Plan	25.36
Unemployment Insurance	22.35
Life, Health, Dental	18.00
Total Deductions	$376.86

The gross pay of $1,075 less the total deductions of $376.86 gives Ron Davies a net pay of $698.14. These figures are shown on an **Employee Earnings Record** (Figure 12.6), which will record Ron Davies's cumulative payroll information for the entire year.

All the payroll information for the employees of Jestadt Industries, including Ron Davies, is summarized on the **Payroll Record** in Figure 12.7. (The other employees are single with no dependents and pay only $8 each for their group health deduction.)

EARNINGS RECORD

DATE EMPLOYED	12-10-82	NAME	Ronald Davis
TAX CODE	5	ADDRESS	17 President Lane
SOCIAL INS. NO.	609-432-017		Winnipeg, MB R3R 0Y8
MARITAL STATUS	Married	TELEPHONE	889-9629
NO. OF DEPENDANTS	4	CLOCK NO.	103

19— WEEK ENDING		GROSS PAY	INC. TAX	CPP CURRENT	CPP YR. TO DATE	UI	LIFE, HEALTH & DENTAL	TOTAL DEDUCT.	NET PAY
Jan.	8	1075 00	311 15	25 36	25 36	22 35	18 00	376 86	698 14
	15	1112 50	327 10	26 11	51 47	22 35	18 00	393 56	718 94
	22	1000 00	279 25	23 36	74 83	22 35	18 00	342 96	657 04
	29	1150 00	349 15	27 11	101 94	22 35	18 00	416 61	733 39

Figure 12.6   Employee Earnings Record

JESTADT INDUSTRIES
HOURLY PAYROLL RECORD

PAYROLL FOR THE PERIOD ENDED

TAX CODE	EMP. NO.	NAME	DAYS WRKD.	HRS.	REGULAR TIME RATE	OVERTIME HRS.	RATE	GROSS PAY	INC. TAX	CPP	UI	LIFE & HEALTH	TOTAL DEDUCTIONS	NET PAY AMOUNT	CH. NO.
5	103	Ron Davies	5	40	25 00	2	37 50	1075 00	311 15	25 36	22 35	18 00	376 86	698 14	11
1	94	Darwin Gaber	5	40	20 00	4	30 00	920 00	272 00	21 36	22 35	8 00	323 71	596 29	12
1	90	Arthur Jansen	5	39	20 00	4	30 00	900 00	266 70	20 86	22 35	8 00	317 91	582 09	13
								2895 00	849 85	67 58	67 05	34 00	1018 48	1876 52	

Figure 12.7   Payroll Record

RECORDING THE PAYROLL

The sample payroll just discussed has been recorded on the payroll record and on the individual earnings records for each employee. Once completed, totalled, and balanced, this payroll data becomes the source information for recording a general journal entry as follows:

19—Jan.	8	Wages Expense				2	8	9	5	00					
		Income Tax Payable										8	4	9	85
		CPP Payable											6	7	58
		UI Payable											6	7	05
		Group Health Payable											3	4	00
		Wages Payable										1	8	7	6	52
		To record the payroll for the week.													

The debit entry to Wages Expense (or Salaries Expense) is the total gross wage, and the credit entries to the various payable accounts represent the amounts withheld from the employees and are owing to the government (income tax, CPP, UI) and to the insurance company (the group health plan). The Wages Payable amount is the net pay that will be paid to the employees when the paycheques are issued.

A second journal entry is also necessary to record the employer's contributions to the required government plans and to the group health plan:

19—Jan.	8	CPP Expense				6	7	58					
		UI Expense				9	3	87					
		Group Health Expense				3	4	00					
		CPP Payable								6	7	58
		UI Payable								9	3	87
		Group Health Payable								3	4	00
		To record company's contribution to government and										
		group health plans.										

The debit entries to the expense accounts represent the additional payroll costs incurred by the employer; the credit entries to the payable accounts represent the amounts owing to the government and to the insurance company.

The figures in the first compound entry are taken directly from the totals of the payroll record in Figure 12.7. The figures in the second entry (the company contributions) are determined as follows:

- The amount contributed to the Canada Pension Plan is *equal* to the amount contributed by the employees.

- The amount contributed to Unemployment Insurance is 1.4 times the amount contributed by the employees.

- The amount contributed to the health plan will vary depending on the details of the plan offered by the insurance company. In our example, the company will contribute an equal amount.

As an alternative to recording these transactions in the general journal and then posting the transactions to the ledger accounts, the figures could be posted directly from the payroll record to the appropriate ledger accounts. When this method is used, the payroll record becomes a journal, and the postings marks are entered under the column totals that have been posted. However, the general journal method will be used throughout this textbook.

PAYMENTS AND REMITTANCES
Payments to Employees

Payments to employees for their salaries and wages have traditionally been made by paycheque. However, in recent years, it has become increasingly common for employers to arrange for the pay to be deposited directly into the employees' personal bank accounts.

Some companies prefer to utilize the services of the banks or other institutions to complete their payrolls by providing them with the pertinent payroll data. In this case, the bank would deposit the pay directly into the employees' personal bank accounts or prepare the cheques to be handed out or mailed to the employees. The total of the amounts deposited directly to the employees' accounts, or the total of all cheques issued to employees, is equal to the total of the Net Pay column on the payroll record and, therefore, is equal to the balance in the Wages (or Salaries) Payable account. An entry in the cash payments journal (Figure 12.8) when the paycheques are issued will clear the Wages (Salaries) Payable account to a zero balance.

DATE	ACCOUNT DEBIT	MEMO	F.	ACCTS. PAY. DR.	PURCH. DISC. CR.	PURCH. DR.	GST-ITC DR.	GEN. LED. DR.	BANK CR.	CH. NO.
19— Jan. 8	Wages Payable	R. Davies						1 8 7 6 52	6 9 8 14	11
		D. Gaber							5 9 6 29	12
		A. Jansen							5 8 2 09	13
Feb. 15	Income Tax Payable							8 4 9 85		
	Canada Pension Plan Payable	remittance to						1 3 5 16		
	Unemployment Insurance Payable	Receiver General						1 6 0 92	1 1 4 5 93	47
Feb. 19	Group Health Payable	January remittance						6 8 00	6 8 00	52

(CASH PAYMENTS — PAGE ___)

Figure 12.8   Recording Paycheques and Remittances

Remittance of Payroll Deductions and Company Contributions

When the payroll is entered in the general journal, the deductions are recorded as liabilities (amounts owing to the government and the insurance company); and, of course, these liabilities must be paid on specific pre-arranged dates. Usually, remittances to the government from companies with small payrolls are made on a monthly basis, usually payable by the 15th of the month following the pay period. (KBC Decorating Co. will be following this practice.) Companies with large payrolls (those with monthly remittances totalling $15,000 or more) must remit the appropriate deductions *twice* a month: Amounts from payrolls up to the 15th of the month are payable on the 25th of the month, and amounts from payrolls from the 16th to the end of the month are payable on the 10th of the following month. The total amount owing to the Receiver General (the department of the federal government to which all payroll contributions are remitted) consists of the income tax deductions, the employer *and* employee contributions to the Canada Pension Plan, and the employer *and* employee contributions to Unemployment Insurance. The remittance of these amounts is usually recorded in the cash payments journal (Figure 12.8) at the time the cheque is issued.

The income tax portion of the remittance is the amount that was deducted from the employees. Since it was originally credited to the Income Tax Payable account, the debit entry in the cash payments journal will clear the balance of the Income Tax Payable account to zero.

The Canada Pension Plan Payable figure includes the amount that was withheld from the employees *plus* an equal contribution made by the employer. A total of $67.58 was deducted from the employees' pay and an equal amount of $67.58 was contributed by the employer. The CPP Payable account, then, is debited for $135.16 when the remittance is made to the Receiver General, clearing this account to zero.

The Unemployment Insurance Payable figure is the amount withheld from the employees ($67.05) *plus* the employer's contribution of 1.4 times that amount ($67.05 × 1.4 = $93.87). The total of these two amounts ($67.05 + $93.87 = $160.92) is debited to UI Payable when the remittance is made, thus clearing the account to zero.

The remaining deduction for the group health plan is usually paid on a monthly basis to the insurance company that is providing the health and insurance coverage. In this case, the premiums, when paid, would be debited to the Group Health Payable account, thus clearing this account to zero. The entry for this remittance to the insurance company is recorded in the cash payments journal (see Figure 12.8).

These remittance entries have now cleared all the payroll liability accounts. Only the expense accounts remain open. Figure 12.9 shows the T-accounts representing the ledger accounts used in the payroll of Jestadt Industries.

WORKERS COMPENSATION

Each province in Canada has legislation governing workers' compensation for injuries or disabilities that resulted from accidents that occurred while the employee was on the job.

Deductions for compensation coverage are *not* made from the employee's pay. Instead, the employer assumes the entire cost of the premium as set out in the Workers Compensation Regulations. Although it is not mandatory for employers to obtain coverage for compensation, they can receive coverage upon request. (It should be noted, however, that **Workers Compensation** is not applicable to all companies.)

Bank		Wages Payable	
	698.14		1,876.52
	596.29	1,876.52	
	582.09		
	1,145.93		
	68.00		

Wages Expense		CPP Payable	
2,895.00			67.58
			67.58
		135.16	

CPP Expense		UI Payable	
67.58			67.05
			93.87
		160.92	

UI Expense		Group Health Payable	
67.05			34.00
			34.00
		68.00	

Group Health Expense		Income Tax Payable	
34.00			849.85
		849.85	

Figure 12.9   T-accounts for Jestadt Industries' Payroll

The company's expense for Workers Compensation coverage is not calculated at each payroll period as is the case with the usual payroll expenses. An estimate of the projected payroll for the year is submitted to the Workers Compensation Board at the beginning of each year. The Workers Compensation Board uses this estimate for premium billings, which are payable in two or three instalments during the year. At the end of the year, the actual payroll amount is then reported by the company. The Board will then send a bill for the balance or record a credit if the payroll was originally over-estimated.

These premiums paid by the company are considered an operating expense and are charged to the Workers Compensation Expense account.

HOLIDAY PAY

All employees are entitled to a minimum of two weeks' paid vacation time each year. However, in cases when this vacation time is not taken by the employee, Revenue Canada stipulates that all full- and part-time employees must be paid an amount equal to 4% of their annual earnings in lieu of this vacation time. Such payments to the employees are considered part of the wage or salary and are subject to the usual deductions.

▶ **PRACTICE EXERCISE 1**

The following time cards are for the three employees of Widgits Unlimited. These employees are required to punch in each morning and punch out at the end of each regular work day. Those employees working overtime must punch in and out again in the evening. Any employee arriving between five and 15 minutes late is penalized 15 minutes' pay. Each employee takes a half-hour lunch break *without* pay.

The standard work week is 40 hours at a regular rate of $20 per hour. Overtime is paid for all hours worked over 40 hours per week at time-and-a-half ($30 per hour). Any hours worked on Saturday are paid at double the regular rate ($40 per hour).

Calculate the gross pay for each of these employees:

Week ending: April 14, 19—

NAME: EDNA SMITH

			Extra	
	IN	**OUT**	**IN**	**OUT**
Mon.	8:00	4:31	7:00	8:02
Tue.	8:01	4:30		
Wed.	7:58	4:32	7:00	8:15
Thu.	7:59	4:30		
Fri.	9:01	4:31		
Sat.	8:00	12:00		
TOTAL TIME:			hours	
Rates $				
Total Wages $				

Week ending: April 14, 19—

NAME: JOY BAKER

			Extra	
	IN	**OUT**	**IN**	**OUT**
Mon.	7:58	4:00	7:00	8:30
Tue.	8:01	4:31		
Wed.	7:59	4:32	7:00	8:30
Thu.	8:00	4:31		
Fri.	8:30	4:30		
Sat.	8:00	12:00		
TOTAL TIME:			hours	
Rates $				
Total Wages $				

Week ending:	April 14, 19—				
NAME: LUCY CANELLI					
				Extra	
	IN	OUT		IN	OUT
Mon.	7:59	4:32		6:59	8:30
Tue.	8:00	4:01			
Wed.	8:01	4:31		6:58	8:15
Thu.	8:10	3:00			
Fri.	8:00	4:33			
Sat.	8:00	12:00			
TOTAL TIME:				hours	
Rates $					
Total Wages $					

▶ PRACTICE EXERCISE 2

(a) Select a piecework payroll record from your supplies and record the number of pieces completed by each employee of The Fashion Factory:

P. Cardin	1,111
J. Woolly	1,129
T. Bloomer	1,148
R. Napp	1,133

(b) Calculate the gross pay for each employee using this multi-tier incentive plan:

First 500 pieces	$0.50 each
Next 300 pieces	$0.60 each
Next 200 pieces	$0.70 each
Over 1,000 pieces	$0.90 each

(c) Complete the payroll using the payroll deduction tables illustrated in Figures 12.3, 12.4, and 12.5. All employees are Code 1 for income tax purposes. (The Fashion Factory does not have a group health plan.) Total all columns and prove that the payroll balances.

(d) Prepare the compound general journal entry to record this payroll on June 30, 19—.

(e) Prepare the general journal entry on June 30 to record the employer's contribution to CPP and UI.

(f) Prepare the general journal entry to record the remittance to the Receiver General on July 15, 19—.

▶ PRACTICE EXERCISE 3

Select a piecework payroll record from your supplies. Enter the names of these employees and the number of pieces produced by each:

Julie Robinson	2,300
Katie Friesen	2,275

| Mary Boyko | 2,310 |
| Joan Flannery | 2,350 |

These employees are paid according to the following incentive plan: Up to 1,000 pieces, $0.35 each; next 600 pieces, $0.40 each; next 400 pieces, $0.45 each; over 2,000 pieces, $0.50 each.

Determine the income tax and CPP deductions from the tables illustrated in Figures 12.3 and 12.5. All employees are single with no dependents, so Code 1 is used in the income tax table. The UI deduction for each employee is the weekly maximum of $22.35. Company pension is to be calculated at 3% of gross pay.

(a) Total and prove the payroll record.

(b) Prepare a general journal entry dated February 22, 19—, to record the payroll.

(c) Prepare a general journal entry to record the company's expenses for CPP, UI, and company pension. The employer contributes an equal amount to the company pension.

(d) Prepare the general journal entries necessary to record the remittance to the Receiver General and to the insurance company that administers the company pension plan. Assume both remittances are recorded on March 14, 19—.

(e) Post the above entries to T-accounts.

▶ PRACTICE EXERCISE 4

The employees at Klym Construction are members of a closed-shop union. This means that *all* employees are union members. The union dues are deducted from each employee's weekly paycheque and all dues collected are remitted to the union once a month.

Assume that all the employees are paid at the same basic rate of $25 per hour for a regular 8-hour day. The union contract specifies that any time worked on Saturdays and any time worked over 8 hours in any one day will be considered overtime and will be paid at 1.5 times the regular rate (time-and-a-half). Double time is paid for hours worked on Sundays and holidays.

EMP. NO.	NAME	HOURS WORKED						INCOME TAX CODE
		JULY 1 MON.	JULY 2 TUES.	JULY 3 WED.	JULY 4 THUR.	JULY 5 FRI.	JULY 6 SAT.	
27	John Stremich	4	8	8	8	9	1	1
28	Ernie Kull	0	8	9	8	10	2	1
33	John Pattinson	4	8	8	8	10	1	1
35	Bob Norman	0	8	8	8	9	3	1

Other information:

July 1 is Canada Day; therefore, *all* employees will be paid for 8 hours. Those employees who did work on July 1 will be paid double time for their hours worked in addition to their basic 8 hours. Union dues are $12.00 per week per employee. Income tax is determined from the table in Figure 12.3, and Canada

Pension from the table in Figure 12.4. The Unemployment Insurance deduction is the weekly maximum of $22.35.

(a) Complete the payroll on a payroll record selected from your supplies. Total and prove the payroll as usual.

(b) Prepare a general journal entry dated July 8 to record the week's payroll.

(c) Prepare a general journal entry to record the employer's contributions to the government plans. The employer does *not* contribute to union dues.

(d) Prepare a general journal entry for the remittance to the Receiver General and for the remittance to the union. These remittances will be dated August 15, 19—.

► ### PRACTICE EXERCISE 5

The following information is taken from the payroll records of McKnight Manufacturing on June 30, 19—.

Gross Pay	— Production Department	$18,700.00
	— General Office	5,200.00
		23,900.00

Deductions:		
Income Tax	$5,114.00	
CPP	717.00	
UI	574.00	
Company Pension	478.00	
RRSP Contributions	4,000.00	
Medical Plan	239.00	
Canada Savings Bonds	850.00	
Union Dues	748.00	12,720.00
Total Net Pay		$11,180.00

(a) Prepare a compound general journal entry to record the payroll on June 30.

(b) Prepare a compound general journal entry to record the employer's contribution to CPP, UI, the company pension, and the medical plan:

• CPP and UI as usual;

• company pension and medical plan on an equal basis.

(c) Prepare a compound general journal entry to record the remittance to Manufacturers Life Insurance Company on June 30 for the company pension plan, RRSP contributions, and the medical plan.

(d) Prepare a general journal entry to record the payment on June 30 to Canadian Trust for the Canada Savings Bond contributions.

(e) Prepare a general journal entry to remit the union dues on June 30.

(f) Prepare a general journal entry to remit income tax, CPP, and UI to the Receiver General. This remittance is made on July 14.

THINK ABOUT IT!

1. Name three types of payroll systems. Give an example of a type of job that would fit within each system.
2. What information is recorded on a time card?
3. Name the three payroll deductions that by law must be withheld from all employees' pay.
4. Do all employees pay the same amount of income tax? Why? What government form is prepared by every employee for this purpose?
5. What amount must the *employer* contribute to the Canada Pension Plan? to Unemployment Insurance?
6. Name three other common payroll deductions.
7. What is the difference between Gross Pay and Net Pay?
8. What is Workers Compensation? Who pays for it?

▶ **SEPTEMBER TRANSACTIONS: KBC DECORATING CO.**

Record September's activities in the usual journals, posting the customers' and suppliers' transactions on a daily basis.

19—

Sept. 1 Paid Consolidated Freightways $50 plus $3.27 GST for freight charges on the order from Minnesota Decor on August 14.
Received a cheque from Clear-Vu Windows for the September rent, $2,500 plus GST.

1 KBC made arrangements with the bank today to transfer $15,000 from its account into a 30-day term deposit. Debit Investments in the cash payments journal. The bank has given a debit memo; therefore, no cheque was issued.

1 Received a debit memo from the bank for the mortgage payment: principal, $316.63, and interest, $996.87.

3 Donated $50 to the Boy Scouts of Canada.

4 Paid Shell Oil $430 plus $28.13 GST.

11 The cheque received from K. Young Painting and deposited on August 30 for invoice #24 has been returned to KBC's bank marked NSF (non-sufficient funds). The bank has sent a debit memo with the NSF cheque attached. This debit memo for $696.00 includes a handling charge of $12. In the cash payments journal, debit K. Young Painting and Accounts Receivable Control for $684. On the next line, debit Bank Charges & Interest for $12. Both amounts will appear in the General Ledger column, and the total of $696 is credited to the bank. Mr. Martin will phone Mr. Young to ask him to send a certified cheque to cover the NSF cheque and the additional bank charges incurred.

12 Received the bank statement and cancelled cheques for August. Complete the bank reconciliation statement, based on the following

information: The August statement shows a balance on August 31 of $34,205.14. These items do not appear on the statement and are, therefore, considered outstanding: the August 31 deposit of $21,400, cheque #95 for $2,488.32, cheque #97 for $3,000, and cheque #98 for $3,000. Bank charges for the month of August were deducted on the statement, $48.85, but have not yet been recorded on KBC's books. Record and post the necessary journal entry resulting from this bank reconciliation. Refer to last month's entry if necessary.

13   Paid the hydro bill, $60 plus $3.93 GST, and the Intercity Gas bill, $45 plus $2.94 GST. Paid the phone bill, $240 plus $15.70 GST. Paid Minnesota Decor Supply for their invoice #1290, $1,400.

13   Received a bill from Border Brokers for the cost of clearing through customs the shipment from Minnesota Decor Supply (invoice #1290 dated August 14). Their bill covers customs clearance fees, $70, plus the GST on the imported goods (7% of $1,470 = $102.90). Issued a cheque as follows: debit Duty & Brokerage, $70; debit GST-ITC, $102.90; credit Bank, $172.90.

14   Cash sales: paint and supplies, $2,500, and wallpaper, $2,300.

15   Sales on terms of 2/10,n/30: Beavis & Sons, paint and supplies, $1,200, and wallpaper, $500. Jay-Mar Co., paint and supplies, $800, and wallpaper, $200. Edna Morton, paint and supplies, $1,600, and wallpaper, $400. S. Wilkinson, paint and supplies, $800, and wallpaper, $300.

16   Payments from petty cash: coffee, sugar, and creamer, $15 (GST exempt); postage due, $2.20 plus $0.15 GST; sweeping compound for the warehouse, $12 plus $0.79 GST; freight on incoming merchandise, $18 plus $1.18 GST.

16   Issued a cheque to pay freight charges on the order from Minnesota Decor, $38.95 plus $2.58 GST.

19   Remitted the August sales tax: total collected, $917.70; our commission, $37.18; net remitted, $880.52.

20   Bought office supplies inventory of $360.50 plus $23.59 GST from Diswinka Hardware; C.O.D. Paid Mitchell Advertising for the net owing on invoice #39. Paid Coleman Industries for the net owing on invoice #77. (We have lost the discount for failing to pay within the discount period.) Cash sales: paint and supplies, $1,400, and wallpaper, $1,600.

22   Received these purchase invoices: #140 from Reynolds Paper Co. for paint and supplies, $2,000, and wallpaper, $3,000 (plus $350 GST); #120 from Rainbow Supplies for paint and supplies, $3,000, and wallpaper, $2,000 (plus $350 GST); and #51 from Spencer Stucco for paint, $5,000 plus $350 GST. All invoices carry terms of 2/10,n/30 and are dated September 20.

25   Received payment from our customers for the September 15 invoices, less the 2% discount: invoices #27, #28, #29, and #30.

26   Payments from petty cash: postage due, $3.10 plus $0.22 GST; car wash for the van, $10 plus $0.65 GST (Miscellaneous Expense); garbage bags for the warehouse, $20 plus $1.31 GST; wrapping paper and twine for the warehouse, $10 plus $0.65 GST. Issued a cheque to reimburse the petty cash fund.

27   Received a certified cheque from K. Young Painting to cover the NSF cheque previously received for invoice #24. In the cash receipts journal, credit the customer for $684 and credit Bank Charges & Interest for $12.

28   Mr. Martin withdrew paint costing $80 for use in decorating his own home. In the general journal, debit Drawings, H. Martin $85.60; credit GST Payable $5.60; and credit Purchases—Paint & Supplies $80. (Since the owner is taking the paint at cost price, the value is deducted from the Purchases account rather than charging it to Sales. However, the paint is considered to be sold; therefore, GST must be charged on the value of the paint.)

30   The partners have each withdrawn $3,000 cash. Issue separate cheques. (Refer to the August 30 entry if necessary.) Received the balance owing on Job #5, $20,000 plus GST. Cash sales: paint and supplies, $2,000, and wallpaper, $1,700.

30   Complete the payroll for all four employees, using a payroll record sheet. Because you are the bookkeeper, use your own name in the payroll records. Your gross pay is $2,000 and the three service employees' gross pay amount is $2,400 each. Only the required government deductions (income tax, CPP, and UI) will be used in this payroll.

　　　For income tax purposes, Tony Asfour is Code 5 (married with a wife as dependent). Dale Campbell, Rudy Wenzell, and you (the bookkeeper) are Code 1. To determine the deductions for income tax, CPP, and UI, consult the government deductions tables provided.

　　　From the completed payroll record, prepare the general journal entries that are required. For help with this, refer to the entries for Jestadt Industries illustrated earlier in this chapter. Also, record the general journal entries for the company's contributions to CPP and UI. Finally, record the paycheques issued from the cash payments journal: debit Salaries Payable for the total net pay in the General Ledger column, and enter the individual net pay amounts in the Bank column. Show special payroll cheque numbers issued, beginning with cheque #30.

MONTH-END ACTIVITIES

(a) Balance all journals as usual.

(b) Post all remaining transactions and totals. Prepare a trial balance with schedules.

(c) Prepare an interim statement of profit and loss for the nine months ending September 30, 19—. Merchandise inventory on hand at the end of September is $20,376.90. Estimates have determined the following expenses: Insurance expense, $600; Office Supplies expense, $600; and Warehouse Supplies expense, $500. (Do not record journal entries for these figures; they are estimates calculated only for the purposes of preparing this interim statement.

Correcting Entries

CHAPTER OBJECTIVES

After completing this chapter, you will be able to:
- record journal entries to correct errors in entries previously recorded and posted

IMPORTANT WORDS AND TERMS IN THIS CHAPTER

Adjusting Entries
Correcting Entries

Occasionally, errors are made when recording and/or posting a journal entry. When they do occur, some common-sense practices should be observed to maintain the integrity of the financial records:

1. Entries should be corrected as soon as the errors are discovered; otherwise, they could be forgotten, thereby creating further errors.

2. Erasing, writing over figures, and using liquid eradicators should be avoided. These destroy the dependability and integrity of the records.

3. Neatness and legibility are important. An obscured figure could be read incorrectly by the accountant or by other employees. The bookkeeper must keep in mind that others rely on the information contained in the financial records—the accountant, the owner/manager, the auditor, and Revenue Canada.

In order to allow space for possible corrections, it is a common practice to use only half the height of the writing space for recording the original transaction. This leaves sufficient space to make a correction should an error be discovered. Figure 13.1 shows properly written figures on columnar paper.

Figure 13.1   Writing Figures Properly

When an error is found, here are the basic principles that should be observed:

1. If an error in a journal is discovered *before* it has been posted to the ledger, a single line is drawn through the incorrect amount or incorrect word and the corrected amount or word is neatly written above the error. The original error must not be obliterated because it could be questioned later by management or by the auditor. Figure 13.2 illustrates the correction of errors.

2. If the entry in the journal is correct, but an error is discovered in the ledger, the same correcting procedure is used as discussed in item 1.

3. If the error is discovered in an entry that has already been posted *after* the journal is totalled and ruled, or during the preparation of the bank recon-

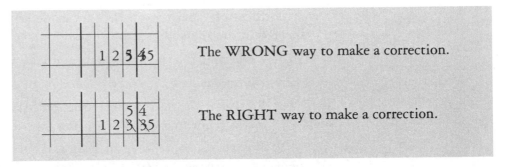

Figure 13.2   Correcting Writing Errors

ciliation or the trial balance, a **correcting entry** (sometimes called an **adjusting entry**) must be recorded and posted. The correcting entry will transfer an amount from the incorrect account(s) to the correct account(s) or adjust the amount of the transaction in the existing accounts.

For example, cheque #53 for $456, issued to the A. Smith Company as payment on account, was entered incorrectly in the cash payments journal (CP6) as $546. This transposition error was not discovered until the preparation of the bank reconciliation. (We will assume that the amount recorded on the cheque is correct.) Because the original journal entry was recorded for an amount greater than the actual amount of the cheque, the following entry is recorded to effectively reduce the amount of the original entry by $546 − $456 = $90:

DATE		DESCRIPTION	F.	DEBIT	CREDIT
19— June	21	Bank		90 00	
		A/P A. Smith Co.			90 00
		To correct error. Cheque #53 for $456 was recorded			
		in cash payments journal, page 6, as $546.			

4. If an amount is posted to the wrong account, a correcting (adjusting) journal entry is necessary to transfer the amount from the wrong account to the proper account. For example, on January 19, a purchase of office supplies for $30 was posted by mistake to the Warehouse Supplies Prepaid account. A correcting entry is required to remove the amount from the Warehouse Supplies Prepaid account and to charge it to the Office Supplies Prepaid account.

DATE		DESCRIPTION	F.	DEBIT	CREDIT
19— Feb.	1	Office Supplies Prepaid		30 00	
		Warehouse Supplies Prepaid			30 00
		To charge Office Supplies account with purchase			
		on Jan. 19, which was erroneously charged to			
		Warehouse Supplies.			

A three-step analysis can be used in determining which account must be affected in the adjusting entries:

1. Determine the entry that was originally recorded.
2. Determine how the entry *should have been* recorded.
3. Prepare the correcting entry that will transfer the value from the incorrect account to the proper account.

To illustrate this three-step analysis, assume that on February 3, office equipment was purchased for $980 from Sunare Office Equipment Co. on terms of n/30. The entry that was originally recorded was:

DATE		DESCRIPTION	F.	DEBIT	CREDIT
19— Feb.	3	Office Equipment		9 8 0 00	
		Capital			9 8 0 00
		Purchased office equipment on terms of 30 days.			

The entry that should have been recorded for this transaction was:

DATE		DESCRIPTION	F.	DEBIT	CREDIT
19— Feb.	3	Office Equipment		9 8 0 00	
		A/P Sunare Office Equipment Co.			9 8 0 00
		Purchased a typewriter on 30-day terms.			

Since the original debit to the Office Equipment account was correct, there is no need to affect that account in the correcting entry. Therefore, we need to transfer $980 from the incorrect account (Capital) to the proper account (A/P Sunare Office Equipment Co.). This general journal entry will make the necessary correction:

DATE		DESCRIPTION	F.	DEBIT	CREDIT
19— Feb.	3	Capital		9 8 0 00	
		A/P Sunare Office Equipment Co.			9 8 0 00
		To remove transaction recorded to Capital that should have been			
		recorded to Accounts Payable.			

Once the correcting entry has been posted, both the Capital account and the A/P Sunare Office Equipment Co. account will reflect the correct balances as if the error had never occurred.

To better understand the relationship between the correcting entry and the original entry, the bookkeeper or accountant will sometimes enter a pencil notation in the margin beside the original journal entry. This notation would identify the date it was corrected, the journal in which the correcting entry was recorded, and any other information that may be helpful.

▶ **PRACTICE EXERCISE 1**

The following errors were discovered on the books of A-Line Distributors. Record the necessary general journal entries, complete with detailed explanations, to correct these errors. The dates of the original transactions appear in parentheses. All correcting entries should be dated December 31, 19—.

(a) An entry of $67 was charged to Office Supplies Expense but should have been charged to Warehouse Supplies Expense. (December 3)

(b) $25 was debited to Sales Discounts instead of Sales Returns & Allowances. (December 5)

(c) $250 was charged to Insurance Prepaid (Stock) instead of Insurance Prepaid (Building). (December 10)

(d) Freight charges on an order of catalogues and other advertising material, $69.50, were charged in error to Freight In. (December 14)

(e) $10.52 was charged to Miscellaneous Expense instead of Delivery Expense. (December 18)

(f) An invoice for the purchase of warehouse supplies ($17.30) and office supplies ($41.70) was charged to Purchases. (December 20)

(g) The Petty Cash account was debited in the cash payments journal (CP5) when the fund was reimbursed for this month's expenditures: Miscellaneous Expense, $14.22; Office Supplies Prepaid, $21.30; Freight In, $17.70; and Delivery Expense, $25.90. (December 28)

(h) The total of the GST-ITC column in the purchase journal (PJ8) for December was posted to the GST Payable account, $744.62. (December 31)

▶ **PRACTICE EXERCISE 2**

The following transactions were recorded in the general journal by your assistant. You may assume that the narratives (memos) are correct; however, the journal entries contain errors. Record the general journal entries necessary to correct these errors. Use December 31, 19—, as the current date.

19— June	4	Utilities				1	5	6	80				
		Cash									1	5	6	80
		To record gas bill ($24.60) and electricity bill ($122.20).												
Aug.	16	Cash				2	1	0	00				
		Sales									2	1	0	00
		To record merchandise sold to customer on account (n/30).												
Sep.	30	Capital				2	0	0	0	00			
		Cash									2	0	0	0	00
		To record cash withdrawn by owner for personal use.												
Oct.	5	Purchases				2	5	0	0	00			
		Accounts Receivable									2	5	0	0	00
		To record purchase of merchandise from our regular supplier												
		on account.												
Nov.	7	Sales				7	2	1	5	00			
		Cash									7	2	1	5	00
		To record over-the-counter cash sales for this week.												
	16	Cash				7	0	5	60				
		Accounts receivable									7	0	5	60
		To record cheque for $705.60 received from customer on												
		Invoice #266 ($720.00) less 2% discount.												
Dec.	3	Telephone Expense					3	2	70				
		Drawings										3	2	70
		To record payment of owner's personal telephone bill using												
		company funds.												

▶ **PRACTICE EXERCISE 3**

For each of the following transactions, prepare the necessary correcting entry in general journal form. If the entry is already correct, just write OK. Use the last day of the month as the date of correction.

Jan.   6   A cash purchase of office stationery, $87.15, was charged to the Office Equipment account.

Jan. 13   Cheque #19 for $13.50 was issued to Apex Courier for the delivery of merchandise to a customer. It was charged to the Freight In account.

Jan. 23   A cheque for $135 received from Susan Curtis, a customer, to apply against invoice #37 was credited to the Sales account.

Mar. 17   Purchased a computer from Western Office Equipment Co. for $1,250 on 90-day terms; invoice #2171. The Purchases account was debited.

Apr. 19   A cash refund of $15 received for an overcharge on the purchase of office supplies was credited to the Purchase Returns & Allowances account.

May 30   A cheque for $500 was issued to the owner, Stan Clives, for his personal use. It was charged to the Salaries Expense account.

June 11   A cheque for $450 received on account from Smith & Sons was credited to the account of A.J. Smith & Co.

July 12   Merchandise valued at $146 was withdrawn by the owner for his personal use. It was credited to the Sales account.

Aug. 9   Express charge on shipping supplies, $3.50, was debited to the Freight In account.

Sept. 11   A credit note for $33 was issued to Henry Ball for an overcharge on an invoice. It was recorded as a debit to Sales and a credit to Accounts Receivable/Henry Ball.

Sept. 29   Sold an old computer to an employee for $200. Bank was debited and Sales was credited.

Oct. 3   A cheque issued for $59 to pay the telephone bill was recorded incorrectly on Sept. 12 in the cash payments journal (page CP12) as $95. The cash payments journal was totalled and posted on Sept. 30.

Nov. 18   Purchased a second-hand truck from Stern Trucks Ltd. for $3,500. The Delivery Expense account was debited.

Nov. 21   A cheque for $821.50 received from Vernon King (a customer) and deposited on Nov. 15 was returned by the bank today marked NSF along with the appropriate debit memo. The entry recorded for this NSF cheque was a debit to Accounts Receivable/Vernon King and a credit to Bank.

Dec. 10   Coffee purchased for the office, $8.50, was charged to the Office Supplies Expense account.

Dec. 19   A cheque received from A.C. Grant (a customer) to pay invoice #67 for $510 was entered on the books as a debit to Bank and a credit to Accounts Receivable/A.C. Grant.

Dec. 21   The GST applicable to the merchandise withdrawn by the owner for his personal use was credited to the GST-ITC account, $21.

▶ **PRACTICE EXERCISE 4**

Prepare the general journal entries, complete with proper explanations, to correct the errors discovered in the books of the Hamilton Distributing Co. All errors are to be corrected on February 1. (All source journals were posted at the end of January.)

1.   A cheque for $200 received from a customer, John Arthurs, on January 10 was credited to Arthur Jones's account in the cash receipts journal (CR5).

2. An invoice dated January 15 for $526.30 entered in the sales journal (SJ9) was posted to Robert Hall's account. This invoice was actually issued to Carl Hull.

3. On January 31, the total of the Sales column in the cash receipts journal (CR6) was posted to the credit of the Purchases account, $9,836.30.

4. On January 30, the owner, Bobbi Hamilton, withdrew $500 worth of merchandise for her personal use. It was recorded as a debit to the Drawings account and a credit to the Sales account. (Disregard GST.)

5. A purchase invoice dated January 31 for $136.50 for office supplies was entered in the Purchases column of the purchase journal (PJ7).

6. Cheque #86 for $47, issued to pay the water bill, was entered in the cash disbursements journal (CD7) charged to the Telephone Expense account.

7. On January 18, a credit note was received from Ajax Supply Co. for an overcharge of $15 on a recent purchase of office supplies. It was recorded in the general journal (GJ5) as a debit to Accounts Payable/Ajax Supply Co. and a credit to Purchases.

8. A cheque for $35, issued to ABC Transport for the delivery of merchandise to a customer, was debited to Freight In in the cash disbursements journal (CD8).

9. A credit note for $22.50 was issued to a customer, Lyn-Tor Industries, for damaged goods returned on invoice #447. It was recorded in the cash disbursements journal (CD8) as a debit to Sales Returns & Allowances.

10. The remittance of the net GST for the last fiscal quarter (October, November, December) was entered in the general journal on January 28 as a debit of $3,456.78 to GST-ITC, a debit of $4,197.54 to Bank, and a credit of $7,654.32 to GST Payable. (Assume that the dollar amounts quoted are correct.)

THINK ABOUT IT!

1. How are entries corrected if they have *not* yet been posted?
2. How are entries corrected if posting has already taken place?
3. Should erasers or liquid eradicators be used for correcting errors on financial records? Why?

► OCTOBER TRANSACTIONS: KBC DECORATING CO.

Job #6 is a two-month contract at the Army Camp painting the barracks buildings, offices, pool building, sports auditorium, and other buildings. The cost of this contract is $42,000 with a payment of $21,000 due at the end of October and again at the end of November. Since there are adequate inventories of supplies, no purchases will be needed this month (the purchase journal is not required).

19—

Oct. 1 Received payment from Clear-Vu Windows for the October rent, $2,500 plus GST. Received a debit memo from the bank for this month's mortgage payment, $1,313.50, covering principal of $319.80 and interest of $993.70. Renewed the $15,000 term deposit and received a credit memo for the interest earned at 5.5%, $68.75. (Interest Revenue)

2 Paid purchase invoices dated September 22 less the 2% discount: Reynolds Paper Co. on invoice #140; Rainbow Supplies on invoice #120; and Spencer Stucco on invoice #51.

4 Paid the water bill for the third quarter, $300 (GST exempt).

5 Bought two extension ladders for $250 plus $16.35 GST from Diswinka Hardware, C.O.D. (Tools & Equipment)

8 Paid Intercity Gas, $70 plus $4.58 GST, and hydro, $50 plus $3.27 GST. Sent a donation to the United Way, $200.

9 Cash sales: paint and supplies, $2,000, and wallpaper, $1,300. Payments from petty cash: postage, $6 plus $0.42 GST; paint roller refills, $20 plus $1.31 GST; felt markers, $12 plus $0.79 GST; and warehouse supplies, $16 plus $1.05 GST.

12 Received the bank statement and cancelled cheques for September. Complete the bank reconciliation statement using the following information: The bank statement shows a balance of $31,846.93 on September 30. The following items do not appear on the statement: deposits of $21,400 and $4,218, cheque #103 for $47.94 and cheque #109 for $4,494. A debit memo for bank charges of $55 has not yet been recorded on KBC Decorating's books. A deposit of $700.00 had been added to KBC Decorating's account, but this deposit does not belong to the company. (The bank has been contacted about this error.) Record and post the necessary journal entry resulting from the bank reconciliation.

15 Remitted to the Receiver General of Canada all payroll deductions and contributions from the September payroll. In the cash payments journal, three lines are required: debit Income Tax Payable $1,764.70; debit UI Payable $662.40; and debit CPP Payable $405.04. Only one cheque is issued for the total of $2,832.14.

16 Refilled the postage meter machine, $98.50 plus $6.90 GST. (Postage)

19 Remitted the September provincial sales tax: total collected, $1,211; commission, $40.11.

20 Remitted net GST for the third quarter: total GST collected, $7,818.30; total GST-ITC, $3,768.45. Issued a cheque for the net amount. Prepare the GST Tax Return. The total sales figure for the fiscal quarter (Line 101 of the return) is determined by adding up all the sales entries posted to the Sales accounts during July

through September. The total of purchases (Line 102) will be determined by adding up the purchases posted to the Purchases accounts during this same period. (For the sake of simplicity, we will ignore the purchases of other expenses and assets, which should normally be included in the total on Line 102.)

22   Cash sales: paint and supplies, $1,500, and wallpaper, $900.

25   Sales on terms of 2/10,n/30: Dayson & Son, paint and supplies, $600, and wallpaper, $400. S. Miller, paint and supplies, $400, and wallpaper, $200. Wm. Zelisko Enterprises, paint and supplies, $500, and wallpaper, $500.

29   Paid from petty cash: purchase of paint and supplies, $18.50 plus $1.21 GST; postage due, $4 plus $0.28 GST; Scotch tape for the office, $10 plus $0.65 GST. Issued a cheque to reimburse the petty cash fund.

30   Cash sales: paint and supplies, $1,400, and wallpaper, $1,600. The owners withdrew $3,000 each (separate cheques). Received a cheque for the first instalment on Job #6, $21,000 plus 7% GST.

31   Complete the payroll. The service employees have been given a raise to $2,600 each. The bookkeeper's salary has been increased to $2,100. Refer to the deductions tables at the end of Chapter 12 to determine the amount to be withheld from each employee. Record the necessary general journal entries (a) to record the payroll and (b) to record the company payroll contributions. Record the issuance of the payroll cheques in the cash payments journal (cheque #34, #35, #36, and #37).

MONTH-END ACTIVITIES

(a)   Balance the journals as usual.

(b)   Complete the posting as usual.

(c)   Prepare a trial balance with schedules.

14

November Transactions: KBC Decorating Co.

. . . .

BC Decorating's service employees are still working on Job #6 at the Army Camp. This job is expected to be completed by the end of the month.

19—

Nov. 1 Received a debit memo from the bank for the mortgage principal, $323, and interest, $990.50; the total mortgage payment is $1,313.50. Received a credit memo from the bank for the October interest earned on the term deposit, $68.75. KBC has increased the amount of the investment to $20,000 and has renewed it for another 30 days. Debit Investments for $5,000 in the cash payments journal.

1 Received a cheque from Clear-Vu Windows for their November rent, $2,500 plus GST.

2 Cash sales: paint and supplies, $1,500, and wallpaper, $1,100.

3 Received payment from Dayson & Son on invoice #31. Payments from petty cash: coffee, sugar, and creamer, $14; typewriter ribbon, $12.60 plus $0.82 GST.

4 Sold to Beavis & Sons, paint and supplies, $600, and wallpaper, $300; to Jay-Mar Co., paint and supplies, $700, and wallpaper, $400; to Edna Morton, paint and supplies, $800, and wallpaper, $300; and to S. Wilkinson, paint and supplies, $500, and wallpaper, $200. All invoices carry the usual terms.

7 Paid the hydro bill, $80 plus $5.23 GST. Paid Intercity Gas for the heating bill, $100 plus $6.54 GST. Received a credit note from Rainbow Supplies for defective wallpaper received on their invoice #120, $160 plus $11.20 GST.

7 Paid the October and November phone bills, $450 plus $29.44 GST. (Last month's phone bill was not paid on the due date because of an error on a long distance charge. The company has received a corrected bill and is now paying both bills together.)

10 The bank statement and cancelled cheques for October have arrived in the mail. Complete the bank reconciliation. The statement shows a balance on October 31 of $30,671.31. These items do not appear on the statement: a deposit of $22,470, cheque #115 for $5,250, and cheque #124 for $1,170.89. A debit memo for October bank charges of $70.00 has not yet been recorded on the books. Included among the cancelled cheques were two cheques that belong to

another company but were deducted from KBC's account in error: $620 and $380 (the company has returned these cheques to the bank and asked that the bank adjust their records accordingly). Record and post the necessary journal entry.

12 Mr. Barker withdrew paint and supplies, $50, and wallpaper, $185, to redecorate his family room at home. (Charge GST Payable $16.45 applicable to the goods withdrawn.)

14 Received payments from Beavis & Sons for invoice #34; Jay-Mar Co. for invoice #35; Edna Morton for invoice #36; and S. Wilkinson for invoice #37. All have earned the discount.

15 Remitted to the Receiver General the payroll deductions and company contributions for the October payroll: income tax, $2,026.65; CPP, $440.04; UI, $712.80.

16 Cash sales: paint and supplies, $1,800, and wallpaper, $1,200.

19 Remitted the October provincial sales tax: total collected, $791; the company's commission, $35.91.

20 Received invoices dated yesterday (usual terms): Coleman Industries, invoice #99, for paint and supplies, $3,500; wallpaper, $800; GST, $301. Tranborg & Noble, invoice #70, for paint and supplies, $1,500; wallpaper, $700; GST, $154. Major Office Supplies, invoice #170 (terms n/30), for furniture, $500; office supplies, $226; GST, $47.50.

21 Payments from petty cash: postage due, $3 plus $0.21 GST; fabric cleaner for cleaning mats (Miscellaneous Expense), $15 plus $0.98 GST. Purchased a computer ($2,000), a printer ($500), and suitable software packages ($275). Issued a cheque for $2,775 plus $181.54 GST (charge Furniture & Equipment).

22 Paid freight on incoming merchandise, $65 plus $4.25 GST.

23 Gave a credit note to Jay-Mar Co. for the inferior supplies they received on their last shipment, $84 plus GST plus sales tax. (Don't forget to credit the control account.)

27 Purchased calendars by cheque and mailed them to customers and suppliers, $150 plus $9.81 GST. (Advertising)

28 Cash sales: paint and supplies, $1,700, and wallpaper, $1,500. Paid Coleman Industries for invoice #99 and Tranborg & Noble for invoice #70. KBC is eligible for discounts on both invoices.

30 The owners withdrew $3,000 each.

30 Complete the November payroll. Use the same figures as for the October payroll.

30 Received the final payment on Job #6, $21,000 plus GST.

MONTH-END ACTIVITIES

(a) Balance the journals as usual.

(b) Post all appropriate transactions and totals.

(c) Prepare a trial balance with schedules.

December Transactions: KBC Decorating Co.

....

The partners have decided to close the office and warehouse during the last two weeks of December to allow the entire staff to take their holidays at the same time. The employees all agreed to this arrangement when they were hired. Because there is an ample stock of merchandise on hand, there will be no purchases of merchandise this month, but orders will be placed with suppliers for January delivery.

The service employees are working on Job #7, painting the interior of a large church. This job will be completed before the December 14 closing and will earn $10,000.

19—

Dec. 1 Received a debit memo from the bank for $1,313.50 covering the mortgage payment: principal, $326.23, and interest, $987.27. Received the monthly rent cheque from Clear-Vu Windows. Received a credit memo from the bank for $91.67 for the interest earned on the term deposit. This investment has been renewed.

2 Paid from petty cash: chocolates for guests visiting the office, $14 plus $0.92 GST; boxes of Christmas cards, $20 plus $1.31 GST.

3 Sales on usual terms: Dayson & Son, paint and supplies, $500, and wallpaper, $200. Edna Morton, paint and supplies, $600, and wallpaper, $400.

4 Paid the November hydro bill, $180 plus $11.78 GST, and the Intercity Gas bill for November service, $350 plus $22.90 GST. Paid the phone bill for November service, $300 plus $19.63 GST.

5 Sent a donation to the Christmas Cheer Board, $300.

5 Payments from petty cash: postage due, $2.80 plus $0.20 GST; a broom for the office, $10 plus $0.65 GST. Reimburse the petty cash fund.

8 Received the bank statement and cancelled cheques for November. Complete the bank reconciliation as usual. The bank statement shows a balance on November 30 of $60,814.95. All deposits have cleared but two cheques have not: #137 to Coleman Industries for $4,515, and #138 to Tranborg & Noble for $2,310. A debit memo was included with the cancelled cheques for bank charges of $66.00, which has not yet been recorded on the books. Record the necessary journal entry.

8 Jay-Mar Co. phoned today and asked for a cheque for the $95.76 credit balance on their account. This will now clear their account

for year end. Send the cheque today. (Remember to post the entry to the Accounts Receivable Control account.) Paid Major Office Supply in full.

9 Received a cheque for $1,154.25 as payment on invoice #33 dated October 25 from Wm. Zelisko Enterprises. This payment includes a half-month's interest at 2.5% for late payment, $14.25. In the cash receipts journal, credit the customer for the amount of the invoice and credit Interest Revenue for the amount of the interest.

10 Cash sales: paint and supplies, $1,200, and wallpaper, $900. Paid the Receiver General for the November payroll deductions and company contributions.

13 Remitted the November sales tax: total collected, $876.12; commission, $36.76. Received payment on invoice #38 from Dayson & Son and on invoice #39 from Edna Morton. Both customers have deducted the discounts earned.

14 Rainbow Supplies has sent us a cheque for the November credit note to clear the company's account at year end. (Be sure to credit the Accounts Payable Control account.) Job #7 was completed yesterday and the cheque for $10,000 plus GST has been received. The owners have withdrawn $5,000 each and have asked you to make up the December payroll today and give a $500 bonus to each employee. Add this bonus to each gross pay before determining deductions; therefore, the service employees' gross salaries will be $3,100 each and the bookkeeper's gross salary will be $2,600. Refer to the deductions tables in Chapter 12. Issue the four paycheques as usual.

14 A review of salaries for Workers Compensation purposes shows that the company owes a balance payable on the difference between the projected salaries for this year and the actual salaries recorded this year. This additional premium will be paid next February when KBC receives the next Workers Compensation statement.

MONTH-END ACTIVITIES

(a) Balance the journals as usual.

(b) Complete the posting as usual.

(c) Prepare a trial balance as usual.

C H A P T E R ·····································

16

Aging of Accounts Receivable and the Suspense Account

CHAPTER OBJECTIVES

After completing this chapter, you will be able to:
- prepare a statement of accounts receivable by age for the purpose of determining an estimate of uncollectible accounts receivable

- record transactions involving the Suspense account

IMPORTANT WORDS AND TERMS IN THIS CHAPTER

Aging of Receivables
Collections Department
Suspense Account

he **aging of accounts receivable** (sometimes called an analysis of accounts receivable by age) is a listing of the customers and their account balances, categorized according to how long the balances are overdue. A business that relies heavily on a steady cashflow will keep a close watch on the status of its receivables to ensure that accounts are collected as soon as possible and not allowed to run overdue any longer than necessary. As well, the process of aging the receivables keeps management informed of the effectiveness of the credit and collection department and is a stepping-stone to determining how much of the customers' balances might eventually be uncollectible. These "bad debts" would then have to be written off (as discussed later in this chapter).

As mentioned, the aging of receivables will draw to the attention of management any customers' accounts that are past due and will show how long they are past due. The longer the account is past due, the greater the likelihood of uncollectibility. If an analysis of receivables by age is prepared at the end of every month, management is kept informed of the status of collections and can immediately take appropriate action concerning its credit policies: Are the terms on credit sales too lenient? Should discounts be offered to encourage prompt payment? How effective and responsible is the collection department? Should collection procedures be stepped up?

ANALYSIS OF ACCOUNTS RECEIVABLE BY AGE

CUSTOMERS	TOTAL	NOT YET DUE	1–30 DAYS PAST DUE	31–60 DAYS PAST DUE	61–90 DAYS PAST DUE	OVER 90 DAYS PAST DUE
R.S. Abbot	$ 650		$ 650			
T.P. Bond	145			$ 145		
L.A. Cooper	700	$ 500	200			
M.T. Dunn	800				$ 500	$ 300
N.D. Ewing	455	455				
Others	25,250	14,300	5,000	4,000	1,050	900
Totals	$28,000	$15,255	$5,850	$4,145	$1,550	$1,200
Percentages	100%	54%	21%	15%	6%	4%

Figure 16.1 Analysis of Accounts Receivable by Age

Figure 16.1 analyzes accounts receivable by age, showing the names of the customers and their balances. These balances are categorized according to the amount of time that the various invoice amounts are overdue (usually measured in days). A comparison can then be made between the total of each group and the total accounts receivable. In the illustration, we can see that $5,850 out of the total of $28,000 of receivables has been overdue up to 30 days. However, the relationship between these two amounts cannot be readily appreciated. A better way to look at each group is as a percentage of the total receivables (represented as 100%). By dividing the group total ($5,850) by the total of receivables ($28,000), we determine that approximately one-fifth (21%) of the total receivables is up to one month overdue. From experience, management would know whether or not this is an acceptable level for this group of receivables.

Such a detailed analysis shows specifically which customers have allowed their balances to run more than two or three months past due. For example, one customer (M.T. Dunn) has two outstanding invoices: one for $500 that is more than two months overdue and one for $300 that is more than three months overdue. The aging of receivables makes such long-overdue balances obvious.

To estimate how much of the total receivables will be uncollectible, we must apply an appropriate percentage to each age group total in Figure 16.1. The actual percentage to be applied to each group will be determined by experience. But for the purposes of our example, we will assume that only about 1% of the "not yet due" group of receivables will be uncollectible; similarly, 4% of the "1–30 days past due" group, 10% of the "31–60 days past due" group, and so on. (See Figure 16.2.)

	Schedule for Estimating Allowance for Doubtful Accounts December 31, 19—		
Amount	**Estimated Uncollectible**	**Allowance for Doubtful Accounts**	
Not yet due	$15,255	1%	$ 152.55
1–30 days over	5,850	4%	234.00
31–60 days over	4,145	10%	414.50
61–90 days over	1,550	20%	310.00
Over 90 days past due	1,200	50%	600.00
Totals	$28,000		$1,711.05

Figure 16.2   Estimated Uncollectibility of Receivables

Although the balances in the "not yet due" group in our example represent 54% of the total receivables, we are making an educated guess that about 1% of this amount will ultimately prove to be uncollectible. The longer the account is overdue, the greater the likelihood that the amount will never be collected.

By applying the percentages to the value of receivables in each category, we can reasonably estimate how much of the present accounts receivable total will likely never be collected; in this case, $1,711.05.

If no provision has yet been made on the books for this estimated uncollectible amount of $1,711.05, the journal entry to record it would be:

DATE		DESCRIPTION	F.	DEBIT	CREDIT
19— Feb.	1	Bad Debts Expense		1 7 1 1 05	
		Allowance for Doubtful Accounts			1 7 1 1 05
		To record estimated uncollectible accounts receivable.			

Such "bad debts" must be absorbed by the business, making the cost of operating the business higher since the goods shipped to the customer are likely no longer recoverable. This additional operating cost is debited to the Bad Debts Expense account. The Allowance for Doubtful Accounts account is a contra-asset showing how much of the current accounts receivable balance is estimated to be uncollectible. If we take the balance of the Accounts Receivable Control account ($28,000) and deduct the balance of the Allowance for Doubtful Accounts account ($1,711.05), we arrive at the estimated amount of receivables that we *do* expect to collect ($26,288.95). This amount is sometimes referred to as the net realizable value of receivables.

WRITING OFF BAD DEBTS

When it has been determined that a customer's account cannot be collected (often because the customer has gone bankrupt), the value of that Accounts Receivable account must be written off against the allowance for doubtful accounts determined earlier.

Let us assume that Emmerson Plastics (a customer) has an account that has been overdue for over six months. The balance owing is $644. If Emmerson declares bankruptcy (declaring through the courts that it is unable to pay its debts and, therefore, is going out of business), their account on the books must be written off. As shown earlier, the balance in the Allowance for Doubtful Accounts account is an estimate of the value of accounts receivable that will likely become uncollectible during this operating year. The Emmerson account, then, confirms in part the estimate of uncollectibility.

To write off the account, the following entry is recorded in the general journal:

DATE			DESCRIPTION	F.	DEBIT	CREDIT
19— Oct.	17		Allowance for Doubtful Accounts		6 4 4 00	
			A/R Emmerson Plastics			6 4 4 00
			To write off the account as uncollectible.			

The credit entry to Emmerson's account will reduce their balance to zero. The debit entry to the Allowance for Doubtful Accounts account will reduce the balance to $1,067.05 ($1,711.05 − $644.00), indicating that management still assumes that over $1,000 of accounts receivable will likely become worthless.

To continue the example, suppose another customer, Axworthy Metals Inc., has a long-overdue balance of $1,567.90. This customer is having financial difficulties and will likely not be able to pay off this balance. To write off this account, the journal entry is:

DATE		DESCRIPTION	F.	DEBIT	CREDIT
19— Nov.	1	Allowance for Doubtful Accounts		1 0 6 7 05	
		Bad Debts Expense		5 0 0 85	
		A/R Axworthy Metals			1 5 6 7 90
		To write off an uncollectible account.			

Because the balance in the Allowance for Doubtful Accounts account ($1,067.05) was not sufficient to fully cover the balance of the account being written off, the difference is charged to Bad Debts Expense in order to recognize this additional cost that must be borne by the company through this bad debt.

RECOVERING A BAD DEBT

Occasionally, a bad debt that was previously written off will be paid, either in full or in part, by the customer. If Emmerson Plastics, for example, sends a cheque for $250 toward their delinquent balance, the account must first be reinstated at a balance of $250 so that the usual entry can be recorded in the cash receipts journal for this receipt on account. The general journal entry to reinstate the account is:

DATE		DESCRIPTION	F.	DEBIT	CREDIT
19— Dec.	15	A/R Emmerson Plastics		2 5 0 00	
		Allowance for Doubtful Accounts			2 5 0 00
		To recover an account previously written off.			

You will notice that this entry is the reverse of the entry that was recorded to write off the account. Now that the customer's account has been reinstated with a balance equal to the amount just received, the usual entry can be recorded to receive the payment on account, reducing the balance of the customer's account to zero:

DATE		DESCRIPTION	F.	DEBIT	CREDIT
19— Dec.	15	Bank		2 5 0 00	
		A/R Emmerson Plastics			2 5 0 00
		Received on overdue account.			

The effects of all the preceding journal entries can be seen in the ledger accounts for Emmerson Plastics and Allowance for Doubtful Accounts (see Figure 16.3).

ACCOUNT A/R Emmerson Plastics   ACCT. NO. 162

TERMS 2/10, n/30 _____ CREDIT LIMIT 2000.00 _____ SHEET NO. 1

DATE		MEMO	DISC. DATE	F.	✓	DEBIT	✓	CREDIT	✓	DR. CR.	BALANCE
19— Mar.	3	Inv. 858	Mar. 13	SJ		6 4 4 00				Dr.	6 4 4 00
Oct.	17	write off		GJ				6 4 4 00			∅
Dec.	15	on Inv. 858		GJ		2 5 0 00					2 5 0 00
	15	on Inv. 858		CRJ				2 5 0 00			∅

ACCOUNT Allowance for Doubtful Accounts   ACCT. NO. 105

_____ SHEET NO. 3

DATE		MEMO	DISC. DATE	F.	✓	DEBIT	✓	CREDIT	✓	DR. CR.	BALANCE
		Balance Fwd.								Cr.	1 7 1 1 05
Oct.	17	Emmerson		GJ		6 4 4 00					1 0 6 7 05
Nov.	1	Axworthy		GJ		1 0 6 7 05					∅
Dec.	15	Emmerson		CRJ				2 5 0 00			2 5 0 00
	31	to increase		GJ				2 0 2 5 00			2 2 7 5 00

Figure 16.3   Ledger Accounts for Emmerson Plastics, Allowance for Doubtful Accounts

INCREASING THE ALLOWANCE

The balance in the Allowance account shown in Figure 16.3 is $250 on December 15. If next year the aging of receivables shows that $2,275 of the total accounts receivable is estimated to be uncollectible, the existing allowance must be increased by $2,025 ($2,275 − $250). The journal entry that increases the allowance is:

DATE		DESCRIPTION	F.	DEBIT	CREDIT
19— Dec.	31	Bad Debts Expense		2 0 2 5 00	
		Allowance for Doubtful Accounts			2 0 2 5 00
		To increase the allowance to the level of estimated uncollectible			
		accounts.			

▶ **PRACTICE EXERCISE 1**

The accounts receivable subsidiary ledger of Dominion Importing Co. shows the following customers' balances on December 31, 19—. Terms on all sales invoices are net 30 days.

Name of Customer	Date on Invoice	Amount
Andrews, Conrad	July 10, 19—	$ 350.00
Bell, Thomas	Sept. 28, 19—	165.50
Decker, Sylvia	Dec. 3, 19—	453.75
Evans, John	Sept. 15, 19—	510.35
Ford, Jane	Nov. 8, 19—	215.25
Graham, Arthur	Oct. 20, 19—	687.10
Hallet, Marie	Oct. 3, 19—	96.00
Moore, Stephen	Aug. 10, 19—	204.30
Russell, Edward	Nov. 30, 19—	260.75
Sanders, Robert	Nov. 16, 19—	528.50
Williams, Michael	Dec. 8, 19—	112.40
Others	Dec. 15, 19—	11,450.00

(a) Prepare a schedule of accounts receivable by age as illustrated in Figure 16.1. (*Remember*: The invoice is due 30 days after the invoice date shown.) Calculate the percentage that each category is of the total accounts receivable.

(b) Using the following percentages for probable loss, compute the estimated loss from uncollectible accounts:

Not yet due	1%
1–30 days past due	4%
31–60 days past due	10%
61–90 days past due	20%
Over 90 days past due	50%

(c) Prepare the general journal entry to record the estimated uncollectible receivables at year end (December 31).

▶ PRACTICE EXERCISE 2

Following are a few of the customers' ledger accounts on the books of Bramer Inc. on December 31, 19—. A total of $9,050 of other customers' balances is not yet due.

(a) Prepare a schedule of accounts receivable by age as illustrated in Figure 16.1. Show the dollar total of each category and the percentage of each category to the total of the accounts receivable.

(b) Using the same percentages of estimated loss as in Practice Exercise 1, compute the estimated loss from uncollectible accounts.

(c) Prepare the general journal entry on December 31 for the estimated uncollectible receivables.

ACCOUNT A/R Bell, Michael   **ACCT. NO.** 14
Selkirk, Manitoba   **SHEET NO.** 3

DATE		MEMO	DISC. DATE	F.	✓	DEBIT	✓	CREDIT	✓	DR. CR.	BALANCE
19— July	31	Balance Forward								Dr.	6 4 8 00
Aug.	15	on acct.		CR				4 8 00			6 0 0 00
Sept.	1	on acct.		CR				2 0 0 00			4 0 0 00
Sept.	5	n/30 days, #21		SJ		1 5 0 00					5 5 0 00
Oct.	20	on acct., #21		CR				1 5 0 00			4 0 0 00
Nov.	1	n/30 days, #38		SJ		2 2 0 00					6 2 0 00

ACCOUNT A/R Duncan, Henry   **ACCT. NO.** 26
Petersfield, Manitoba   **SHEET NO.** 4

DATE		MEMO	DISC. DATE	F.	✓	DEBIT	✓	CREDIT	✓	DR. CR.	BALANCE
19— Sept.	30	Balance Forward								Dr.	1 0 0 00
Oct.	25	n/30 days, #34		SJ		3 5 0 00					4 5 0 00
Oct.	31	on acct.		CR				1 0 0 00			3 5 0 00
Nov.	1	n/30 days, #39		SJ		4 5 0 00					8 0 0 00
Nov.	25	on acct., #34		CR				2 0 0 00			6 0 0 00
Dec.	10	n/30 days, #50		SJ		1 5 0 00					7 5 0 00

ACCOUNT A/R Kramer, Edward   **ACCT. NO.** 30
Elie, Manitoba   **SHEET NO.** 3

DATE		MEMO	DISC. DATE	F.	✓	DEBIT	✓	CREDIT	✓	DR. CR.	BALANCE
19— Oct.	31	Balance Forward								Dr.	5 7 5 00
Nov.	15	on acct.		CR				3 0 0 00			2 7 5 00
Nov.	20	n/30 days, #41		SJ		2 0 0 00					4 7 5 00
Nov.	30	on acct.		CR				2 7 5 00			2 0 0 00
Dec.	12	n/30 days, #56		SJ		1 2 5 00					3 2 5 00

ACCOUNT A/R Nash, Francis   **ACCT. NO.** 39
Portage La Prairie, Manitoba   **SHEET NO.** 2

DATE		MEMO	DISC. DATE	F.	✓	DEBIT	✓	CREDIT	✓	DR. CR.	BALANCE
19— Aug.	31	Balance Forward								Dr.	9 0 0 00
Sept.	12	on acct.		CR				3 0 0 00			6 0 0 00
Sept.	30	on acct.		CR				4 0 0 00			2 0 0 00
Oct.	1	n/30 days, #15		SJ		3 7 5 00					5 7 5 00
Oct.	31	on acct.		CR				2 0 0 00			3 7 5 00
Nov.	15	n/30 days, #40		SJ		4 0 0 00					7 7 5 00
Nov.	30	on acct., #15		CR				3 7 5 00			4 0 0 00
Dec.	15	n/30 days, #59		SJ		1 6 0 00					5 6 0 00

▶ ### PRACTICE EXERCISE 3

Prepare general journal entries for the following transactions affecting the books of Hascus & Skeaters Enterprises. Disregard GST and sales tax. Set up a T-account to keep track of the transactions affecting the Allowance for Doubtful Accounts account, which shows a credit balance of $2,500 on December 31, 19-1.

19-2

Jan.   3   Sold merchandise to Peter Nelson, $675, terms 30 days.

5   Received a cheque from James Waters to apply against his invoice dated Dec. 6, $890. Not eligible for a discount.

6   Sold merchandise on account to Ethel Hall on terms 2/10,n/30; $743.

7   Sold merchandise to Neil Ritchie, $540. Terms 1/5,n/30.

9   Issued a credit note for $40 to Neil Ritchie for unsatisfactory goods returned.

10   Received a notice from the bank that the cheque from James Waters on Jan. 5 has been returned NSF.

11   Received a cheque from Neil Ritchie to cover the invoice dated Jan. 7.

12   James Waters has declared bankruptcy. Write off this uncollectible account.

13   A customer, Al Roftu (balance owing on Dec. 31 was $1,500), has returned to his home country and cannot be located to settle his account. Make the entry necessary to write off his uncollectible account.

16   Received a cheque from Ethel Hall to cover the invoice dated Jan. 6.

18   James Waters has contacted us agreeing to make a partial payment of $500 on his account. Record the necessary entry to re-open his account, then record the receipt of his payment on account.

20   Sold merchandise, $550, to William Jensen on terms of 10 days.

31   William Jensen has changed residence. After failing to locate him, we have decided to write off his account. Record the necessary entry.

31   Tom Harper showed a long overdue balance on Dec. 31 of $739. He had promised to pay this account by Jan. 31. He is currently unemployed and his account is now deemed to be uncollectible. Record the write-off of this account. (*Hint:* The Allowance for Doubtful Accounts account does not have a sufficient balance to fully write off this account.)

▶ ### PRACTICE EXERCISE 4

On December 31, assume the following balances appear in these general ledger accounts:

Accounts Receivable Control	$ 50,000.00
Allowance for Doubtful Accounts	1,200.00
Sales	110,000.00
Sales Returns & Allowances	1,900.00
Sales Discounts	2,300.00

(a) Prepare a general journal entry that will increase the Allowance for Doubtful Accounts balance to 5% of the existing accounts receivable.

(b) Prepare a general journal entry that will increase the Allowance for Doubtful Accounts balance by 1% of net sales (gross sales minus returns and discounts).

SUSPENSE ACCOUNT

The **Suspense account** is a general ledger account for recording temporarily those transactions for which sufficient information is not available at the time the entry is recorded. When the required information is eventually received, another entry will be recorded to transfer the value from the Suspense account to the proper account.

To illustrate, on June 12, an invoice is received from Selkirk Paper Co. for the purchase of wrapping paper, $155, on terms of n/30. The manager was on vacation at the time and did not inform the bookkeeper whether the paper is for resale or for use within the warehouse.

Since the purpose of the paper is unknown, the bookeeper does not know whether to debit Purchases or Warehouse Supplies Prepaid. Instead, the Suspense account is debited until the intended purpose of the wrapping paper becomes known. This entry would normally appear in the purchase journal:

DATE		DESCRIPTION	F.	DEBIT	CREDIT
19— June	12	Suspense		1 5 5 00	
		A/P Selkirk Paper Co.			1 5 5 00
		To record temporarily the purchase of paper.			

Upon his return, the manager decided that the paper would be used within the business; therefore, a general journal entry will be necessary to transfer the value from the Suspense account to the Warehouse Supplies Prepaid account:

DATE		DESCRIPTION	F.	DEBIT	CREDIT
19— June	30	Warehouse Supplies Prepaid		1 5 5 00	
		Suspense Account			1 5 5 00
		To transfer from Suspense the purchase of paper for use in the			
		warehouse.			

In another example, the owner is planning a trip to Montreal to attend a new-products convention and has asked the bookkeeper to give him $500 as spending money. Since it is yet unknown how the money will be spent, the entry in the cash payments journal for the issuance of the cheque will debit and credit these accounts:

DATE		DESCRIPTION	F.	DEBIT	CREDIT
19— July	17	Suspense		5 0 0 00	
		Bank			5 0 0 00
		To record cheque for Montreal convention;			
		purposes unknown.			

When the owner returns from the convention and presents all the receipts for his purchases, a general journal entry is recorded to transfer the value out of the Suspense account to the appropriate accounts, such as:

DATE		DESCRIPTION	F.	DEBIT	CREDIT
19— July	26	Travel & Accommodations		3 4 4 00	
		Convention Expense		1 5 6 00	
		Suspense			5 0 0 00
		To transfer Montreal convention costs to appropriate			
		expense accounts.			

▶ **PRACTICE EXERCISE 5**

Prepare general journal entries for each of the following transactions. Disregard GST and sales tax in all entries.

1. On May 31, your employer has left word that he/she has taken cheque #179 to Edmonton to cover an auction item purchased for $520. It was not stated what the item purchased was.

2. On June 10, your employer has returned from Edmonton and has indicated that cheque #179 (see above) was used for the purchase of merchandise.

3. On June 28, a $260 cheque is received. No company name is printed on the cheque and the signature is difficult to read. Because there are several outstanding invoices for this amount, you cannot be sure who has made this payment.

4. On August 7, Reverend Carter of the Holy Ghost Church calls for a repeat of their May order for merchandise. You mention to him that his May order has not yet been paid. He replies that the church treasurer sent a cheque on June 26. You are now able to correct the June 28 entry. Also record today's sale of merchandise to the church on account.

5. On September 7, payment is received from the Holy Ghost Church for their August 7 order.

THINK ABOUT IT!

1. What is aging of accounts receivable? Why is it used?
2. How are percentages of estimated loss determined?
3. Explain the purpose of the Suspense account.

17

At Year End

CHAPTER OBJECTIVES

After completing this chapter, you will be able to:

- close the books at the end of the operating year
- prepare a worksheet
- record adjusting and closing journal entries
- prepare the balance sheet and income statement to reflect the financial position of the company

IMPORTANT WORDS AND TERMS IN THIS CHAPTER

Accounting (Fiscal) Period
Accrued Expenses
Accumulated Depreciation
Bad Debts Expense
Balance Sheet
Book Value of Assets
Closing the Books
Contra Account
Current Assets
Current Liabilities
Depreciation
Financial Statement
Fixed (Long-Term) Assets
Income Statement

Income Summary
Inventory (Periodic & Perpetual)
Long-Term Liabilities
Net Income (or Loss)
Post-Closing Trial Balance
Prepaid Expenses
Present Market Value of Assets
Temporary Accounts
Unearned Revenues
Worksheet

· · · · · · · · · ·

Once a year, every business is required to prepare an accurate and detailed statement showing how it earned its revenue and what expenses it incurred in the process of generating that revenue. This statement, known commonly as an income statement, is submitted to Revenue Canada with the owner's personal income tax return as evidence of the earnings of the business. Since proprietorships and partnerships do not themselves pay income tax on their earnings, the owner(s) must report the business's net profit as personal income and, as a result, must pay income tax on it.

The operating year chosen for reporting purposes may be the calendar year (January 1 to December 31) or a fiscal year (any 12-month period); however, once chosen, the operating year must remain consistent from year to year unless Revenue Canada permits a change to a different 12-month period. KBC Decorating, for example, has been following a calendar year for reporting purposes primarily because it anticipates the lowest level of business activity in late December and early January, and thus would have the lowest level of inventory on hand. Other businesses, on the other hand, might find it more advantageous to use a fiscal year, such as a 12-month period beginning July 1 and ending June 30, because that time of year is its slowest season. The Government of Canada's operating year is April 1 to March 31.

Regardless of the operating year chosen, the process for measuring the financial information required for reporting purposes remains the same. An accurate inventory value of merchandise and supplies on hand must be determined; journal entries must be recorded for any adjustments in the values of assets, liabilities, revenues, and expenses carried from one operating year to the next; and the resulting financial statements (an income statement and a balance sheet) must be prepared.

INVENTORY

The merchandise kept on hand for the purpose of selling it to customers at a profit during the regular operations of business is termed inventory. It is important to determine a reasonable value for year-end inventory because it is the key figure in establishing the cost of goods sold during the year. An understatement or overstatement of the value of an inventory will result in an understatement or overstatement of the net income, which in turn affects the owner's equity. Also, the value of the total assets owned by the business would be misstated as well. Such errors in accounting destroy the significance and integrity of the information portrayed by the financial statements.

There are several ways of computing inventories for the preparation of financial statements: (1) the periodic inventory method, (2) the perpetual inventory method, (3) the retail method, and (4) the gross profit method. The periodic and perpetual inventory methods, if applied correctly, require an accurate physical count and valuation for inventory on hand. The retail and gross profit methods are used to determine a reasonable estimate of the value of inventory in circumstances when a physical count of goods on hand is either impossible (such as when goods were destroyed by fire) or impractical (when the time and cost of determining the value of inventory is not warranted by the need for this information, such as monthly financial statements for which estimates are suitable for decision-making purposes). For the purposes of recording inventories in this textbook, only the first two methods (periodic and perpetual) will be discussed.

The balances of all asset accounts are kept up to date during the accounting period, with the exception of Inventory. As explained in the early chapters, goods purchased for resale are recorded in the Purchases account and the sale of these goods is recorded in the Sales account. However, the merchandise that remains unsold at the end of the financial period is recorded in the Inventory account.

Periodic inventory involves a systematic count of all goods on hand, usually at the end of the financial year but more often if necessary. When the physical count is complete, a statement of inventory is prepared by making a list of all items on hand and multiplying each item by its unit price (using either the cost price or the present market value of the item, whichever is lower). The total of this statement of inventory (see Figure 17.1) is known as the *closing inventory*.

STATEMENT OF INVENTORY
DECEMBER 31, 19—

ITEM	QUANTITY ON HAND	COST	PRESENT MARKET	INVENTORY VALUE
Angle Bolts	10	$110.00	$100.00	$1,000.00
Buckle Pins	6	190.00	220.00	1,140.00
Card Flange	30	50.00	60.00	1,500.00
Drop Cables	25	80.00	70.00	1,750.00
End Wings	24	65.00	50.00	1,200.00
False Plates	18	75.00	85.00	1,350.00
Total Inventory				$7,940.00

Figure 17.1 Statement of Inventory

The cost figures for each item of inventory should include freight, duty, brokerage, repackaging, and other costs incurred to bring the goods into the warehouse or store and make them ready for resale. These costs are allocated to each item of inventory on the basis of a suitable ratio determined by the accountant or by management.

Perpetual inventory is used by businesses that sell high-price items, such as cars, televisions, computers, and furniture. In such a system, a separate inventory card or stock sheet is prepared for each type of merchandise. A running record is kept for each unit purchased (added to stock) and for each unit sold (deducted from stock), thus showing constantly the number of units on hand (see Figure 17.2). In the perpetual inventory system, purchases of goods are debited to the Inventory account rather than to the Purchases account. To confirm and ensure the accuracy of the perpetual records, a physical count is taken occasionally, and the total number of units on hand is compared with the quantities shown on the perpetual inventory cards.

PERPETUAL INVENTORY CARD

| CODE | Brand A | | MAXIMUM | 30 |
| ITEM | Colour TV | | MINIMUM | 5 |

| DATE | | QUANTITIES | | | SOURCE DOCUMENT # | UNIT COST PRICE | | DOLLAR COST | | |
		IN	OUT	BALANCE				IN	OUT	BALANCE
19— May	1			10		200	00			2,000	00
	31	20		30	P.O. 130	200	00			6,000	00
	31		22	8	Inv. 1001	200	00			1,600	00

Figure 17.2   Perpetual Inventory Card

Although the procedure for inventory control, as described above, appears to be very simple, it is, without a doubt, a very important and responsible operation. One responsibility of the inventory clerk is to have sufficient quantities of merchandise in stock to fill all incoming orders without delay. The quantity of goods on hand should not fall below a required minimum, nor should any item be overstocked to the point that it is unsalable or becomes obsolete.

Inventory, like cash, is a popular object of theft. The use of the perpetual system, if conducted properly, provides excellent internal control over merchandise. Some of the elements of internal control are: subdivision of duties the person physically handling the inventory should not have access to the inventory records), the use of serially numbered documents, and separating the accounting functions from the custody of the inventory. Every reasonable precaution should be taken to ensure that the inventory system does not fall prey to unscrupulous employees or other dishonest individuals.

A very important accounting concept is the matching of expenses with related revenues for a given accounting period. This means that the expenses that have been incurred during the current accounting period, for example, must relate to (or have contributed toward) the revenue that has been generated during this same accounting period. Some business transactions are attributed completely to one accounting period, such as one month's rent paid at the beginning of the month, thereby being "consumed" by the end of each month.

Other transactions, however, may benefit more than one accounting period, such as the purchase of a building with an estimated useful life of 40 years or the purchase of enough office supplies to last for many months. To match expenses with related revenues for one accounting period, it is essential to apportion those expenditures that overlap two or more accounting periods. This can be accomplished by making **adjusting entries**, which are a means of achieving the correct amount for each asset, liability, revenue, and expense applicable to the same accounting period.

TYPES OF ADJUSTING ENTRIES

a. Prepaid Expenses (or Unexpired Expenses): When supplies are purchased for the office or store, often little thought is given to the length of time required to use them up. Only part of a quantity of supplies might be used (or consumed) in the current financial period; the remainder, then, would be consumed in the next period. Such expenditures are commonly known as prepaid expenses—paid for in advance and used up over the next months or years.

An insurance policy on the building or the merchandise, for example, is likely to apply to two financial periods. A one-year insurance policy on the building was purchased on August 1 for $480. The journal entry recorded at the time was:

19— Aug.	1	Insurance Prepaid (or Unexpired)			4 8 0 00		
		Bank				4 8 0 00
		To record purchase of one-year insurance				
		policy on building.				

At year end (assuming a December 31 year end), only five months of the policy has expired; therefore, an adjusting entry is needed to transfer five months' worth of the insurance cost ($480 × 5/12 = $200) from the Insurance Prepaid account to the Insurance Expense account.

19— Dec.	31	Insurance Expense			2 0 0 00		
		Insurance Prepaid				2 0 0 00
		To transfer 5 months' insurance to expense				
		for this period.				

The five months of insurance expired, $200, is recognized as an operating cost attributed to the operating year just ended and will be shown as an operating expense on the income statement (discussed later). The portion of the cost that has not yet expired, $280, will be carried forward into the next operating year as an asset.

In another example, a large quantity of office supplies was purchased on September 20 for $625. The journal entry to record this purchase was:

19— Sept.	20	Office Supplies Prepaid			6 2 5 00		
		Bank				6 2 5 00
		Bought supplies for the office.				

By year end (assuming December 31), the inventory value of the supplies still on hand was $450; therefore, $175 worth of supplies had been used up. An adjusting entry is needed to transfer the value of the supplies used up to an expense account:

19— Dec.	31	Office Supplies Expense			1 7 5 00		
		Office Supplies Prepaid				1 7 5 00
		To allocate to expense the supplies used during this				
		operating year.				

The amount of the expense, $175, represents an operating cost attributed to the year just ended. The unused quantity of supplies, $450, will be consumed in the next financial period.

b. Unearned Revenue (Revenue Received in Advance)   An unearned revenue is a payment made by the customer in advance for goods or services that are to be provided in the near future. By year end, all or part of the order may already have been delivered to the customer and must then be recognized on the books as a revenue *earned.*

For example, a cheque for $800 was received on November 30 for two months' rent paid in advance for part of the office space sublet to another small business. The entry recorded on November 30 was:

19— Nov.	30	Bank		8 0 0 00	
		Unearned Rental Revenue			8 0 0 00
		Received 2 months' rent in advance.			

At year end (assuming December 31), only one month of the rental revenue has so far been earned; therefore, one month's worth of the prepaid rent will be transferred from the Unearned Rental Revenue account to the Rental Revenue Earned account.

19— Dec.	31	Unearned Rental Revenue		4 0 0 00	
		Rental Revenue Earned			4 0 0 00
		To transfer one month's unearned revenue to revenue earned for			
		this period.			

Rental Revenue Earned, $400, is then recognized as revenue earned during the operating year just ended and will be shown on the income statement. The portion of prepaid rent that has not yet been earned, $400, will be carried into, and recognized as revenue in, the next operating year. This unearned revenue is treated as a *liability* because the service is still owed to the company that is subletting the office space.)

In another example, a client has contracted on December 15 for plumbing work to be done in his new house. He has agreed to pay $600 in advance and the balance when the job is completed. When the down payment is received on December 15, it was charged to the Unearned Service Revenue account:

19— Dec.	15	Bank		6 0 0 00	
		Service Revenue Unearned			6 0 0 00
		To record payment of fees received in advance.			

At year end (assuming December 31), approximately $400 worth of work was completed for the client; therefore, $400 must be transferred to the Service

Revenue Earned account to be recognized as revenue earned in the operating year just ended. The adjusting entry is:

19—							
Dec.	31	Service Revenue Unearned		4 0 0 00			
		Service Revenue Earned				4 0 0 00	
		To allocate portion of fees received in advance to this					
		year's revenue.					

The balance of the Service Revenue Unearned, $200, will eventually be recognized as earned revenue in the next financial year and will be transferred into the Service Revenue Earned account at that time using a similar adjusting entry.

c. Unpaid Expenses: At the end of the operating year, any expenses that have been incurred, but have not yet been paid for, must be recorded on the books so that they may be properly allocated to the year just ended. Employees' salaries totalling $1,600, for example, are paid on the fifteenth of each month. On December 15, the usual paycheques are issued and the usual journal entry is recorded. On December 31, half the month's salaries, $800, has accrued (December 15 to December 31) but will not be paid until the 15th of January. An adjusting entry is required on December 31 (year end) to record the accrual of the half-month's expense. The following entries illustrate the sequence of events:

19–1							
Dec.	15	Salaries Expense		1 6 0 0 00			
		Bank				1 6 0 0 00	
		Paid monthly salaries for pay period of Nov. 15–Dec. 15.					
Dec.	31	Salaries Expense		8 0 0 00			
		Salaries Payable				8 0 0 00	
		To record accrued and unpaid salaries as an expense for this period.					
19–2							
Jan.	15	Salaries Expense		8 0 0 00			
		Salaries Payable		8 0 0 00			
		Bank				1 6 0 0 00	
		Paid salaries for pay period of Dec.15–Jan.15.					

The adjusting entry on December 31 (year end) allocates the accrued expense for the operating year just ended and establishes a liability for the amount owing to the employees at year end. On the next regular payday (January 15), Salaries Payable will be cleared when the usual cheques are issued.

d. Unrecorded Revenues: Revenues that have been earned but have not yet been recorded on the books must also be recorded at year end, whether paid at that time or not, in order that they will be recognized as revenue earned in the year just ended. On December 29, for example, a broker concluded negotiations on behalf of its client for the purchase of specialized equipment and has earned a commission of $1,400, but payment for it has not yet been received. The adjusting entry is:

19— Dec.	31	Commission Receivable		1 4 0 0 00	
		Commission Earned			1 4 0 0 00
		To record revenue earned in this period but not yet received.			

Commission Receivable (an account similar to Accounts Receivable) represents an asset of $1,400 to be received in the near future. Commission Earned of $1,400 is recognized as a revenue earned during the operating year just ended.

e. Depreciation (or Capital Cost Allowance): The cost of a long-term asset cannot be totally written off as an expense in only one year. Instead it should be allocated (converted) to expense over its useful life. For example, a building costing $250,000 is estimated to have a useful life of 25 years. One twenty-fifth of the cost ($250,000 × 1/25 = $10,000) should be allocated to expense each year. This expense is called **Depreciation**. Although depreciation is an expense that does not require an outlay of cash, it is considered an operating expense just the same.

19— Dec.	31	Depreciation Expense—Buildings		10 0 0 0 00	
		Accumulated Depreciation—Buildings			10 0 0 0 00
		To allocate a portion of the cost of the building to expense.			
		($250,000 x 1/25 = $10,000).			

The **Accumulated Depreciation** account is a contra-asset account (a negative asset account) representing the total amount of the asset cost that has so far been written off to expense since the asset was purchased.

Plant & Equipment			
Buildings	250 0 0 0 00		
less Accumulated Depreciation	10 0 0 0 00	240 0 0 0 00	

The amount of $240,000 shown above is called the **book value** of the asset. Book value should not be confused with the market value (the amount that would be received if the asset were sold or traded). Simply stated, the book value is the portion of the original cost of the asset that has *not* yet been depreciated.

There are several methods of depreciating long-term assets; however, only two of these methods will be discussed in this text.

(i) Straight-Line Method: Under the straight-line method, an equal portion of the cost of the asset is allocated to expense each year until the full value of the asset has been written off. For example, a computer system is purchased at a cost of $3,500 with an estimated useful life of seven years. The annual depreciation would be $3,500 ÷ 7 = $500. After seven years of depreciation, this asset would be fully depreciated and would be carried on the books at a zero book value. This does not mean, however, that the computer no longer has any value; if it is still being used by the business, it will continue to be shown on the books at a zero book value, but no additional depreciation will be recorded.

(ii) Declining-Balance (Diminishing-Balance) Method: Under the declining-balance method, depreciation is computed on the reduced book value each year. For example, a delivery truck is purchased for $20,000 with depreciation to be calculated at an annual rate of 25%. The calculations for the first two years are as follows:

Cost of Delivery Truck	20	0	0	0	00
1st Year Depreciation (20,000 x 25%)	5	0	0	0	00
Book Value at end of Year 1	15	0	0	0	00
2nd Year Depreciation (15,000 x 25%)	3	7	5	0	00
Book Value at end of Year 2	11	2	5	0	00

Here are the general journal entries that would be recorded at the end of Year 1 and Year 2:

Yr.	1	Depreciation Exp. (Trucks)	5 0 0 0 00	
		Accumulated Deprec. (Trucks)		5 0 0 0 00
		To depreciate 25% on $20,000 using declining-balance method.		
Yr.	2	Depreciation Exp. (Trucks)	3 7 5 0 00	
		Accumulated Deprec. (Trucks)		3 7 5 0 00
		To depreciate 25% on $15,000 using declining-balance method.		

When the declining-balance method of depreciation is used, a book value is carried on the books for as long as the asset is used in the business. In theory, the book value will never reach zero.

f. Bad Debts: One additional expense that must be considered is the portion of Accounts Receivable that is estimated to be uncollectible. This is known as **Bad Debts Expense** (or Uncollectible Accounts Expense). Bad debts must be recognized in the year in which the sales were made and should be recorded as an expense for that period. This expense is offset by the contra-asset account called **Allowance for Doubtful Accounts**.

A reasonable estimate of the amount of uncollectible accounts can be determined by two methods:

Method 1: The income statement approach is used in estimating the Bad Debts Expense as a percentage of the net sales value (which is determined by subtracting Sales Returns & Allowances and Sales Discounts from the value in the Sales account). The percentage used is based on past years' experience with uncollectible accounts. Any existing balance in the Allowance for Doubtful Accounts account is *not* taken into consideration when this method is used. If, for example, total sales for the year just ended amount to $150,000 and it is estimated that 1% will likely be uncollectible, the amount recorded this year as Bad Debts Expense will be $150,000 × 1% = $1,500. The adjusting entry, then, is:

19— Dec.	31	Bad Debts Expense			1 5 0 0 00		
		Allowance for Doubtful Accounts				1 5 0 0 00	
		To record expense for estimated uncollectible accounts;					
		1% of total sales.					

Method 2: The balance sheet approach involves aging the accounts receivable as explained in Chapter 16. The balance required in the Allowance for Doubtful Accounts account is arrived at by aging the receivables and applying a percentage to each category. If the estimated uncollectible accounts receivable value is $800, any existing balance in the Allowance for Doubtful Accounts account will be subtracted to arrive at the amount of the Bad Debts Expense.

Estimated uncollectibles	8 0 0 00
Existing balance in the allowance account	2 0 0 00
Bad Debts Expense for this year	6 0 0 00

The journal entry to record such an adjustment is:

19— Dec.	31	Bad Debts Expense			6 0 0 00		
		Allowance for Doubtful Accounts				6 0 0 00	
		To increase the allowance for doubtful accounts to $800.					

The Allowance for Doubtful Accounts account is a contra-asset account that is deducted from the Accounts Receivable balance to show the expected net realizable value of receivables.

<u>Current Assets</u>			
Accounts Receivable	32 0 0 0 00		
less Allowance for Doubtful Accounts	8 0 0 00	31 2 0 0 00	

▶ **PRACTICE EXERCISE 1**

October 31 is the fiscal year end for the Spring Hill Ski Complex. From the information below, prepare the adjusting journal entries with suitable explanations (including any necessary calculations).

(a) Depreciation on the lodge and restaurant for the current year ending October 31 is $23,600.

(b) Salaries owing to employees but not yet paid are $2,750.

(c) Snow-grooming equipment was leased on October 15 at a daily rate of $45. Began using the equipment immediately. No lease payments have yet been made.

(d) The Spring Hill Restaurant was leased to a local catering company on September 1 at a yearly rate of $7,200. One year's rent was received in advance on the day the lease contract was signed and was credited to the Unearned Rent Revenue account.

(e) A five-month bank loan was negotiated on October 1 for $24,000 at an annual interest rate of 10%. No interest expense has yet been recorded. (Interest = Principal × Rate × Months ÷12)

(f) Depreciation on the shuttle bus for the current year ending October 31 is $4,200.

(g) A lease agreement was signed today (October 31) for the use of a second shuttle bus during the winter months, beginning November 1. The lease rate will be $350 per month plus 27 cents per kilometre.

▶ **PRACTICE EXERCISE 2**

Record the following year-end adjustments in the general journal of Spencer Distributing Co. on December 31, 19—.

(a) The Insurance Prepaid account includes the following expired insurance coverage: $250 on stock, $300 on the building, and $150 on furniture and equipment.

(b) The Office Supplies Prepaid account includes $1,200 worth of supplies used in the current year.

(c) The Unearned Rent Revenue account shows a balance of $1,600 that includes $800 for January of the *new* year.

(d) The Advertising Prepaid account includes $750 used in the current year.

(e) Salaries accrued but not yet paid on December 31, $2,700.

▶ **PRACTICE EXERCISE 3**

In the general journal of Krywa TV Service, prepare the adjusting entries for the three-month period ending March 31, 19—.

(a) On January 1, rent was paid in advance for six months at $250 per month. The total paid was $1,500 debited to Rent Prepaid.

(b) A one-year insurance policy was purchased on January 2, $600, and was charged to Insurance Prepaid.

(c) The value of office supplies on hand, based on a physical count on March 31, is $85. The present balance in the Office Supplies Prepaid account shows $315.

(d) On January 1, advertising costs were prepaid for six months, $360.

(e) Salaries earned by the employee but not yet paid on March 31, $205.

(f) Services to customers who have paid in advance have been completed in March, $560.

(g) Interest accrued on a bank loan for three months, $375.

(h) Depreciation on Tools & Equipment is to be calculated on the book value of $1,600 at an annual rate of 25% for three months.

(i) The balance in the Repair Parts & Supplies Prepaid account is $1,050. A physical inventory of the parts and supplies on hand on March 31 is now $165.

THE WORKSHEET

The columnar **worksheet** (often 10 to 14 columns wide) is designed to arrange systematically all the accounting data required for the preparation of the financial statements (the income statement and the balance sheet) and for closing the revenue and expense accounts by means of adjusting and closing journal entries. It is the accountant's tool for simplifying the volume of data to be handled at the end of the financial period and minimizing potential errors. Each pair of columns on the worksheet (see Figure 17.3) represents a different stage in the closing process and ensures that each stage is balanced before the next stage is started. Because the worksheet is not part of the permanent records, it is usually prepared in pencil to allow erasures and alterations.

Although a worksheet can be prepared at any time during the financial period as the preliminary step in preparing interim financial statements, its primary use is to organize the data necessary for the closing of the books at year end.

The worksheet in Figure 17.3 contains five pairs of columns. One pair will be used for each of the five steps necessary to complete the worksheet.

1. The trial balance prepared at year end is copied into the first two columns of the worksheet, including the totals. The totals are ruled as usual. These trial balance figures become the basis for the next four steps.

2. The debit and credit entries for the adjustments are entered in the Adjustments columns. For example, the adjustment for the expired insurance discussed earlier calls for an entry that will debit Insurance Expense and credit Insurance Prepaid. Any account names that are needed to complete the adjustments but are not already included in the trial balance listing are written in the "Name of Account" column on the first available line below the trial balance totals. In order to relate the debit and credit sides of each adjustment, these entries are usually keyed using (a), (b), (c), etc., to show the relationship between the accounts affected by the adjustment. The Adjustments columns are totalled to ensure that they are in balance.

3. Each account balance is then transferred into the Adjusted Trial Balance columns, taking into consideration the effects of the adjustments. For example, the adjusted balance for the Office Supplies Prepaid account is $500, determined from the original trial balance value of $1,600 minus the $1,100 portion of the supplies inventory that has been used up. The Adjusted Trial Balance columns are also totalled and checked for equal debits and credits.

4. The amounts in the Adjusted Trial Balance columns are extended to the Income Statement columns or the Balance Sheet columns, depending on the classification of each account. To ensure that these figures are extended properly, they should be taken in order beginning with the first account

listed on the worksheet. Revenue and expense accounts are extended into the Income Statement columns. Assets, liabilities, and owner's equity accounts are extended into the Balance Sheet columns. Care must be taken when extending "contra-asset" accounts, such as the Allowance for Doubtful Accounts, which are extended to the credit column of the Balance Sheet columns.

COMPANY Webster Milton Company   **WORKSHEET**   **FOR** One Year **ENDED** October 31, 19—

ACCOUNT TITLE	TRIAL BALANCE DEBIT	TRIAL BALANCE CREDIT	ADJUSTMENTS DEBIT	ADJUSTMENTS CREDIT	ADJUSTED TRIAL BALANCE DEBIT	ADJUSTED TRIAL BALANCE CREDIT	INCOME STATEMENT EXPENSE	INCOME STATEMENT REVENUE	BALANCE SHEET ASSETS	BALANCE SHEET LIAB. & EQUITY
Bank	7600 00				7600 00				7600 00	
Accounts Receivable	12000 00				12000 00				12000 00	
Allowance for Doubtful Accounts		600 00		(g) 600 00		1200 00	40000 00			1200 00
Inventory (Opening)	40000 00				40000 00					
Office Supplies Prepaid	1600 00			(c) 1100 00	500 00				500 00	
Insurance Prepaid	1300 00			(b) 900 00	400 00				400 00	
Land	25000 00				25000 00				25000 00	
Building	54000 00				54000 00				54000 00	
Accumulated Depreciation—Bldg.		2700 00		(f) 2700 00		5400 00				5400 00
Equipment	20000 00				20000 00				20000 00	
Accumulated Depreciation—Equip.		2000 00		(f) 2000 00		4000 00				4000 00
Accounts Payable		23400 00				23400 00				23400 00
Capital, Michael Fraser		104000 00				104000 00				104000 00
Drawings, Michael Fraser	15700 00				15700 00				15700 00	
Sales		242000 00				242000 00		242000 00		
Sales Returns and Allowances	1400 00				1400 00		1400 00			
Sales Discounts	3200 00				3200 00		3200 00			
Purchases	143800 00				143800 00		143800 00			
Purchase Returns and Allowances		1800 00				1800 00		1800 00		
Purchase Discounts		2100 00				2100 00		2100 00		
Transportation In	400 00				400 00		400 00			
Delivery Expense	1100 00				1100 00		1100 00			
Selling Commission Expense	8500 00		(e) 500 00		9000 00		9000 00			
Salaries & Wages Expense	37000 00				37000 00		37000 00			
Property Taxes	2400 00		(d) 1200 00		3600 00		3600 00			
	378600 0	378600 00								
Insurance Expense			(b) 900 00		900 00		900 00			
Office Supplies Expense			(c) 1100 00		1100 00		1100 00			
Property Taxes Payable				(d) 1200 00		1200 00				1200 00
Selling Commissions Payable				(e) 500 00		500 00				500 00
Depreciation—Building			(f) 2700 00		2700 00		2700 00			
Depreciation—Equipment			(f) 2000 00		2000 00		2000 00			
Bad Debt Expense			(g) 600 00		600 00		600 00			
			9000 00	9000 00	385600 00	385600 00				
Inventory (closing)								33800 00	33800 00	
							250400 00	279700 00	169000 00	139700 00
Net Income							29300 00			29300 00
							279700 00	279700 00	169000 00	169000 00

Figure 17.3 Worksheet

You will note that the year end inventory value is not treated as an adjusting entry. Instead, it is entered as a credit in the Income Statement columns. This credit entry is not interpreted as another revenue but, instead, is a reduction of expenses since the goods were not sold during the operating year just ended. These goods on hand are being carried forward into the next financial year; therefore, the closing inventory figure is extended to the debit column of the Balance Sheet columns as an asset. This is the only figure, aside from the net income (or net loss) figure, that appears on *both* financial statements. All others appear on only one statement or the other.

5. The worksheet is not complete without the net income (or net loss) figure, which is necessary to balance the Income Statement columns and the Balance Sheet columns. The net income (or loss) is determined by taking the difference between the subtotal of the revenue column and the subtotal of the expense column. This income (or loss) figure is entered into whichever column has the smaller subtotal. The words "Net Income" or "Net Loss" are written in the "Account Name" column on the left side of the worksheet.

A **net income** will increase the owner's equity, so it is extended into the same column as the owner's Capital account; that is, the credit column. A **net loss** and the Drawings account both decrease the owner's equity, so they should be extended into the column opposite that of the Capital account; that is, the debit column.

The Income Statement columns and the Balance Sheet columns are now totalled and ruled as usual.

▶ ## PRACTICE EXERCISE 4

Atlas Drafting Service was started on January 2, 19—, by Howard Pollard. The trial balance that follows was prepared on June 30, 19—, after six months of operations. From the trial balance and the additional information provided below:

(a) Complete the worksheet for six months ending June 30, 19—.

(b) Record the adjusting entries in the general journal. Provide suitable memos for these entries.

Additional information:

(1) Drafting supplies on hand on June 30, $384.

(2) Office rent of $4,000 for one year paid on January 2 was charged to Prepaid Office Rent.

(3) Interest accrued on the bank loan to June 30, $50.

(4) Drafting services to clients but not yet billed or collected, $940. (Drafting Fees Receivable)

(5) A number of clients had made payments in advance for services to be provided over a considerable period. On June 30, the value of services provided and chargeable against Unearned Fees was $7,000.

(6)   Salaries accrued and unpaid on June 30, $500.

(7)   Drafting equipment purchased on January 2 has an estimated useful life of 10 years. (Use straight-line depreciation.)

Atlas Drafting Service
Trial Balance
June 30, 19—

ACCOUNT NAME	DEBIT					CREDIT				
Bank	10	9	3	0	00					
Office Rent Prepaid	4	0	0	0	00					
Drafting Supplies Prepaid	1	5	0	0	00					
Drafting Equipment	7	6	0	0	00					
Bank Loan						8	0	0	0	00
Unearned Fees						12	9	8	0	00
Capital, Howard Pollard						11	1	0	0	00
Drawings, Howard Pollard	4	9	9	0	00					
Fees Earned						12	9	4	0	00
Salaries Expense	15	5	0	0	00					
Miscellaneous Expense		5	0	0	00					
	45	0	2	0	00	45	0	2	0	00

▶ **PRACTICE EXERCISE 5**

Dauphin Supply Co. is owned and operated by Jack Clements. He has just given to you the following trial balance dated December 31, 19—, and the additional information that follows. From this information:

(a)   Prepare a 10-column worksheet for the year ending December 31, 19—.

(b)   Prepare the adjusting entries in general journal form, complete with proper narratives.

Additional information:

(1)   Physical inventory on December 31, 19—, $35,440.

(2)   Accrued unpaid salaries: office, $935; sales, $1,050.

(3)   Insurance expired, $740.

(4)   Store supplies used, $1,850.

(5)   Uncollectible accounts are estimated at 5% of accounts receivable.

(6)   Depreciation is to be calculated using the *declining-balance method:* buildings, 10% per annum; delivery equipment, 20% per annum.

Dauphin Supply Co.
Trial Balance
December 31, 19—

ACCOUNT NAME	DEBIT					CREDIT				
Bank	10	3	1	0	00					
Accounts Receivable	12	3	8	0	00					
Allow for Doubtful Accounts						1	2	0	0	00
Inventory, January 1, 19—	38	0	0	0	00					
Store Supplies Prepaid	2	2	7	0	00					
Insurance Prepaid	1	4	1	0	00					
Land	90	0	0	0	00					
Building	100	0	0	0	00					
Accum. Deprec.—Building						17	6	5	0	00
Delivery Equipment	55	0	0	0	00					
Accum. Deprec.—Del. Equip.						15	8	0	0	00
Accounts Payable						32	4	5	0	00
Salaries Payable										
Capital, Jack Clements						296	1	6	5	00
Drawings, Jack Clements	50	0	0	0	00					
Sales						271	2	2	0	00
Sales Returns & Allowances	3	4	3	0	00					
Purchases	213	0	0	0	00					
Purchase Returns & Allowances						2	8	2	0	00
Transportation-In	2	6	5	0	00					
Delivery Expense	3	8	0	0	00					
Office Salaries Expense	20	0	0	5	00					
Sales Salaries Expense	35	0	5	0	00					
Store Supplies Expense										
Insurance Expense										
Bad Debts Expense										
Deprec. Expense—Buildings										
Deprec. Expense—Del. Equip.										
	637	3	0	5	00	637	3	0	5	00

▶ ### PRACTICE EXERCISE 6

Below is a partially completed worksheet for the Clarke Supply Co. You have been asked to assist with their year end by completing the following tasks:

(a) Record the adjusting entries in the general journal from the keyed entries in the Adjustments columns of the worksheet.

(b) Complete the worksheet by extending the appropriate amounts to the remaining columns (see Figure 17.3). Inventory at year end is valued at $32,440.

COMPANY Clarke Supply Co.   **WORKSHEET**   FOR One Year   ENDED December 31, 19—

NAME OF ACCOUNT	TRIAL BALANCE DEBIT	TRIAL BALANCE CREDIT	ADJUSTMENTS DEBIT	ADJUSTMENTS CREDIT
Bank	10 760 00			
Petty Cash	100 00			
Accounts Receivable	9 380 00			
Allowance for Doubtful Accounts		450 00		(e) 469 00
Inventory (Jan. 2, 19—)	28 650 00			
Store Supplies	1 270 00			(d) 950 00
Insurance Prepaid	710 00			(c) 270 00
Land	49 700 00			
Building	100 000 00			
Accum. Deprec. (Building)		17 650 00		(a) 8 000 00
Delivery Equipment	45 000 00			
Accum. Deprec. (Del. Equip.)		15 340 00		(a) 1 500 00
Accounts Payable		21 450 00		
Salaries Payable				(b) 1 795 00
Capital, Michael Clarke		205 000 00		
Drawings, Michael Clarke	30 000 00			
Sales		217 220 00		
Sales Returns & Allowances	2 730 00			
Purchases	138 900 00			
Purchase Returns & Allowances		2 385 00		
Freight In	17 620 00			
Delivery Expense	2 500 00			
Bad Debts Expense			(e) 469 00	
Deprec. Exp. (Building)			(a) 8 000 00	
Deprec. Exp. (Del. Equip.)			(a) 1 500 00	
Insurance Expense			(c) 270 00	
Office Salaries Expense	18 125 00		(b) 835 00	
Sales Salaries Expense	24 050 00		(b) 960 00	
Store Supplies Expense			(d) 950 00	
	479 495 00	479 495 00	12 984 00	12 984 00

CLOSING JOURNAL ENTRIES

Revenue and expense accounts are often referred to as temporary accounts because they are closed at the end of each financial year. The credit balances of the revenue accounts and the debit balances of the expense accounts are transferred into an account called Income Summary or Revenue & Expense Summary). The balance in the Income Summary account should equal the net income or net loss calculated at the bottom of the Income Statement columns of the worksheet. If the total revenues exceed the total expenses, the balance in the Income Summary account will represent a net income. If, on the other hand, the total expenses exceed the total revenues, the balance in the Income Summary account will represent a net loss.

The purpose of closing accounts at the end of the year is two-fold:

1. to reduce the balances in the temporary accounts to zero, thus preparing the accounts to receive transactions in the new financial year; and

2. to transfer the balance in the Income Summary account to a permanent account; namely, the owner's Capital account.

Since revenue accounts have credit balances, they are debited in order to close them, and the Income Summary account is credited. To simplify the process of closing the revenue accounts, they can be closed in groups by means of a compound journal entry.

19— Dec.	31	Sales Revenue			xx	x	x	x	xx						
		Rental Revenue				x	x	x	x	xx						
		Income Summary									xx	x	x	x	xx
		To close revenue accounts.													

Expense accounts have debit balances; therefore, the expense accounts are credited in order to close them and the Income Summary account is debited. A compound entry simplifies the closing of expense accounts.

19— Dec.	31	Income Summary			x	x	x	x	xx					
		Delivery Expense								x	x	x	xx
		Telephone Expense								x	x	x	xx
		Utilities Expense								x	x	x	xx
		Salaries Expense								x	x	x	xx
		To close expense accounts.											

Closing the Income Summary account to the owner's Capital account follows the same idea. If Income Summary has a credit balance (representing a net income), it will be debited in the closing entry in order to reduce the balance to zero. Capital will be credited.

19— Dec.	31	Income Summary			xx	x	x	x	xx					
		Capital									xx	x	x	x	xx
		To close net income for this financial period to Capital.												

If Income Summary has a debit balance (representing a net loss), it will be credited in order to close it, and Capital will be debited.

19— Dec.	31	Capital			xx	x	x	x	xx					
		Income Summary								xx	x	x	x	xx
		To close net loss for this financial period to Capital.												

The owner's Drawings account must also be closed so that it can be made ready to receive transactions in the new financial year.

19— Dec.	31	Capital			xx	x	x	x	xx					
		Drawings								x	x	x	x	xx
		To close Drawings to Capital.												

As explained in a previous chapter, Drawings is not an expense; it is a reduction of the owner's equity, representing the amounts withdrawn by the owner throughout the year.

▶ **PRACTICE EXERCISE 7**

From the worksheet prepared in Practice Exercise 4, record the closing entries in general journal form, with suitable explanations, for the Atlas Drafting Service.

▶ **PRACTICE EXERCISE 8**

From the worksheet prepared in Practice Exercise 5, record the closing entries in general journal form, with suitable explanations, for the Dauphin Supply Co.

▶ **PRACTICE EXERCISE 9**

From the worksheet prepared in Practice Exercise 6, record the closing entries in general journal form, with suitable explanations, for the Clarke Supply Co.

POST-CLOSING TRIAL BALANCE

After the adjusting and closing journal entries have been recorded and posted, one last trial balance is taken of the accounts in the general ledger. While most of the accounts will have zero balances, the asset, liability, and owner's equity accounts are still open and the **post-closing trial balance** will prove that the ledger is still in balance. Figure 17.4 shows a sample post-closing trial balance.

The closing of the books is now complete and the books are ready to receive the transactions that will be recorded in the new financial year. The recordkeeping cycles starts all over again.

Webster Milton Company
Post-Closing Trial Balance
October 31, 19—

ACCOUNT NAME	DEBIT					CREDIT				
Bank	7	6	0	0	00					
Accounts Receivable	12	0	0	0	00					
Allowance for Doubtful Accounts						1	2	0	0	00
Inventory	33	8	0	0	00					
Office Supplies Prepaid		5	0	0	00					
Insurance Prepaid		4	0	0	00					
Land	25	0	0	0	00					
Building	54	0	0	0	00					
Accumulated Depreciation (Building)						5	4	0	0	00
Equipment	20	0	0	0	00					
Accumulated Depreciation (Equipment)						4	0	0	0	00
Accounts Payable						23	4	0	0	00
Property Taxes Payable						1	2	0	0	00
Selling Commissions Payable							5	0	0	00
Capital, Michael Fraser						117	6	0	0	00
	153	3	0	0	00	153	3	0	0	00

Figure 17.4　Post-Closing Trial Balance

INCOME STATEMENT

The objective of every business organization (with the exception of not-for-profit organizations) is to earn a profit. Such profits can be retained in the business in order to finance future expansion or may be withdrawn by the owner(s) as compensation for managing the business and as a return on the investment in the business.

Since earning a profit is the goal of running a business, it follows that one of the accounting functions is to compile the necessary information in order to measure the profitability of that business. Such information is summarized in an **Income Statement** (Figure 17.5), which measures the success or failure of a business by matching the revenues earned during the financial period with the related expenses incurred during the same period. As seen during the preparation of the worksheet, the difference between the total revenues and the total expenses is the net income (or net loss) earned at the end of the accounting period.

The accounting period is the length of time covered by the statement, whether one month, six months, or one year. The income statement is usually prepared at the end of each financial (fiscal) period for the benefit of all interested parties, such as the owner(s) of the business, the company's banker, Revenue Canada, shareholders, and creditors. In addition, interim monthly statements are often prepared for internal decision-making purposes so that management can keep a close watch on the trend of operations in order to control, and perhaps avoid, incurring operating losses. These monthly statements are called interim financial statements (discussed in Chapter 11).

FINANCIAL STATEMENTS

Webster Milton Company
Income Statement
For one year ended October 31, 19—

Revenue:			
Gross Sales			242 0 0 0 00
Less Sales Returns & Allowances		1 4 0 0 00	
Sales Discounts		3 2 0 0 00	4 6 0 0 00
Net Sales			237 4 0 0 00
Cost of Goods Sold:			
Inventory (opening)		40 0 0 0 00	
Purchases	143 8 0 0 00		
Less Purchase Returns & Allowances	1 8 0 0 00		
Purchase Discounts	21 0 0 0 00 → 3 9 0 0 00		
Net Purchases	139 9 0 0 00		
Add Transporation-In	4 0 0 0 00		
Cost of Goods Purchased		143 9 0 0 00	
Cost of Goods Available for Sale		183 9 0 0 00	
Less Inventory (closing)		33 8 0 0 00	
Cost of Goods Sold			150 1 0 0 00
Gross Profit on Sales			87 3 0 0 00
Operating Expenses:			
Delivery Expense		1 1 0 0 00	
Selling Commission Expense		9 0 0 0 00	
Salaries and Wages Expense		37 0 0 0 00	
Property Taxes Expense		3 6 0 0 00	
Insurance Expense		9 0 0 00	
Office Supplies Expense		1 1 0 0 00	
Depreciation—Building		2 7 0 0 00	
Depreciation—Equipment		2 0 0 0 00	
Bad Debt Expense		6 0 0 00	
Total Operating Expenses			58 0 0 0 00
Net Income			29 3 0 0 00

Figure 17.5 Income Statement

Other titles for the income statement are: profit and loss statement, statement of earnings, and statement of operations. However, throughout this text, "income statement" is used. A properly classified income statement should answer such questions as: how much income was earned? how was it earned? and how long did it take to earn it?

BALANCE SHEET

A financial statement of equal importance is the **Balance Sheet** (Figure 17.6). This is a classified statement of assets, liabilities, and owner's equity, and summarizes the financial position of a business at the end of an accounting period. The balance sheet will help to provide answers to such questions as:

1. Do we have sufficient resources (current assets) to pay our short-term liabilities (current liabilities)? In other words, is the business solvent?

2. Do we require a bank loan to cover our short-term obligations?

3. Should excess cash, if any, be placed in a short-term investment or a long-term investment?

4. Are the resources that were contributed by the creditors too large in ratio to the resources contributed by the owner(s)? If so, such a situation could result in foreclosure of the business.

Webster Milton Company
Balance Sheet
October 31, 19—

ASSETS														
Current Assets														
Bank						7	6	0	0	00				
Accounts Receivable	12	0	0	0	00									
Less Allowances for Doubtful Accounts	1	2	0	0	00	10	8	0	0	00				
Inventory (closing)						33	8	0	0	00				
Office Supplies Prepaid							5	0	0	00				
Insurance Prepaid							4	0	0	00				
Total Current Assets											53	1	0	0	00
Plant and Equipment						25	0	0	0	00				
Land	54	0	0	0	00									
Building	5	4	0	0	00	48	6	0	0	00				
Less Accumulated Depreciation—Building	20	0	0	0	00									
Equipment	4	0	0	0	00	16	0	0	0	00				
Less Accumulated Depreciation—Equipment											89	6	0	0	00
Total Plant and Equipment											142	7	0	0	00
LIABILITIES AND OWNER'S EQUITY														
Current Liabilities														
Accounts Payable						23	4	0	0	00				
Property Tax Payable						1	2	0	0	00				
Selling Commission Payable							5	0	0	00				
Total Current Liabilities											25	1	0	0	00
Owner's Equity														
Capital, Michael Fraser						104	0	0	0	00				
Net Income	29	3	0	0	00									
Less Drawing, Michael Fraser	15	7	0	0	00	13	6	0	0	00	117	6	0	0	00
											142	7	0	0	00

Figure 17.6 Balance Sheet

A classified balance sheet shows the subdivisions of each general classification of account. Assets, for example, are divided into current assets, long-term assets, and other assets. Liabilities can be similarly divided.

Current assets are those that can be readily converted into cash, usually within one year. These include cash, accounts receivable, inventories of merchandise and supplies on hand, and marketable securities (investments). **Long-term assets** are usually land, buildings, and equipment owned and utilized by the business in the process of earning revenue. Other assets are those assets that cannot be classified as either current or long-term assets. These might include patents, copyrights, and assets owned but not presently used by the business in the process of earning revenue.

Current liabilities are those debts that must be paid within the operating cycle or one year (whichever is longer). These debts are paid out of current assets.

The comparison of current assets with current liabilities is known as a Current Ratio, which is a measurement of the firm's short-term debt-paying ability. To qualify as a good financial risk, the ratio should be at least 2:1. This means that for every dollar of current liabilities, the business should have at least $2 of current assets.

Long-term liabilities are those debts that are to be paid at some time beyond the term of one operating year or one calendar year, such as mortgages and bank loans.

The owner's equity section is a statement of the effects on the owner's Capital account as a result of recording a net income (or net loss) and any contributions and withdrawals by the owner during the financial period.

Financial statements can be prepared at any time during the accounting period for management use. Whereas interim statements do not require that the accounts be closed through the recording of closing entries, the preparation of the formal income statement and balance sheet is part of the accounting cycle performed at the end of the accounting period when the books are "closed" and made ready for the next financial year.

▶ **PRACTICE EXERCISE 10**

From the worksheet prepared for Atlas Drafting Service in Practice Exercise 4:

(a)   Prepare a classified income statement for six months ending June 30, 19—.

(b)   Prepare a classified balance sheet as at June 30, 19—.

▶ **PRACTICE EXERCISE 11**

From the worksheet prepared for Dauphin Supply Co. in Practice Exercise 5:

(a)   Prepare an income statement for one year ending December 31, 19—.

(b)   Prepare a classified balance sheet as at December 31, 19—.

▶ **PRACTICE EXERCISE 12**

From the worksheet prepared for Clarke Supply Co. in Practice Exercise 6:

(a)   Prepare an income statement for one year ending December 31, 19—.

(b)   Prepare a classified balance sheet as at December 31, 19—.

▶ **PRACTICE EXERCISE 13**

From the following trial balance and additional information provided, prepare:

(a)   a worksheet;

(b)   adjusting and closing journal entries;

(c)   a classified income statement;

(d)   a classified balance sheet.

ACCOUNT NAME	DEBIT					CREDIT				
Thomas Wong & Company **Trial Balance** **June 30, 19—**										
Bank	2	4	1	5	00					
Accounts Receivable	5	3	2	0	00					
Allowance for Doubtful Accounts									∅	
Office Supplies Prepaid		8	9	0	00					
Insurance Prepaid		9	3	5	00					
Inventory				∅						
Equipment	12	0	5	0	00					
Accum. Depreciation—Equipment									∅	
Accounts Payable						8	7	3	0	00
GST Payable							7	2	5	00
GST–ITC		3	2	0	00					
Salaries Payable									∅	
Capital, T. Wong						16	7	1	0	00
Drawings, T. Wong	5	4	5	5	00					
Sales						27	2	5	0	00
Sales Returns & Allowances	1	7	5	0	00					
Rental Revenue						4	1	4	0	00
Purchases	19	3	0	0	00					
Purchase Returns & Allowances						2	7	1	0	00
Advertising Expense	2	4	2	0	00					
Bad Debts Expense				∅						
Depreciation Expense–Equipment				∅						
Insurance Expense				∅						
Miscellaneous Expense		2	1	0	00					
Office Supplies Expense				∅						
Salaries Expense	9	2	0	0	00					
	60	2	6	5	00	60	2	6	5	00

Additional information available on June 30:

(1)   Inventory of merchandise on hand, $1,200.

(2)   Inventory of unused office supplies on hand, $130.

(3)   Unexpired insurance, $230.

(4)   Salaries accrued but not yet paid to the employee, $700.

(5)   Depreciation on the equipment is to be calculated for three months on the declining balance at a rate of 20% per annum.

(6)   The allowance for doubtful accounts is estimated to be 5% of the current Accounts Receivable balance.

► **PRACTICE EXERCISE 14**

From the following trial balance and additional information for Brandon Importing Co., prepare:

(a)   a worksheet;

(b)   adjusting and closing journal entries, complete with suitable explanations;

(c)   a classified income statement for the year ending October 31, 19-8;

(d)   a classified balance sheet as at October 31, 19-8.

Brandon Importing Co.
Trial Balance
October 31, 19–8

ACCOUNT NAME	DEBIT	CREDIT
Cash	8 3 0 0 00	
Petty Cash Fund	1 0 0 00	
Accounts Receivable	12 0 0 0 00	
Allowance for Doubtful Accounts		5 0 0 00
Inventory (November 1, 19-7)	40 0 0 0 00	
Insurance Prepaid	1 3 0 0 00	
Supplies Prepaid	1 6 0 0 00	
Land	25 0 0 0 00	
Building	54 0 0 0 00	
Accumulated Depreciation—Building		2 7 0 0 00
Equipment	20 0 0 0 00	
Accumulated Depreciation—Equipment		2 0 0 0 00
Accounts Payable		25 4 0 0 00
Capital, Michelle Foster		104 0 0 0 00
Drawings, Michelle Foster	15 7 0 0 00	
Sales		235 0 0 0 00
Sales Returns & Allowances	1 4 0 0 00	
Sales Discounts	3 2 0 0 0	
Rental Revenue		4 5 0 0 00
Purchases	139 8 0 0 00	
Purchase Returns & Allowances		2 0 0 0 00
Purchase Discounts		2 3 0 0 00
Freight In	4 0 0 0 00	
Bank Charges	2 0 0 00	
Delivery Expense	1 5 0 0 00	
Miscellaneous Expense	1 0 0 00	
Property Tax Expense	2 2 0 0 00	
Salaries & Wages Expense	37 0 0 0 00	
Selling Commission Expense	8 5 0 0 00	
Telephone Expense	8 0 0 00	
Utilities Expense	1 7 0 0 00	
	378 4 0 0 00	378 4 0 0 00

The following information is also available on October 31:

(1) The physical count of merchandise on hand at the end of the fiscal year was determined to be $31,000.

(2) Insurance expired during the year, $600.

(3) Supplies on hand at year end, $600.

(4) Accrued property taxes not yet recorded, $1,500.

(5) Selling commissions accrued but unpaid, $700.

(6) Depreciation rates: 5% on building, 10% on equipment (both calculated using the straight-line method).

(7) Uncollectible accounts are to be increased by 5% of the current value of accounts receivable.

▶ ### CLOSING THE BOOKS: KBC DECORATING CO.

KBC Decorating uses the calendar year (January 1 to December 31) as its financial period. To assist you in the closing of the books and the preparation of the financial statements, the following information has been compiled:

1. A physical count of inventory on hand was taken on December 31, 19—:

Paint and Supplies	$5,211.50	
Wallpaper	2,500.00	$7,711.50

2. Inventory of unused supplies:

Office Supplies	$342.60	
Warehouse Supplies	132.20	$474.80

3. All fixed assets are depreciated on the cost value (at the annual rate stated) from the date of purchase:

Building (depreciation rate of 10%) from July 1 for six months, calculated as:

$$\$100,000.00 \times 10\% \times 6/12 = \$5,000$$

Office furniture and equipment (depreciation rate of 20%):

Jan.	1	$2,000.00	1 year	$400.00	
July	2	2,000.00	6 months	200.00	
Nov.	19	3,275.00	$1\frac{1}{2}$ months	81.87	$681.87

Service Vehicles (depreciation rate of 30%):

Jan.	1	$10,000.00	1 year	$3,000.00	
Mar.	30	15,000.00	9 months	3,375.00	$6,375.00

Tools and Equipment (depreciation rate of 30%):

Jan.	2	$ 1,500.00	1 year	$ 450.00	
Mar.	1	10,000.00	10 months	2,500.00	
Jun.	16	600.00	$7\frac{1}{2}$ months	112.50	
Aug.	30	5,400.00	4 months	540.00	
Oct.	5	250.00	3 months	18.75	$3,621.25

4. A customer's account (S. Miller, account #153) has been determined to be uncollectible, $684.

5. All employees have been given appropriate vacation time based on length of employment; therefore, no holiday pay has accrued to year end.

YEAR-END ACTIVITIES

1. Set up a worksheet using the column headings shown in Figure 17.3. Three pages of working paper will be required for this worksheet.

2. In the Name of Accounts column, copy the names of all the accounts listed on the December 31 trial balance (Chapter 15). Include these accounts:

    #521 Insurance Expense

    #525 Office Supplies Expense

    #535 Warehouse Supplies Expense

    Do not include Salaries Payable (#218) since this account has a zero balance and will have no effect on the closing of the books.

3. In the Trial Balance columns, copy the figures from the December 31 trial balance. Rule the totals as usual.

4. Complete the worksheet as described in this chapter using the adjustments listed above. Extend the figures to the other columns as required.

5. Prepare the adjusting entries in the general journal and post them to the ledger accounts. Open new accounts as required.

6. Prepare the journal entry required to write off S. Miller's uncollectible account for $684.

7. Record and post the following journal entries:

(a) a compound entry to close the revenue accounts to the Income Summary account and to record the closing inventory;

(b) a compound entry to close the expense accounts into the Income Summary account and to remove the opening inventory ($13,000);

(c) an entry to close the balance of the Income Summary account into the partners' Capital accounts, divided in ratio to the partners' Capital balances;

(d) an entry to close the partners' Drawings accounts to their respective Capital accounts.

8. Prepare a properly classified income statement for the year ended December 31, 19—.

9. Prepare a properly classified balance sheet dated December 31, 19—.

10. Prepare a post-closing trial balance.

CHAPTER

18

Other Record-keeping Systems

CHAPTER OBJECTIVES

After completing this chapter, you will be able to:
- utilize other recordkeeping systems:
  the One-Write System, the synoptic journal, and
  the voucher system

IMPORTANT WORDS AND TERMS IN THIS CHAPTER

Cheque Register
One-Write System
Pegboard
Synoptic Journal
Voucher
Voucher Register

ONE-WRITE SYSTEM

The one-write system (or peg board system) is a time-saving and labour-saving bookkeeping procedure that utilizes a pegboard and specially designed stationery for processing daily business transactions (see Figure 18.1). The pegboard is a flat sheet of metal or plastic/vinyl with pegs mounted along one side. Special preprinted forms are aligned on these pegs and adjusted line by line as the accounting transactions are recorded. This system allows for several accounting records to be created at the same time by writing the transaction only once.

The manual system, as discussed in previous chapters, requires a step-by-step sequence of events, first evidenced by a source document from which the information is entered in a journal and later posted to the ledger. Because the figures in such transactions are copied several times in the manual system, the possibility of errors always exists. The one-write system minimizes recording and copying errors because each transaction is written only once; the data entered is transferred to the journals and ledger accounts by means of carbon paper or chemically treated paper. Therefore, the recording process is not only more accurate but also faster.

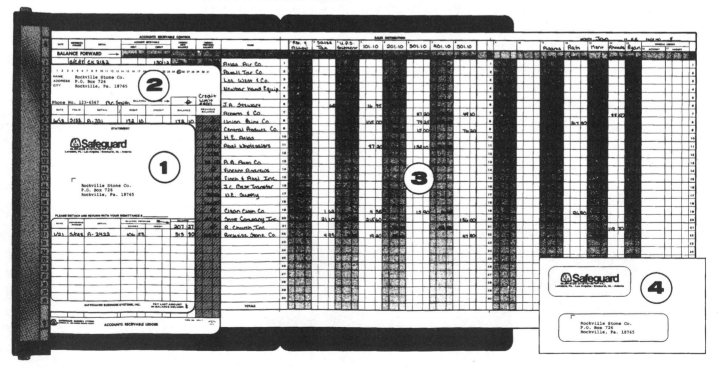

Figure 18.1   One-Write System

Source: Courtesy of Safeguard Business Systems Ltd.

Although the one-write system can be adopted for virtually every phase of accounting, it is most commonly used for processing accounts receivable, payroll, perpetual inventory, and cash payments.

In processing accounts receivable, for example, the forms would consist of a sales journal, the customers' ledger accounts, and statements to be sent to the customers at the end of each month. Each form would be mounted on the pegs, one overlaying the other, with the first available writing line on each appropriately aligned. As the sale to the customer is entered on the statement, the carbon paper would transfer the same information through to the customer's ledger card positioned below, and through to the sales journal sheet positioned below the ledger card. Therefore, by writing the transaction only once, the journal and the ledger are recorded simultaneously.

Similarly, the forms for recording payroll would be the payroll summary sheet, the employee earnings records, and the paycheques. Again, the forms would be positioned appropriately on the pegboard with the first available writing line of each correctly aligned. As the cheque and the payroll stub are filled out, the information is transferred by carbon paper through to each employee's earnings record and to the payroll summary sheet. As the information is being written on the top-most form, it is transferred through to all the forms positioned below it.

The main advantage of the one-write system is the time saved in recording the transactions, thus eliminating the need to recopy information from the source document to the journal and to the ledger accounts or other data sheets. A possible disadvantage of this system is the cost of having the special journals and other forms printed for use on a one-write system.

With the development and availability of low-cost computer software for common bookkeeping and accounting functions, many businesses are moving away from paper-intensive accounting systems such as one-write systems in favour of computerization. Computerized accounting is discussed in Chapter 19.

SYNOPTIC JOURNAL

Not all businesses require the full range of journals discussed throughout the previous chapters of this textbook. A small business, such as a bowling alley or a convenience store, will not likely have enough purchase transactions to warrant the use of a purchase journal or enough cash receipt entries each month to warrant the use of the cash receipts journal. For such businesses with a very small number of transactions to record each month, the five traditional journals (sales, purchases, cash receipts, cash payments, and general journals) can be combined into one synoptic journal.

The multi-columned **synoptic journal** can be easily designed using ordinary columnar paper available from any stationery store and tailored to suit the changing needs of any type of business. Because it is the only journal utilized in this recordkeeping system, several advantages can be appreciated:

1. All the business activities are recorded in one journal rather than in a variety of journals.

2. Special columns are established for those transactions that occur frequently (like those created in the purchase journal and the sales journal). These special columns reduce the amount of recording and the number of entries to be posted.

3. The cost of bookkeeping supplies is reduced. Simple multicolumn accounting stationery can be used instead of specially designed and printed journals and forms.

The only disadvantage of the synoptic journal is that, because only one person is responsible for recording a transaction from beginning to end, there is a greater possibility of errors going undetected. However, the relative simplicity of the synoptic journal allows someone with little or no bookkeeping experience to record the most common business transactions with ease.

The structure of the synoptic journal will vary. The journal illustrated in Figure 18.2 is typical of most. The first three pairs of money columns (general ledger, accounts receivable ledger, and accounts payable ledger) are set up for transactions that occur relatively infrequently.

1. General Ledger Dr. and Cr. columns are for transactions affecting any accounts for which no special columns are provided.

2. Accounts Receivable Dr. and Cr. columns are for transactions affecting customers' accounts.

3. Accounts Payable Dr. and Cr. columns are for transactions affecting creditors' accounts.

The accounts affected by amounts entered into any of these first six money columns must be identified in the "Name of Accounts" column and would be posted individually. In the first entry, for example, the owner has invested $15,000 into the business. The typical entry is to debit Bank (or Cash) and to credit Capital. Because there is no special column in this synoptic journal for capital entries, the credit side of the transaction is entered into the General Ledger Cr. column and the account *Capital* is named in the "Name of Accounts" column.

The remaining special columns are for transactions that occur often: Bank (or Cash), Sales, Purchases, and frequently charged taxes and expenses. By using these special columns, only the month-end total of each column is posted to the respective account instead of the individual entries recorded in the column.

The following basic principles of recording transactions in the synoptic journal should be observed:

1. The name of the account is written in the "Name of Account" column only for entries that are recorded in the first three pairs of money columns (general ledger, accounts receivable ledger, and accounts payable ledger). If the transaction can be accommodated entirely within the various special money columns, the "Name of Account" column can be left blank, such as for a cash sale entry where both the debit entry to Bank and the credit entry to Sales are accommodated by the appropriate special columns.

2. Some transactions require that *both* the debit and credit entries be written in the "Name of Account" column. The purchase of a computer on credit, for example, would require a debit entry to Office Equipment and a credit entry to the appropriate accounts payable account. Since special columns are not provided for either Office Equipment or the specific supplier, both account names are identified in the "Name of Account" column.

SYNOPTIC JOURNAL

PAGE 51

DATE 19—	ACCOUNTS	MEMO	✓	GENERAL LEDGER DEBIT	GENERAL LEDGER CREDIT	A/R LEDGER DEBIT	A/R LEDGER CREDIT	A/P LEDGER DEBIT	A/P LEDGER CREDIT	BANK DEBIT	CH.	BANK CREDIT	PURCH. DEBIT	GST-ITC DEBIT	STORE SUPPLIES DEBIT	SALES CREDIT	GST PAYABLE CREDIT	SALES TAX CREDIT
Mar. 1	Capital	investment			15 000 00					15 000 00								
2	Rent Expense	for March		8 41 12							1	9 00 00		5 8 88				
2	Store Fixtures			1 6 05 00										1 0 5 00				
	Winters Furniture	n/90							1 7 1 0 00									
3		cash purch.									2	1 3 1 6 64	1 2 3 0 50	8 6 14				
4		cash sale								1 8 8 1 00						1 6 5 0 00	1 1 5 50	1 1 5 50
7	Central Fruit	n/30							3 4 3 47				3 2 1 00	2 2 47				
7	Freight In	on above		1 1 77							3	1 2 54		77				
10	Ron Abbot	n/30				4 9 02										4 3 00	3 01	3 01
	Ann Black	n/30				3 3 06										2 9 00	2 03	2 03
	Shirley Curtis	n/30				2 0 52										1 8 00	1 26	1 26
11		refund									4	5 1 30				(4 5 00)	(3 15)	(3 15)
29	Shirley Curtis	on acct.					2 0 52			2 0 52								
31	Salaries Payable			2 3 0 0 00							5	2 3 0 0 00						
31		supplies									6	1 0 6 54		6 54	1 0 0 00			
				4 7 5 7 89	15 0 0 0 00	1 0 2 60	2 0 52		2 0 5 3 47	16 9 0 1 52		4 6 8 7 02	1 5 5 1 50	2 7 9 80	1 0 0 00	1 6 9 5 00	1 1 8 65	1 1 8 65

Figure 18.2   Synoptic Journal

3. If a separate Memo (or Explanation) column is not provided, it is suggested that memos be written in parentheses in order to distinguish between an account name and a memo. For entries recorded entirely in the special columns, a memo should be recorded to provide a quick reference as to the nature of the transaction since the "Name of Account" area has been left blank.

4. Most small businesses will usually require only a few adjustments (credit notes and refunds) to purchases and sales; therefore, they are not likely to use Purchase Returns & Allowances or Sales Returns & Allowances accounts. Such adjustments are usually made directly to the Purchases and Sales accounts. For example, if a credit note is received from a supplier for defective merchandise that had been returned, the entry would be recorded as a debit to Accounts Payable/(supplier's name) and a credit to Purchases. If, on the other hand, a credit note is issued to a customer for a shortage on an invoice, we would debit Sales and credit Accounts Receivable/(customer's name).

If the synoptic Journal does not provide a Purchases Cr. column, the credit notes and cash refunds received from suppliers are recorded in the Purchase Dr. column with the amount shown in parentheses. The use of parentheses indicates that the value is to be *deducted* from the Purchases account. Likewise, an amount shown in parentheses in the Sales Cr. column indicates that the amount is to be *deducted* from the Sales account.

To demonstrate the use of the synoptic journal, the following transactions are illustrated and explained initially as general journal entries. Compare each general journal entry with the same entry as it would be recorded in the synoptic journal in Figure 18.2.

March 1   Peter Greene invests $15,000 to open grocery store.

19— Mar.	1	Bank			15	0	0	0	00					
		Capital									15	0	0	0	00
		Owner's initial investment.												

In the synoptic journal, the debit to Bank is accommodated by recording $15,000 in the Bank Dr. column. However, because there is not a special column for Capital, *Capital* is written in the "Name of Account" column and the amount is entered in the General Ledger Cr. column.

March 2   Cheque #1 for $900 is issued to Smith Leasing Agency for the March rent. The rental payment includes $58.88 GST.

Mar.	2	Rent Expense			8	4	1	12					
		GST-ITC				5	8	88					
		Bank								9	0	0	00
		Paid rent for March. Issued cheque #1.											

Because rent transactions would occur only once a month, a special column has not been provided. The debit entry to Rent Expense is identified in the "Name of Accounts" column and the amount attributed to rent ($841.12) is entered in the General Ledger Dr. column. The appropriate amount of GST is recorded in the GST-ITC column and amount of the cheque issued is entered in the Bank Cr. column. The cheque number is also identified. When recording compound entries in a journal with so many columns, extra care must taken to ensure that the transaction is balanced; that is, Debits = Credits.

March 2   Bought store fixtures at a cost of $1,605 (plus $105 GST) from Winters Furniture Co. on terms of 90 days.

Mar.	2	Store Fixtures		1 6 0 5 00		
		GST-ITC		1 0 5 00		
		A/P Winters Furniture				1 7 1 0 00
		Bought display fixtures on terms n/90.				

March 3   Purchased merchandise from West Wholesalers, $1,230.50 (plus $86.14 GST). Issued cheque #2.

Mar.	3	Purchases		1 2 3 0 50		
		GST-ITC		8 6 14		
		Bank				1 3 1 6 64
		Cash purchase of merchandise; issued cheque #2.				

March 4   Cash sales during opening week, $1,650 plus 7% GST and 7% sales tax.

Mar.	4	Bank		1 8 8 1 00		
		Sales				1 6 5 0 00
		GST Payable				1 1 5 50
		Sales Tax Payable				1 1 5 50
		Cash sales.				

This cash sale transaction is accommodated entirely within the special columns of the synoptic journal; therefore, nothing is written in the "Name of Accounts" column, but a memo is entered to easily identify the nature of this transaction.

March 7   Bought merchandise, $321.00 plus $22.47 GST, from Central Fruit Co. on 30-day terms.

Mar.	7	Purchases			3	2	1	00				
		GST-ITC				2	2	47				
		A/P Central Fruit							3	4	3	47
		Terms n/30.										

March 7   Issued cheque #3 for $11.77 (plus $0.77 GST) to ABC Truckers for the freight on merchandise delivered to the store.

Mar.	7	Freight In			1	1	77				
		GST-ITC					77				
		Bank							1	2	54
		Issued cheque #3 to ABC Truckers for freight charges.									

March 10   Sold merchandise on 30-day terms to Ron Abbot, $43; Ann Black, $29; and Shirley Curtis, $18. Add 7% GST and 7% sales tax.

Mar.	10	A/R Abbot, Ron			4	9	02				
		A/R Black, Ann			3	3	06				
		A/R Curtis, Shirley			2	0	52				
		Sales							9	0	00
		GST Payable								6	30
		Sales Tax Payable								6	30
		Sales on account; terms n/30.									

March 11   A refund was given to a cash customer for damaged goods returned, $45 plus adjustment to taxes.

Mar.	11	Sales			4	5	00				
		GST Payable				3	15				
		Sales Tax Payable				3	15				
		Bank							5	1	30
		Issued Cheque #4 as refund for damaged goods.									

The adjustments to Sales, GST Payable, and Sales Tax Payable in the synoptic journal are made by recording the amounts in parentheses in their respective columns. The amounts in parentheses will be deducted from the other amounts in the column when the column is totalled.

March 29   Received payment from Shirley Curtis on the sale of March 10, $20.52.

Mar.	29	Bank			2 0 52	
		A/R Curtis, Shirley				2 0 52
		Received amount owing on account for invoice dated Mar. 10.				

March 31   Issued paycheque to our employee, $2,300.

Mar.	31	Salaries Payable			2 3 0 0 00	
		Bank				2 3 0 0 00
		Issued cheque #5 for month-end payroll.				

We are assuming that the usual payroll entry had already been recorded, including deductions, and that this entry represents the net pay.

March 31   Issued cheque #6 for the purchase of store supplies, $100 plus $6.54 GST.

Mar.	31	Store Supplies			1 0 0 00	
		GST-ITC			6 54	
		Bank				1 0 6 54
		Cheque #6.				

POSTING FROM THE SYNOPTIC JOURNAL

The procedure for posting from the synoptic journal is similar to that of posting from the other special journals discussed in earlier chapters:

1. Total the columns in pencil and prove equal debits and credits for the journal overall.

2. Total and rule the columns in ink.

3. Post the amounts in the General Ledger columns individually to their respective accounts, either daily or at the end of the month, using the date of entry as recorded in the Date column.

4. Post daily the amounts in the Accounts Receivable Ledger columns to the customers' accounts.

5. Post the totals of the Accounts Receivable Ledger columns to the Accounts Receivable Control account in the general ledger.

6. Post daily the amounts in the Accounts Payable Ledger columns to the creditors' accounts.

7. Post the totals of the Accounts Payable Ledger columns to the Accounts Payable Control account in the general ledger.

8.   Post the total of each of the special columns to the debit or credit of the appropriate account in the general ledger.

9.   Prepare a trial balance as usual, supported by a schedule of accounts receivable and a schedule of accounts payable.

▶ **PRACTICE EXERCISE 1**

Harvey Shortt has just opened a grocery store in Winnipeg, Manitoba, and has decided to utilize a synoptic journal. The headings he will use are the same as those illustrated in Figure 18.2.

The following ledger accounts will be required. Each account is to be numbered as indicated and each will be labelled Sheet #1.

Bank	101
Petty Cash	102
Accounts Receivable Control	103
Office Supplies Prepaid	105
Store Supplies Prepaid	106
Store Fixtures & Equipment	110
Accounts Payable Control	201
GST Payable	205
GST-ITC	207
Sales Tax Payable	210
Capital, H. Shortt	301
Drawings, H. Shortt	302
Sales	401
Sales Discounts	403
Purchases	501
Purchase Discounts	503
Freight In	505
Advertising	511
Donations	512
General Expense	513
Office Postage	514
Rent Expense	518
Salaries—Office	521
Salaries—Sales	522
Telephone Expense	525
Utilities	527

Accounts Receivable:
Grant, Edward	131
Hobson, Jack	133
Lamb, Stephen	135
Lawson, Joe	137

Accounts Payable:
Kildonan Lumber Co.	231

(a)   Record the following transactions for the month of February. Add 7% GST and 7% sales tax to all sales, based on the selling price quoted. GST on items purchased is indicated in parentheses. Eligible discounts will be calculated on the value of the goods (before taxes). All transactions affecting customers and suppliers should be posted on a daily basis to their accounts. All payments are to be made by cheque beginning with cheque #1.

19—

Feb.   1   Harvey Shortt invests $22,000 in his grocery business.

1   Issued cheque #1 for $75 to establish a petty cash fund.

1   Issued cheque #2 to J. Patterson for February rent, $950.00 (includes $62.15 GST).

5   Received the following invoices for items recently purchased: Starr Equipment Co., $3,990 (includes $245 GST) for display counters, cash register, and show cases; terms n/10; invoice dated February 3. National Printing Co., $65.35 (includes $4.01 GST) for office stationery; terms 2/10,n/30; invoice dated February 4. Kildonan Lumber Co., $205.20 (includes $12.60 GST) for lumber and other materials for building shelves; terms net 60 days; invoice dated February 5.

6   Issued a cheque to Speedy Delivery, $49.50 (includes $3.04 GST), for delivery charges on the purchase from Starr Equipment Co. on February 3.

7   Issued a cheque to Weekly News to advertise the store's upcoming grand opening on February 12, $45.65 (includes $2.80 GST).

11   Purchase invoices received today: Neepawa Abattoirs Ltd., $875.60 for fresh and cured meats; terms net 10 days; dated February 10. Wholesale Grocers Ltd., $3,778.50 for groceries; terms n/30; dated February 10. California Fruit Distributors Ltd., $350.60 for fruit; terms C.O.D.; dated February 10. *Food orders are GST exempt.*

11   Issued a cheque to ABC Truckers for delivering the meat from Neepawa Abattoirs Ltd., $71.50 (includes $4.39 GST).

11   Purchased packaging and wrapping supplies, $484.50 (includes $29.75 GST), from Wilkinson Paper Co. by cheque.

11   Paid express charges, $29 (includes $1.78 GST), on packaging and wrapping supplies delivered by Speedy Delivery.

12   Cash sales, $753.60.

12   Credit sale to Joe Lawson, $48.90. (Terms on all credit sales will be 2/10,n/30.)

13   Issued a cheque to Starr Equipment Co. for their invoice dated February 3.

14   Issued a cheque to National Printing Co. for their invoice dated February 4.

14   Paid salaries: sales clerks, $475; bookkeeper, $450. Two cheques are to be issued.

14   Cash sales, $954.75.

14   Credit sales: Jack Hobson, $35.60; Edward Grant, $42.30.

15   Harvey Shortt withdrew $500 cash for personal use.

16   Paid Wilfred Green $150 plus $10.50 GST for building the shelves in the store.

At this point, subtotal all columns, prove equal debits and credits, and forward all subtotals to page 2 of your journal.

18   Cash sales, $986.10.

18   Sales on account: Joe Lawson, $29.50; Stephen Lamb, $36.20.

20   Issued cheques to: California Fruit Distributors, $295.10, for an order of fruit C.O.D.; Neepawa Abattoirs Ltd. to cover their invoice dated February 10.

23   Purchase invoices received: Neepawa Abattoirs Ltd., $410.60; net 10 days; dated February 22. Wholesale Grocers Ltd., $615; net 30 days; dated February 23. (These invoices are GST exempt.)

24   Issued a cheque to ABC Truckers for delivering meats from Neepawa Abattoirs Ltd., $64.50 (includes $3.96 GST).

24   Received cheques from Jack Hobson and Edward Grant to cover invoices dated February 14.

25   Cash sales, $782.45.

25   Sales on account: Joe Lawson, $18.65; Jack Hobson, $24.70; Edward Grant, $33.95.

26   Issued a cheque for $62.50 plus $4.09 GST to the *Weekly News* for month-end advertising.

28   Received cheque from Joe Lawson for the sale dated February 12; and from Stephen Lamb for sale dated February 18.

28   Issued a cheque to reimburse the petty cash fund for this month's expenditures: stamps for the office, $3.70 plus $0.26 GST; sundry office supplies, $28.35 plus $1.85 GST; express charges on office supplies, $5.35 plus $0.35 GST; donation to Boy Scouts, $10; cleaning supplies, $17.10 (includes $1.05 GST).

28   Paid salaries (same as February 14).

28   Issued a cheque to Provincial Gas Co. for $178.50 (includes $10.96 GST) for heating.

28   Paid telephone bill, $23.50 plus $1.54 GST.

(b) Total all columns in pencil and prove equal debits and credits.

(c) Total and rule the journal in ink.

(d) Post the remaining transactions and appropriate totals to the ledger accounts.

(e) Prepare a trial balance with schedules of accounts receivable and accounts payable.

▶ **PRACTICE EXERCISE 2**

Robert Campbell is the owner/operator of Fit-Well Shoes in Red Deer, Alberta. Record his transactions for the month of May, 19—.

Set up a synoptic journal with the following headings: General Ledger Dr., General Ledger Cr., Accounts Receivable Dr., Accounts Receivable Cr., Accounts Payable Dr., Accounts Payable Cr., Bank Dr., Cheque Number, Bank Cr., Purchases Dr., GST-ITC Dr., Sales Cr., GST Payable Cr., and Salaries Dr.

Open the following accounts in the general ledger: Bank, 101; Accounts Receivable Control, 102; Insurance Prepaid, 107; Office Supplies Prepaid, 109; Counters & Displays, 115; Accounts Payable Control, 201; GST Payable, 202; GST-ITC, 203; Capital, R. Campbell, 301; Sales, 400; Purchases, 501; Postage, 503; Rent Expense, 505; Salaries, 507; Telephone, 509; Utilities, 511.

The accounts receivable subsidiary ledger will consist of these customers' accounts: Blaine Mitchell, 110; Clint Prior, 111; David Poyser, 112; Brian Sutherland, 113; and Wendy Suderman, 114.

The accounts payable subsidiary ledger will consist of these suppliers' accounts: Best Shoes, 210; John Pattinson, 211; The Shoe Factory, 212; The Bootery, 213; and Major Office Supply, 214.

Record the following transactions in the synoptic journal, charging 7% GST on all sales:

19—

May 1 Mr. Campbell invested $20,000 in a retail shoe business.

2 Issued a cheque for rent of the store for the month of May, $1,000 (includes $65.42 GST); cheque #1. Bought counters and display shelving from John Pattinson on invoice #47, $3,500 plus $245 GST; terms n/30.

3 Bought merchandise from Best Shoes, $2,800 plus $196 GST; terms n/10.

4 Cash sales, $870. Bought insurance on merchandise, $250 (GST exempt); cheque #2.

5 Credit sales: Blaine Mitchell, $140; Clint Prior, $280; and David Poyser, $226. All invoices carry terms of n/15.

8 Paid freight on merchandise purchased in Regina, $65.00 plus $4.55 GST; cheque #3. (Debit this freight cost directly to Purchases.)

9 Purchased shoes from The Shoe Factory, $3,000 plus $210 GST; terms n/30.

10   Credit sales on terms n/15: Brian Sutherland, $95; Wendy Suderman, $125; and Blaine Mitchell, $70.

11   Cash sales, $525.

12   Bought fashion boots from The Bootery, $2,889 (includes $189 GST), on terms of n/10. Paid CN Express for freight on purchase of May 9, $70 plus $4.90 GST.

15   Bought postage stamps, $43 plus $3.01 GST, by certified cheque. Paid salaries, $1,600.

16   Received a credit note from The Shoe Factory for $50 plus GST for laces missing in the order of May 9. (This will be recorded as a direct reduction from Purchases; therefore, enter the amount in the Purchases Dr. column with the amount shown in parentheses. Adjust GST-ITC in the same manner.)

18   Gave a credit note to Blaine Mitchell for imperfect insoles, $12.84, on the May 5 sale. (This will be recorded as a reduction from Sales in the Sales Cr. column. Show the amount in parentheses. Also, enter $0.84 as a reduction to GST Payable.)

At this point, you should subtotal your journal and check that these subtotals balance. Carry the subtotals forward to page 2 of the journal and continue recording the transactions.

21   Cash sales, $1,729.

22   Received cheques for sales of May 10 from Brian Sutherland and Wendy Suderman, and a cheque from Blaine Mitchell for his May 5 invoice (less credit note).

23   Bought office supplies from Major Office Supply, $116.30 (includes $7.61 GST); terms n/20.

24   Paid the hydro bill, $78 plus GST, and the telephone bill, $110 plus GST. Separate cheques were issued.

25   Cash sales, $975.

30   Paid salaries, $1,600. Paid J. Pattinson for the May 2 invoice.

Total all columns and balance the journal. Post all appropriate entries and column totals to the ledger accounts. Prepare a trial balance with schedules.

THE VOUCHER SYSTEM

If a business sees the need to adopt tighter controls on the purchase of assets and expenses and for the payments of such expenditures, it might choose the **voucher system**. In addition to the usual sales journal and cash receipts journal, a voucher register (which replaces the purchase journal) and a cheque register (which replaces the cash payments journal) would be utilized.

The adoption of the voucher system would necessitate a change in purchasing and payment routines. Authorization is required for each step of the process to ensure that no one person has complete control over the acquisition of assets and supplies and that payments are made only for those acquisitions that have been properly authorized.

A properly completed and authorized voucher (Figure 18.3) becomes the source document for an entry in the voucher register. This voucher provides evidence that a liability is owing to the company named and that payment is to be made by the due date specified. If a discount is eligible for early payment of the voucher, the amount of the discount is noted along with the net amount due.

When the cheque is issued in payment of the authorized voucher, an entry is recorded in the cheque register, paying off the liability that was originally recorded in the voucher register.

KBC Decorating Co.			**Voucher # 1**
Account Debit	**Amount**	Invoice #	214
Purchases—Paint & Supplies	200.00	Invoice Date	Feb. 7, 19—
Purchases—Wallpaper	355.00	Terms	2/10, n/30
Freight In		Due Date	Feb. 17, 19—
Office Supplies			
Warehouse Supplies		Supplier:	Rainbow Supplies
Rent			2007 Jasper Ave.
Telephone			Edmonton, AB
Utilities			T5G 3W7
Miscellaneous			
Other:		**Summary:**	
GST-ITC	38.85	Invoice Total	593.85
		Discount	11.10
Total Debit	593.85	Net Payment	582.75
		Date Paid	Feb. 17, 19—
Total Credit to		Cheque #	242
Vouchers Payable	593.85	Approved By	H. Martin

Figure 18.3   Voucher

VOUCHER REGISTER

The **voucher register** (Figure 18.4) is a journal resembling an expanded purchase journal. Whereas the purchase journal is used to record all purchases of assets and expenses on account, the voucher register is used to record *all* types of expenditures. Every entry in the voucher register consists of a credit to Vouchers Payable (a liability account much like Accounts Payable) and a debit to an appropriate account representing the asset and expense acquired, whether purchased on account or to be paid by cheque immediately, or the payment of a liability.

A typical voucher register (Figure 18.4) uses these basic columns: Date, Voucher Number, Name of Creditor, Date of Payment, Cheque Number, and Vouchers Payable Cr. The Vouchers Payable column is similar to the Accounts Payable column in the purchase journal, representing the amount of the invoice or bill that is to be paid. Other columns and account titles can be added to suit the needs of each particular business. When each entry is recorded in the voucher register, the total of the voucher is recorded under Vouchers Payable and is then allocated to the respective asset or expense column or is charged to a specified account under Other Accounts.

At the end of the month, the columns are totalled and posted in a manner similar to that for other special journals.

VOUCHER REGISTER

PAGE VR19

DATE		VO. NO.	CREDITOR	PAYMENT		VOUCHERS PAYABLE CR.	PURCHASES DR.	GST-ITC DR.	FREIGHT IN DR.	ADVERT. DR.	SUPPLIES DR.	OTHER ACCOUNTS DEBIT		
				DATE	CH. NO.							ACCOUNT	F.	AMOUNT
19—Mar.	1	41	Atlas Agency	Mar. 1	26	1250 00		81 78				Rent Exp.		1168 22
	1	42	Manitoba Supply Co.	11	30	1140 00	1070 00	70 00						
	2	43	Redwood Furniture Co.	12	31	1710 00		105 00				Off. Equip.		1605 00
	2	44	Berger Freight Co.	3	27	53 50		3 50	50 00					
	5	45	National Bank	5	28	566 00						Bank Loan		500 00
												Int. Exp.		66 00
	5	46	Berger Freight Co.	6	29	37 00		2 42				Off. Equip.		34 58
	30	87	Addison Advertising	30	43	125 40		7 70		117 70				
	30	88	Manitoba Supply Co.			1311 00	1230 50	80 50						
	30	89	Berger Freight Co.	30	44	32 10		2 10	30 00					
	31	90	O.K. Supply Co.			109 44		6 72			102 72			
	31	91	Payroll	31	45	2250 00						Salaries		2250 00
						8584 44	2300 50	359 72	80 00	117 70	102 72			5623 80

Figure 18.4   Voucher Register

The **cheque register**, used in conjunction with the voucher register, is a simplified version of the cash payments journal. It has only three money columns: Vouchers Payable Dr., Purchase Discounts Cr., and Bank Cr. Every cheque issued is recorded as a debit to Vouchers Payable (offsetting the liability originally recorded in the voucher register) and a credit to Bank. (See Figure 18.5.)

CHEQUE REGISTER

PAGE CqR 12

DATE		NAME OF PAYEE	VOUCHER NO.	VOUCHERS PAYABLE DR.	PURCHASE DISCOUNT CR.	BANK CR.	CHEQUE NO.
19—Mar.	1	Atlas Agency	41	1250 00		1250 00	26
	3	Berger Freight Co.	44	53 50		53 50	27
	5	National Bank	45	566 00		566 00	28
	6	Berger Freight Co.	46	37 00		37 00	29
	11	Manitoba Supply Co.	42	1140 00	20 00	1120 00	30
	12	Redwood Furniture Co.	43	1710 00		1710 00	31
	30	Addison Advertising	87	125 40		125 40	43
	30	Berger Freight Co.	89	32 10		32 10	44
	31	Payroll	91	2250 00		2250 00	45
				7164 00	20 00	7144 00	

Figure 18.5   Cheque Register

When payment for an approved voucher is recorded in the cheque register, a notation of the cheque number and the date of the cheque is made beside the original entry in the voucher register, thus providing a cross-reference between the entries in the two journals.

At the end of the month, the totals of the columns in the cheque register are posted to their respective accounts in the ledger. The individual entries in these columns are not posted since all transactions will affect the Vouchers Payable account and the Bank account.

When the voucher system is used, the Accounts Payable subsidiary ledger is eliminated. The total amount owing to creditors is represented by the *unpaid* vouchers in the voucher register and should, therefore, equal the balance in the Vouchers Payable account.

The main advantage offered by the voucher system is that it eliminates the accounts payable ledger. This, in turn, reduces the amount of detailed recording and posting that would otherwise be necessary, eliminates the costs required to maintain an accounts payable ledger, and maintains a stronger control over cash expenditures.

The disadvantages to be considered are that the invoices are not classified according to creditors' names; there is no record of the total purchases from a given supplier over a period of time; and there is no record of the total amount owed to a given creditor for whom we might have several outstanding invoices.

▶ ### PRACTICE EXERCISE 3

(a) Set up a voucher register with the headings illustrated in Figure 18.4. Also, set up a cheque register with the headings illustrated in Figure 18.5.

(b) Open a ledger account for Vouchers Payable, #222, showing the total of the unpaid vouchers on June 30, as listed here:

DATE DUE		VOUCHER NO.	PAYEE	AMOUNT					TERMS
19— July	3	339	Black Co.	1	8	0	0	00	n/30
	6	361	Jones Inc.	3	0	0	0	00	2/10, n/30

(c) Enter the following approved vouchers for the month of July in the voucher register. *Disregard GST-ITC in this exercise.*

DATE DUE		VOUCHER NO.	PAYEE	AMOUNT					TERMS	ACCOUNT DEBIT
19— July	1	362	Randall Co.	4	0	0	0	00	2/10, n/30	Purchases
	7	363	Fast Freight		2	0	0	00	cash	Freight In
	10	364	Winnipeg Furniture	1	6	5	0	00	n/30	Office Equip.
	12	365	Marco Ltd.	4	6	0	0	00	2/10, n/30	Purchases
	13	366	Fast Freight		1	5	0	00	cash	Freight In
	15	367	National Bank	5	0	0	0	00		Bank Loan Pay.
					7	0	0	00		Interest Expense
	17	368	Argue Co.		2	2	5	00	cash	Office Suppl. Prep.
	18	369	Randall Co.	1	0	0	0	00	2/10, n/30	Purchases
	20	370	The Enterprise		2	3	0	00	cash	Advertising
	25	371	Willson Stat'ry		1	9	0	00	n/30	Office Suppl. Prep.
	29	372	B & A Service		4	6	0	00	n/30	Repairs
	31	373	Payroll	10	0	0	0	00	cash	Salaries

(d) Enter the following cheques issued for the month of July in the cheque register. Copy the date and the cheque number of each paid voucher into the appropriate columns of the voucher register. Be sure to check invoices for eligible discounts on purchases.

DATE DUE		CHEQUE NO.	PAYEE	VOUCHER NO.	AMOUNT				
19— July	3	501	Black Co.	339	1	8	0	0	00
	6	502	Jones Inc.	361	2	9	4	0	00
	7	503	Fast Freight	363		2	0	0	00
	11	504	Randall Co.	362	3	9	2	0	00
	13	505	Fast Freight	366		1	5	0	00
	15	506	National Bank	367	5	7	0	0	00
	17	507	Argue Co.	368		2	2	5	00
	20	508	The Enterprise	370		2	3	0	00
	22	509	Marco Ltd.	365	4	5	0	8	00
	28	510	Randall Co.	369		9	0	8	00
	30	511	Payroll	373	10	0	0	0	00

(e) Total and rule the journals; prove equal debits and credits.

(f) Post to the Vouchers Payable account only.

(g) Prepare a schedule of unpaid vouchers by listing the vouchers in the voucher register that have not yet been paid. The total of the unpaid vouchers should equal the balance of the Vouchers Payable account in the general ledger after the posting is complete.

▶ **PRACTICE EXERCISE 4**

The voucher system is used by the Johnston-Stiller Company of Medicine Hat, Alberta.

(a) Set up a voucher register and a cheque register with the same headings as those used in Figures 18.4 and 18.5.

(b) Record the April total of the unpaid vouchers in the Vouchers Payable account (#236) in the general ledger:

DATE DUE		VOUCHER NO.	PAYEE	DATE ON INVOICE	AMOUNT					TERMS
19— May	2	712	Starr Co.	Apr. 2	2	6	7	5	00	n/30
	4	723	Standard Co.	Apr. 24	8	5	6	0	00	2/10, n/30

(c) Enter the following vouchers and cheques for the month of May in the appropriate registers. If the voucher is to be paid immediately, enter the transaction in the voucher register, then record the payment in the cheque register.

19—

May 1 Received invoice #56 from Payne Co. for $4,000 (plus $280 GST) for merchandise purchased; terms 2/10,n/30; voucher #728.

2 Cheque #401 is issued to Starr Co. to cover voucher #712.

4 Received a freight bill for $435 (plus $30.45 GST) from CN Express on incoming merchandise and issued cheque #402. (Both voucher and cheque are to be recorded.)

4 Issued cheque #403 to Standard Co. to cover invoice dated April 24 less the 2% discount on $8,000.

9 Purchased office supplies from Portage Supply, $235.40 (includes $15.40 GST); terms n/30; invoice #73.

11 Issued a cheque to Payne Co. for voucher #728.

12 Purchased office equipment from Hammond Equipment Co., $3,648 (includes $238.65 GST); terms n/30; invoice #63 dated May 11.

14 Received invoice #79 dated May 12 from Penners Ltd. for merchandise purchased, $780 (plus $54.60 GST); terms 2/10,n/30.

15 Paid Expressways $95 (plus $6.65 GST) for merchandise delivered from Penners Ltd. (Both voucher and cheque are to be recorded.)

17 Issued a cheque to the Canadian Bank to cover the monthly bank loan payment, $1,000, and interest to date, $275. (Enter both the voucher and the cheque.)

22 Received invoice #89 dated May 21 for merchandise purchased, $4,012.50 (includes $262.50 GST), from Krahns Inc.; terms 2/10,n/30.

22 Received invoice #101 dated May 21 for advertising in *The Towne Herald,* a local community paper, $561.75 (*plus* $39.32 GST); terms n/30.

22 Issued a cheque to Penners Ltd. for invoice #79 dated May 12. The discount is to be calculated on the value of the goods ($780).

24 Received invoice #103 from Beck Suppliers for wrapping paper and twine to be used in the shipping room, $104.88 (includes $6.86 GST); terms n/30.

30 Paid Portage Supply for the purchase of May 9.

31 Issued a cheque to pay salaries, $12,500. (Record both the voucher and the cheque.)

31 Issued a cheque to reimburse the petty cash fund: general expense, $30. (plus $2.10 GST); office supplies, $18 (plus $1.26 GST); advertising, $41 (plus $2.87 GST); freight-in, $16 (plus $1.12 GST); postage, $64.20 (*includes* $4.20 GST). (Record both the voucher and the cheque.)

(d) Total and rule the journals; prove equal debits and credits.

(e) Post to the Vouchers Payable account only.

(f) Prepare a list of unpaid vouchers for May 31.

CHAPTER

19

Computers and Accounting

CHAPTER OBJECTIVES

After completing this chapter, you will be able to:
- apply the fundamental principles of manual bookkeeping to a computerized accounting environment

· · · · · · · · · ·

Until now, we have been concentrating on keeping financial records manually. Until recently, this was the only way a small or medium-sized business was able to keep track of its transactions and prepare its financial statements. The computer, however, has effectively changed all that. The computer is a tool used to help minimize the repetitive and routine office processing tasks—and bookkeeping certainly falls into that category.

The computer may provide a different means of entering and storing financial data, but the principles of bookkeeping and accounting remain the same. The same importance is placed on the accuracy of the information obtained from source documents; and the same importance is shown in the recording of balanced entries and in the preparation of accurate and meaningful financial statements.

ACCOUNTING SOFTWARE

Since 1981, when microcomputers became generally available to the business market, many accounting software packages have been developed to assist the bookkeeper or accountant with the more routine aspects of his or her duties. Some of these software packages are basic and inexpensive; others are sophisticated and costly. Choosing the right accounting package for the business is much like buying a new car. You must decide how big the car should be, what options you wish to have, and how much money you can afford to spend. The choice of software depends on a number of similar factors, such as the size of the business, the nature of that business, the amount of detailed information required by management for decision-making purposes, and the amount of money that can reasonably be spent in order to achieve the benefits of such a conversion to a computerized accounting system.

Most software packages are divided into modules that reflect the different processing activities within the accounting function. The most common modules are general ledger, accounts receivable, accounts payable, payroll, and inventory.

In the accounts receivable module, for example, sales are recorded using the same data that would have been required when recording them in the manual sales journal; but, in this case, no posting is required because the computer handles posting automatically. Not only are the individual sales posted to the respective customers' accounts, but the total of the sales is also posted to the Sales account and the Accounts Receivable Control account in the general ledger. The receipt of cash from the customer on account would also be recorded in this module, with the transaction posted to the customer's account as usual and the cash automatically posted to the Bank account.

Accounting programs that allow information to be exchanged between modules are referred to as *integrated programs.* The general ledger module can be thought of as the hub of a wheel, and the other modules as the spokes of the wheel (see Figure 19.1). Any information recorded in the subsidiary modules (the spokes of the wheel) will automatically be posted to the appropriate control accounts in the general ledger (the hub of the wheel).

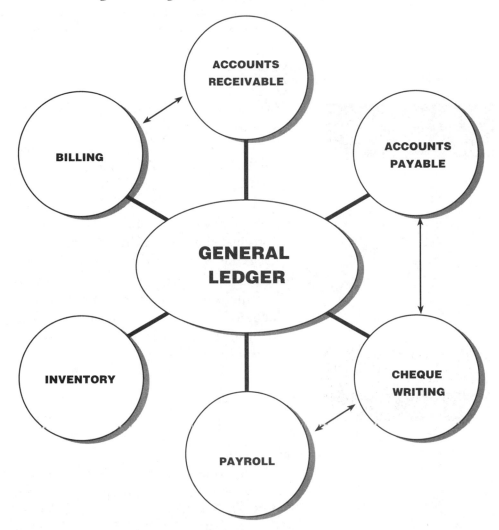

Figure 19.1   Integrated Accounting Software

The advantages of such an accounting system should be fairly obvious: no need to post and no need to physically prepare statements and reports, such as trial balances, aging of receivables, and financial statements. The bookkeeper or accountant simply records the transactions, after which the computer will produce, on demand, a variety of listings and reports. Whereas the time necessary to prepare monthly interim financial statements in the past was often prohibitive, they can now be produced literally at the push of a button.

CHART OF ACCOUNTS

Computerized accounting systems identify the various ledger accounts in the same way as in a manual system; that is, by account number. Some programs will allow you to freely assign account numbers as you might with the manual ledger system. If, for example, your business has many expense accounts, you might require a wide range of account numbers, such as 500 to 799. Other programs are restricted to predefined number ranges. In this case, the program is very strict about what numbers can be assigned to asset accounts, to liability accounts, to owner's equity accounts, etc.

During the process of opening each new account on the computer, you will be asked to assign an account number, to enter the appropriate account title, and in some cases to indicate whether it is a balance sheet account or an income statement account. If the account has been identified as a balance sheet account, the program will know to list that account on the balance sheet whenever one is prepared. If it is identified as an income statement account, it will appear on the income (profit and loss) statement.

OPENING THE ACCOUNTS

After all the accounts have been opened on the computer, and even after the computerized accounting system is in full operation, the program will still allow new accounts to be added to the ledger provided no attempt is made to assign an existing account number. Naturally, the computer would have difficulty distinguishing between two accounts if both were numbered 101.

Under certain circumstances, accounting programs will allow account numbers to be changed. If so, the program usually keeps documentary evidence of the original number and the new number.

Deleting existing accounts is usually possible only if no transactions have been recorded in that account. Just as throwing away a page from the manual ledger file is unethical (not to mention illegal), deleting an account from the computer cannot be done. An audit trail is maintained in all computerized accounting programs to ensure the accuracy and legitimacy of the financial records in the system.

ENTERING DATA

Once the accounts have been opened, transactions can be entered. In the manual accounting system, certain information must be recorded for each transaction, such dates, descriptions, amounts, etc. This holds true for the computerized system as well.

The *transaction date* must be entered in a format that is acceptable by the program. Some programs require that the date be entered in the format YY-MM-DD, where YY is the last two digits of the year, MM is two digits for the month, and DD is two digits for the day of the month. If, for example, the date to be recorded is June 15, 1993, it would be entered as 93-06-15. Other programs require the date to be entered as MM-DD-YY. The operating manual that accompanies the accounting software package will specify which date format is required.

Source codes are labels to identify transactions of a similar nature. For example, if all sales transactions are recorded with a source code of "SJ," it would be possible to print a listing of all sales transactions recorded in the last month, in the last year, or for whatever period of time is desired. Other source codes might be PJ, CR, CP, and PR (payroll register). Not all programs refer to these labels as source codes, but most programs have some means by which to identify like transactions, whether they are called journal codes, batch codes, or group codes.

Many accounting programs provide a field into which *reference* information may be keyed. This information might include invoice numbers, document codes, or some other unique information that will more readily identify certain transactions.

All programs provide a field for the *description* of the transaction, much like the Memo column in the manual cash journals or in the ledger accounts. Such descriptions will help the bookkeeper to understand the transaction more easily should it be necessary to look back on the records six months or a year from now.

The dollar amount of the transaction must be recorded with great care in order to ensure accuracy. Many accounting programs have an implied two-decimal-place amount field. This means that if the amount keyed is 5000, the last two digits are assumed to be the decimal places, so it will be interpreted as $50.00. If the amount to be recorded is actually $5000, it would have to be entered as *500000* or as *5000.00*. By physically keying the decimal point, there is no question about what the correct amount should be.

DEBIT VS. CREDIT

In the manual accounting system, distinguishing the debit entry from the credit entry is a matter of writing the amount in the appropriate column already labelled Debit or Credit. In the computerized accounting system, we must be more cautious about how the amount is entered. In this respect, computer programs vary.

Some programs interpret all positive values as debit entries and all negative values as credit entries. For example, 5000.00 would be read as a debit entry, and −5000.00 (or 5000.00−) would be read as a credit entry.

In other programs, debit and credit are determined by the account number. The computer would know that if a transaction is posted to an account with a number between 100 and 199 (an asset), a positive value is the debit entry and a negative value is the credit entry. In this case, the negative value would reduce the balance of the ledger account. If a transaction is posted to an account with a number between 200 and 299 (a liability), a positive value is the credit entry and a negative value is the debit entry. Here, the negative entry would reduce the balance of the liability on the debit side (in accordance with the rules of bookkeeping).

CORRECTING ERRORS

In the manual system, you learned the importance of correcting errors by marking a single line through the incorrect figure and neatly writing the correct figure above it. Both the correct value and the error always remain clearly visible. In computerized accounting, the program will allow figures to be changed but will provide documented evidence of these changes. With such a detailed audit trail, the opportunity to manipulate the data illegally is kept to a minimum and preserves the integrity of the information.

TRIAL BALANCE

Although the accounting software keeps all ledgers in balance by keeping all transactions in balance, the trial balance is still a necessary and useful statement. It is still the same concise listing we are familiar with after each month's transactions have been recorded and posted; but in a computerized environment, the trial balance can be printed with additional working columns for noting adjustments, for showing budgeted amounts, or for showing balances from previous months or previous years.

FINANCIAL STATEMENTS

Traditionally, financial statements are prepared manually from the balances listed on the trial balance. Now, the balance sheet and income statement are available on demand "at the push of a button." This includes not only year-end statements, but monthly, quarterly, semiannual, and year-to-date statements as well. Besides the ease with which such statements are made available, an important advantage is the availability of comparative statements, those that compare current balances with those of last month, last year, or with budgeted amounts (including percentages of budget).

Because of the flexibility of the computerized system, departmental accounting is made easier. Transactions posted to departmental revenue and expense accounts are transferred automatically to the control accounts in the general ledger; therefore, statements are just as easy to prepare for a company with many departments as they are for the small store that has no distinguishable departments.

RECORDING FROM JOURNALS

The processes of recording transactions on the computer are generally of two kinds: (1) *POS (Point of Sale)* entries, whereby the transaction is recorded in the computer at the time the transaction occurs; and (2) *batch entries*, whereby the usual journals prepared in a manual system are used as data input forms on a weekly or monthly basis.

The POS system is generally used by medium-sized and large retail stores, such as Eaton's, K-Mart, and Sears. A credit card sale is posted to the customer's account at the moment the sales clerk enters the sale on the cash register.

The number of entries recorded by a small retail store would probably not be great, so the POS system would be impractical. In this case, the daily or weekly transactions would be recorded in the manual journals as usual; at the end of the month, the bookkeeper would then enter the transactions on the computer using a procedure very much like that used for posting to the ledgers. Special column totals in the sales, purchase, cash receipts, and cash payments journals can be recorded as single entries, just as they would be when posted manually to the respective general ledger accounts. (The batch system just described will be used with the transactions that affect KBC Decorating in this chapter.)

▶ **JANUARY TRANSACTIONS FOR KBC DECORATING CO.**

Martin and Barker, the owners of KBC Decorating Co., have made the decision to computerize their accounting procedures. As is usually the case, the newly computerized accounting system is to be run parallel with the manual system to ensure that consistent and reliable results are achieved from the computerized process.

The manual journals for the January and February activities appear on the next few pages. These will be used as the source information when you are ready to record the transactions on the computer. But first, you will need to create this computerized accounting system. To do so, follow these steps:

1. Create the Chart of Accounts. On the computer, open the accounts that you have been using for the KBC Decorating activities throughout this textbook. To simplify this task, use the chart of accounts printed at the

back of this text. Be sure to answer all the pertinent questions asked by the computer about the account number and the type of account. (These questions will vary depending on the accounting software you are using. If necessary, consult an instructor or the software manual for a full explanation of the requirements for your program.)

2. Record the balances forward from December. Use the post-closing trial balance from December 31 (Chapter 17). Be sure to distinguish clearly whether the balances are debits or credits. Because this is the beginning of a new fiscal year, all revenue and expense accounts will have zero balances.

3. Use the journals that follow to record the transactions that occurred during January. Post each journal separately to ensure that each batch of transactions is balanced. Also, look for ways to simplify the recording process; for example, in the cash payments journal, the entries in the Purchase Discounts column would be posted only as a total. They would not be recorded individually.

4. After all journals have been recorded on the computer, be sure to print listings of all transaction batches. Most businesses with computerized accounting functions will keep back-up copies of their financial records on diskette, but they also keep printed listings for ready reference.

5. Print a trial balance. Compare this trial balance with those you had prepared for KBC Decorating in previous months, noting particularly how the information is displayed on the computer printout.

▶ FEBRUARY TRANSACTIONS FOR KBC DECORATING CO.

Using the same process described above for the January transactions, record the information found on the source journals for the month of February. Your accounting software may require that you change the processing date to February 28, 19—, before you can proceed with the February transactions. Consult your instructor or the software manual for details.

1. Record all transactions.

2. Print a listing of each batch of transactions.

3. Print a trial balance.

PURCHASE JOURNAL (JANUARY)   PAGE PJ21

INVOICE DATE	ACCOUNT	INV. NO.	TERMS	F.	ACCOUNTS PAYABLE	PURCHASES PAINT & SUPPL. DR.	PURCHASES WALLPAPER DR.	GST-ITC DR.	OTHER ACCOUNTS DEBIT ACCOUNT	F.	AMOUNT
19—Jan. 10	Coleman Industries	113	2/10, n/30		2652 90	1050 00	1440 00	162 90			
	Rainbow Supplies	191	2/10, n/30		1145 33	1075 00		70 33			
	Spencer Stucco	127	2/10, n/30		1310 47	1230 00		80 47			
24	Reynolds Paper Co.	183	n/30		912 00		856 00	56 00			
	Tranborg & Noble	100	2/10, n/30		1140 00	749 00	321 00	70 00			
27	Mitchell Advertising	63	n/30		570 00			35 00	Advertising		535 00
28	Major Office Supply	205	n/30		136 80			8 40	Office Supplies		128 40
					7867 50	4104 00	2617 00	483 10			663 40

SALES JOURNAL (JANUARY)   PAGE SJ 21

DATE	ACCOUNT DEBIT	INV. NO.	TERMS	F.	ACCOUNTS REC. DR.	SALES PAINT & SUPPL. CR.	SALES WALLPAPER CR.	GST PAY. CR.	SALES TX. PAYBL. CR.
19—Jan. 6	Beavis & Sons	91	2/10, n/30		1567 50	675 00	700 00	96 25	96 25
	Dayson & Son	92	2/10, n/30		2023 50	850 00	925 00	124 25	124 25
	Jay–Mar Co.	93	2/10, n/30		883 50	375 00	400 00	54 25	54 25
10	Edna Morton	94	2/10, n/30		997 50	450 00	425 00	61 25	61 25
11	Beavis & Sons	95	2/10, n/30		640 68	332 00	230 00	39 34	39 34
24	Wm. Zelisko Enterprises	96	2/10, n/30		1083 00	600 00	350 00	66 50	66 50
	S. Miller	97	2/10, n/30		655 50	575 00		40 25	40 25
26	Dayson & Son	98	2/10, n/30		570 00	330 00	170 00	35 00	35 00
					8421 18	4187 00	3200 00	517 09	517 09

CASH RECEIPTS (JANUARY)   PAGE CR21

DATE	ACCOUNT CREDIT	MEMO	F.	ACCTS. REC. CR.	SALES DISC. DR.	SALES PAINT & SUPPL. CR.	SALES WALLPAPER CR.	GST PAYABLE CR.	SALES TAX PAYABLE CR.	GENERAL LEDGER CR.	BANK DR.
19—Jan. 2	Rental Revenue	Clear-Vu						175 00		2500 00	2675 00
	Interest Revenue	on T.D.								72 31	72 31
4		cash sales				840 00	395 00	86 45	86 45		1407 91
10		cash sales				720 00	525 00	87 15	87 15		1419 30
16	Dayson & Son	on #92		2023 50	35 50						1988 00
	Jay-Mar Co.	on #93		883 50	15 50						868 00
	Beavis & Sons	on #91		1567 50	27 50						1540 00
17		cash sales				920 00	400 00	92 40	92 40		1504 80
20	E. Morton	on #94		997 50	17 50						980 00
21	Beavis & Sons	on #95		640 68	11 24						629 44
24		cash sales				750 00	350 00	77 00	77 00		1254 00
30	Sales-Service	Contract 8						420 00		6000 00	6420 00
				6112 68	107 24	3230 00	1670 00	938 00	343 00	8572 31	20758 75

CASH PAYMENTS (JANUARY)

PAGE CP21

DATE	ACCOUNT DEBIT	MEMO	F.	ACCTS. PAY. DR.	PURCH. DISC. CR.	GST-ITC DR.	GEN. LED. DR.	BANK CR.	CH. NO.
19—Jan. 4	Utilities	heat				11 34	173 40	184 74	46
	Purchases—Wallpaper	special order				19 07	291 50	310 57	47
6	Utilities	gas				4 95	75 60	80 55	48
7	Telephone					8 19	125 25	133 44	49
	Mortgage Payable						347 41		
	Interest on Mortgage	on above					966 09	1313 50	DM
12	Delivery Expense	to S. Miller				1 30	18 50	19 80	50
13	Drawings, Barker						1000 00	1000 00	51
15	Income Tax Payable						2807 80		
	UI Payable	Dec. payroll					856 80		
	CPP Payable						539 80	4204 40	52
19	Rainbow Supplies	on #191		1145 33	21 50			1123 83	53
20	Coleman Industries	on #113		2652 90	49 80			2603 10	54
	Spencer Stucco	on #127		1310 47	24 60			1285 87	55
26	Drawings, Martin						2000 00	2000 00	56
29	Miscellaneous Expense						23 41		
	Freight In						18 90		
	Office Supplies Prepaid						31 75		
	Donations					4 85	15 00	93 91	57
				5108 70	95 90	49 70	9291 21	14353 71	

PURCHASE JOURNAL (FEBRUARY)

PAGE PJ22

INVOICE DATE	ACCOUNT	INV. NO.	TERMS	F.	ACCOUNTS PAYABLE	PURCHASES PAINT & SUPPL. DR.	PURCHASES WALLPAPER DR.	GST-ITC DR.	OTHER ACCOUNTS DEBIT — ACCOUNT	F.	AMOUNT
19—Feb. 1	Coleman Industries	134	2/10, n/30		812 50	441 60	321 00	49 90			
	Rainbow Supplies	217	2/10, n/30		2166 00	428 00	1605 00	133 00			
3	Mitchell Adertising	78	n/30		741 00			45 50	Advertising		695 50
5	Spencer Stucco	150	2/10, n/30		615 60	577 80		37 80			
	Tranborg & Noble	181	2/10, n/30		2793 00			171 50	Tools & Equip.		2621 50
21	Reynolds Paper Co.	200	n/30		798 00	749 00		49 00			
26	Rainbow Supplies	230	2/10, n/30		1509 18		1350 00	159 18			
					9435 28	2196 40	3276 00	645 88			3317 00

SALES JOURNAL (FEBRUARY)

PAGE SJ 22

DATE		ACCOUNT DEBIT	INV. NO.	TERMS	F.	ACCOUNTS REC. DR.	SALES PAINT & SUPPL. CR.	SALES WALLPAPER CR.	GST PAY. CR.	SALES TX. PAYBL. CR.
19— Feb.	1	S. Wilkinson	99	2/10, n/30		193 80	70 00	100 00	11 90	11 90
	3	Dayson & Son	100	2/10, n/30		604 20	300 00	230 00	37 10	37 10
		Jay-Mar Co.	101	2/10, n/30		307 80	120 00	150 00	18 90	18 90
	19	Edna Morton	102	2/10, n/30		342 00	150 00	150 00	21 00	21 00
		Wm. Zelisko Enterprises	103	2/10, n/30		433 20	280 00	100 00	26 60	26 60
	28	Dayson & Son	104	2/10, n/30		1026 00	650 00	250 00	63 00	63 00
		Edna Morton	105	2/10, n/30		684 00	600 00		42 00	42 00
						3591 00	2170 00	980 00	220 50	220 50

CASH RECEIPTS (FEBRUARY)

PAGE CR22

DATE		ACCOUNT CREDIT	MEMO	F.	ACCTS. REC. CR.	SALES DISC. DR.	SALES PAINT & SUPPL. CR.	SALES WALLPAPER CR.	GST PAYABLE CR.	SALES TAX PAYABLE CR.	GENERAL LEDGER CR.	BANK DR.
19— Feb.	1	Rental Revenue	Clear-Vu						175 00		2500 00	2675 00
		Interest Revenue	on T.D.								72 40	72 40
			cash sales				625 00	375 00	70 00	70 00		1140 00
	3	W. Zelisko Enterprises	on #96		1083 00	19 00						1064 00
		S. Miller	on #97		655 50	11 50						644 00
	5	Dayson & Son	on #98		570 00	10 00						560 00
	6		cash sales				950 00	320 00	88 90	88 90		1447 80
	11	S. Wilkinson	on #99		193 80	3 40						190 40
	13	Jay-Mar Co.	on #101		307 80	5 40						302 40
		Dayson & Son	on #100		604 20	10 60						593 60
			cash sales				1020 00	640 00	116 20	116 20		1892 40
	15	Sales—Service	Contract 9						245 00		3500 00	3745 00
	20		cash sales				840 00	990 00	128 10	128 10		2086 20
	26		cash sales				900 00	570 00	102 90	102 90		1675 80
	28	E. Morton	on #102		342 00	6 00						336 00
	28	W. Zelisko Enterprises			433 20	7 60						425 60
		Sales—Service	Contract 10						287 00		4100 00	4387 00
					4189 50	73 50	4335 00	2895 00	1213 10	506 10	10172 40	23237 60

CASH PAYMENTS (FEBRUARY)   PAGE __CP22__

DATE		ACCOUNT DEBIT	MEMO	F.	ACCTS PAY. DR.	PURCH. DISC. CR.	GST—ITC DR.			GEN. LED. DR.	BANK CR.	CH. NO.
19— Feb.	2	Utilities	heat				12 08			184 65	196 73	58
	3	Tranborg & Noble	on #100		1140 00	20 00					1120 00	59
	6	Utilities	gas				6 11			93 40	99 51	60
	7	Telephone					10 75			164 30	175 05	61
		Mortgage Payable								356 10		
		Interest on Mortgage	on above							957 40	1313 50	DM
	11	Coleman Industries	on #134		812 50	14 25					798 25	62
		Rainbow Supplies	on #217		2166 00	38 00					2128 00	63
	15	Spencer Stucco	on #150		615 60	10 80					604 80	64
		Tranborg & Noble	on #181		2793 00	49 00					2744 00	65
	20	Freight-In					1 86			26 55	28 41	66
	22	Reynolds Paper	on #183		912 00						912 00	67
	26	Drawings, Barker								4000 00	4000 00	68
		Drawings, Martin								2000 00	2000 00	69
		Mitchell Advertising	on #63		570 00						570 00	70
	27	Major Office Supplies	on #205		136 80						136 80	71
					9145 90	132 05	30 80			7782 40	16827 05	

APPENDIX A   ANSWERS TO THINK ABOUT IT!

CHAPTER 1

1. True
2. True
3. False
4. False
5. True
6. A proprietorship is owned by one person; a partnership is owned by two or more persons. In proprietorships and partnerships, the owners are directly involved in the operation of the business. A corporation is a separate legal entity for which ownership is divided into shares; the stockholders (or shareholders) are not usually involved in the ongoing operation of the business.
7. Assets are items of value owned by the business that are expected to contribute to the ongoing operation of the business. Expenses are the costs of operating the business, contributing to operations during only the current operating period.
8. See examples in Figure 1.10.
9. Capital refers to the owner's financial interest (equity) in the business. Assets – Liabilities = Owner's Equity.
10. A person's source of earnings is his or her salary or wage earnings (paycheque). A business's earnings are from sales of merchandise and sales of services.

CHAPTER 2

1. True
2. True
3. False
4. True
5. False. The accounting equation can be expressed as

   Assets – Liabilities = Owner's Equity (or Capital), or as

   Assets = Liabilities + Owner's Equity (or Capital).
6. True
7. False. Financial records are maintained in a permanent form; that is, in ink or on a computer.
8. A journal is a chronological (day-by-day) record of the financial activities of the business. It is sometimes referred to as a book of original entry.
9. (a) Debit. (b) No. (c) In consecutive order.
10. All financial records must be kept by the business for at least six years. Without year dates on each page, one year's activities cannot be distinguished from those of another year.
11. Yes

CHAPTER 3

1. Purchases

2. general ledger, accounts receivable ledger, accounts payable ledger

3. To accumulate in one place all the activities that affect each specific asset, liability, owner's equity, revenue, and expense.

4. Posting Reference or Ledger Reference. Folios provide a cross-reference between the entry in the journal and its corresponding entry posted to the ledger account.

5. Posting is the procedure of accurately transferring all transactions from the journal to the ledger accounts. Each debit and credit entry is posted in the order in which it was entered into the journal.

6. Accounts appear on the trial balance in the order in which they are arranged in the general ledger.

7. No. The trial balance proves only that equal debits and credits have been maintained. Other errors are possible that would not affect the balance between the debits and the credits.

8. Double-check the addition of the columns. Compare the amounts in the trial balance with those in the ledger accounts. Calculate the difference between the debit and credit totals to determine the amount out of balance. Divide the difference by 2 and look for this amount within the trial balance or in the ledger accounts. Divide the original difference by 9 to determine if a transposition error was made. Recalculate the balances in the ledger accounts if necessary. Check to see that all entries have been posted from the journals to the ledger accounts correctly.

9. We need the year date because financial records must be kept at least six years in the event of a government audit.

10. Errors should be neatly crossed out without obliterating the original figures. The correct figures or words are then written neatly above.

CHAPTER 4

1. The purchase journal records the purchase of assets and expenses for which payment has not yet been made. The sales journal records the sale of goods and services for which the customer has not yet paid.

2. Special journals reduce the amount of repetitive recording that is otherwise necessary if only the general journal were used. Posting is also simplified because column totals are posted rather than individual entries.

3. The terms of payment extend from the date of the invoice, not the date on which the transaction is eventually recorded.

4. No. If payment was not made when the item was purchased, the entry is recorded in the purchase journal.

5. No. The sales journal has no column for incoming cash. Only sales of goods and services made on account (on credit) are recorded in the sales journal.

6. Same as Question 2 above.

7. Sequentially numbered sales invoices ensure that all invoices are accounted for. They also provide a means of identifying the document.

8. Not usually. The Sales account shows the amount of the sale *before* taxes are added. Sales tax and GST are recorded in their respective liability accounts representing the amounts owing to the governments.

9. A control account is a single ledger account that represents a group of subsidiary ledger accounts. Control accounts appear in the general ledger.

10. The balance in the control account must be equal to the sum of the individual accounts it represents.

CHAPTER 6

1. The cash receipts journal records all money received. The cash payments journal records all money paid out (usually by cheque).

2. Special journals reduce the amount of repetitive recording that is otherwise necessary if only the general journal were used. Posting is also simplified because column totals are posted rather than individual entries. Division of labour can also be achieved when using special journals; that is, more than one employee can record transactions at the same time.

3. The total of the Bank column in the cash receipts journal is added to the current balance in the Bank account in the general ledger. Then the total of the Bank column in the cash payments journal is deducted. The resulting balance in the Bank account represents the actual amount of money on hand.

4. Not necessarily. The bookkeeper may choose to extend each transaction to the Bank column; or the bookkeeper may choose to extend only the total of the day's receipts to the Bank column. Both methods are acceptable provided equal debits and credits are maintained.

5. No. The entries that appear in the General Ledger column have nothing in common; therefore, the total is not posted.

6. All cheques in the number sequence must be accounted for.

7. A single line is ruled above the totals; a double line is ruled below the totals.

8. Just as every general journal entry must balance, the journals themselves must balance. If the journals do not balance, the trial balance will not balance.

9. When a transaction cannot be accommodated in the special journals, it goes in the general journal.

10. Cash is a common target of theft. If cash is deposited daily, the potential loss from a theft will be kept to a minimum.

CHAPTER 7

1. No. A refund is granted only if cash was paid at the time the goods were purchased. Instead, a credit note will be issued.

2. Not usually. If cash was paid at the time of the purchase, cash will be refunded when the goods are returned. However, some stores now issue vouchers that can be applied against the value of a future purchase instead of giving a cash refund.

3. Returns & Allowances accounts provide clearer evidence of the amount of damaged or inferior goods that have been received from suppliers or unwanted goods returned by customers.

4. In small businesses that have few returns or price allowances, separate accounts for returns and allowances are unnecessary.

5. Office Supplies Prepaid is credited because the refund must reverse part of the original debit entry to Office Supplies Prepaid.

6. 2/20,n/60 means that a 2 percent discount on the value of the purchase or sale may be taken if the invoice is paid within 20 days of the invoice date; otherwise, the total invoice value must be paid within 60 days. Terms of 3/5,1/20,n/45 means that a 3 percent discount may be taken if the invoice is paid within the first 5 days, or a 1 percent discount may be taken if the invoice is paid between the 6th and the 20th day; otherwise the invoice must be paid by the 45th day.

7. Yes, $6.40.

8. C.O.D. means Cash on Delivery. C.O.D. purchases are recorded in the cash payments journal and C.O.D. sales are recorded in the cash receipts journal. When the goods are delivered to the customer, the driver waits for the customer to make payment.

CHAPTER 8

1. The Freight In account is used to record the transportation costs on incoming goods that were purchased for resale.

2. Delivery Expense (sometimes called Transportation Out).

3. Duty & Brokerage is recorded when import duties/tariffs and brokerage fees are paid on merchandise purchased outside Canada.

4. If freight charges are incurred on goods other than those purchased for resale, such charges are debited to the account charged for the goods themselves; such as Office Supplies Prepaid or Advertising Expense.

5. The difference is charged to the "Cash Over or Short" account.

6. Petty cash is used for making small expenditures for which writing a cheque would be impractical.

7. To increase the fund, the Petty Cash account is debited and the Cash (or Bank) account is credited. To decrease the fund, the Cash (or Bank) account is debited and the Petty Cash account is credited.

8. The accounts representing the various expenses incurred when payments were made are debited in the reimbursing entry so that these costs can be posted to their respective accounts. The Cash (or Bank) account is credited.

CHAPTER 9

1. No. Some of the entries on the company's books have not yet appeared on the bank statement.

2. Some of the cheques and deposits have not yet cleared the bank; therefore, the bank was not aware of them when the bank statement was printed.

Also, the bank has likely recorded transactions in the account for which the company's books have not yet recorded entries.

3. As soon as the bank statement is received from the bank, it is reconciled.

4. Cancelled cheques and advices (commonly called debit memos and credit memos).

5. A cheque that has been recorded in the cash payments journal but has not yet been cleared by the bank is known as an outstanding cheque.

6. When a cheque is certified, a guarantee is made by the bank that sufficient funds will be available when the cheque is cleared. Because both the company and the bank now have a record of the cheque, it cannot be considered as outstanding.

7. An NSF cheque is a cheque that has been dishonoured by the bank because the account does not have sufficient funds.

8. Bank charges are fees charged by the bank each month for servicing an account. These charges cover clearing cheques, printing cheques, rental of safety deposit box, etc. The account debited for such charges is *Bank Charges* or *Bank Service Charges*. (KBC Decorating Co. calls this account Bank Charges & Interest.)

CHAPTER 11

1. Proprietorship: owned by one person.

   Partnership: owned by two or more persons.

   Corporation: a separate entity operating under government charter; shareholders or stockholders usually have no direct involvement in the operation of the business.

2. Advantages of a partnership: ease of combining resources and skills; less expensive to establish than a corporation; enjoys more freedom from government regulation.

   Disadvantages of a partnership: each partner is personally responsible for all the debts of the firm.

3. The respective asset accounts are debited; Capital is credited.

4. The Drawings account records the values withdrawn from the business by the owner(s). The Salaries account records the payroll paid to employees only. In a proprietorship or a partnership, an owner cannot be an employee of his or her own company; therefore, any money paid to him or her is a withdrawal from equity.

5. Cash withdrawals, payment of home utility bills using a company cheque, withdrawal of merchandise for personal use, etc.

6. Purchases is credited. The owner is removing the goods from the inventory of saleable merchandise at the cost price; therefore, the cost price must be deducted from the account to which that cost was originally recorded. (Some businesses record all purchases of merchandise into the Inventory account; therefore, a withdrawal would be deducted from the Inventory account.)

7. Office Supplies Prepaid is credited. When items are removed from the business by the owner for personal use, the value is deducted from the same account to which the original purchase was charged.

8. Interim statements can be prepared any time they are requested by management. Usually interim statements will be prepared monthly, quarterly, or half-yearly.

9. Management can more closely watch trends in revenues and expenses if profit statements are prepared more regularly than yearly. Without a close eye on such trends, avoidable operating losses might be incurred.

CHAPTER 12

1. Piecework: factory workers, fruit and vegetable pickers, etc.

   Salary: office workers, sales clerks, police/fire workers, etc.

   Commission: sales representatives.

2. Time cards record the time work was started and ended each day and total regular and overtime hours worked.

3. The three payroll deductions are income tax, Unemployment Insurance, Canada Pension Plan.

4. No. The income tax deduction is based on the amount of gross pay and the employee's claim code (determined from the TD1 form.)

5. The employer contributes an amount *equal* to the total of the employees' contributions to the Canada Pension Plan. The employer also contributes 1.4 times the UI contribution made by the employees.

6. Other deductions include union dues, group life insurance, company pension plan, hospitalization/accident insurance, dental insurance, Canada Savings Bonds, and RRSPs.

7. Gross pay is the amount of employee payroll *before* deductions are withheld. Net pay is the amount paid to the employee *after* deductions are withheld.

8. Workers Compensation is a form of insurance coverage providing financial and medical compensation to employees for injuries or disabilities resulting from accidents in the workplace. The employer pays the premiums for this coverage.

CHAPTER 13

1. A single line is drawn through the incorrect figure or word; the new figure or word is neatly written immediately above the error. Both the incorrect and the correct data must be legible.

2. A general journal entry is recorded and posted, which transfers an appropriate amount from the incorrect account affected to the correct account.

3. No, erasers and liquid eradicators should not be used. The incorrect figures or words must not be obliterated.

CHAPTER 16

1. Aging of receivables is an analysis of the accounts receivable based on the length of time the balance is overdue. This information alerts management to customers' accounts that may be in danger of becoming

uncollectible; the longer an account is overdue, the less likely it will be collected.

2. Percentages of estimated loss are determined from experience. After several years of keeping track of receivables, management will know approximately what percentage of the current receivables might eventually become uncollectible.

3. Suspense is a general ledger account used for recording transactions temporarily when insufficient information is available at the time the transaction is originally recorded. Once the correct information is determined, an adjusting entry is made to transfer the value from Suspense to the appropriate account.

GLOSSARY

Account A concise record of the increases and decreases affecting a particular financial item.

Accountant A skilled person who designs accounting systems, prepares financial statements, and has the ability to analyze and interpret financial information so that management can make sound business decisions.

Accounting The process of interpreting and communicating the financial information compiled in the bookkeeping records. The vast field of accounting includes many important phases performed by accountants, such as income tax, budgeting, forecasting, etc.

Accounting Cycle A standard sequence of accounting procedures performed during an accounting period.

Accounting Equation Total assets are equal to total liabilities plus total owner's equity, as illustrated by the balance sheet.

Accounting Period The period of time covered by the income statement, usually one year.

Accounts Payable Amounts owed by the business to creditors for goods and services purchased on credit.

Accounts Payable Ledger A subsidiary ledger that contains the individual ledger accounts of all creditors, arranged in alphabetical or numerical order.

Accounts Receivable Amounts owed to the business by customers for goods and services sold on credit.

Accounts Receivable Ledger A subsidiary ledger that contains the individual accounts of all customers, arranged in alphabetical or numerical order.

Accrued Expenses Expenses that have accrued or accumulated but have not yet been paid or recorded on the books at the end of the accounting period.

Accumulated Depreciation A contra-asset account used to accumulate the dollar amount of the cost of a fixed asset that has been allocated to expense (depreciation) over its useful life. The contra-asset account is shown as a deduction from the related asset on the balance sheet.

Adjusting Entry A journal entry required at the end of the accounting period to adjust those costs that overlap two or more accounting periods.

Aging of Accounts Receivable A breakdown of the balances in customers' accounts categorically: amounts not yet due; amounts due now; amounts past due, due in 1–30 days, due in 31–60 days, etc. Also called *analysis of accounts receivable by age.*

Allowance for Doubtful Accounts A contra-asset account to show the portion of the total of accounts receivable that has been estimated to be uncollectible.

Articles of Partnership The terms and conditions outlined in a partnership agreement to avoid disputes that may arise in the future among the partners.

Assets Economic resources; things of value owned by the business to benefit future operations.

Audit Trail The process of following a transaction through the entire accounting cycle, from the source document to the journal to the ledger accounts to the trial balance and the financial statements (and back again) through the use of folios or posting references.

Bad Debts Expense An expense account representing the estimated losses allocated to the current year because of uncollectible accounts receivable. See also *Allowance for Doubtful Accounts.*

Balance Sheet A financial statement of the assets, liabilities, and owner's equity properly classified to show the financial position of a business on a specific date.

Balance Sheet Approach for Probable Losses A method of estimating probable losses from uncollectible accounts receivable, based on the aging of the accounts receivable and taking into consideration the existing balance of the Allowance for Doubtful Accounts.

Bank Charges Charges made by the bank for maintaining its customers' chequing accounts. Also called *bank service charges* or *service charges*.

Bank Draft A negotiable document drawn by a bank on one of its branches. Similar to a money order or a cashier's cheque.

Bank Errors Mistakes made unintentionally in the customer's bank account by a bank employee.

Bank Loan A liability account representing money borrowed from the bank, giving the bank a legal claim against the assets of the borrowing company.

Bank Loan Interest An expense account representing the interest paid by the borrower for the temporary use of the bank's money. Also called *Interest on Bank Loan*.

Bank Reconciliation Statement A summary of the financial items that cause the bank statement balance to differ from the cash book balance and that brings these two independent records into agreement.

Bank Statement A complete record of the customer's banking transactions during the month, itemizing all cheques issued, deposits made, and pre-authorized debits and credits.

Book Errors Errors made by the bookkeeper when recording transactions on the company books.

Bookkeeper The person responsible for recording and maintaining business transactions in a set of books.

Bookkeeping The process of recording daily the monetary values of business transactions in a set of books.

Book Value of Assets The cost of assets minus the amounts in the related contra-asset accounts (cost of fixed assets minus accumulated depreciation).

Business Entity A business enterprise, separate from its owner, for which transactions are recorded, summarized, and reported in accordance with the generally accepted accounting principles (accounting rules).

Calendar Year An accounting period beginning January 1 and ending December 31.

Canada Pension Plan A bill enacted by the Canadian government requiring both the employer and the employee to make contributions to a plan that provides funds for employee retirement, disability, and benefits to widowed spouses and orphans.

Cancelled Cheques Issued cheques that have been cleared by the bank and charged to the company's account.

Capital The equity account that represents the net amount contributed by the owner to his or her business. See also *Owner's Equity*.

Cash Over or Short An account to record the amounts by which the actual cash received differs from the amount of cash recorded on the cash register tapes.

Cash Payments Journal A book of original entry designed specially for all cash payment transactions. Also called *cash disbursements journal*.

Cash Receipts Journal A book of original entry designed specially for receipts of cash and cheques.

Cash Refunds Cash adjustments made for allowances or returns on cash sales and cash purchases.

Certified Cheque A cheque that guarantees sufficient funds will be available when the cheque is presented for payment; the amount of the cheque is withdrawn by the company's bank from the company's bank account at the time the cheque is certified.

Certified Invoice An incoming purchase invoice that has been properly checked for quantities, prices, and extensions before it is entered in the purchase journal.

Chart of Accounts The list of ledger account titles used within the books of a given company, with an identification number assigned to each account.

Cheque A negotiable document ordering the bank to pay a specific sum of money to the holder or bearer of the cheque.

Cheque Register A book of original entry used in the voucher system to record all cheques issued in payment of approved vouchers.

Cheque Stub The part of the issued cheque retained by the office, providing the information required for recording the transaction in the cash payments journal. Also called *cheque rider*.

Chequing Account A bank account for the purposes of making disbursements by cheque for all business obligations. Cheques drawn on such an account are cleared (cancelled) by the bank and returned to the company each month with the bank statement. Also called a *current account*.

Closing the Books The process of removing the balances in the temporary accounts (revenue, expense, and drawings accounts) by transferring their balances to the owner's equity account and preparing these accounts for the next accounting period by reducing their balances to zero. Also called *closing the accounts*.

C.O.D. (Cash on Delivery) An immediate cash payment is required at the time of delivery in order to take possession of the goods. Always treated as a cash transaction.

Collateral Documents or securities pledged to the bank and held as security in the event of default in the repayment of a loan or mortgage.

Collections Department The department of a business that is responsible for collecting due and past due accounts receivable.

Compensating Errors An error on the debit side of an account is counter-balanced by an error of an equal amount on the credit side of the same or another account.

Compound Entry A transaction consisting of any number of debit entries that are offset by one or more credit entries; the total of the debit entries must equal the total of the credit entries.

Compulsory Deductions Deductions from employees' earnings, enforced by acts of the Canadian government and constitutions (such as those of labour unions); includes Canada Pension Plan, Unemployment Insurance, Income Tax, and union dues.

Contra Account An account that fully or partially offsets the corresponding balance sheet or income statement account to produce the proper value of that financial item.

Control Account A general ledger account that takes the place of numerous accounts of a similar nature that have been removed from the general ledger to form a subsidiary ledger.

Corporation A separate legal entity organized under a federal or provincial charter, owned by shareholders and managed by a board of directors.

Cost Price The purchase price of goods plus all incidental costs, such as freight, duty, insurance, etc.

Credit An accounting term that refers to the right side of an account.

Credit Balance The balance of an account in which the total amount of the credit entries exceeds the total amount of the debit entries.

Credit Card A document in the form of a card allowing the cardholder to purchase goods and services without an immediate cash outlay.

Credit Department A segment of a business whose duty it is to investigate the debt-paying ability and the credit status of prospective customers and to determine the maximum credit to be granted to customers.

Credit Memo A document or notice sent by a bank to inform its customer of transactions that have been credited (added) to the customer's bank account. Also called a *credit slip* or *credit advice*.

Credit Note A statement of particulars relating to returns or allowances made on credit sales and credit purchases. Also called a *credit invoice*.

Credit Terms A stipulation on an invoice that determines the last day of credit allowed before payment is due. The terms may also include the last day on which to take advantage of a cash discount.

Current Assets Assets that can be converted into cash within one year or the operating cycle (whichever is longer) without interfering with the normal operations of the business.

Current Liabilities Debts or obligations that are to be paid within one year or the operating cycle, whichever is longer.

Customs Duties A tax levied by the government on goods purchased from other countries. This cost is recorded in an account called Duty & Brokerage and is added, at the end of the financial period, to the cost of goods purchased.

Debit An accounting term that refers to the left side of an account.

Debit Balance The balance of an account in which the total amount of the debit entries exceeds the total amount of the credit entries.

Debit Memo A document or notice sent by a bank to inform its customer of transactions that have been deducted from the customer's bank account. Also called a *debit slip* or a *debit advice*.

Declining Balance Method of Depreciation The calculation of depreciation based on the net value of the asset after each period of use. Also referred to as the *diminishing balance method*.

Delivery Expense An account for recording costs incurred for delivering merchandise to customers.

Demand Promissory Note A signed promissory note giving the bank the legal right to demand repayment on a loan before the due date.

Depositor One who opens and operates a bank account.

Deposit Slip A bank document on which are recorded the cheques, coins, and currency deposited into a bank account.

Depreciation The allocation of the cost of an asset to expense over the useful life of the asset.

Dissolution of Partnership A change in the partnership ownership as the result of the admission of a new partner or the withdrawal of a partner.

Donations A general ledger account into which are recorded contributions made to charities and other organizations.

Double-Entry System A system of accounting for business transactions requiring equal debit and credit values.

Drawee The bank on which a cheque is drawn.

Drawer The individual or company that issued a cheque. Also called the *maker*.

Drawings An account used exclusively for recording withdrawals of cash or other items by the owner. Drawings is not an operating expense; it is a decrease in the owner's equity. Also called *Withdrawals*.

Duty & Brokerage See *Customs Duties*.

Employee Earnings Record A payroll record maintained for each employee regarding the gross earnings, deductions, net pay, and other information accumulated for the year to date.

Employee Tax Deduction Return (TD1) A form prepared for the payroll department and signed by the employee, showing the total amount of authorized exemptions and payroll deductions.

Endorsement An authorized signature or rubber stamp impression on the back of a cheque or other negotiable instrument by which the document is transferred to another party or to the bank.

Expenses The cost of goods and services consumed in the process of generating revenues; the cost of operating the business.

Filled Order A merchandise order that is packed and ready for shipment to the customer.

Financial Statements Types of accounting reports that show the financial position and operating results. These reports portray the financial strength, profitability, and forecasts of the business.

Fiscal Year Any 12 consecutive months chosen for an accounting period. Also called the *financial year*.

Fixed Assets Long-term assets acquired for use in the operation of the business; asset life generally is considered to be two years or more. Also called *Long-Term Assets* or *Plant and Equipment*.

F.O.B. (Free on Board) Destination An accounting term that indicates that the seller bears the cost of shipping the goods to the buyer's place of business.

F.O.B. Shipping Point An accounting term that indicates that the buyer of the goods bears the cost of transportation from the seller's place of business.

Folio A reference mark recorded during the posting process to identify the source journal in which the transaction is recorded or the ledger account to which a journal entry has been posted.

Freight & Express Prepaid and Charged An account for recording freight costs paid by the seller and then charged to the customer. Prepaid freight charges are deducted from the sales revenue to compute the net sales for the period.

Freight In An account on the buyer's books for recording the cost of transporting merchandise from the supplier. Freight In is included in the total cost of goods purchased.

General Journal The simplest type of book of original entry, consisting of two money columns: one for debit entries and one for credit entries.

General Ledger The file of ledger accounts on which financial statements are based.

Gross Earnings The amount earned, before deductions, by the employee during a payroll period.

GST The federal government's Goods and Services Tax chargeable on almost all goods and services sold to customers. The liability account GST Payable represents the amount of tax charged to customers and the gross amount owing to the Receiver General of Canada. See also GST–ITC.

GST–ITC The Goods and Services Tax–Input Tax Credit, representing the amount of GST paid on goods and services acquired in the process of conducting business. This contra-liability account balance is deducted from the GST Payable amount to determine the net amount owing to the Receiver General of Canada.

Imprest Fund See *Petty Cash Fund*.

Income Statement A financial statement that measures the profitability of a business by matching the revenues and related expenses for a chosen period of time, whether one month, one year, or some other period. Also called *profit and loss statement*. See also *Interim Financial Statements*.

Income Statement Approach for Probable Losses The allowance for uncollectible accounts is based on a percentage of net sales. The percentage is determined for past years' experience. The existing balance in Allowance for Doubtful Accounts is not taken into consideration.

Income Summary A temporary equity account opened specifically for accumulating all the balances of revenue and expense accounts to determine the net income or loss for the period. A credit balance indicates a net income; a debit balance indicates a net loss. The account is closed at the end of the period by transferring the balance to the owner's Capital account.

Income Tax A compulsory payroll deduction from the employee's earnings.

Interest Expense The cost of borrowing, for example on a bank loan or on a mortgage, or the overdue cost of an account owing to a supplier. This account name may vary depending on specific purposes; that is, Interest on Bank Loan or Interest on Mortgage.

Interim Financial Statements Those financial statements prepared for management and outsiders' use at intervals shorter than one year.

Inventory An asset account representing the value of goods on hand at the end of the financial period; all goods owned by the business for the purpose of resale in the regular course of operations.

Invoice A statement itemizing the sale of goods or services to a customer; important details include the date of sale, quantity, terms, price, etc.

Journal Any book of original entry in which business transactions are recorded in chronological order.

Journalize The process of recording business transactions in a journal.

Ledger A record accumulating all the increases and decreases of all accounts in one file. See also *General Ledger*.

Liabilities Debts owing by the business; creditors' claims against the assets of a business.

Limited Life A partnership is legally ended by the withdrawal or death of a partner in the firm.

Liquidation of Partnership The end of the business operation when assets are sold, creditors are paid, and the remaining assets are distributed among the owners.

Long-Term Liabilities Existing liabilities that are not due within one year.

Mark down A reduction of the initial selling price to attract customers and dispose of slow-moving merchandise.

Mark up The dollar amount added to the cost price of goods to compensate the owner for managing his or her business.

Merchandise Goods purchased by the business for the purpose of selling them to its customers at a profit.

Mutual Agency Each partner acts as an agent of the partnership and has the legal right to enter into contracts that are acceptable to the other partners and within the scope of normal operations.

Negotiability of Cheques The legal transferability of cheques by means of endorsement. See *Endorsements*.

Net Income The excess of revenues earned over expenses incurred during a financial period; results in an increase in the owner's equity. Also called *net profit*.

Net Loss Expenses incurred have exceeded the revenues earned during the financial period, resulting in a decrease in the owner's equity. Also called deficit.

Net Purchases Total purchases of merchandise less returns and allowances and discounts.

Net Sales Total sales revenue less returns and allowance and discounts.

Net Worth See *Owner's Equity*.

Noncash Assets All assets (other than cash) of a physical or nonphysical nature, such as equipment, franchises, trademarks, etc.

NSF (Non-Sufficient Funds) Cheque A cheque rejected by the bank because the amount of the cheque is greater than the balance in the account.

One-Write System An accounting system designed to process several phases of bookkeeping simultaneously by writing the transactions only once. Also called the *pegboard system*.

Outstanding Cheque A cheque issued by the company and entered in the cash payments journal, but not yet cleared by the bank.

Outstanding Deposit Cash and cheques received at month end that have been entered in the cash receipts journal, but were deposited too late at the bank to appear on that month's bank statement.

Owner's Equity Total assets minus total liabilities. The owner's investment into the business, plus profits that are retained by the business, less losses incurred and the owner's withdrawals of assets.

Partnership A business owned by two or more persons. An agreement is drawn up to join the partners legally.

Payee The person or company to which a cheque is issued.

Payroll The process of recording the names of employees, pay rates, and hours worked, and calculating gross earnings, deductions, and net pay for a given pay period.

Payroll Register A record of all payroll information relating to one pay period.

Pegboard A flat sheet of plastic or light metal with built-in posts on which to assemble special forms designed for the one-write system of recordkeeping. See also *One-Write System*.

Periodic Inventory The method under which the value of inventory on hand is determined regularly at the end of an accounting period (monthly, quarterly, yearly, etc.) by a systematic physical count of all goods on hand.

Permanent Accounts Assets, liabilities, and owner's equity accounts, which remain on the ledger after the books are closed at the end of the financial year for the purpose of continuing the operations of the business.

Perpetual Inventory A daily record of all merchandise bought and sold, with the balance on hand noted after each transaction.

Petty Cash Fund A small sum of money set aside from the regular bank account for making payments that are deemed too small to pay by cheque. Also called *Imprest Fund*.

Petty Cash Sheet A multicolumn sheet for recording and categorizing petty cash expenditures.

Petty Cash Voucher A document prepared for every petty cash payment. Serves as a receipt for the expenditures and as the source of the entry recorded on the petty cash sheet.

Post-Closing Trial Balance A trial balance prepared after the books are closed to prove that the equality of debits and credits in the ledgers has been maintained in the process of closing. Also called an *after-closing trial balance*.

Posting The process of transferring the debit and credit entries recorded in the journals to the proper accounts in the ledgers.

Posting Marks The number of the journal page from which the entry is posted and number of the ledger account to which the entry is posted. They are written into the reference columns in the journals and the ledger accounts affected by the transaction, providing a cross-reference. Also called *posting references* or *folios*.

Prepaid Expense An expense paid in advance, a portion of which is deferred (to be consumed or used up in the next accounting period). The unused (unexpired) costs are shown as a current asset on the balance sheet.

Present Market Value of Assets The current cost of replacing an asset.

Profit (Income) Revenues in excess of related operation expenses. See also *Net Income*.

Proof A process of ascertaining that the total of the debit columns is equal to the total of the credit columns.

Proprietorship A business owned by one person.

Purchase Discounts An account for recording cash reductions taken on purchases. Purchase discounts are used by the selling company to induce prompt payment for a credit purchase of merchandise. The amount of the discount allowed and the expiry date are stipulated in the terms of the invoice.

Purchase Invoice A document received from the seller confirming that the goods have been shipped and that payment is requested as stipulated by the terms of the invoice.

Purchase Journal A special journal used exclusively for recording the purchases of assets and expenses on credit.

Purchase Order A list of goods required to replenish the stock of merchandise; prepared by the purchasing department.

Purchase Requisition A notice sent by an inventory clerk to the purchasing department itemizing those goods in inventory for which on-hand quantities have fallen below the established reorder level.

Purchase Returns & Allowances An account for recording adjustments made for returns and allowances on purchases of merchandise; decreases the cost of goods purchased.

Reimbursing Cheque A cheque issued to replenish or replace the money spent from the petty cash fund; recorded at the end of the month or whenever the fund is exhausted or depleted.

Revenue & Expense Summary See Income Summary.

Revenue Earnings An inflow of assets in the form of cash or receivables from the sales of goods and/or services.

Sales Discounts An account for recording cash reductions allowed to customers to induce prompt payment on an invoice. The amount of discount allowed and the expiry date are stipulated in the terms of the invoice.

Sales Invoice A document itemizing the goods sold to a customer; serves as a billing to the customer and as the source document for entry into the accounting records.

Sales Journal A special journal used exclusively for all credit sales of merchandise.

Sales Ledger See *Accounts Receivable Ledger.*

Sales Returns & Allowances An account to record adjustments made for allowances on returned merchandise and for unsatisfactory goods retained by the customer; decreases the total sales revenue.

Sales Tax The provincial tax on goods and services sold to customers. The liability account Sales Tax Payable represents the amount charged to customers and owing to the provincial government.

Schedule of Accounts Payable A list of balances owing to creditors; the total is equal to the balance of the Accounts Payable Control account in the general ledger. Also called an *analysis of accounts payable.*

Schedule of Accounts Receivable A list of balances due from customers; the total is equal to the balance of the Accounts Receivable Control account in the general ledger. Also called an *analysis of accounts receivable.*

Selling Price The cost price of a product or service plus a substantial mark-up for what might be a profit allowance on sales.

Signature Card A document retained by the bank showing a specimen of an authorized signature; used for comparing signatures on cheques issued by the company.

Simple Entry A transaction recorded in the journal consisting of one debit entry and a credit entry of equal value.

Single Proprietorship A business owned by a single proprietor who usually performs the duties of both owner and manager.

Slide Error Transplacing some or all of the digits of a number one or more places to the right or left without any change in the order of the numbers; for example, 3.27 written instead of 327.

Source Documents Business forms that contain information supporting the original facts of a business transaction; the basis for recording transactions in the books.

Special Journals Journals other than the general journal used for recording transactions of the same class or nature; developed to simplify the recording and posting processes.

Spoiled Cheques Cheques containing written errors on the face. Both the cheque and stub are carefully voided and filed with the cancelled cheques. Spoiled cheques are never destroyed.

Statement of Inventory A detailed listing of all merchandise on hand; consists of a description of each item, the quantity, the price, and the value of the total inventory at the end of an accounting period.

Statement of Remuneration (T4 slips) A formal summary of an employee's gross earnings and deductions for the calendar year. Required by Revenue Canada for income tax purposes.

Straight-Line Method of Depreciation A method of calculating depreciation by allocating the cost of the asset to expense equally for each period of use.

Subsidiary Ledgers Supplementary records in the form of secondary ledgers containing detailed information for a related control account in the general ledger. The total of the accounts in the subsidiary ledger must equal the balance of the related control account in the general ledger.

Suspense Account A general ledger account used for temporarily recording transactions for which there is not sufficient information or evidence at the time of the original entry. Upon receipt of documented evidence, another transaction will be recorded to transfer the amount from the Suspense account to the proper account.

Synoptic Journal A multicolumn journal designed for a specific business; serves as the only book of original entry.

T-Account A simple T-shaped representation of an account to show the effects of debit and credit entries.

Temporary Accounts Revenue and expense accounts that are closed at the end of the accounting period to determine the net income or loss.

Time Card A source document used by employees paid on an hourly basis, showing the number of hours worked during each pay period.

Transactions Business events that can be expressed in monetary values and must be recorded in the books of the business.

Transportation In See *Freight In*.

Transportation Out See *Delivery Expense*.

Transposition of Figures Changing the natural order of the digits of a value from one side to the other; for example, 627 instead of 672.

Trial Balance A list of all the open accounts in the ledger to prove that the total of the debit balances is equal to the total of the credit balances.

Uncollectible Accounts Expense See *Bad Debts Expense*.

Unearned Revenues A portion of a revenue that has been received and recorded in the accounts but has not yet been earned by the business. Also called *deferred revenues* or *revenues received in advance*.

Unemployment Insurance A federal government insurance plan composed of funds contributed by both employee and employer to provide temporary financial relief to the employee during periods of unemployment.

Unexpired Costs See *Prepaid Expenses*.

Unlimited Liability Each partner is personally liable for the debts of a partnership.

Voluntary Deductions Payroll deductions authorized by the employee for such items as savings bonds, health and dental plans, etc.

Voucher A document prepared to describe and authorize an expenditure to be recorded in the voucher register.

Voucher Register A book of original entry used exclusively for recording expenditures or liabilities that have been approved for payment.

Voucher System An accounting system that requires that every expenditure be properly verified and approved before payment is made.

Withholding Statements Payroll documents prepared by the employer for amounts withheld for Unemployment Insurance, Canada Pension, and income tax; submitted by the employer to Revenue Canada accompanied by the remittance of these deductions.

Worksheet   A multicolumn sheet used by the accountant to assemble all the accounting data required for the preparation of adjusting and closing entries and financial statements at the end of an accounting period.

Workers Compensation   A fund providing compensation, including medical costs, to employees who have suffered injury from accidents while on the job; contribution is made by the employer to the Workers Compensation Board as required by provincial law.

CHART OF ACCOUNTS
KBC DECORATING CO.

ASSETS

101	Bank
102	Investments (Term Deposits)
103	Petty Cash Fund
104	Accounts Receivable Control
105	Allowance for Doubtful Accounts
106	Inventory of Merchandise
110	Insurance Prepaid
111	Office Supplies Prepaid
112	Warehouse Supplies Prepaid
120	Land
121	Building
122	Accumulated Depreciation—Building
123	Office Furniture & Equipment
124	Accumulated Depreciation—Furniture & Equipment
125	Service Vehicles
126	Accumulated Depreciation—Service Vehicles
127	Tools & Equipment
128	Accumulated Depreciation—Tools & Equipment

LIABILITIES

201	Accounts Payable Control
206	GST Payable
207	GST-ITC
208	Canada Pension Plan Payable
209	Income Tax Payable
210	Sales Tax Payable
216	Unemployment Insurance Payable
218	Salaries Payable
224	Mortgage Payable

OWNERS' EQUITY

301	Capital, Henry Martin
302	Drawings, Henry Martin
303	Capital, John Barker
304	Drawings, John Barker
310	Income Summary

REVENUES

401	Sales—Paint & Supplies
402	Sales—Wallpaper
403	Sales—Service
406	Sales Discounts
407	Commission Revenue
409	Interest Revenue
412	Rental Revenue

EXPENSES

501	Purchases—Paint & Supplies
502	Purchases—Wallpaper
504	Purchase Discounts
505	Duty & Brokerage
506	Freight In
510	Advertising Expense
511	Bad Debts Expense
512	Bank Charges & Interest
513	Business Tax Expense
514	Canada Pension Plan Expense
515	Delivery Expense
516	Depreciation Expense—Building
517	Depreciation Expense—Furniture & Equipment
518	Depreciation Expense—Service Vehicles
519	Depreciation Expense—Tools & Equipment
520	Donations
521	Insurance Expense
523	Interest on Mortgage
524	Miscellaneous Expense
525	Office Supplies Expense
526	Postage
527	Rent Expense
528	Salaries Expense—Office
529	Salaries Expense—Service
530	Telephone Expense
532	Unemployment Insurance Expense
533	Utilities Expense
535	Warehouse Supplies Expense
537	Workers Compensation Expense

ACCOUNTS RECEIVABLE SUBSIDIARY LEDGER

150	Beavis & Sons	2000 Regent Ave., Transcona, MB
151	Dayson & Son	3007 Roblin Blvd., Winnipeg, MB
152	Jay-Mar Co.	Forest Park Mall, Charleswood, MB
153	S. Miller	300 Scotland Ave., Winnipeg, MB
154	Edna Morton	1100 Manitoba Ave., Portage La Prairie, MB
155	S. Wilkinson	16 Heather St., Morden, MB
156	K. Young Painting	St. Norbert, MB
157	Wm. Zelisko Enterprises	15 Byars Bay, Selkirk, MB

ACCOUNTS PAYABLE SUBSIDIARY LEDGER

250	Coleman Industries	10-110 Avenue, Brandon, MB
251	Major Office Supplies	22 Victoria Ave., Regina, SK
252	Minnesota Decor Supply	1600-27 Ave. North, Minneapolis, MN, U.S.A.
253	Mitchell Advertising	1200 Floom St., Regina, SK
254	Rainbow Supplies	2007 Jasper Ave., Edmonton, AB
255	Reynolds Paper Co.	1200 Main St., Saskatoon, SK
256	Robinson Insurance	1100 Grant Ave., Winnipeg, MB
257	Spencer Stucco Ltd.	720 Main St., Dauphin, MB
258	Tranborg & Noble	Box 670, Steinbach, MB

To the owner of this book

We hope that you have enjoyed *Basic Bookkeeping: An Office Simulation,*
Second Edition, and we would like to know as much about your experiences
with this text as you would care to offer. Only through your comments and
those of others can we learn how to make this a better text for future readers.

School _____   Your instructor's name _____

Course _____   Was the text required? _____   Recommended? _____

1. What did you like the most about *Basic Bookkeeping?*

_____

_____

_____

2. How useful was this text for your course?

_____

_____

_____

3. Do you have any recommendations for ways to improve the next edition of
this text?

_____

_____

_____

4. In the space below or in a separate letter, please write any other comments
you have about the book. (For example, please feel free to comment on
reading level, writing style, terminology, design features, and learning aids.)

_____

_____

_____

_____

Optional

Your name _____   Date _____

May Nelson Canada quote you, either in promotion for *Basic Bookkeeping* or in
future publishing ventures?

Yes _____   No _____

Thanks!

Nelson

TAPE SHUT

0107077099-M1K5G4-BR01

TAPE SHUT

Nelson Canada
College Editorial Department
1120 Birchmount Rd.
Scarborough, ON M1K 9Z9

PLEASE TAPE SHUT. DO NOT STAPLE.

FOLD HERE